COLONIAL AMERICA

Jerome R. Reich
Chicago State University

Prentice-Hall, Inc., Englewood Cliffs, N.J. 07632

Library of Congress Cataloging in Publication Data

REICH, JEROME R.
    Colonial America.

    Includes bibliographies and index.
        1. United States—Civilization—To 1783.   I. Title.
E162.R44 1984   973   83-9460
ISBN   0-13-151167-X

Editorial/production supervision: Joyce Turner
Cover design: Diane Saxe
Manufacturing buyer: Ron Chapman
Cover photo: Courtesy, Library of Congress

Printed in the United States of America

10   9   8   7   6   5   4   3   2   1

ISBN 0-13-151167-X

Prentice-Hall International, Inc., *London*
Prentice-Hall of Australia Pty. Limited, *Sydney*
Editora Prentice-Hall do Brasil, Ltda., *Rio de Janeiro*
Prentice-Hall Canada Inc., *Toronto*
Prentice-Hall of India Private Limited, *New Delhi*
Prentice-Hall of Japan, Inc., *Tokyo*
Prentice-Hall of Southeast Asia Pte. Ltd., *Singapore*
Whitehall Books Limited, *Wellington, New Zealand*

Contents

Preface

It is now more than half a century since Carl Becker enunciated his relativistic approach to history in "Every Man His Own Historian," the presidential address delivered at the 1931 meeting of the American Historical Association. In that address Becker drew a distinction between a series of events that actually occurred and our memory, or "idealization," of these events. The first is immutable; the second is dynamic—"always changing in response to the increase or refinement of knowledge." Thus, history "cannot be precisely the same for all at any given time or the same for one generation or for another."

Recent scholarship on the colonial period of American history confirms the validity of Becker's contention. Studies highlighting the role of American Indians, blacks, women, the "middling sort of people," and even the "rabble" have done much to modify, if not transform, our long-held views of the early history of our nation. This is a significant accomplishment. Our colonial period—if dated from Sir Humphrey Gilbert's ill-fated attempt to found a colony in 1583—lasted 200 years, exactly half our history to date. Further, it was during the first two centuries that the social, intellectual, economic, and political patterns which we designate as peculiarly "American" were formed.

This volume, then, attempts—within a limited number of pages—to provide its readers with a survey of all facets of colonial life, utilizing the cogent and wide-ranging research undertaken in the last two decades as well as that done in the past. (The bibliographies found at the conclusion of each chapter supply a sample of these books.) My thanks to Stephen Dalphin, Joyce Turner, and their colleagues at Prentice-Hall for their cooperation, and to the members of my family for their patience with a sometimes difficult-to-live-with author.

J. R. Reich

I
European
Backgrounds

As Walter Durant recounts in his volume, *The Age of Faith,* "libera nos a furore Normanorum"—from the fury of the Northmen deliver us—was a common prayer during the ninth century. It might have been uttered by an inhabitant of England, Ireland, Russia, Sicily, or present-day Turkey. The Northmen—or Norsemen, or Vikings—attacked and plundered all these areas. What impelled the Norsemen to leave their homelands—Norway, Sweden, and Denmark—is still uncertain. Some postulate that a shortage of good land coupled with an expanding population caused them to leave. Others attribute their leaving to dynastic strife in the newly unified Scandinavian kingdoms. Further, one cannot overlook the fact that fame and fortune could be won by a successful freebooter.

NORSE DISCOVERIES

By the end of the tenth century, over 20,000 Norsemen were living in Iceland. A few thousand more lived in Greenland, which had been discovered only a few years earlier by Eric the Red. In the opening decade of the eleventh century, Leif, one of the sons of Eric the Red, sailed west and discovered three "lands." He named them Helluland (Flatland), Markland (Timberland), and Vinland (which may be translated either as Wine Land—from the grapes which grew there—or Meadow Land—from the archaic Norse word *vin*).

Authorities differ widely on the location of these three lands, but the most widely accepted theory is that they are Baffin Island, Labrador, and Newfoundland—all of which are only a few hundred miles from Greenland. Archaeological studies made by Helge and Anne Stine Ingstadt at L'Anse aux Meadows, Newfoundland, during the 1960s appear to buttress the belief that a Viking settlement existed there. The Ingstadts found the remains of houses, boat sheds, a cooking pit, a smithy, a bronze pin, and other artifacts of the type used by the Norsemen. Radiocarbon analysis dates these remains at about the year 1000.

The Greenlanders' saga and the saga of Eric the Red tell about several attempts to colonize Vinland, but none of these attempts seems to have enjoyed long-term success. Leif's brother Thorvald was killed by the Indians, who were called *skraelings*, or screechers, by the Norsemen. These *skraelings* were described as "swarthy . . . with ugly hair on their heads . . . they had great eyes, and were broad of cheek." Other expeditions were also harassed by the Indians and were forced to return to Greenland. Thus, the Norse discovery of America proved to be a false start: even its memory faded away. In the eleventh century Europeans were not prepared economically, politically, or technologically to settle new, far-off continents. It was another 500 years before that state of readiness was achieved.

THE CRUSADES

Before the end of the eleventh century, however, the first link was forged in the long and intricate chain leading from Leif Ericsson to Christopher Columbus. That link was the calling of the First Crusade by Pope Urban II at the Council of Clermont in 1095. The primary goal of the First Crusade and of later Crusades—the capture of the Holy Land from the Moslems—was never attained. However, as so often happens with great historical movements, the unforeseen results of the Crusades proved to be more significant and far-reaching than its sponsors ever imagined.

The feudal system—the political, social, and economic regime which dominated western Europe at that time, never fully recovered from the Crusades. The lands of knights who perished in these expeditions without leaving heirs reverted to the king. Those who did survive were often forced to sell or mortgage their lands, or to grant privileges to the towns on their estates in order to raise the money needed to finance their participation in a Crusade. By 1300 most towns had bought or won charters, which made townspeople free and virtually self-governing. Countless serfs won their freedom either by joining a Crusade or by running away to one of these towns, where residence for a year and a day gave serfs their liberty.

The Crusades also had important effects on European culture. European contacts with the Byzantine and Moslem empires—which had preserved classical philosophy, medicine, mathematics, astronomy, and geography—facilitated the reintroduction of this body of thought and knowledge into European life. Contrary to accepted belief, Europeans did not merely accept classical Moslem and Oriental knowledge but, particularly in the sciences, built upon it as well. The result was a series of technological improvements which were to prove crucial in the rediscovery and settlement of America.

Chief among these technological accomplishments were improvements in the compass, the astrolabe, and gun powder. Europeans borrowed the compass from Moslem navigators, who probably learned about it from the Chinese. The astrolabe was a device which measured the height of the sun at noon, thereby indicating approximate latitude. It was used by the Greeks, preserved by the Moslems, and passed on to European sea captains. Gun powder, also a Chinese invention, was put to military use by Europeans, thus making it possible for them to overpower the inhabitants of the Americas. No longer would the *skraelings* (or Indians) be able to impede European settlement permanently.

FIGURE 1A (From Hofstadter, et al. *United States: Brief Edition.* Englewood Cliffs, N.J.: Prentice-Hall, Inc., ©1979, p. 4. By permission of the publisher.)

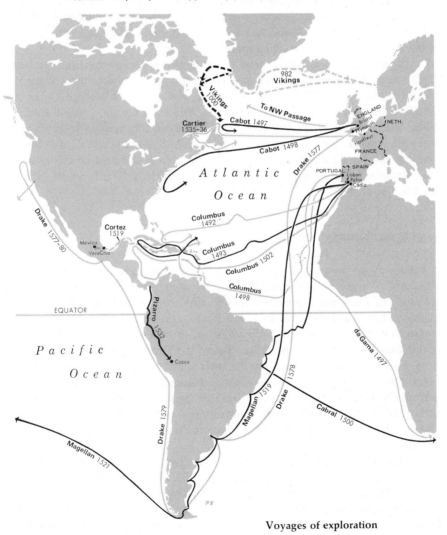

Voyages of exploration

European shipbuilders also made important contributions to marine technology. The galleys that sailed the Mediterranean Sea during the period of the Crusades were low, bulky ships which depended on their rowers as much as on their sails for power. Gradually, however, vessels (called caravels) became larger, longer, narrower, and higher, with multiple decks. Caravels had three masts and depended entirely upon their sails, which had become bulkier and more complex. These improvements made ships speedier, more maneuverable, and better able to take advantage of wind direction.

Closely allied to the improvements in shipbuilding were the improvements in map making. The forerunners of the modern map were marine charts which described the coastlines, first of the Mediterranean, and later of the Atlantic coast of Europe. By the beginning of the fifteenth century, a Latin translation of Ptolemy's (second-century) work on geography reminded Europeans of what their scholars had never completely forgotten—that the world was round. The exact circumference of the globe, however, was still in dispute.

Ptolemy, who was followed by fifteenth-century geographers such as Pierre d'Ailly and map makers such as Paolo Toscanelli, greatly underestimated the size of the world. Both d'Ailly and Toscanelli, who greatly influenced Columbus, theorized that the distance from Europe to Asia was only about 6,000 to 6,500 miles, with Japan and several other islands conveniently located in between to break the voyage. By the first half of the fifteenth century, the Canary Islands, Madeira, and the Azores had already been rediscovered, and most experts expected other islands to be found as navigators sailed farther and farther west into the Atlantic Ocean.

THE RENAISSANCE

Another step on the road to the rediscovery of America was the Renaissance. The Renaissance, or rebirth of classical learning, began in thirteenth-century Italy. There the study of Latin and Greek literature became known as the humanities, the study of human beings and their literature. The Renaissance also stimulated European art, architecture, science, and technology. Perhaps most importantly, it led to a new outlook on life that was very unlike that of the Middle Ages. During the Middle Ages people had concentrated on the next world; during the Renaissance they concentrated on this world. People of the Renaissance tended to be more skeptical, individualistic, and optimistic than their forebears of the Middle Ages. The psychology of the Middle Ages tended to hinder the search for, and exploration of, new parts of the world; the psychology of the Renaissance positively encouraged such ventures.

This adventurous spirit is perhaps best illustrated by the missionaries and traders who, long before Europeans began to think of sailing westward to reach the Orient, attempted to reach India and China by following the caravan routes across Asia. The first recorded visit of a European to the Far East was made in 1241 by a Franciscan monk named John of Plano Carpini, an envoy of Pope Innocent IV to

Ghengis Khan. Twelve years later another Franciscan, William de Rubruquis, was sent on a similar mission by King Louis IX of France. Both men left detailed accounts of their visits; but the most famous—and influential—account of the Orient was written by Marco Polo, a young Venetian trader who traveled throughout the Orient between 1274 and 1295.

Marco Polo might never have written his famous account of the wonders of the East if he had not been captured and imprisoned by the Genoese during the course of a war with Venice. Fortunately for us, if not for him, he spent his time in prison writing about his adventures. His narrative excited generations of Europeans with accounts about the wealth and grandeur of China, India, Persia (which he saw with his own eyes), and islands such as Japan, Zanzibar, and Madagascar (about which he had learned second hand). When the first printed edition of his adventures appeared in 1477, it became a best seller. Columbus felt the book was important enough to take with him on his first voyage to America. The wide circulation of Marco Polo's book is only one example of the effect of the invention—in the mid-fifteenth century—of movable metal type for the printing press which made it possible to mass produce books and maps.

TRADE AND THE NATION-STATE

While the Crusades increased knowledge, they increased trade between Europe and the Far East even more. During the course of the Crusades, the merchants of the Italian cities (which were the jumping-off places for the Crusades) had accumulated the ships, the know-how, and the large amounts of capital needed for trade with the Orient. Soon textiles such as silk, satin, velvet, taffeta, and damask; spices (necessities, not luxuries, in the days before refrigeration) such as pepper, cinnamon, ginger, nutmeg, and cloves; as well as rugs, tapestries, gems, china, glassware, perfumes, dyes, and steel weapons began arriving in European markets. Further, hitherto exotic fruits such as cherries, melons, apricots, peaches, and dates became commonplace on the tables of Europeans wealthy enough to afford them.

These goods were transported thousands of miles by land and sea before arriving at the port cities at the eastern end of the Mediterranean or at Constantinople. Because of agreements negotiated during the period of the Crusades, merchants from one or another of the Italian cities (most often from Venice, Genoa, or Pisa) held a virtual monopoly of all trade at these ports. They alone were eligible to purchase the oriental products, and the rest of Europe was forced to go to Italy to obtain these products—at exorbitant prices.

Italy was not the only area of Europe to benefit from the increase in trade. Important mercantile towns and seaports developed in the Low Countries (present-day Holland and Belgium), Portugal, Spain, France, England, and the Hanseatic League towns along the Baltic and North seas. Merchants from all these parts of Europe purchased oriental goods and, in return, sold the hides, timber, furs, tin, lead, woolen goods, and leather products which were produced in their own areas. These towns also became centers of industry and banking. The wealthy bourgeoisie (town dwellers) who controlled them gradually attained a position of power and influence in the medieval world.

The bourgeoisie resented the limitations placed upon them by the feudal nobility. Whenever a noble's land was crossed, merchants faced, at best, the payment of a fee. At worst, merchants faced confiscation of their goods or loss of their lives. The lack of any ruler strong enough to protect merchants against these depredations or against robbers and pirates was a severe handicap to trade. The fact that each petty principality had its own system of coinage and code of laws further worked against mercantile prosperity.

It was not long before merchants began to discern the solution to their problem—supporting the monarchs in their struggle to assert authority over nobles. The details of this strategy need not concern us here. Suffice it to say that with the financial support of the merchant class, kings were able to hire mercenaries and to equip them with the guns and cannon necessary to subdue the recalcitrant nobles and destroy their castles. During the fifteenth century Portugal, Spain, France, and England became true nation-states. Their rulers showed their appreciation of bourgeois support (and recognized their own self-interest) by giving full support to commercial development.

However, all these new nations found themselves with a common problem: an unfavorable balance of trade, or, more precisely, an unfavorable balance of payments. In other words, they were spending more on the goods they imported than they received for the goods they exported. As a result, bullion (gold and silver) was being drained out of all these new nations. According to the economic doctrine which developed concurrently with the rise of the nation-state, nothing could be more disastrous. Without an ample supply of gold and silver, how could merchants carry on their trade? How could a king support an army and navy to protect his, and his nation's, interests?

The cause of this unfavorable balance of payments was obvious. The prices these nations had to pay for oriental products reflected the intrinsically high value of the goods, the huge distances over which they had to be transported, the innumerable tolls which were levied on them, the number of middlemen through whose hands they passed, and the monopolistic prices charged by the Italian merchants. On the other hand, the prices which the new nations were able to charge for their raw materials and even for their manufactured goods were much more modest. The solution to this problem was equally obvious: Find an alternative route to the Far East. The nation that discovered such a route would break the monopoly of the Italian merchants and possibly even replace them as the purveyor of oriental goods to the rest of Europe.

PORTUGUESE EXPLORATION

Portugal was the first nation-state to institute the search for such a route. Several factors help explain Portugal's precedence in this enterprise: It was unified at an early date; it was barred from eastward expansion by the powerful Spanish state of

Castile; it had many good harbors; and its seamen were seasoned by a long series of naval wars against the Moors of North Africa. Further, from 1422 to 1460 Portuguese exploration had the unflagging support of Prince Henry the Navigator, a younger son of the Portuguese royal family. Prince Henry's motives were mixed. He planned to spread Christianity to the peoples of Africa and, perhaps, with the aid of the legendary Christian kingdom ruled by Prester John, drive the Moors from North Africa. He also hoped to reach Guinea, on the Atlantic coast of Africa, where caravans from central Africa reportedly delivered ivory, gold, and slaves. Finally, he hoped to find a passage through, if not around, Africa to the Far East.

Prince Henry was no idle dreamer. He endowed a naval observatory at Cape St. Vincent, on the southwestern tip of Portugal, where navigators, astronomers, and map makers—Moslem and Jewish as well as Christian—worked to conquer unchartered seas. For almost forty years Prince Henry sent one expedition after another down the west coast of Africa. In 1434 a Portuguese sea captain returned safely home after sailing beyond Cape Bojador into waters which had hitherto been thought to be boiling hot, thick with salt, and full of sea monsters. In 1441 Antan Goncalves, another of Prince Henry's captains, landed just south of Cape Bojador and kidnapped ten or twelve Africans and brought them back to Portugal as slaves. From this small beginning grew the gigantic slave trade.

Not even the Prince's death could deter Portuguese exploration. In 1471 Portuguese explorers sailed south of the equator; in 1484 they reached the mouth of the Congo River; and in 1486 Bartholomew Diaz rounded the Cape of Good Hope. In 1497–1498 Vasdo da Gama sailed to India, returning to Lisbon the following year with a cargo of pepper, cinnamon, cloves, nutmeg, and gems worth a sizable fortune.

Portugal had won the race to the Far East, and it moved quickly to consolidate its advantage. Within the first years of the sixteenth century, Portugal established trading posts along the east coast of Africa, conquered the Indian city of Goa, and forged commercial ties with China, Burma, Siam (modern-day Thailand), and the Malay Peninsula. Portuguese merchants rapidly displaced Italian merchants as the suppliers of oriental goods to Europe, and Portugal grew wealthy on the proceeds. The commercial revolution—the shift of economic power from the Mediterranean world to the new nation-states bordering the Atlantic Ocean—had begun.

SPANISH EXPLORATION

Spain, France, and England were no happier to see their gold and silver disappear into Portuguese coffers than they were to see it channeled into the Italian cities. Even before da Gama reached India, the two able Spanish rulers, Queen Isabella and King Ferdinand, had taken steps to find a route to the Far East that would be dominated by Spain. Spain had only recently been united: Ferdinand was king of Aragon and Isabella was queen of Castile, but after 1479 the two nations were ruled as one. With the aid of the bourgeoisie, Ferdinand and Isabella were able to assert their authority over the nobles and over the powerful military orders which had grown up in Spain during the centuries of warfare against the Moors. This "crusade" against the Moors culminated in 1492 when Granada, the last Moorish foothold on the Iberian Peninsula, surrendered to Ferdinand and Isabella. Spain was now a powerful, united nation that was ready to challenge Portugal in the race for new trade routes to the Far East.

In the Treaty of Alcacovas in 1479, however, Spain had agreed to accept Portuguese domination of African waters. If the Spanish navigators were going to reach the Far East, it would have to be by an entirely different route. In the mid-1480s a man appeared at the Spanish court who claimed to know of such a route. This man was Christopher Columbus. Columbus was born in Genoa sometime in the middle of the fifteenth century and went to sea at an early age. From the mid-1470s to the mid-1480s, Columbus lived in Portugal, where he married the daughter of one of Prince Henry's sea captains. He is known to have made voyages down the coast of Africa and to have been on board a Portuguese ship that sailed to England. There he boarded a Bristol ship which traded with Iceland.

Columbus was greatly influenced by those geographers and map makers who felt that Asia was only a bit more than 6,000 miles from Europe. His own calculation was that the distance was only 4,500 miles; information culled from Bristol seamen about islands in the North Atlantic only made him more confident that a westward voyage across the Atlantic was the shortest and easiest route to Asia. Columbus attempted unsuccessfully to convince the king of Portugal of the validity of his theory. Portuguese experts insisted that the distance from Europe to Asia was closer to 10,000 miles. In any case, the Portuguese were already fully committed to the African route.

Columbus then sent his brother Bartholomew to France and England to win the support of their sovereigns for his plan, but he enjoyed no success with either king. Columbus himself went to Spain, where he was repeatedly turned down. However, the conquest of Granada soon made the Spanish monarchs more receptive to new projects. On August 3, 1492, Columbus—having received royal permission—set sail from the town of Palos with three ships—the Santa Maria, the Nina, and the Pinta—and about ninety men. Columbus was to receive a share of any profits deriving from the voyage and was to be named admiral and governor of any territories he might discover. The small fleet sailed to the Canary Islands, where some repairs were made on the Pinta. Then, on September 6 Columbus headed directly west. Although the weather was calm, his crew was terrified, and on October 10 Columbus barely prevented a mutiny. Fortunately, two days later a landing was made, probably on Watling Island (called San Salvador by Columbus) in the Bahamas. Columbus also visited Cuba and Haiti (which he called Hispaniola). Leaving the crew of the Santa Maria (which had been wrecked) to build a fort on Haiti, Columbus sailed home, bringing a small amount of gold, some coconuts, and a few natives—whom he called Indians—back with him.

Columbus may have been perplexed by the disparity between the islands he had visited and the glowing accounts of Marco Polo, but if he was, he did not share his doubts with the Spanish authorities. On the contrary, the report he sent to

Ferdinand and Isabella promised that on future voyages he would "procure as much gold as they [the Spanish sovereigns] need" as well as spices, cotton, and drugs. This report impressed the Spanish monarchs more than the meager booty with which Columbus returned; before the end of 1493, Columbus led a fleet of seventeen ships back to the West Indies. On this voyage he reinforced the original settlement of Haiti and explored Puerto Rico, Jamaica, and the Lesser Antilles before returning to Spain in 1496. On his third voyage (1498-1500) Columbus sailed along the coast of South America, and on his final voyage (1502-1504) he sailed along the coast of Central America, still insisting that the riches of Asia could not be far away. Two years later he died—poor, bitter, and definitely out of favor at the Spanish court.

Columbus's first voyage was a terrible shock to the Portuguese, coming just a few years before da Gama reached India. Were seventy years of hazardous expeditions down the coast of Africa to prove futile? The king of Portugal was unwilling to admit defeat. At first he claimed that the lands reached by Columbus were within the Portuguese sphere of influence as laid down in the Treaty of Alcacovas. However, this claim was patently false. After first appealing to the pope, Spain and Portugal negotiated the Treaty of Tordesillas in 1494. This treaty gave Spain title to all non-Christian lands discovered west of an imaginary line drawn pole to pole at 370 leagues (about 1,100 miles) west of the Cape Verde Islands (the pope had drawn a line only 100 leagues west) and gave Portugal similar lands to the east of the line.

Within a few years da Gama reached India, but Portugal was still unwilling to surrender the right to what it had already begun to suspect was a potentially rich new continent. In 1500 Pedro Cabral, a Portuguese sea captain (accidentally?) crossed the South Atlantic while sailing down the African coast and reached what is now Brazil. According to the Treaty of Tordesillas, this territory belonged to Portugal. In the following year another Portuguese expedition explored the coast of South America. One of the members of this expedition was Americus Vespucius, a Florentine merchant who claimed to have crossed the Atlantic as early as 1497. A letter from Vespucius in which he called this region a new world was included in a geography book published in 1507. The editor of this volume, Martin Waldseemüller, suggested that the area be called Americ's land, or America, in Vespucius's honor, and the designation was soon accepted all over Europe.

The competition between Spain and Portugal led to still another epoch-making voyage. In 1518 Spain claimed that the line drawn by the Treaty of Tordesillas ran all the way around the globe, giving Spain a claim to part of the Eastern Hemisphere. Ironically, it was a Portuguese sea captain, Ferdinand Magellan, who persuaded the king of Spain of the existence of a passage through the American continent that might prove to be a shortcut to Asia. In 1519 Magellan left Spain with a fleet of five ships. Not finding any transcontinental passage, he was forced to sail through the straits which now bear his name. There followed an arduous trip across the Pacific Ocean to the Philippine Islands, where Magellan was killed in a skirmish with the natives. One of his ships, however, did sail around the Cape of

Good Hope and finally returned to Spain in 1522. The earth had been circum-navigated. Magellan's voyage gave Spain a claim to the Philippines, but Portugal retained all its possessions in the Far East.

ENGLISH AND FRENCH EXPLORATION

Spain and Portugal might have thought that they had divided up all the newly dis-covered parts of the world between them, but the rulers of England and France strongly dissented. In 1497 King Henry VII sponsored a voyage by John Cabot (really Giovanni Caboto), a Genoese sea captain. Like Columbus, Cabot believed that Asia could be reached by sailing west; like Columbus he tried, and failed, to convince the monarchs of Portugal and Spain to finance such an attempt. Cabot was apparently still in Spain when Columbus returned from his first voyage. How-ever, by 1495 he was in England, where he made an unsuccessful voyage into the Atlantic. In 1497, however, he successfully sailed west until he landed on the coast of Newfoundland. This discovery gave England its claim to North America. Cabot was lost at sea in an unsuccessful follow-up expedition in 1498. Although Cabot's son Sebastian attempted to find a northwest passage around North America (1508-1509) and English fishermen visited the Grand Banks regularly, political, religious, and economic turmoil forced England to wait more than half a century before again seriously endeavoring to challenge Spain and Portugal.

France, too, hoped for colonial empire and was somewhat more persistent than England. The French king commissioned Giovanni da Verrazano (note the continued dependence on Italian navigators) to search for new lands. In 1524 Verrazano sailed along the coast of North America from about the present-day Carolinas to what is now Maine. Ten years later Jacques Cartier, a French sea cap-tain, sailed into the St. Lawrence River. In two subsequent expeditions (1535-1536 and 1541) he (and the Sieur de Roberval) sailed up the St. Lawrence as far as Montreal and tried unsuccessfully to found a settlement at Quebec. French motives for the settlement of Canada were varied. Initially the hope for precious metals was preeminent, but soon the value of the fisheries and the fur trade became ap-parent. Nevertheless, when the French failed to find gold in Canada, they turned their attention to more southerly climes, even though it meant directly challenging Spain and Portugal. In 1555 French Protestants, called Huguenots, were encouraged to found a settlement called La France Antarctique on an island off the coast of Brazil near Rio de Janeiro. However, the Portuguese captured and destroyed the colony in 1560. A similar attempt to found a Huguenot colony in South Carolina in 1562 collapsed because of famine and internal dissension. A third Huguenot colony was founded in 1564 on the St. Johns River in Florida. This colony was a potential danger to Spanish shipping, and Pedro Menendez de Avila, the Spanish governor of Florida, massacred all 132 inhabitants of the settlement. He then wiped out another group of Huguenots who tried to attack the recently established Spanish fort at St. Augustine. Religious and political dissension at home soon ended all French attempts at colonizing America. Later French rulers were able to turn their attention once again to Canada at the very end of the sixteenth century.

As this chapter has pointed out, Europe (at least western Europe) at the end of the sixteenth century bore little resemblance to the Europe of the eleventh century. Feudalism had been replaced by the nation-state and a capitalistic economic system. Old knowledge had been rediscovered, new knowledge was developed, and both were disseminated more quickly and widely than ever before in human history. Where once, human thought and effort had been devoted almost entirely to the next world, the focus shifted to this world. Where once, people had lived and died within a few narrow acres, intrepid explorers now stretched their horizons thousands of miles to include Asia, Africa, and the Americas. With the first flush of exploration over, Europeans began to think of colonizing the "New World" which they had rediscovered.

BIBLIOGRAPHY

JONES, GWEN. *A History of the Vikings.* New York, 1968.
MORISON, SAMUEL E. *The European Discovery of America: The Northern Voyages.* Boston, 1971.
MORISON, SAMUEL E. *The Discovery of America: The Southern Voyages.* New York, 1974.
PARRY, J. H. *The Age of Reconnaissance.* Cleveland, 1963.
PARRY, J. H. *The Discovery of South America.* New York, 1974.
PENROSE, BOIES. *Travel and Discovery in the Renaissance, 1420–1620.* Cambridge, 1952.
QUINN, DAVID B. *North America from Earliest Discovery to First Settlements: The Norse Voyages to 1612.* New York, 1977.
SCAMMELL, G. V. *The World Encompassed: The First European Maritime Empires.* Berkeley, 1981.

2

The Indians
of the Americas

Christopher Columbus, Americus Vespucius, and even Leif Ericsson must be classed as latecomers to the Americas. According to contemporary experts, the "discovery" of America took place approximately 40,000 years ago. While no one knows the name of the person who first stepped on our shores, he or she was probably the leader of a group of nomads who crossed from Siberia to Alaska by way of a land bridge which, at that time, connected Asia and North America.

INDIANS SETTLE THE AMERICAS

The first settlers of America were food gatherers and hunters. Very slowly—perhaps over a period of 20,000 years—they spread southward and eastward until they occupied all of North, Central, and South America. In the course of this long migration, groups of Indians lost contact with each other and cultural differentiation began to occur. It is estimated that by the time Europeans arrived in America, Indians spoke about 2,000 different languages.

Cultural diversity also manifested itself in many other ways. The food a group consumed, the clothing it wore, and the type of shelter it constructed were all strongly determined by the natural environment. The Indians of the Amazon basin wore little or no clothing, while those of the Hudson Bay area wore furs. The Indians of the eastern woodlands or of the northwestern part of the United States built their homes of timber; the Plains Indians covered their tepees with buffalo skins;

and the Indians of the southwest constructed their pueblos of sun-dried adobe bricks.

Archaeological findings seem to indicate that up to about 10,000 years ago, hunting supplied a large portion of the diet of most Indian groups. Then, remarkable though it seems, the Indians managed—with only stone weapons—to kill off the mastadon, the woolly mammoth, the giant bison, the American horse (horses had to be reintroduced by the Spanish), and, in South America, a llama-like camel. The only other plausible explanation is that climatic changes caused these animals to become extinct, but no real evidence for this theory has been discovered.

Scarcity of game accelerated the agricultural revolution—the process by which Indian groups learned to domesticate plants. The agricultural revolution took place gradually over thousands of years. Its beginnings are estimated at between 7000 and 8000 B.C., and some Indian groups had not yet entered the agricultural stage at the time Europeans reached the Americas. Even in those groups which practiced agriculture, hunting and fishing continued to be important and prestigious occupations. So prestigious, in fact, were these two activities that they were performed by men while women were relegated to agricultural labor.

We do not know which plant was first domesticated by the Indians, but certainly maize, or Indian corn, was the most important. Other plants developed in the Americas include white potatoes, sweet potatoes, tomatoes, avocados, pumpkins, squashes, lima beans, and tobacco.

Agriculture seems to have developed first among the Indians of Central America and later in Peru. Indian farming is called hoe culture because the hoe was the Indians' main farm implement. No Indian group ever developed the plow, probably because they lacked draft animals such as the horse or ox. With the increased importance of agriculture came settled villages and the production of pottery and textiles—again usually by the women. The Indians of both Central America and Peru domesticated the dog and the turkey (also the llama in Peru), which supplied them with meat, skins, and wool. Also, both societies—using only stone tools—built huge pyramids decorated with massive sculptures. However, neither society put the wheel to practical use, although the Indians of Mexico made toys which ran on rollers.

THE INDIANS OF CENTRAL
AND SOUTH AMERICA

The earliest-known people of Central America were the Olmecs, whose civilization flourished somewhat after 1000 B.C. They are credited with the invention of the type of writing and system of mathematics which the Maya Indians perfected and the Aztecs later copied. The writing has not yet been deciphered, but we are now familiar with the number system as it was developed by the Mayas after the year 300 A.D.

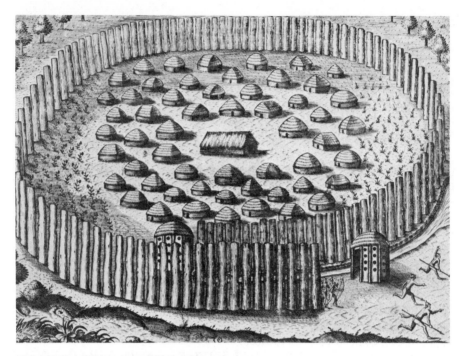

FIGURE 2A (New York Public Library.)

Like our number system, the Mayan system included the concepts of zero and place value. Mayan mathematical knowledge was used to develop an unusually accurate series of calendars. One was a lunar calendar; another, based on the planet Venus, consisted of 584 days; and the sacred calendar consisted of twenty groups of thirteen days. The last—the most precise calendar—consisted of 365 days divided into eighteen groups of twenty-day periods, with five days (which were considered unlucky) added to round out the year. This was a far more accurate calendar than the one used in Europe (or anyplace else in the world) at the time.

While their systems of mathematics and astronomy were quite sophisticated, the Mayan people lived simple lives. Corn was their staple food and chocolate their favorite drink. They varied their diet with beans, squash, fish, turkey, wild pigs, and dog meat. The Mayas were the first people to enjoy chickle, the base for modern chewing gum. In the climate of Central America, the common man and woman wore relatively little clothing: a loin cloth and cape for the men and a tunic of decorated cloth for the women. Both also had a larger cloak to be used in colder weather or as a blanket at night.

The upper classes ate the same food as the lower classes, but their costumes were more ornate and decorative. They valued cloaks and headdresses made of feathers, and both men and women wore necklaces, earrings, bracelets, and nose plugs made of metal, jade, or jewels. Tattooing was popular with all classes, and each group painted itself a different color: Priests were blue; warriors, red and black;

and slaves, black and white. Teeth were filed to sharp points and were often covered with precious metals.

Mayan children were carefully brought up. When a baby was born, a priest cast the child's horoscope and told the parents which would be the child's lucky and unlucky days. Mayan mothers placed their babies' heads within boards so that the children's skulls would be elongated and the top end pointed. A ball of wax was often suspended between a baby's eyes because a squint was considered a mark of beauty. In addition, mothers scalded their boys faces with hot cloths in order to prevent the growth of facial hair. At the age of three months for girls and four months for boys, babies went through a ceremony that introduced them to the type of work they would do in later life. At the age of puberty, another ceremony took place which ushered them into the adult community. Marriage usually occurred by the age of twenty for men and a few years younger for women.

Mayan society was highly stratified. The king ruled with the aid of an advisory council, which probably was made up largely of members of the royal family. Emissaries from the noble class were sent to each city to hold court and to see that taxes were paid promptly and fully. Other nobles served as commanders in the army, which was made up of mercenaries and peasant conscripts. The Mayan priesthood was a large and varied body. Priests conducted the (often human) sacrifices, treated the sick, and observed the stars in order to advise on crucial questions such as when to plant the crops or when to initiate a war.

Mayan merchants journeyed far beyond the limits of Mayan political control, trading cotton, skins, pottery, and textiles for cocoa, beans, feathers, and jade, which was even more highly valued by the Mayas than gold. The peasants were forced to pay taxes in produce and labor. The men also had to serve in the army; however, wars were only fought between the agricultural seasons, and battles ended at sunset. At the bottom of the social scale were the slaves—either prisoners captured in war or the children of peasants who had sold them to pay their debts.

The Mayan cities controlled Central America for about a thousand years. Each city seems to have been independent at first, but gradually they formed confederations and even planted new colonies. From about 1200 to 1400, the capital of the Mayan confederation was located in the city of Mayapan. However, a great revolt took place, Mayapan was destroyed, and the individual cities resumed their independence; however, the constant warfare severely crippled Mayan civilization.

Even before the fall of Mayapan, the Aztecs, a warlike group of Indians, conquered most of Mexico and borrowed much of the Mayan culture. The Aztecs were not the first group of Mexican Indians to have imitated the Mayan way of life. The Toltec Indians, the Aztec's predecessors as rulers of Mexico, had already rebuilt the pyramids of the sun and moon and the huge temples which dominated the city of Teotihuacan, the religious center of Mexico. The Aztec Indians, however, controlled a larger area and ruled it more ruthlessly than any of their forerunners.

The leader of the Aztecs exercised absolute rule but was aided by the advice of three major officials: the chief priest (for religious ceremonials); the chief justice (for legal affairs); and the chief of markets, who regulated the trade of the Aztec

Empire. Aztec traders were organized in a guild and carried on an extensive trade, by land and sea, all over Central America. They also served as spies, ensuring that conquered tribes remained loyal and determining if free tribes were ripe for conquest.

The Aztec capital, Tenochtitlan, was a beautiful city built on a series of islands on the site of present-day Mexico City. Its population is estimated to have reached 300,000, but even a third of that number would have placed it among the largest European cities of the time. The city was divided into twenty neighborhoods (one for each clan), each with its own temple and arsenal. The men of each neighborhood farmed a common area and served in the army as a unit. The Aztecs forced tributary tribes to pay heavy taxes in gold, silver, jade, jaguar skins, cotton, and all types of foodstuffs. In addition, they required a human tribute of thousands of people, who were sacrificed each year to satisfy the voracious Aztec deities. At the dedication of one temple alone, 20,000 victims (by conservative estimates) were sacrificed to the gods. As can easily be imagined, revolt was endemic in the Aztec empire.

The Indians of Peru also built a highly advanced civilization. The high point of Peruvian political organization—though not necessarily of Peruvian civilization—was reached under the rule of the Incas, which began in about the year 1100. The Inca rulers claimed to be descendants of the sun. To keep their line pure, the eldest son of the royal family always married his eldest sister. The Incas had a well-trained army in which all young men between the ages of fifteen and twenty were expected to serve. The army was well fed and clothed, and entry to government office might be won by acts of bravery. This army soon conquered the small states along the western coast of South America and created an empire with its capital at Cuzco.

The Inca empire was divided into tribal districts, each with its own capital city. Each tribe wore a distinctive form of dress. This made it possible for the government to recognize any strangers who might be in the tribal area and to ascertain why they were there. The huge quantities of gold and silver which were mined in the Inca empire all belonged to the ruler. In addition, each tribe was responsible for a quota of various other products. Failure to meet this quota was met with stern punishment. Disrespect for the ruler or for the official religion (which were virtually synonymous) was punishable by death. Lesser crimes were punished by mutilation—cutting off the offender's ear, nose, hand, or foot. Imprisonment was reserved only for the nobility.

The Inca empire was a flourishing economic unit united by a network of roads, bridges, and inns. The people living along these routes had to help build them and keep them in repair. Goods were carried by llamas (who could carry only about forty pounds) or by men (who were often able to carry more than a hundred pounds). The Indians ruled by the Incas were outstanding artisans. Their pottery, woven cloth, and metal work were magnificent. A brisk trade in these items took place all over the Inca empire. The roads also served a basic military purpose. The army used them to put down revolts within the empire and to march against unconquered tribes on the borders of the empire.

The Inca empire was a bureaucratic welfare state. Priests, merchants, and artisans made up virtually closed classes. The masses of the people were farmers. Girls were taught to spin and weave. Those girls, of whatever class, who exhibited the most skill in these arts might become Virgins of the Sun, who served in the temples, and later might marry into the nobility or even into the royal family.

After completing their military service, young men were encouraged to marry. Village officials would allot to the young couple a plot of land and a house. The couple was exempt from taxation for the first year of their marriage and for one year after the birth of each child. They then farmed their land, labored on public projects, and paid their taxes just as their parents had done before them. When people became old, their taxes and forced labor were remitted, and—if necessary—they received food and clothing from the government warehouses scattered all over the empire.

Not all the Indians with whom the Spanish made contact were as advanced as the Indians of Central America and Peru. The Arawak Indians of the West Indies, the first to be seen by Columbus, probably arrived there from South America about 1,500 years before Columbus did. These Indians were peaceful farmers who grew maize and sugar cane. However, a much fiercer tribe, the Caribs—also from South America—followed them to the West Indies. The Caribs gave their name to the sea surrounding the West Indies, and by literally eating up the Arawaks, they added the word *cannibal* to the English language.

THE INDIANS OF THE SOUTHWEST AND WEST

Later, as the Spanish moved north from Mexico, they came into contact with the Indians of the southwestern part of the United States. The ancestors of the Pueblo, Hopi, and Zuni Indians—known variously as the Basketmakers, or the Anasazi, or Ancient Ones—lived in the area for at least 2,000 years. The Basketmakers were an advanced agricultural people who used irrigation to help grow their crops. They lived in houses of adobe and wood which were originally built in pits and were entered from the roof.

In about the year 700, the Basketmakers began to build their homes above ground and joined their homes together into a rambling multistoried complex which the Spanish called *pueblos,* or villages. Separate, subterranean rooms in these pueblos—known as *kivas,* or chapels—were set aside for religious ceremonials. Each kiva had a fire pit and a hole that supposedly lead to the underworld. The largest pueblos had five stories and more than 800 rooms. Rooms were about twelve feet square and had a fireplace.

The Pueblo Indian family was matrilinear (that is, descent was traced through the female) and consisted of a grandmother, her daughters, and her granddaughters plus their husbands and unmarried sons. The sacred objects of the family were under the control of the oldest female, but the actual ceremonies were conducted by her brother or son. Women owned the rooms in the pueblo and the crops, once they were harvested. (While still growing, crops belonged to the men, who in contrast to most Indian groups, planted them.) The women made the splendid baskets and pottery; the men wove the equally beautiful textiles, crafted the turquoise jewelry, and made the small images which represented the family's ancestors.

Each village had two chiefs: the war chief and the village chief. The village chief dealt with land disputes and religious affairs. The war chief led the men in fighting during the occasional conflicts which broke out with neighboring villages and the defensive battles against raiding Apaches and Navajos. (The Apaches continued their nomadic ways; the Navajos later settled down.) He also directed the men in community building projects. The cohesive political and social organization of the Pueblo Indians made it difficult for the Spanish to conquer them and almost impossible for these Indians to change their traditional way of life.

Most of the Indians of California, with whom the Spanish were to come into contact, were still in the food-gathering stage. The only art in which they excelled was basket weaving. During the colonial period Europeans did not have many direct or continuous contacts with the much more advanced Indians of the northwest, who had war canoes, elaborately carved totem poles, and potlatches, or lavish gift-giving parties.

THE PLAINS INDIANS

However, one group of Indians, the Plains Indians (with whom Europeans had little contact during the colonial period), were nevertheless to have their lives revolutionized by the newcomers. The Plains Indians did some farming but gradually became more and more nomadic as they followed the buffalo herds. Dogs, their only domesticated animal, pulled the Plains Indians' possessions along on a pair of A-shaped poles, later called a *travois* by the French. These same poles were utilized to form the framework of their tepees.

Hunting buffalo on foot was not easy. When horses (which escaped—or were stolen—from Spanish settlers) reached the Great Plains by the beginning of the eighteenth century, the Indians found a solution to many of their problems. On horseback they were able to encircle and kill entire herds of buffalo. The Plains Indians now had more meat for food, more skins for clothing, and more bones for their tools and weapons. Horses also made it possible for them to increase the amount of their possessions, since their goods could be so much more easily transported from place to place. Later, when guns from the east began to reach the Plains Indians, this group emerged as the formidable and archetypal Indians of our "last frontier."

The most culturally advanced Indians of North America were known as the Mound Builders. The Mound Builders lived in the Ohio River valley and were the progenitors of the Creek and Choctaw Indians. Their name derived from the thousands of huge mounds they built in the shape of humans, birds, or snakes. They built most of these mounds to bury their dead, but others must have served as fortification. Judging from archaeological remains, the Mound Builders were primarily an agricultural people, but they engaged in trade in metals, textiles, and pearls with Indians from the Rocky Mountains to the Atlantic coast. Beginning in about 500 A.D., however, the Mound Builders were challenged by another cultural group, who were known as the Mississippians. The Mississippians also built mounds—one near Cahokia, Illinois, is one hundred feet high and has a base slightly larger than the Great Pyramid of Egypt. The Mississippi culture died out before the European discovery of America, but some of the agricultural knowledge it acquired spread to the Indians living along the eastern coast of North America.

THE EASTERN WOODLAND INDIANS

The Indians with whom the English, the Dutch, and the French were to come into contact were known as the Eastern Woodland Indians. The eastern tribes were primarily agricultural, although the men spent considerable time hunting and fishing. Both farming and hunting were communal enterprises, and private ownership of land did not exist among these tribes. The major crops were corn, beans, squashes, pumpkins, and tobacco. In addition to doing the farm work, women also gathered nuts and berries to supplement their families' diet. When the hunters were successful, these Indians also enjoyed deer, moose, beaver, turkey, and duck meat. All types of fish were eaten as well as lobsters, clams, and oysters.

The Eastern Woodland Indians lived in an egalitarian society. There were no extremes of wealth or poverty. Even the chief lived in much the same way as the other members of his tribe. A man who was a better hunter than his fellows was still expected to share equally with them. No one went hungry as long as some food remained in the village. Child raising was, on the whole, permissive, with the aim of developing a young man or woman with loyalty to the group and the requisite skills to be a useful member of it. These Indians had no elaborate law codes or penal system. Such systems were unnecessary because all members of the tribe knew what was expected of them. If a violation of the norms did take place, it was immediately followed by public ridicule and/or ostracisim.

Eastern Woodland villages were small, perhaps numbering only one hundred people. Usually they were surrounded by a wall of earth topped by a wooden stockade. Wigwams were made of small tree trunks placed in the ground in a circle and pulled together at the top, leaving just enough space for a smoke-hole. The wigwam was covered with woven bark or rushes and skins when the weather was colder. Benches were placed around the insides of the wigwam for sitting or sleeping. Most wigwams held only one family. However, certain tribes built long-houses, so-called because they were over one hundred feet in length and housed up to twenty families. The Eastern Woodland Indians did not live in their villages all year round but wandered around following the game.

The Eastern Woodland Indians were living in Stone Age conditions during the age of discovery. Their utensils and tools, and weapons such as the tomahawk, war club, knife, spear, blow gun, and bow and arrow were made of stone, bone, or wood. Pipes were made of pottery or stone. They did, however, develop the light and convenient birch-bark canoe and the toboggan and showshoe for winter travel. Their agricultural implements were extremely simple—the hoe often being nothing more than a clamshell tied to a stick. Clothes were equally simple, depending on the weather. In summer a breechclout for the men and a skirt for the women (both made out of skins) were sufficient. In the winter men added trousers, leggings, and shirts; women wore blouses and capes. Furs were worn by both sexes in the colder areas. Typical ornaments were necklaces and pendants made of bone, shell, or animal teeth. Feathered headdresses were worn by the men, but they were not as elaborate as those of the Plains Indians.

The Eastern Woodland Indians worshiped many gods, of whom the Great Spirit was preeminent. As animists they believed that trees, stars, animals—the entire environment—had souls. Their main religious functionary was a medicine man who combined the duties of priest and physician. The dead were buried in cemeteries along with lavish offerings. Gift giving was extremely important in this society. However, the recipient of a gift was expected to return a gift of equal, or even greater, value. From this comes the expression "Indian giver."

This custom also helps explain why after Europeans arrived, certain chiefs who were in severe financial straits because of the gifts they were expected to give, sold tribal lands to white settlers in order to augment their fortunes. Skins, furs, and tobacco were among the common gifts, but the most prized was wampum. White wampum (made from the inside of a conch shell) and the even more highly valued dark wampum (made from the shell of a clam or mussel) were both generally in the form of small beads which were either strung together or woven into a belt. Before the arrival of Europeans, wampum was not used as money but had great ritual significance and could be constructed to convey a message.

The head of the tribe was a hereditary chief. Generally, however, he met with his council, whose consent was necessary for all important decisions. At these council meetings a pipe full of tobacco would be passed around, since it was thought that tobacco had the magical property of clearing the mind and leading to correct decisions. The Iroquois Indians, who lived between New York State and the Great Lakes, are the best known of the Eastern Woodland Indians. They had the most complex form of government found among North American Indians. In the sixteenth century five tribes—the Mohawks, Oneida, Cayuga, Onondaga, and Seneca—formed the Five Nations (which grew to six when the Tuscarora were admitted to membership 200 years later). This was also known as the Iroquois Confederacy. Council meetings were held at least once a year to decide questions of importance to all members of the confederacy. The council had about fifty regular members (plus "Pine Tree chiefs" who were allowed to speak but not to vote). Each tribe had only one vote, and a decision to go to war required a unanimous vote.

It appears that Iroquois women had a greater voice in decision making than the women of most Indian tribes. The Iroquois family was matrilinear, and groups of families headed by women who were related formed an *ohwachira,* or kinship group. These kinship groups, in turn, combined to form a clan. The heads of clans were always women, and these leaders had the power to name the men they wished to serve on the tribal councils and the council of the confederacy. While men did all the talking at these council meetings, they were always aware that they could be removed if they did not meet the expectations of the women who appointed them.

Games were important among the Eastern Woodland Indians. Games of chance, particularly those involving the use of dice, were extremely popular. Lacrosse contests, spear-throwing contests, and all types of races took place within, and even between, villages. Local pride and large bets were involved in these contests, and the competition resulted in numerous, and serious, injuries. Some psychologists have viewed these contests as substitutes, as well as preparation, for actual warfare.

Yet, warfare itself was very common. After the formation of their confederacy, the Iroquois deliberately expanded their power by destroying or cowing neighboring tribes. The approximately 3,000 warriors they could muster at the height of their power wore reed breastplates and used common Indian weapons as well as unusual (for North American Indians) weapons such as the blowpipe and poisoned darts. Generally, the Iroquois fought the hit-and-run style of warfare typical of most Indians. Like most other tribes, they took scalps and subjected their prisoners to hideous torture before finally eating their hearts.

Nevertheless, recent studies, particularly those by Anthony Wallace, have indicated that the Iroquois brave was not as self-assured as legend would have us believe. The Iroquois had a Society of Faces (or False Face Society) which allowed the men to conceal themselves behind masks and act our forbidden or shameful fantasies. In addition, the Iroquois, like many other tribes, believed that the wishes of the "soul"—as manifested through dreams—must be fulfilled. Therefore, they were allowed to discuss their dreams before a special council which attempted to interpret them and to facilitate their realization. For example, an unfavorable dream was considered an acceptable and legitimate excuse for a brave to refuse to join a war party.

The Indians of the southwest—the Creeks, Choctaws, Cherokees, and Chicasaws—lived very much like the tribes that lived farther north. They did, however, depend more on agriculture, which meant that they were more sedentary and had more time to perfect the arts of pottery making and basket weaving. Each village was independent, but villages of one tribe never fought one another. It was only later, when European settlers began treating them as a unit, that tribal councils developed.

To the west of these tribes, along the eastern bank of the Mississippi, lived one of the most interesting Indian groups of North America, the Natchez Indians. The Natchez Indians had a complex political and religious system which almost surely was influenced by the Indians of Mexico. The leader of the Natchez Indians was

INDIAN TRIBES OF EASTERN NORTH AMERICA
ON THE EVE OF EUROPEAN CONTACT

FIGURE 2B (From Gary B. Nash, *Red, White, and Black,* 2nd ed. Englewood Cliffs, N.J.: Prentice-Hall, Inc., ©1982, p. 15. By permission of the publisher.)

called the Great Sun. In his capital city stood two mounds: one for his residence, the other for a temple in which a perpetual fire was kept burning and the body of his immediate predecessor was kept. The Great Sun was both king and god. During his life his word was law, and he was carried on a litter and seated on an elaborate throne. At his death wives and servants were executed to serve him in the next world. Upper-class members of the tribe and outstanding warriors were elaborately tattooed and dressed more ornately than the common people. The Natchez Indians withstood both the Spanish and French for most of the colonial period.

ESTIMATES OF INDIAN POPULATION

The foregoing account has merely highlighted a few of the Indian groups living in the Americas in 1492. Estimates of the total Indian population at that time vary from 10 million (1 million in North America; 4 million in Central America and the West Indies; and 5 million in South America) to 100 million (multiplying each area projection by 10). Whatever the exact number, the crucial fact so often overlooked in studying colonial history is that the Indian population along the west coasts of both continents, in Central America, and—to a lesser degree—on the east coast of North America, was considerable—seventy-five people per one hundred square kilometers. Europeans were *not* entering empty continents, as is so often implied.

However, Europeans, wittingly or unwittingly, did their best to empty these continents as speedily as possible. Millions of Indians were killed off by war and slavery, but many more millions were wiped out by disease. The three main scourges were smallpox, typhus, and measles, which were new to the Americas and against which the Indians had absolutely no immunity. Malaria was also imported into the New World from Europe. (Contrary to common belief, Europeans in South America discovered the value of chinchoma bark [quinine] in combating malaria only in the seventeenth century.) It was once taken for granted that the Indians obtained a measure of revenge by bequeathing syphilis to the Old World. The men of Columbus's expeditions were supposed to have brought it back to Europe after contact with Indian women. Now, however, scientists claim to have found types of syphilis—of which there are several—in Europe long before 1492.

In any case, it has been estimated that the Indian population of Haiti declined from 200,000 in 1492 to 29,000 in 1514. It is a fact that hardly an Indian was left alive in all of the European-occupied West Indies by the middle of the sixteenth century. The Indian population of Mexico was reduced by 80 percent within thirty years after the Spanish conquest and continued to decline for another century before it once again began to rise. In North America the story was similar, except on a slightly smaller scale. By 1660 the estimated 3,000-member Massachusetts Indian tribe (from which the state takes its name) was virtually extinct. Gradually, 400 other tribes suffered a similar fate. This was, as in South America, partly a result of war and disease but even more a result of the clearing of land and preempting of water sources by settlers.

BIBLIOGRAPHY

AXTELL, JAMES. *The European and the Indian: Essays in the Ethnohistory of Colonial North America.* New York, 1981.

BOWDEN, HENRY WARNER. *American Indians and Christian Missions: Studies in Cultural Conflict.* Chicago, 1981.

CASTILE, GEORGE PIERRE. *North American Indians.* New York, 1979.

COLLIER, GEORGE. *Inca & Aztec States, Fourteen Hundred–Eighteen Hundred: Anthropology & History.* New York, 1982.

CROSBY, ALFRED W., JR. *The Columbian Exchange: Biological and Cultural Consequences of 1492.* Westport, Conn., 1972.

DAVIES, NIGEL. *The Aztecs: A History.* New York, 1973.

DENEVAN, WILLIAM M., ed. *The Native Population of the Americas in 1492.* Madison, 1976.

GORENSTEIN, SHIRLEY, et al. *Prehispanic America.* New York, 1974.

HENDERSON, JOHN S. *The World of the Ancient Maya.* Ithaca, 1981.

HUDSON, CHARLES. *The Southeastern Indians.* Knoxville, 1976.

KUPPERMAN, KAREN ORDAHL. *Settling with the Indians: The Meeting of English and Indian Cultures in America, 1580–1640.* Totowa, N.J., 1980.

NASH, GARY, B. *Red, White, and Black: The Peoples of Early America.* Englewood Cliffs, N.J., 1974.

RUSSELL, HOWARD S. *Indian New England Before the Mayflower.* Hanover, N.H., 1980.

SALISBURY, NEAL. *Manitou and Providence: Indians, Europeans, and the Making of New England, 1500–1643.* New York: Oxford University Press, 1982.

WRIGHT, J. LEITCH. *The Only Land They Knew: The Tragic Story of the American Indians in the Old South.* New York, 1981.

3
The Spanish Empire in America

In 1518 Montezuma II, the emperor of the Aztec Indians, was a worried man. The portents were ominous: A temple was struck by lightning; a comet flashed through the skies; and a flood destroyed homes in his capital city. Were these omens announcing the imminent return of Quetzalcoatl—the Plumed Serpent, the Lord of Life, the God of the Morning, the Bringer of Civilization—who was portrayed as a pale, bearded man destined to return to his kingdom on the back of a deer? Could it be true that this prophecy was at long last to be fulfilled?

SPANISH CONQUESTS

To answer this question, let us look back a few years. In the early 1500s Spanish colonization was largely confined to Haiti, Puerto Rico, Cuba, and Jamaica. Several expeditions had attempted to colonize the isthmus of Panama, but all had failed because of Indian opposition. Vasco Nuñez de Balboa, a colonist of Haiti who was so poor that he had to stow away aboard a ship bound for Panama, realized the futility of trying to fight the Indians. He married the daughter of one Indian chieftain and made friends with the son of another. In 1513, with their help, he led an expedition of about 200 men (only 60 survived) across the jungles of Panama to the South Sea (Pacific Ocean), which he claimed for the king of Spain. Balboa found just enough gold and pearls to whet the appetite of other Spaniards for the wealth of the New World.

In the same year Ponce de Leon, the governor of Puerto Rico, sailed northward looking for two things—gold and the fountain of youth. Ponce de Leon landed in Florida, dug for gold, and bathed in all the springs; but on this and on a later expedition, he was disappointed in both quests. Nor did the Spanish government do much to follow up his explorations. Only when the French tried to start a settlement in Florida did the Spanish establish a fort at St. Augustine, around which developed the first town in what is now the United States. However, very few Spaniards ever settled in Florida, and it remained an isolated outpost all during the colonial period.

It was Hernando Cortés who proved in 1519 that playing off one Indian group against another could lead to fame and fortune. Cortés landed on the coast of Mexico, burned his ships, and marched directly toward the Aztec capital of Tenochtitlan. On the way, with the aid of his Indian mistress—the lady Marina (as she was called after being baptized)—Cortés won the Aztec tributary tribes to his side. Without these allies Cortés and his 500 men—even with their horses, armor, and cannon—would have been annihilated.

Montezuma tried to bribe Cortés not to visit Tenochtitlan by sending him gifts of silver and gold. Nothing could have been more illadvised. The sight of these treasures only intensified Cortés's determination. Soon Montezuma, still not sure of Cortés's status, welcomed him to the Aztec capital. Before long he was Cortés's prisoner.

The next threat to Cortés's success came not from the Aztecs but from a Spanish force that had arrived from Cuba with orders to capture him dead or alive. Cortés swiftly defeated this force and convinced its survivors to join him. However, during his absence the Aztecs decided to drive the Spaniards out of Tenochtitlan. Despite Cortés's return, the uprising succeeded. Montezuma was killed—whether by the Spanish or by the Aztecs is unknown—and Cortés barely managed to escape from the city with less than half of his forces left alive. Now the real conquest of Mexico began: It was not primarily accomplished by Cortés's few hundred men but by the literally hundreds of thousands of Indians that flocked to his standard. Finally, in August 1521, Cortés and his allies again captured Tenochtitlan, massacred its inhabitants, and razed it to the ground. The Aztec empire had fallen, but as we shall see later, Cortés's allies were not destined to celebrate their victory for long.

The riches of Mexico were exceeded only by those of Peru. The Indians of Panama had told Balboa about the wealth of the Inca empire, but it was not until 1532 that a successful expedition was mounted against it. The leader of this expedition was Francisco Pizarro, a veteran of Balboa's expedition and of many years of Indian fighting in Central America. Pizarro landed on the coast of Peru with only 164 men and 62 horses and marched toward Cuzco, the Inca capital. Pizarro took Cuzco with practically no opposition, partly because of disease—which had killed off many Indians just before his landing—and partly because of dissension within the Inca ruling family. Nevertheless, in outlying areas the Indians continued to resist Spanish rule until 1572, when the last Inca ruler was finally defeated.

THE EXPLORATION AND SETTLEMENT
OF THE WEST

From Mexico and Peru *conquistadores* marched out to conquer all of Central and South America. These areas were to form the core of the Spanish empire in America. However, we, like those Spaniards who continued to search for gold and silver, will now turn our attention to North America. In 1528 Pánfilio de Narváez landed on the coast of the Gulf of Mexico with an expedition of 400 men. Eight years later, four survivors—including Cabeza de Vaca, a Spanish nobleman and Estevan (or Estevanico), a black slave originally captured in Morocco—reappeared in northern Mexico. De Vaca wrote a book about their ordeal in which he repeated the tales told him by the Indians of the Seven Cities of Gold. De Vaca's book triggered several expeditions to discover these cities. One of them, led by Hernando de Soto, who had served with Pizarro in Peru, landed in Florida and wandered through (what is now) Alabama, Georgia, the Carolinas, Tennessee, Mississippi, Louisiana, Arkansas, Texas, and Oklahoma between 1539 and 1542. De Soto died of a fever in 1542 and was buried secretly in the Mississippi River so that the Indians would believe that he was a god who had temporarily ascended to heaven.

In the same year that De Soto landed in Florida, an expedition led by a Franciscan, Friar Marcos, set out to search for the Seven Cities of Gold in the southwest. Estevan, who accompanied the expedition, dressed as an Indian medicine man—a role he had played to save his life earlier—and went out with a few Indians as an advance scouting group for the party. At first the Indians welcomed him, but when he reached one of the pueblos of the Zuni Indians, he was locked in a hut and killed when he tried to escape. In the following year a much larger expedition under the command of Francisco de Coronado reached the pueblo where Estevan had been killed. Seeing that it was obviously not one of the Seven Cities of Gold, he continued to search elsewhere until 1642. He, too, covered immense stretches of territory. He was the first European to view the Grand Canyon, but he never found the treasure he was seeking.

The Indians of the southwest were left in peace (except for sporadic slave-raiding expeditions) until 1598, when Juan de Oñate, a large Mexican landowner (who was married to the great granddaughter of Montezuma) settled about 400 colonists in the southwest. He founded Sante Fé in about 1610, and by 1680 approximately 2,500 Spaniards lived in the area. In that year, however, the Indians, tired of the exactions of the Spanish and of their attempts to extirpate the native religion, rose up in revolt under the leadership of a medicine man named Pope. About 500 Spanish settlers were killed, and the rest fled all the way to El Paso, Texas. Not until 1692 was a Spanish army strong enough to return. It then took four more years of fighting before the southwest returned to Spanish control and settlement.

Spanish ships sent out by Cortés traveled along the coast of California as early as the 1530s, and in 1542-1543 Juan Rodriguez Cabrillo (and his pilot Bartolomé Ferrelo, after the former's death) sailed along the Pacific coast as far north as

Oregon. However, it was not until the beginning of the eighteenth century that missions were founded in Arizona and Lower California by the heroic Eusebio Francisco Kino, a Jesuit father. Over the course of the next sixty years, the Jesuits managed to found fourteen missions in Lower California, but they lacked the resources to continue into Upper California. However, at the end of the Seven Years' War (1763), threats of Russian and/or English settlement in that area impelled the Spanish government to conquer and settle Upper California as soon as possible. The Franciscans took over religious authority in California in 1767 when the Jesuits were expelled from Spanish America. Under the leadership of Father Junipero Serra, a string of twenty missions was founded, extending as far north as San Francisco.

The Indians of California, who were nomadic, were herded into these missions in order that their souls be saved and their labor exploited. They were taught the elements of Christianity, the Spanish language; European methods of farming and of raising cattle, sheep, and horses; and the practice of crafts such as carpentry, tanning, tailoring, metalworking, shoemaking, and whatever else was needed for their economy. Mission Indians were allowed to regulate most of their everyday affairs, but ultimate authority over them resided in the Church.

Whether the mission was located in the southwest or in California, a *presidio*, or garrison, was usually coupled with it. These frontier posts were manned by about sixty soldiers, their families, and Indian servants. They kept the supply routes to Mexico open and protected the missions from attacks by unconverted Indians. Gradually, though in relatively small numbers, settlers moved north out of Mexico into these new areas. Most of these settlers engaged in either farming or ranching. In California olives, grapes, fruit, and grain were raised in large quantities. Many of these crops—wheat, rice, oranges, cherries, figs, watermelons, peaches, and onions—had been introduced to the Americas in the early sixteenth century and were gradually accepted by the Indians, including those not confined to missions.

However, in the southwest, and even in California, ranching was the dominant occupation. Ranches, as such, did not exist. Thousands of heads of cattle and large numbers of horses grazed on the rich grass of the open, unfenced range. This necessitated the use of branding so that owners could identify their cattle. It also led to the rodeo, or roundup (the original meaning of the word), in which the cattle were encircled by horsemen, separated out by their owners, and then driven to market. This type of ranching, including its terminology, costumes, and techniques, was later imitated almost exactly by the American post-Civil War cattle industry.

THE GOVERNMENT
OF THE SPANISH EMPIRE

Let us now return to Central and South America during the last quarter of the sixteenth century. This was when the frantic search for gold and silver came to an end and the Spanish government remained determined to develop strong, stable colonies under firm royal control. Two agencies had already been organized to accomplish these ends. The first, the Casa de Contratación, or House of Trade (established in 1503), regulated all aspects of economic life in the colonies. It granted the merchant guild of Seville (later Cadiz) a monopoly of all trade with the colonies. Ships trading with Spanish America had to sail in regular convoys and could only land at designated ports. This facilitated the collection of a wide variety of taxes on colonial commerce including an export tax, an import tax, and a sales tax. The Casa de Contratación attempted to prevent any foreign nation from trading with the Spanish colonies. However, by the seventeenth century this had already become impossible because of the decline of the Spanish merchant marine, the desire for lower-priced goods, and the inefficiency and corruption of the colonial bureaucracy. The Casa de Contratación also failed in its efforts to prevent the colonists from raising products which would compete with those grown in Spain. Nevertheless, even though these commercial regulations were later modified (and always loosely enforced), Spanish colonists in America resented the heavy-handed attempts of the home government to regulate their economic life.

The second governmental agency (formed in 1524) to assist the king in ruling his American possessions was the Consejo de Indias, or Council of the Indies. Through this council laws were promulgated, appointments made, and judicial appeals heard. The Spanish empire in America was ultimately divided into four "kingdoms": New Spain—including Mexico, the West Indies, and Central America; New Granada—including Venezuela, Colombia, and Ecuador; New Castile—including Peru and Chile; and La Plata Uruguay, Paraguay, Bolivia, and Argentina. Each of these major political divisions was headed by a viceroy who had full political and military powers, subject only to instructions from Spain and the advice of *audiencias,* or councils. The most important political offices were always held by appointees sent out from Spain. Lesser officials were at first appointed by the viceroys, but later they, too, became royal appointees. Towns were ruled by *cabildos,* or municipal councils, headed by two *alcaldes,* or judges. Although in theory all these officials were expected merely to see that the laws promulgated in Spain were enforced to the letter, in practice all levels of officials from viceroys down often altered or disregarded these laws. To counteract this trend, the Spanish government sent *visitadores,* or inspectors, to the colonies with power to discipline offending officials. Another practice, the *residencia,* or formal hearing at the conclusion of an official's term of office, was designed to reduce official inefficiency and corruption. However, it tended to generate into a mere formality. In the eighteenth century another layer of royal officials, the intendants, was added to the bureaucracy. This multiplicity of officials, and laws, and taxes—even if they were not always enforced—still weighed heavily on most Spanish colonists.

It is difficult to categorize the Spanish colonists in America. They were predominantly male and included government officials, large landowners, traders, doctors, lawyers, artisans, farmers, and churchmen. The number of Spanish settlers grew from about 100,000 in the middle of the sixteenth century to over 3 million by the end of the colonial period. Whites who were born in Spain held all the highest positions and considered themselves superior to the creoles, or whites who were born in the colonies. All whites considered themselves better than mestizos (of mixed Indian and white descent) and mulattoes (of mixed African and white descent) and infinitely superior to pure-blooded Indians or Africans.

RACE RELATIONS
IN THE SPANISH EMPIRE

Mention of the latter two groups necessitates a review of Spanish theories about and treatment of Indians and Africans. Not only were these people important in Spanish colonial life, but Spanish theories, and the practices resulting from them, affected the other European empires in the New World. The Spanish had no doubt that the Indians were an inferior group of pagan barbarians who must be converted to Christianity; however, just what degree of force was to be allowed to accomplish this end was not certain.

Between 1512 and 1556 Spanish commanders were expected to read a document known as the Requerimiento (Requirement) to the Indians before attacking them. This document described some of the tenets of Christianity, ordered the Indians to accept it and acknowledge the authority of the pope and the king of Spain, and threatened them with loss of their land and their freedom if they refused. The Requerimiento assumed that the Indians were rational beings and not brutes. This question was itself the subject of a long and heated debate before Paul III declared in a Papal decree (1537) that "Indians are truly men, and . . . capable of understanding the Catholic faith."

The Requerimiento was actually read by the conquistadores—though in Spanish and probably at a safe distance—before attacking the Indians. This placed the Spaniards in the position of fighting a "just war" and laying all the blame for what happened on the Indians themselves. If sword and steel were necessary to bring the Indians to Christianity, as apparently they were, then their use was legitimate and proper.

Once the conquest of the Indians was completed, the next task was to exploit their labor. For this purpose the *encomienda* system was instituted in the West Indies as early as 1503. Under this system the Indians of a certain area were "commended" to the rule of a Spanish overlord called an *encomiendero*. This official was expected to Christianize and "civilize" the Indians; they, in turn, were to work part time for him as well as contribute to him a share of the crops they raised for themselves. Although the Spanish government always insisted that these Indians were free citizens who must be treated humanely, in practice they were bought and sold, worked (literally) to death, and forced into virtual slavery.

The great opponent of the encomienda system and defender of Indian rights in general was a churchman, Bishop Bartolomé de Las Casas. Las Casas insisted that Indians were rational beings who could, and should, be converted without force. In fact, he and a group of Dominican friars actually did convert a group of Indians in a section of Guatemala without the use of force. In 1520 Las Casas's arguments convinced the new king, Charles I, to order the abolition of the ecomienda system. However, the conquest of Mexico induced the king to rescind this edict. Later, however, in 1542-1543, a series of enactments known as the New Laws forbid the creation of any new encomiendas, strictly regulated conditions on those that already existed, and made it impossible for them to be bequeathed to any heirs.

Even at this date colonial opposition was strong enough to have the ban on inheritance removed. However, Indians were exempted from personal service and their contributions were strictly limited. These restrictions, plus the high death rate among the Indians, severely reduced the profits of the encomienderos, and the institution was moribund long before the eighteenth-century legislation which finally abolished it.

However, Las Casas's vivid accounts of the cruelties of the conquistadores and the sufferings of the Indians on the encomiendas (exaggerated, perhaps, because he was trying to convince the king to abolish the institution) were later translated by authors in nations hostile to Spain in order to prove that Spaniards were too cruel to be permitted to rule any part of the New World. Thus arose the so-called Black Legend of fiendish Spanish cruelty. Still, whether Spain's record was any blacker or more legendary than that of other European nations is questionable.

The abolition of the encomienda did not completely free the Indians. Royal officials still collected taxes in kind from them and allotted Indian workers to private landowners when they felt additional labor was necessary. In addition, royal policy and Indian depopulation encouraged the gathering of Indians into villages and the expropriation of their lands. These lands tended to fall into the hands of a small number of Spaniards, whose huge estates became known as *haciendas*. Gradually, the Indians living on or near these estates became virtually attached to them as peons. This form of landholding and labor system persisted in Spanish America well into the twentieth century.

However, no system of Indian labor was able to meet the ever-increasing demand for workers in the Spanish colonies. Disease, suicide, and the running away of slaves made Indian slavery uneconomic. Also, the efforts of Las Casas soon made it technically illegal. The obvious alternative (it had already been introduced into Spain) was African slavery. As early as 1501 the king approved the shipment of African slaves from Spain to the West Indies, and by 1516 the Spanish government initiated the policy of granting a foreign nation the *Asiento,* or monopoly of African slave trading with its colonies. During the course of the ensuing three centuries, a wide variety of companies and nations enjoyed this concession and imported millions of slaves into Spanish America. Las Casas also attempted to prevent Africans from being condemned to perpetual slavery, but the demand for cheap labor was too strong and he reluctantly capitulated.

Slaves worked in the fields, in the mines, and in the cities, largely as servants and artisans. With some exceptions in the city, working conditions were harsh. Strict rules were designed to control every aspect of a slave's life, and whipping and mutilation were common punishments for violation of these rules. As a natural result, slave revolts were endemic in Spanish America.

Yet, in theory at least, slavery in Spanish America was not as brutal as it was to be in the English colonies. Even though Las Casas was not able to prevent African slavery, the Catholic Church was able to mitigate some of its inhumanity. Slaves were baptized—thus, they were acknowledged as human beings with souls, not mere chattels. Slave marriages were recognized, and family life was respected. Owners were expected to meet the minimum physical needs of their slaves and to keep their punishments within reasonable limits. Slaves were allowed to earn money which could be utilized to purchase their own, and their family's, freedom. Manumission of slaves was a much easier and much more common process in Spanish America than in the English colonies. Further, Spaniards—whether because of lack of women and/or due to relative lack of race prejudice—were not adverse to marrying African women. As a result of all these factors, free blacks outnumbered slaves in the Spanish colonies by the end of the colonial period.

RELIGIOUS AND CULTURAL LIFE
IN THE SPANISH EMPIRE

The Catholic Church was the most important institution in Spanish America. It was well organized (five archbishoprics and twenty-seven bishoprics by 1600) and extremely wealthy—owning from one-third to one-half of all private property in the colonies. The Inquisition—the arm of the Church designated to uproot heresy and dissent—was authorized to act in America, and over the years trials were held in Mexico City, Lima, and Cartegena. However, Indians were not subject to its jurisdiction and, with the exception of its prosecution of secret Jews, it concentrated primarily on cases of immorality and the censorship of books and plays.

In addition to its concern for Indians and slaves, the Church attempted to minister to the medical and educational needs of its Spanish congregants as well as meet their spiritual needs. Hospitals, orphanages, and shelters for the elderly were all sponsored by the Church. It was also in full control of primary and secondary education as well as the ten major and fifteen minor institutions for higher education which existed in Spanish America. The two most important universities—those in Mexico City and in Lima, Peru—were chartered as early as 1551. Yet, the honor of being the first institution of higher learning in the Spanish colonies belongs to the College of Santa Cruz, which was founded in Mexico City in 1536 to serve Indian students.

Books from Spain were allowed into the colonies duty free, and personal libraries of over 4,000—and institutional libraries of 6,000-8,000—books were not unknown. Irregular issues of newspapers began to appear as early as 1560, and by the middle of the eighteenth century, most provincial capitals had well-established journals which contained European and local news as well as reports on bullfights and religious festivals. Many colonists were also avid readers of *El Espiritu de los Mejores Diarios,* Madrid's major newspaper. Dissemination of news was aided by the postal service. During the seventeenth century mail boats sailed regularly between

Spain and the major ports of the New World. From these ports couriers, often using old Indian routes, transported letters all over the empire.

The Spanish colonists also enjoyed the theater. At first plays were strictly religious in nature, but gradually they became more secular. By the beginning of the seventeenth century, Mexico City and Lima had permanent theaters with regular troupes who performed plays written either in Spain or locally.

In 1536 the first printing press arrived in Spanish America, and many important works were produced there during the colonial period. Perhaps the outstanding poet of seventeenth-century Spanish America was Juana Inés de la Cruz, a brilliant young woman who became a nun after being denied entrance to the university. Most of what we know about the pre-Columbian life of the Indians of Central and South America is based on the anthropological and linguistic (as we would call them today) studies made by scholars in Spanish America. Friar Bernardino de Sahagún in Mexico and Sarmiento de Gamboa in Peru preserved, with the help of the Indians themselves, much of the Aztec and Incan civilizations.

As would be expected, most of the literary and artistic works produced in the colonies was influenced by Spanish models. However, original scientific writing was done by Fray Alonzo de la Veracruz in the sixteenth century; Pedro de Peralta Barnuevo, José de Acosta, and José Celestino Mutis of Peru in the eighteenth century; and Antonio Alzate of Mexico also in the eighteenth century. As Bernardo Babluena, the bishop of Puerto Rico (and himself a scientist and poet) wrote with some hyperbole in his poem "Grandeza Mexicana" "Here [in Mexico] you will find more persons eminent in science and all the other faculties than grains of sand in Ganges might flow."

The revolts which broke out in South America during the early part of the nineteenth century overthrew Spanish political control in most of its American empire. Nevertheless, the Spanish empire was the first, the longest-lasting, the largest, the richest, and the most cultured of the American empires. Further, it was the one which most influenced the other European empires in the New World.

BIBLIOGRAPHY

BANNS, JOHN FRANCIS. *The Spanish Borderlands Frontier, 1513–1821.* New York, 1970.

GIBSON, CHARLES. *The Aztecs Under Spanish Rule.* New York, 1964.

GIBSON, CHARLES. *Spain in America.* New York, 1966.

HANKE, LEWIS. *The Spanish Struggle for Justice in the Conquest of America.* Philadelphia, 1949.

JONES, OAKAH L., JR. *Los Paisanos: Spanish Settlers on the Northern Frontier of New Spain.* Norman, Okla., 1979.

LOCKHART, JAMES. *Spanish Peru: A Colonial Society, 1532–1560.* Madison, 1968.

MACLACHLAN, COLIN M., and RODRIGUEZ, JAIME E. *The Forging of the Cosmic Race; A Reinterpretation of Colonial Mexico.* Berkeley, 1980.

PICÓN-SALAS, MARIANO. *A Cultural History of Spanish America from Conquest to Independence.* Berkeley, 1962.

STERN, STEVE J. *Peru's Indian Peoples and the Challenge of Spanish Conquest.* Madison, 1982.

ZAVALA, SILVIO. *New Viewpoints on the Spanish Colonization of America.* New York, 1968.

4

The Portuguese, French, and Dutch Empires in America

Spain and Portugal were not destined to enjoy their American possessions undisturbed. Francis I of France is reputed to have said that he doubted whether Adam's will granted the Americas to Spain and Portugal. Similar sentiments were voiced by English rulers beginning with Henry VIII; and the actions, if not the words, of the leaders of the Dutch Republic indicated that they, too, were ready to challenge Spain's hegemony over the Americas.

THE PORTUGUESE IN THE NEW WORLD

As discussed above, Portugal had the only claim to territory in South America which Spain recognized—albeit reluctantly. The area which fell under Portuguese rule received its name from the large number of valuable red-trunked dyewood trees found there, which were similar to the so-called brazil trees of the Far East. For about thirty years after the discovery of this land by Cabral, Portugal was too wrapped up in its Far Eastern trade to pay much attention to Brazil. Only a few scattered Portuguese settled in Brazil, where, if they survived, they usually took Indian wives and "went native." However, as the profits of the Far Eastern trade began to decline, the realization grew that dyewood was an extremely valuable product. Fear of French and/or Spanish encroachment on Brazil grew too.

    In 1530 Martin Alfonso de Souza was sent with five ships to clear French ships from the coast of Brazil and to plant two Portuguese settlements there. Three years later King John III divided Brazil into fifteen east-west strips about 150 miles wide, called *capitanias,* or captaincies. Each captaincy was granted to a Portuguese nobleman. This noble would then be responsible for the conversion of the Indians, the recruiting of settlers, and the economic development of his grant—a system resembling the Spanish encomienda. In 1549 the king appointed a governor-general to rule the entire colony. Under the royal regime Brazil prospered, and by 1680 it had a population of about 20,000 Portuguese, 18,000 Christianized Indians, and 14,000 African slaves—all engaged in the production of sugar, cotton, tobacco, and dyewoods.

In 1580 the king of Spain usurped the throne of Portugal, but life went on in Brazil much as before. However, in the 1620s Dutch attacks began, which were eventually to result in Dutch occupation of more than a thousand-mile stretch of the Brazilian coast. When Portugal regained its independence in 1640, the settlers themselves, with virtually no assistance from Portugal, attacked the Dutch. By 1654 these settlers drove the Dutch completely out of Brazil. This action was typical of the settlers of Brazil, who felt that they knew best how to deal with their own problems and did not hesitate to ignore Portuguese edicts—such as those abolishing Indian slavery—which they felt were against their self-interest.

Not only was Indian slavery retained, but after gold and diamonds were found in Brazil at the beginning of the eighteenth century, slave hunting became one of the main Brazilian occupations. *Bandeiras,* or military companies, were formed to venture into the interior and capture Indians. Members of these groups did not hesitate to kidnap thousands of Indians from the mission villages established by the Jesuits. The only positive side to these slave-hunting expeditions was that they expanded the western boundaries of Brazil.

However, Indian slaves did not satisfy the insatiable demand for labor in Brazil. African slaves began arriving in the 1530s and continued to be imported at the rate of 40,000 a year throughout the seventeenth century, until they far outnumbered the rest of the population. Like the slaves in the Spanish empire, Brazilian slaves were baptized and were supposedly protected by law. A few fortunate slaves lived in the towns, where they worked as servants and laborers. In the towns slaves were often hired out by their owners, and sometimes they were able to earn some money of their own. Manumission of slaves was encouraged, and it was possible for slaves to buy their freedom. The vast majority of Brazilian slaves, however, worked from sunrise to sunset in the fields or in the mines under the most brutal conditions.

Running away was the most common reaction to this type of treatment. Very often runaway slaves joined together in groups to protect their new-found freedom. The largest and most famous of these groups existed from 1630 to 1697 in the virtually independent Republic of Palmares in northeastern Brazil. This republic had an organized government, an elected ruler, and a walled capital city. The inhabitants of Palmares lived by farming and trading. Runaway slaves kept coming to Palmares for refuge, and it is estimated that its population reached 20,000. The Dutch attacked Palmares in 1644 and the Portuguese in 1676, but it survived until 1697, when an army of over 7,000 captured its capital city and destroyed Palmares forever. However, the fall of Palmares did not mean the end of slave revolts.

Because the number of Portuguese settlers was small and predominantly male, it is not surprising that the Portuguese married, or at least mated with, Indian and African women. Although much less stigma attached to miscegenation there than in North America, or even in Spanish America, race still played an important role in determining social status in Brazil. The highest class was all-white, often Portuguese-born, and its members held the chief political and ecclesiastical posts. Just below them were the white, Brazilian-born landowners, who controlled local government. Next came the *mamelucos,* or descendants of Portuguese and Indians, who were small farmers or ranchers, skilled artisans, or foremen on large estates. Although mamelucos were full citizens and in theory had the right to hold office, in practice they rarely did.

Free blacks, both full-blooded and mulatto, ranked next in the social scale. This group was legally barred from holding political or clerical office, but no objection was made when exceptions were made. Christianized Indians, who worked as farmhands or house servants, formed the lowest free class of citizens. At the very bottom of the social ladder were the slaves, while the "wild" Indians of the interior were outside the system altogether.

In a sense, women were also outside the system. Perhaps because of Moorish influence, upper-class Portuguese, more than any other people of western Europe, kept their women in seclusion—honored in theory but ignored in practice. Education for women was nonexistent. They learned cooking, sewing, and other domestic duties from their mothers. Most were not taught to read or write lest they acquire and disseminate sinful knowledge. Brazilian churchmen complained that not only were young girls not allowed to attend classes (even though they were conducted by nuns), but they were not even allowed to attend mass. No wonder a Portuguese proverb claimed that a virtuous woman only left her home three times during her lifetime: for her christening, for her marriage, and for her funeral.

The Catholic Church in Brazil was not as well organized, as rich, or as prestigious as its counterpart in the Spanish colonies. Perhaps for this reason education lagged in Brazil. Though the Church established schools, all attempts at founding a university failed during the colonial period. Further, the Portuguese government refused to sanction the operation of a printing press in its American colonies. The Inquisition never set up its machinery in Brazil, but those accused of heresy could be sent to Lisbon for trial. The Brazilian church tended to be more tolerant of the remnants of paganism among its Indian and African followers than the Spanish colonial church. On the other hand, the Brazilian clergy, with the exception of the Jesuits (who were expelled in 1759), was not as zealous as the Spanish clergy in the protection of Indian rights.

In theory Brazil was ruled from Portugal by the king, with the advice of the Conselho Ultramarino (Overseas Council), and the home country was represented in Brazil by a viceroy. In practice, however, the viceroy had little power outside the captaincy in which he resided (before 1763 in Bahia; after 1763 in Rio de Janeiro), and local landowners ruled their own estates virtually as feudal overlords. A complex network of mercantile regulations attempted to force Brazilians to sell their valuable products only to Portugal, to prevent Brazilian competition with Portuguese products, and to guarantee that all goods transported to and from Brazil were carried in Portuguese ships. However, the shortage of Portuguese shipping, the uncooperativeness of the Brazilians, and the competitiveness of English and Dutch traders made these regulations unenforceable.

THE FRENCH IN THE NEW WORLD

As we have seen, France was unsuccessful in planting any settlements in North America during the sixteenth century. However, French fishermen continued to visit the Grand Banks regularly and began to trade with the Indians for beaver skins. These skins were very much in demand in Europe for the making of fashionable hats because the European beaver had become extinct. In the early 1600s Samuel de Champlain, the father of New France, founded fur trading posts at Port Royal (Annapolis) in Acadia (Nova Scotia) and at Quebec. Fortunately for the success of this enterprise, the warlike Iroquois Indians had, for unknown reasons, evacuated the area and left it to more peaceful tribes who were eager to trade their furs for European goods.

In order to retain the support of his Indian allies, particularly the Hurons (an Iroquois people who were not part of the Iroquois Confederation), Champlain was forced to aid them in their battles against the Mohawks and other Iroquois tribes. These campaigns had a lasting effect on colonial history. First, they gradually revolutionized Indian warfare in eastern North America by substituting firearms for spears, clubs, and bows and arrows. Second, Indian warfare changed from intermittent skirmishing for the winning of glory and petty booty into serious, sustained contests for the purpose of controlling the fur trade with the European settlers. Finally, Champlain's consistent support of the Hurons transformed the Iroquois first into allies of the Dutch and later into allies of the English when the latter fought the French for control of trade and territory.

Champlain kept urging the French government to send settlers to Canada, but very few had arrived by the time an English expedition took over Port Royal in 1627 and Quebec in 1629. These conquests might have aborted the French empire in America and prevented the later struggle between England and France for control of North America. However, a peace treaty soon returned these settlements to France.

In 1633 Champlain returned to Quebec with a group of settlers sent by the Company of New France, which had been granted a monopoly of the fur trade with Canada. However, profits were small, since the Iroquois badly defeated the Hurons, who had become the middleman of the fur trade between the Indians of the north and west and the French at Quebec. The Iroquois preferred to trade with the Dutch at present-day Albany rather than with the French because Dutch goods were less expensive. Even the French settlement of Montreal farther down the St. Lawrence River in 1642 (originally planned as a mission to convert the Indians) failed to ameliorate the situation.

However, in the 1660s French colonial policy was reorganized and strengthened by Louis XIV's chief minister, Jean-Baptiste Colbert. Canada was removed from the control of the company and was made a royal colony. In 1665 a governor, intendant, some settlers, and, most importantly, over a thousand soldiers, arrived in Quebec. Within a few years these troops broke the Iroquois blockade of the fur trade, and peace and relative prosperity were enjoyed in New France.

Taxes—an import duty on liquor and tobacco and an export duty on beaver and moose skins—were levied from France by the Ministère de la Marine, or Ministry of Maritime Affairs. Otherwise, the French government did not attempt to rule its American empire completely from France. A great deal of latitude was always allowed its three main colonial officials: the governor, the intendant, and the bishop. The governor was in charge of military and Indian affairs; the intendant was in charge of judicial and commercial affairs and local administration. This system operated well when the holders of these two offices cooperated with each other, but this was the exception rather than the rule. The governor, the intendant, and the bishop (in charge of religious affairs) sat on the council (which eventually numbered twelve men) which served primarily as a judicial, rather than as a lawmaking, body. The other nine members of the council were appointed by the king on the recommendation of the governor and intendant. On occasion the governor or the intendant called the permanent settlers, or habitants, together to discuss an important issue, but their opinion was merely advisory. The parish served as the governmental unit in the outlying areas. No official in New France was elected by the people.

Colbert realized that if Canada were to become self-sustaining (hopefully even food exporting) as well as to provide France with naval stores and other products which it lacked, its population would have to be greatly expanded. He sent hundreds of young men and marriageable girls to Canada, until in 1680 its population reached about 10,000. By that time all the land along the St. Lawrence River from Quebec to Montreal was under cultivation. Much of this land was held by *seigneurs,* or lords, who let it out to *censitaires,* or vassals. Although this sounds like, and technically was, a feudal landholding system, the shortage of settlers resulted in very low rents (paid in kind) and fewer—and much more modest—dues and fees than were collected by the nobility in France. Profits for the seigneurs, therefore, turned out to be so paltry that no large landholding class, such as appeared in the Spanish colonies, ever developed in New France. Nor, was there any cash crop which required cheap labor and a demand for slavery.

Despite Colbert's efforts, the fur trade remained the basis of the Canadian economy. Colbert encouraged the Indians to come to Montreal or Quebec once a year so that all traders would have an opportunity to purchase their furs. These "fairs" were held every spring, when the Indians bartered their furs for knives, kettles, axes, guns, blankets, and brandy. A fair might last for weeks, and it usually ended with drunken sprees. However, Canadian fur traders, with the blessing—and often the partnership—of the governor, the Count de Frontenac, preferred to open trading posts farther west near the Great Lakes, where furs could be bought more cheaply. Many of the famous explorations of the interior, Father Jacques Marquette

FIGURE 4A   (New York Public Library.)

and Louis Jolliet's "rediscovery" of the Mississippi River in 1673, and Robert Cavelier de La Salle's voyage to the mouth of the Mississippi in 1682 were connected with this expansion of the fur trade.

Another purpose of these and of similar exploring expeditions was to locate the elusive Northwest Passage. Although none attained this goal, La Salle's expedition gave France its claim to the Mississippi River valley. The expansion of New France encouraged hundreds of adventurous young Canadians (called *coureurs de bois,* or runners of the wood) not only to trade with the Indians but also to live and intermarry with the Indians and adopt their way of life.

Another group which went into the woods—but for a far different purpose— was the Jesuits. The Jesuits were not the first, nor the only, religious order to be interested in the conversion of the Indians, but they dominated religious endeavors in New France. Their efforts to convert the Indians were heroic, but the results did not measure up to their hopes. Most Indians were perfectly satisfied with their own religion and could see no advantage in exchanging it for one which seemed illsuited to their way of life. They were not impressed by the promise that any Indian who converted to Catholicism would become a French subject equal to a native-born white Frenchman. (Nevertheless, France deserves credit for being the only European nation to make this offer to the American Indians.) Nor were they impressed by being allowed to intermarry with French settlers. On the contrary, many Frenchmen seemed to deem it an honor to intermarry with them. Many a courageous Jesuit met martyrdom because he refused to accept these facts. However, by dint of continued and faithful exertion, the Jesuits were able to convert some Indians to at least the outward trappings of Christianity.

The Jesuits also ministered to the needs of the French settlers. As in the Spanish colonies, the Church sponsored the schools for both boys and girls, as well as orphan asylums, hospitals, old age homes, and all other social services. A seminary in Quebec successfully trained a large number of Canadians for the ministry, and a Jesuit college—opened as early as 1635—provided a first-class education all during the period of French control. However, general cultural life in Canada was meager, and no printing press existed in New France.

During the first half of the eighteenth century, French posts were established at Detroit, Niagara, Kaskaskia, and Cahokia in the Illinois country and at New Orleans at the mouth of the Mississippi River. These posts put France in control of the entire area from the Allegheny Mountains to the Mississippi River, from Canada all the way to Louisiana.

In the middle of the eighteenth century, the French population of this huge area was only about 8,000. At least one-third of the French settlers made their living from the fur trade. The rest were farmers, fishermen, soldiers, or churchmen. All were Catholic, because the French government consistently refused to allow Huguenots or any foreigners to settle in its colonies. All men between the ages of sixteen and sixty were liable for military service, and they had all too frequent opportunities for actual fighting. Although relations with the English colonies were officially hostile, a large contraband trade existed between them in wartime as well as in peacetime.

Although the French government resented the loss of Canada in the peace treaty ending the Seven Years' War, it was more concerned over the loss of a few islands which have not as yet been mentioned. During the course of the seventeenth century, France conquered St. Christophe, Guadaloupe, Martinique, St. Vincent, Grenada, St. Domingo, St. Martin, St. Croix, St. Bartholomew, Tortuga, and Marie Galante—all islands in the West Indies. Large planters found that they could make fortunes on these islands by growing sugar cane, cotton, rice, indigo, tobacco, cocoa, and, later, coffee. All that was missing was the necessary labor supply.

The planters, who often resided in France, were able to persuade the French government to import African slaves into the West Indies. By the middle of the eighteenth century, slaves outnumbered settlers more than ten to one. Colbert prepared a Code Noir (Black Code), effective 1685 which attempted to mitigate the conditions under which the planters had been forcing their slaves to live. The code regulated the amount of food and clothing to which slaves were entitled. The slaves were not to be sent out to work before dawn or to remain in the fields past sunset. Slave marriages were recognized, and young children were not to be separated from their parents. Execution or mutilation of slaves was only allowed if approved by a court of law.

However, this code, like most slave codes, was not rigidly enforced, and slavery in the French West Indies was as harsh as it was anywhere in the New World. Estimates indicate that a third of all newly imported slaves died within the first three years of their arrival in the West Indies; the survivors were worked to death in fifteen more years. Thousands of runaway slaves, known as maroons, fled into the jungle and formed bands that raided plantations and kept the islands in fear and turmoil. Black women might escape slavery by becoming concubines. They, and their offspring, generally received their freedom, and by the middle of the eighteenth century, mulattoes slightly outnumbered whites. They competed with whites for positions as overseers, artisans, shopkeepers, and even as professionals. Mulattoes tended to identify with the white settlers; however, in 1771 an edict was issued forbidding anyone descended from a slave to enter the professions or to hold public office.

Slaves also provided the labor supply in Louisiana, which in the eighteenth century gradually developed a plantation economy similar to, but far less remunerative than, that of the West Indies. In fact, no colony rivaled the West Indies as a source of wealth to France. Thus, when England captured Guadaloupe, Martinique, and other French West Indian islands during the Seven Years' War (1756–1763), it was a more severe blow to France than the loss of Canada. That is why at the peace conference ending the war, France ceded Canada to England; transferred Louisiana to Spain (to compensate Spain for its loss of Florida to England); but insisted on the return of Guadaloupe, Martinique, and a few other West Indian islands. Nevertheless, the dream of a French empire in America had come to an end.

THE DUTCH IN THE NEW WORLD

Holland (or the Netherlands) did not win its independence from Spain until the beginning of the seventeenth century and was, therefore, late in entering the race for a colonial empire. In North America the beginnings of the Dutch empire may be traced to 1609, when Henry Hudson, an English sea captain in the employ of the Dutch East India Company, sailed along the Atlantic coast and up the river which now bears his name as far as Albany. Even though Verrazano—sailing under the flag of France—had visited this area over eighty years earlier, the Netherlands claimed the Atlantic coast between Virginia and Canada on the basis of Hudson's voyage.

Dutch merchants, well aware of the high profits to be made in the fur trade, formed the New Netherland Company (which gave its name to the area) in 1614. By 1621 the New Netherland Company was superseded by the West India Company, which established settlements (or more properly, trading posts) on the Delaware and Connecticut rivers as well as at New Amsterdam and Fort Orange (now New York and Albany) on the Hudson River. The famous purchase of Manhattan Island (22,000 acres) for $24 worth of trading goods was made by Governor Peter Minuit in 1626. While that may not sound like much money, there is a great deal of doubt whether the tribe that sold Manhattan Island really owned it.

The West India Company turned over the settlement of New Netherland to private individuals. In 1629 it voted to offer tracts of land of sixteen miles on one side of the Hudson River or of eight miles on both sides to stockholders of the company who promised to bring fifty colonists over the age of fifteen to New Netherland within four years. These *patroons,* as they were called, were to supply their tenants with homes, cattle, and tools. The tenants were to pay rent to the patroon, use his mill, keep up roads and bridges on his estate, and accept the jurisdiction of his manorial court. The West India Company granted the patroons an eight-year exemption from the taxes on trade; still, only five individuals undertook to become patroons. Few settlers chose to become tenants under these conditions, and four of the five patroonships failed, with their land returning to the company. Only Kiliaen Van Rennsselaer's patroonship in the Albany area survived.

In order to promote immigration to New Netherland, in 1639 the West India Company surrendered its monopoly of the fur trade and allowed all settlers to trade with the Indians. The Mohawk Indians, the chief purveyors of furs to the Dutch traders, were soon being plied with firearms and "fire water" as well as with less dangerous trade goods. The Indians in the immediate vicinity of New Amsterdam, however, were—after many bloody encounters—either killed off or driven away. In contrast to the European empires already studied, the Dutch—though firm in their own Calvinist beliefs—did not actively attempt to convert the Indians.

The Netherlands were so prosperous and religiously tolerant during this period that few Dutch people cared to come to America. However, people from less fortunate areas of Europe settled in the Dutch colonies, and a report of 1643 indicates that eighteen different languages were spoken in New Amsterdam. At first the West India Company insisted that all colonists be Calvinist, but this requirement soon lapsed, and the same 1643 report mentions Catholics, Puritans, Lutherans, Anabaptists, and Mennonites worshiping in New Netherland. In the 1650s, Quakers and Jews (from the recently conquered Dutch colonies in Brazil) arrived in New Amsterdam. In spite of Governor Peter Stuyvesant's heated protests, the company allowed them to worship as they pleased and to enjoy civil rights.

The lack of laborers was met in New Netherland, as in so many other European empires, by the importation of slaves. The first African slaves arrived in the 1620s, and by 1664 slaves constituted one-tenth of the population (which is a higher proportion than in any other colony that far north). Under Dutch law manumission was relatively easy, and many slaves were granted "half freedom" in which they had to work for the West India Company part time but otherwise were free (though their children remained slaves). Freed slaves were under no legal disabilities and were able to intermarry with whites.

The government of New Netherland was autocratic. The States-General, the Dutch parliament, granted the West India Company full political and economic control over the area. In turn, the company appointed the governor, who was responsible only to the company and to his own conscience. In the 1640s the governor organized a council of twelve leading citizens but disbanded it when it tried to play what he considered to be too active a role in the government (though he later reconstituted a council of eight). In 1645 Peter Stuyvesant, an experienced (if choleric) soldier and administrator, became governor. After receiving many complaints about his arrogant behavior, the company ordered him to institute a municipal council in New Amsterdam. This council was composed of five aldermen, two burgomasters, and a sheriff—all appointed by the governor. It passed local ordinances and acted as a court of appeals. Officials in other towns in the colony were also appointed by the governor from among the residents.

The Dutch had to face stiff competition in the New World. They not only competed with the French for control of the fur trade but faced a threat to their territorial integrity. In 1638, with—ironically—the backing of Dutch merchants, Sweden, then one of the most prosperous and powerful nations of Europe, founded New Sweden on the west bank of the Delaware River. The head of the colony was the former governor of New Netherland, Peter Minuit. In spite of complaints by the Dutch government and by Dutch traders, the Swedes refused to evacuate their trading posts and actually seized one of the Dutch forts in the area. Governor Stuyvesant then led an expedition against the Swedes, and by 1655 they were forced to accept Dutch rule. However, the main legacy of the approximately 400 Swedes and Finns who settled on the Delaware—the log cabin—was to play an important role in American life for well over 200 years.

The most serious, and ultimately fatal, competition faced by New Netherland came from the English colonies. Friction between English and Dutch settlers was of long standing. The Dutch attempted to claim Connecticut but were soon forced to back down and even, in 1650, to cede the eastern half of Long Island to the English. Gradually, English settlers moved westward into the Dutch sector of Long Island, often because of the religious toleration they were able to enjoy there, but they were resentful at the lack of political democracy. Many boundary disputes exacerbated relations between the New England colonies and New Netherland, and both sides complained of violations of their trade regulations. It was not until the 1650s and 1660s, however, when warfare broke out between the two home countries, that New Netherland and its 8,000 inhabitants were swallowed up by their English neighbors.

Dutch contributions to American life remain with us even today. We owe Santa Claus and Easter eggs to the Dutch. The sleigh and the ice skate came from Holland. Dutch words such as *yacht, boss, stoop,* and *cookie* became part of our language. Although the patroon system failed during the Dutch period, it was revived by the English as the manorial system and persisted along the Hudson River into the nineteenth century. Further, it is particularly important that the English continued the trade and military arrangements made by the Dutch with the Iroquois Indians which were to be so crucial for the remainder of our colonial history.

COMPARING AND CONTRASTING
THE NON-ENGLISH EMPIRES

All four non-English empires in the New World (those of Spain, Portugal, France, and the Netherlands) failed to attract large numbers of settlers to their colonies. Except for the Netherlands, religious and political dissidents were barred from the colonies, and the ordinary citizen preferred to remain at home. All four nations attempted to institute a feudal system of landholding (the encomienda, the captaincy, the seigneurial system, and the patroonship), but only the first two enjoyed any success, probably because of their larger and more settled Indian populations. These experiments with feudalism reflected the reluctance of the governments of all these nations to throw their own resources into colonization efforts.

There were also significant differences between the various colonial empires. The Spanish and Portuguese colonies were considered royal colonies from their inception; the French government only took control of its colonies after the failure of the Company of New France; while New Netherland remained under the control of the West India Company for its entire forty-year history (although the inhabitants had begun to petition for direct governmental rule).

The government of all four European empires was autocratic. Whether the laws were enacted by a governmental body in Europe, by a commercial company, or by a colonial oligarchy, it was clear that the purpose of the laws was to benefit the group which made them. The needs and interests of the average settler were, by and large, ignored; and if they benefited from a particular piece of legislation, it was usually coincidental. However, while social distinctions were critical in all these colonial societies, social mobility reached proportions undreamed of in any of their homelands.

The economic policies of four colonial empires were almost identical: All were dictated by the tenets of mercantilism, which required that all colonial products and natural resources be sold only to the mother country; that all products be obtained from, or at least through, the mother country or its duly authorized representative; and that all traffic to or from the colonies be carried in ships of the mother country unless specifically exempted. Further, colonies were not to compete commercially or industrially with the motherland. Size of territory, value and type of product, extent of the merchant marine, and efficiency and honesty of the bureaucracy varied from empire to empire, but the mercantilist ideal was common to all.

The three Catholic nations made strenuous efforts to convert the Indians, with the French enjoying the least success because the fur trade played such a crucial role in their own and "their" Indians' lives. The Dutch took the least interest in the religious sphere, since the West India Company was interested solely in the commercial aspect of its settlements. Because of their interest in the fur trade (and relative lack of interest in agriculture), the Dutch and French did not attempt to interfere with the Indian way of life. However, they still called them *sauvages* or *wilden* (wild ones) and like the settlers of the Spanish and Portuguese colonies, they looked down on the Indians and believed that Indian land was theirs for the taking or, at best, purchasing.

All these nations condoned, or even defended, African (and Indian) slavery as a source of cheap labor. The demand for slaves was greatest in the more tropical areas, and it was there that racial mixture was most common and most acceptable. Blacks, too, were viewed as inferiors by settlers of all four nations, but all treated them—in theory at least—as human beings with souls who should enjoy certain elemental rights and the possibility of winning their freedom.

In the next chapter, and for the remainder of this volume, we shall concentrate on the English colonies in North America. It will be worthwhile to note in which aspects they imitated, modified, and departed completely from the precedents established by their European rivals.

BIBLIOGRAPHY

BOXER, CHARLES R. *The Dutch Seaborne Empire.* New York, 1965.
BOXER, CHARLES R. *The Portuguese Seaborne Empire.* New York, 1969.
ECCLES, W. J. *France in America.* New York, 1972.
KENNEY, ALICE P. *Stubborn for Liberty: The Dutch in York.* Syracuse, 1975.
LANG, JAMES. *Portuguese Brazil: The King's Plantation.* New York, 1979.
MORISON, SAMUEL E. *Samuel de Champlain: The Father of New France.* Boston, 1972.
PRADO, CAIO, JR. *The Colonial Background of Modern Brazil.* Berkeley, 1967.
SMITH, GEORGE L. *Religion and Trade in New Netherland: Dutch Origins and American Development.* Ithaca, 1973.
WUORINEN, JOHN H. *The Finns on the Delaware: An Essay in Colonial American History.* New York, 1966.

5

The Background of English Colonization

Large crowds attended the performances of *Eastward Hoe*, a play about the riches of Virginia which opened in 1605. George Chapman, one of the authors has a character in the play claim that "all their (the Indians') dripping pans and their chamber pots are pure gold . . . and for rubies and diamonds they go forth on holidays and gather 'em by the sea shore. . . . " It is impossible to assess how completely the audience accepted such statements, but it is certain that its call for the settlement of the New World was welcomed by many of the humbler members of the audience standing in the pit as well as by the notables sitting above them. At this time the English people and their rulers were virtually in complete accord that the colonization of the New World would be of inestimable benefit to the entire nation.

This consensus has not always existed. England's claim to the North American continent was based on John Cabot's voyage of 1497. However, neither the contemporary ruler (Henry VII) nor his successor (Henry VIII) were inclined to pursue this claim. Part of their hesitation was dictated by domestic concerns—the need to cure the old wounds caused by the Wars of the Roses (1455-1485) and the need to cure the new wounds caused by Henry VIII's split with the Church of Rome. The hesitation of these two monarchs was compounded by a desire to avoid conflict with Spain, a possible ally against the traditional enemy, France.

This lack of interest in colonization continued through the brief reigns of Edward VI and Mary. During the reign of Queen Elizabeth I (1558-1603), however, the English government's attitude toward colonization changed greatly. The Wars of the Roses were now only a memory. The religious problems caused by the English

Reformation proved (as will be seen later in this chapter) to be an incentive, rather than an obstacle, to colonization. Indeed, the English Reformation added religious motivation to the already existing economic and political reasons for challenging Spain's hegemony over the New World.

ECONOMIC MOTIVES

Economic, religious, and political factors all contributed to the change in the attitude of both the English government and the people toward colonization. Agriculture had changed greatly in England during the sixteenth century. At the beginning of the century, the large estates which had evolved from the old medieval manors were worked by tenant farmers who grew grains, vegetables, and fruits. However, as the English woolens industry developed and the demand for wool increased both at home and abroad, manorial lords transformed their estates into sheep farms.

The enclosure movement, as it was called, resulted in the displacement of the majority of tenant farmers. As Sir Thomas More wrote in the *Utopia,* "Your sheep that were wont to be so meek and tame . . . become . . . so wild that they eat up, and swallow down the very men themselves. . . . " Some of the displaced people were able to find employment in the expanding woolens industry or in other areas of the English economy. However, thousands suffered from seasonal unemployment, and others were demoted to the status of "sturdy beggars," a large army of able-bodied men and women who were condemned to more or less permanent unemployment. Not surprisingly, many of them turned to petty crime. They were held responsible for the lawlessness which was plaguing both the countryside and London, to which thousands of the unemployed eventually migrated. Neither they nor the government were satisfied with this explosive situation. Would they not be far better off outside England?

Small landowners in many regions of England who were not in a position to benefit from the effects of the enclosure movement were also suffering from economic dislocation. The inflation which spread over western Europe during the sixteenth century (largely because of the great influx of gold and silver from the New World) had affected them adversely. The prices of most goods and products had risen far faster than the prices of their agricultural products. Tax rates had also greatly increased. As a result, the real income of these small farmers declined, and their social status and feeling of well-being declined as well. Many of these small landowners began to think of selling their farms in England and using the proceeds to purchase huge amounts of the cheap land available in the New World.

The same thought entered the minds of those English families who had the problem of taking care of younger sons. The law of primogeniture and entail required (with some exceptions) that the eldest son inherit a family's entire landed estate. Other sons might go into the army, navy, or clergy; but for the adventurous younger son, what better start in life was there than the purchase of a tract of land in the New World?

RELIGIOUS MOTIVES

Religious factors also played an important role in the desire for English colonization. When Henry VIII detached England from the Catholic Church in the 1530s
and organized the Anglican Church with himself as its head, he set off a chain of
events that was to create turmoil in English religious life for centuries. A byproduct
of this turmoil was to be the English colonization of the New World.

As long as Henry VIII lived, the Anglican Church deviated little from Catholic
doctrine and ritual. However, the guardians of his young son and successor Edward
VI (1547-1553) moved the Anglican Church much closer to the Protestant ideas
then current in Germany and Switzerland. Upon Edward's death his eldest sister,
Mary, became the ruler of England. Mary was a devout Catholic; she married King
Philip of Spain and reinstituted Catholicism as the official religion of England—her
methods earning her the appellation of "Bloody Mary." This return to Rome
however, was only temporary, since Mary died in 1558 and was succeeded by her
half-sister, the famous Queen Elizabeth I.

Queen Elizabeth was a Protestant and a consummate politician. She was determined to use religion as a means of uniting her subjects. In 1559, therefore,
Elizabeth maneuvered the Anglican Church to its present position of mild Protest-
ism just a few degrees farther removed from Catholicism than its original position
under Henry VIII. Clergymen were allowed to marry, English replaced Latin in the
service, and baptism and communion were the only two sacraments celebrated. On
the other hand, the hierarchy of archbishops and bishops, ecclesiastical courts, and
tithes—all integral features of the Catholic Church—were preserved. (However, as
under Henry VIII, the ruler remained head of the Church.)

Nevertheless, the religious efforts of Queen Elizabeth failed to satisfy all the
varied religious groups in England. A segment of the English people never relinquished their loyalty to the Catholic Church. As Catholics, these people found
themselves subject, particularly when England was at war with Spain, to religious
persecution and loss of civil and political rights. At such times the possibility of a
Catholic refuge in the New World seemed very attractive.

On the other hand, large numbers of English people known as Puritans felt
that the Elizabethan religious settlement had not gone far enough in the direction
of Protestantism. The Puritans believed that people were able to communicate
directly with God and felt, therefore, that much of the Catholic ritual and symbol-
ism retained by the Anglican Church was unnecessary. For this reason they opposed
the sign of the cross at baptism, the practice of kneeling at communion, the playing
of organ music, and the wearing of caps and surplices by the clergy.

Perhaps most threatening of all to both religious and secular authorities was
the Puritan demand for the abolition of the authority of archbishops, bishops, and
other ecclesiastical officials. Instead, the Church was to be placed under a Presbyterian form of government in which general policies were to be made by synods, or
regional governing bodies, made up of ministers and lay elders. Further, individual
churches were to maintain a large measure of autonomy.

When King James I succeeded to the throne of England in 1603, the Puritans presented him with the Millenary Petition (so-called because it was signed by a thousand people) requesting that the Anglican Church accept their proposed reforms. King James, however, viewed the Puritan movement as a threat to his own power. At the Hampton Court Conference of 1604, he declared "No Bishop, No King" in response to the Puritan request for a Presbyterian form of church government and he threatened to "harry them [the Puritans] out of the land." When he began to oust clergymen with Puritan leanings and enforce the laws against those who refused to attend Anglican services, the Puritans, too, turned their thoughts to the New World.

A third group, known as Separatists, was even more disillusioned with the Anglican Church than the Puritans. The members of this group felt that there was no hope whatsoever of purifying the Anglican Church of its Catholic tendencies. They believed, therefore, that they must separate from the Anglican Church and form their own completely independent congregations. The Separatists were persecuted even more stringently than Puritans or Catholics: two of their leaders were hanged, others were imprisoned. The Separatists responded by leaving England.

The three religious groups already discussed were all active at the beginning of the seventeenth century. Toward the middle of the century, they were joined by a fourth, and even more "radical," religious group, the Society of Friends—popularly known as the Quakers. George Fox, the founder of Quakerism, began preaching in 1649. By 1665 he had over 80,000 followers. Fox preached that religion was a matter of individual conscience. Churches, doctrine, and ritual were all obstacles to true faith. The Quakers abhorred violence and therefore refused to serve in the militia or even to pay taxes that might be devoted to military purposes. They also refused to take oaths or to show respect to civil, or earthly, authorities—no matter what their rank—by removing their hats.

The Quakers of the seventeenth century were not the staid individuals that we have come to know as Quakers of later generations. To convince others of the truth of their doctrines, Quakers did not hesitate to interrupt church services, assault clergymen, or even on occasion run through the streets completely nude. To the English government the Quakers were the ultimate threat to both church and state. The government imprisoned literally thousands of Quakers and deported hundreds of others. No wonder, then, that the Quakers turned their eyes westward toward the New World.

POLITICAL MOTIVES

As the seventeenth century progressed, political factors also served to encourage migration to the New World. It will be helpful, therefore, to survey briefly English political institutions of the Tudor and early Stuart periods. Much stress is laid on Tudor "absolutism" among political theorists. However, the very fact that Parliaments were called, and that their approval of legislation was required, served as a check on royal absolutism. The House of Lords, comprised of the nobility and the higher clergy, generally agreed with the monarch; but the House of Commons, made up primarily of country gentlemen with a sprinkling of merchants and lawyers, had a mind of its own. Also, during the period when Henry VIII and his successors needed support for their religious policies, or funds with which to carry on their foreign wars, the opinions of the House of Commons had to be heeded. Under the Tudors members of the House of Commons won the right to judge disputed elections, speak on the floor of the House without fear of reprisal, and enjoy freedom from arrest while Parliament was in session. They soon also learned to circumvent the power of the Speaker of the House (a royal nominee) by sitting as a committee of the whole House and naming a chairman of their own choice. When the English colonists in America later won a voice in their own government, they attempted to model the procedures and rights of their own representative assemblies on those won by the House of Commons.

However, at this period it was the local, or county, government which touched the lives of English citizens most closely. Justices of the peace—with the aid of their constables and churchwardens—maintained law and order, held court, collected taxes and tithes, supervised the building and repair of roads and bridges, administered the Poor Law and other welfare services, dealt with religious affairs, regulated wages and prices, and served as liaison officers for the central government. Another royal appointee, the sheriff, had the responsibility of seeing that court procedures and decisions were properly carried out and that elections were conducted according to law. Both these offices, those of sheriff and justice of the peace, were to be transported to America, where—with some modifications—they played important roles in local government.

England underwent two major and one minor political upheavals during the seventeenth century: the Puritan Revolution of 1642-1649, the Glorious Revolution of 1688-1689, and Monmouth's Rebellion of 1685. The Puritans were completely unwilling to accept the religious dictates of James and his son Charles I. Neither did they approve of the political or economic policies of these two monarchs, who levied taxes without consulting Parliament, created innumerable monopolies, and limited legal rights by declaring martial law and refusing to recognize the writ of habeas corpus. When political means failed to solve these disputes, open warfare broke out between King Charles and the Puritans in 1642. Seven years of bitter civil war followed, at the conclusion of which the Puritans defeated and beheaded the king.

The Puritans ruled England until 1660. During this so-called Interregnum period, many royalists found it wise to leave England and settle in the New World. In 1660, upon the restoration of the Stuart monarchy under King Charles II, a substantial number of Puritans were exiled, or found it expedient to flee, to the New World.

At the death of King Charles in 1685, his illegitimate son—the Duke of Monmouth—attempted to seize the throne from the rightful, but highly unpopular, heir—the King's brother, the Duke of York—who became King James II. The suppression of this rebellion led to the deportation of hundreds of Monmouth's followers to the New World.

It took the English people only three years to realize that King James's autocratic tendencies and Catholic faith made him unsuitable to rule them. As long as James's immediate successor was presumed to be his Protestant daughter Mary (wife of William of Orange, the Dutch ruler), they hesitated to act. However, the birth of a son to James and his queen in 1688 meant that a Catholic dynasty was in the process of being established. This contingency was not acceptable to the majority of the English people, and seven leaders of Parliament invited William and Mary to ascend the throne of England. While it did not result in a large wave of immigration to the New World, the Glorious Revolution had tremendous political and religious consequences for the English colonies.

The first half of the eighteenth century was not much more peaceful. In 1714 Queen Anne, the successor to King William III, died with no surviving children, and the Elector of Hanover ascended the English throne as George I. Although the mass of the English people accepted this new Hanoverian dynasty, the supporters of the deposed James II twice (in 1715 and again in 1745) attempted to restore the Stuart family to the English throne. Both of these attempts proved abortive, and the second, particularly, resulted in the deportation or self-exile of large numbers of Scottish people to the New World.

GOVERNMENTAL INTEREST
IN COLONIZATION

These, then, were the economic, religious, and political factors which impelled English people—in substantial numbers—to settle in the New World: but what were the factors which impelled the English government to encourage their settlement? To a large extent they overlap. The horde of "sturdy beggars" was a serious concern to the English government in a period when police forces did not exist. Also, parishes resented having to levy "poor rates" for those unable to work.

In addition, the English government, unlike the governments of France and Spain, was not unwilling to see its dissident religious and political minorities settle in colonies ruled by England. It was generally felt by English rulers that with the poor transportation and communication of this period, sheer distance would negate the effectiveness of their opposition.

However, to more fully understand the extent of the English government's enthusiasm for colonization projects during the first half of the seventeenth century, it is necessary to reintroduce the basic principles of mercantilism. This economic outlook governed the policy of England, as well as that of the other nations of western Europe, during the sixteenth and seventeenth centuries. One of the basic tenets of mercantilism was that a nation's wealth could best be assessed by the amount of gold and silver it controlled. The larger the amount of bullion, the stronger the nation. Obviously, a nation's supply of bullion depended to a large extent on its balance of trade, or its balance of payments. In other words, if it sold to other nations goods of greater value than the goods bought from these nations, its supply of bullion would increase. Conversely, an unfavorable balance of payments would deplete the nation's bullion supply.

During the sixteenth century England was in the latter, unfortunate position. The income from its primary exports of wool, or (increasingly) of woolen goods, did not equal its outlay for the purchase of foreign wines, silks, spices and timber—to name just a few of its crucial imports. How could this situation be remedied? To the mercantilist the answer was simple: build up a colonial empire which would supply the raw materials which England could not produce at home.

Mercantilism was based on a psychology of scarcity that stemmed from medieval conditions and which was still prevalent in the first half of the seventeenth century. If material wealth was limited, one nation could increase its share of the wealth only at the expense of some other nation(s). Similarly, according to this theory, individuals could enlarge their portion of a nation's wealth only by reducing the wealth of a fellow citizen. One can then understand why early seventeenth-century English people were appalled by the increase in their nation's population from about 2.5 million in 1485 (when Henry VII became king) to almost 5.5 million by the middle of the seventeenth century. To them it seemed that England was like a "swarming beehive" and that only emigration or "hiving out" could avert a potential national disaster.

Mercantilism, then, was the English government's basic rationale for encouraging colonies. Colonies would serve as sources of much-needed raw materials. They would serve as markets for the ever-increasing volume of manufactured goods produced in England. In addition, the constant traffic in goods between the mother country and the colonies would bring prosperity to the English shipbuilding industry, enlarge the English merchant marine (which doubled as the English navy in time of war), provide work for countless English seamen, and benefit the royal treasury because of the taxes that the government planned to levy on all goods coming to and from the colonies. Finally, colonies would solve the problem of overpopulation.

As can be seen from this brief survey, developments in English economic, religious, and political life during the sixteenth century and the first part of the seventeenth century were all "push factors" that led many English people to consider migration to the New World. Often a variety of these factors led to a final decision. A Puritan or Separatist family might suffer from hard times, religious persecution, and fear of political reprisal; the English government, for reasons already explained, would be content to see them leave. It was this harmony of interests (temporary, as we shall see later) between segments of the English people and their government as well as the "pull factor" after 1620 of successful colonies that led to the "Great Migration" of about 58,000 people from England to America between 1607 and 1642 (and of another 20,000 people to other parts of the world).

THE BEGINNINGS
OF ENGLISH COLONIZATION

Almost thirty years of trial and error elapsed before the Great Migration got success-fully underway. The forerunner of active governmental support of colonization was the tacit approval given by the English government after 1560 to the depredations of the "Sea Dogs" John Hawkins, Francis Drake, and Richard Grenville against Spanish treasure ships. The fact that Queen Elizabeth responded to Spain's de-mand that Drake be punished for plundering £600,000 worth of treasure from Spanish ships and towns by honoring him with a knighthood indicated clearly that England was readying itself to make a serious challenge of Spain's domination of the New World.

Obviously, this challenge was more likely to succeed in North America, where practically no Spanish colonization had yet taken place and where Cabot's explo-rations had given England a valid claim. As Richard Hakluyt, the great propagandist for English colonization, advised, in his "A Discourse concerning Western Planting" (1584) the time was long overdue when England must settle "those lands which of equity and right appertain unto us." Hakluyt's advice was accepted by Sir Humphrey Gilbert, an English country gentleman and soldier. Gilbert had two main goals in mind. One was to find a northwest passage to Asia. The other was to plant English colonies in North America which would serve as a source of raw materials for England, as a refuge for religious dissenters and the destitute, and as basis for at-tacks on the Spanish empire in America.

In 1578 Gilbert received a charter from Queen Elizabeth which allowed him six years to form a colony or colonies in North America. Toward the end of the year, he set out with seven ships and about 400 men, but storms and an encounter with Spanish ships forced him to return to England. Gilbert spent the next several years raising the money for a second expedition. Finally, in 1583 he reached New-foundland with five ships and about 250 men. Gilbert claimed the territory for England, but the settlers refused to remain there; on the voyage back to England, Gilbert was lost at sea.

Sir Walter Raleigh, a favorite of Queen Elizabeth, continued the task left un-finished by his half-brother, Sir Humphrey Gilbert. In 1584 the queen granted Raleigh a charter that was substantially the same as Gilbert's. Raleigh sent two cap-tains to reconnoiter the Atlantic coast of North America, and they recommended that Roanoke Island off the coast of present-day North Carolina be chosen as the site for his colony. They even brought back two Indians to prove how gentle, lov-ing, and faithful the natives were.

By 1585 Raleigh had raised enough money to send a group of just over one hundred men to form a colony on Roanoke, which was renamed Virginia in honor of Queen Elizabeth. The colonists included an experienced soldier, Ralph Lane, who acted as governor; Thomas Harriot, a mathematician and astronomer; and John White, a painter whose sketches of the Indians and of the flora and fauna of the region still exist. However, the colonists spent too much time searching for precious metals. Supplies ran out; the weather was stormy; the Indians became less friendly as the colonists continued to steal their food; and in 1586, when Sir Francis Drake sailed up to Roanoke Island, the settlers decided to return to England with him.

Raleigh considered this expedition merely an advance party for his main colonizing attempt. Moreover, all reports indicated that Virginia was capable of producing many valuable crops as well as supplying England with furs and timber. In 1587, therefore, after raising additional funds, he sent another group of more than one hundred people—including seventeen women and nine children—to form an agricultural settlement on the mainland near Chesapeake Bay. We know that John White returned as governor; that his daughter, Elenora Dare, gave birth to a girl named Virginia (the first white child born in English America) and that Manteo, a friendly, English-speaking Croatoan Indian (he had been one of the Indians brought back to England and had been taught English by Harriot) was baptized and granted the title of Lord of Roanoke. We are less sure why Governor White ignored his instructions and resettled on Roanoke Island, or why he felt he had to return to England for supplies only a month after reaching the island.

However, the greatest mystery of all is what happened to the remaining settlers. Because of events connected with the beginning of war with Spain and the defeat of the Spanish Armada, White was not able to return to Virginia until 1591. When he did arrive, he saw only scattered debris and the letters *CRO* carved on a tree and the entire word *Croatoan* carved on a post. White interpreted this to mean that the colonists had moved, as planned, into the territory of the Croatoan Indians, but he had no facilities to search for them and was forced to return to England. By this time Raleigh was out of money and out of favor with the queen; therefore, he made no attempts to rescue the settlers (if, indeed, they were still alive) or to resuscitate the Virginia colony. Thus, the mystery of the so-called lost colony has never been solved, although it is generally thought that the remaining colonists must have been dispatched by the Indians.

The war with Spain continued for sixteen years after the defeat of the Spanish Armada in 1588. During this period outfitting privateers to attack Spanish shipping was a much more attractive investment than attempting to plant colonies in America. Only in the early years of the seventeenth century, when the war was virtually over, did encouraging reports on the availability of furs, fish, and timber (made by Bartholomew Gosnold, Martin Pring, and George Weymouth after voyages along the coast of New England) revive English interest in colonization. However, one difficulty still remained. The abortive attempts of Gilbert and Raleigh demonstrated that the resources of an individual, or even of a small group of investors, were insufficient to finance a successful colonial venture. Nevertheless, Queen Elizabeth (and her successors) followed the precedent established by the other European nations—giving only moral, not material, support to efforts at colonization.

Fortunately, the solution to the financial problem was already at hand in the form of the joint stock company. This was a business organization granted a monopoly of trade with distant areas where large amounts of capital were needed but the risks were extremely high. The Muscovy Company, which opened up the Russian trade in the 1550s, was the first such company. The East India Company of 1600 was the most famous and longest lasting of the joint stock companies. Individuals could buy as many shares as they wished, thus making possible the raising of substantial amounts of capital while spreading the risk among many. All shareholders were eligible to attend a general court (shareholders meeting) which elected officers and assistants (the modern board of directors). Profits or losses were calculated at the conclusion of each venture, and new shares were sold for succeeding ventures. The joint stock company was usually also given political privileges—the right to govern any colonists whom they might settle in their trading area.

By 1589 Raleigh, who claimed to have spent £40,000 of his own money, realized that he lacked the resources to plant and nurture a colony. Therefore, he attempted to raise additional funds by selling the right to trade with Virginia to a group of London merchants. However, Raleigh lost all rights to colonize Virginia in 1603 when he was convicted of treason. Nevertheless, as the following chapter will show, the merchants of London as well as of other English towns did not intend that the dream of an English empire in America remain unfulfilled.

BIBLIOGRAPHY

BRIDENBAUGH, CARL. *Vexed and Troubled Englishmen, 1590-1642.* New York, 1968.

ELLIOT-BINNS, LEONARD. *The Reformation in England.* Hamden, Conn., 1966.

NOTESTEIN, WALLACE. *The English People on the Eve of Colonization, 1603-1630.* New York, 1954.

QUINN, DAVID B. *England and the Discovery of America, 1481-1620.* New York, 1974.

RABB, THEODORE K. *Enterprise and Empire: Merchant and Gentry Investment in the Expansion of England, 1575-1630.* Cambridge, 1967.

ROWSE, A. L. *The Elizabethans and America.* New York, 1959.

WRIGHT, LOUIS B. *Religion and Empire: The Alliance between Piety and Commerce in English Expansion, 1558-1625.* Chapel Hill, 1943.

6
The Tobacco Colonies: Virginia and Maryland

When as the luscious smell
Of that delicious land
Above the seas that flows
The clear wind throws
Your hearts to swell
Approaching the dear strand.*

While this *Ode to the Virginia Voyage* by Michael Drayton is lyrical, the motives of the men who financed the voyage which inspired the poem were primarily mercenary. The merchants of London, Plymouth, and Bristol were all eager to begin colonization in Virginia, a territory which at that time included the entire Atlantic coast from present-day North Carolina to southeastern Canada. Their hope was to discover a water route through America and/or to profit from the sale of the fish, furs, timber, metals, and other natural resources found on the continent itself.

THE LONDON AND PLYMOUTH COMPANIES

In 1606, to satisfy these competing interests, King James I issued a charter which divided Virginia between a London company and a Plymouth company (which included Bristol). The London Company was authorized to make settlements from

Ode to the Virginian Voyage by Michael Drayton. Reprinted by permission of Routledge and Kegan Paul Ltd., London, England.

North Carolina to New York (from 31 to 41 degrees north latitude) and the Plymouth Company from Virginia into Canada (from 38 to 45 degrees north latitude). In the overlapping area which both were authorized to colonize, their settlements were to be at least one hundred miles apart.

Virginia was to be supervised by a thirteen-man royal council (the Council of Virginia), resident in England. However, this council was empowered to appoint local councils, also of thirteen men, which were actually to govern the colonies. This first charter of 1606 further provided that the settlers were to enjoy "all Liberties, Franchises, and Immunities . . . as if they had been abiding and born within this our Realm of England."

In 1607 Sir Ferdinando Gorges, the governor of the Plymouth Company, sent out an expedition of over one hundred men headed by George Popham and Raleigh Gilbert (Sir Humphrey's son). They founded a colony at the mouth of the Kennebec River in Maine. The colony failed within a year because of lack of supplies, cold weather, hostile Indians, and internal dissension. This failure so discouraged the members of the Plymouth Company that they confined their activities to fishing and trading and made no further efforts to found a permanent colony.

THE FOUNDING OF JAMESTOWN

In December 1606 the London Company sent three ships and 144 colonists—all male—to Virginia. Four months later, the 105 survivors of the voyage landed in Virginia and formed a settlement, which they called Jamestown, on a peninsula extending into the James River about thirty miles from the ocean. The site proved to be illchosen because, though it was easy to defend, it was low, marshy, and malarial. The settlers were too busy digging for gold to plant food; by September 46 had died. Twenty-one more were to perish during the winter, leaving only 38 of the original 105 settlers alive.

During 1608, however, 200 additional settlers arrived, and Captain John Smith assumed the leadership of the settlement. Smith was an experienced military man who knew the importance of discipline. In his *General History of Virginia* (1624) he recounted how he ordered any malingerer to be "banished from the fort as a drone"—in other words, sent out to certain death. The many "gentlemen" of the colony who had hitherto found it beneath their dignity to do any sort of work now found themselves raising crops, tending the livestock, or constructing palisades.

Relations with the Indians had been, at best, touchy ever since Jamestown was founded. One tribe attacked the English almost as soon as they landed. However, Powhatan, who ruled most of the small tribes in the area, may have seen the English as possible allies against those tribes which still resisted his authority. In any case, when the colony's food supply ran out in 1607, the Indians brought, as Smith reported, "such plenty of their fruits and provisions that no man wanted." Later that same year, the famous incident occurred in which Smith was captured by the Indians and saved by Pocahontas. It is now thought that Powhatan staged the entire

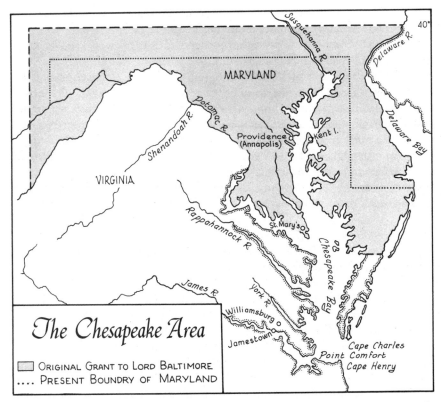

MARYLAND

Providence
(Annapolis)

Kent I.

VIRGINIA

St. Mary's

Chesapeake Bay

The Chesapeake Area

Williamsburg

Jamestown

Cape Charles
Point Comfort
Cape Henry

◻ ORIGINAL GRANT TO LORD BALTIMORE
.... PRESENT BOUNDRY OF MARYLAND

FIGURE 6A   (From *Colonial America* by Oscar T. Barck and Hugh T. Lefler. Copyright©
1958, 1968 by Macmillan Publishing Company.)

incident to point out to Smith that, although the Indians were friendly to the settlers, the lives of the English were really in Indian hands. Smith, however, either
misinterpreted, or decided to ignore, this message and proceeded to use force to
exact food from the Indians. Powhatan's response was to cut off all trade with the
colonists and attack them whenever possible.

It was at this stage that what seems to us today to be a curious order arrived
from England. Powhatan was to be formally crowned to indicate that he and his people were subjects of the English king. Powhatan refused to travel to Jamestown for
his coronation, but when the English came to him, he accepted a bed, a red woolen
robe, and some utensils, and he allowed the crown to be placed on his head (although he refused to kneel as demanded by protocol). Then Powhatan graciously
responded by giving the English his old moccasins and deerskin mantle to bring to
King James.* Smith was probably correct when he complained in his *General*

*They are still in the Ashmolean Museum at Oxford.

History of Virginia that the coronation only made Powhatan "so much overvalue himself that he respected us as much as nothing at all."

Jamestown consisted of perhaps one hundred settlers who lived in some twenty cabins and subsisted on fish, oysters, and whatever corn they were able to grow on about forty acres of cleared land. Still, the London Company was determined to make the colony a success and persuaded King James to grant it a revised charter completely separating it from the Plymouth Company. The new charter set the boundaries of Virginia at 200 miles north and south of Point Comfort, extending north and northwest from sea to sea. (At this time it was still thought that the distance from the Atlantic to the Pacific was relatively short.) Effective control of Virginia passed from the royal council to a company council dominated by the company's treasurer. The company also granted its nominee for governor, Lord Delaware (De La Warr), full powers over the colonists, subject only to its own supervision.

The London Company undertook a large-scale campaign to raise funds and recruit additional settlers for its colony. Shares in the company were sold at £12 10 s (the estimated cost of equipping and transporting one settler to Virginia), and any person who paid his own way to the colony was to receive a free share for himself and for every individual he brought with him, as well as a bonus of a hundred acres of land per person at the end of seven years. (All land was owned by the company.) Those who were unable to pay their way received their transportation free of charge but, in return, had to work as servants for the company for seven years. The campaign was a success—over 1,000 shares were sold and a fleet of nine vessels carrying 600 people set off for Virginia. One ship was lost, one was wrecked on Bermuda (thus giving England a claim to the island), and only about 400 men, women, and children arrived in Jamestown in August 1609.

Ironically, the London Company's campaign almost proved the undoing of the entire colony. The fewer than one hundred settlers at Jamestown were completely unable to support these new arrivals. The winter of 1609-1610 is known in the history of Virginia as the "starving time." The colonists were forced to eat nuts, berries, and herbs. But this was not the worst of it. As John Smith reported

> . . . a savage we slew and buried, the poorer sort took him up and ate him. . . .
> And one amongst the rest did kill his wife, powdered [salted] her, and had
> eaten part of her before it was known; for which he was executed as he well
> deserved.

When Sir Thomas Gates and 175 people who had been marooned on Bermuda finally arrived in Jamestown in May 1610, they found only 60 settlers still alive. Gates and the others were determined to abandon the colony and return to England. However, as they sailed down the James River, they encountered an expedition headed by Lord Delaware, who persuaded them to try once again. Lord Delaware remained in Virginia only about a year, but he left instructions with his deputy governor, Thomas Dale, to govern under a strict set of military rules, known as Dale's Laws. In 1612 the London Company received a third charter which gave its shareholders even greater control of the colony and of Bermuda, which was added to its territory. With the additional money the company was now able to raise, it regularly sent settlers and provisions to Virginia. By 1616 several new settlements had been founded, but the total English population of Virginia was still only about 350 people.

VIRGINIA PROVES A SUCCESS

What turned Virginia into a successful colony was a product that King James condemned in his tract "A Counter-Blast to Tobacco" (1604) as "loathsome to the eye, hateful to the nose, harmful to the brain, dangerous to the lungs"—in a word, tobacco. As early as 1612 John Rolfe was growing tobacco in Virginia, but this tobacco was considered far inferior to that grown in the Spanish colonies. Rolfe then imported tobacco plants from the West Indies. However, it was not until his wife (none other than Pocahontas) taught him the Indian method of curing tobacco that the Virginia product began competing in the European market.

Tobacco growing accelerated the trend toward private ownership of land in Virginia. Initially all land was to remain under the ownership of the London Company until 1616. However, in 1614 Governor Dale, seeing that this system was fatal to individual initiative, gave settlers three acres to farm on their own if they agreed to work on company land for one month a year and to donate two and a half barrels of corn to the company storehouse. Later, all pre-1616 settlers were granted a minimum of one hundred acres (plus one hundred acres for every share of company stock they owned), and anyone who subsequently came to Virginia was to receive fifty acres of land plus a headright of fifty more acres for any person over fifteen they brought with them. The London Company also made large grants of land to individuals or companies who agreed to transport settlers to their grants, or, as they came to be called, plantations. The new problem caused by the success of tobacco production was how to force landowners to devote enough of their land to growing food products instead of tobacco.

The year 1619 turned out to be a momentous one for Jamestown. Two English women had come to the colony as early as 1608, but the population had always remained almost completely male. In 1619, however, the London Company sent out ninety young women to become wives of the settlers. Because a bachelor could purchase a bride for 120 pounds of tobacco, all the young women were soon married. Another group of fifty potential wives arrived in 1621, and even at the increased price of 150 pounds of tobacco, all met the same happy fate. These marriages testified to the fact that the settlers of Virginia thought of themselves as permanent residents of the New World.

Another crucial event of 1619 was the arrival of a Dutch ship at Jamestown with a cargo of, in John Rolfe's words, "twenty Negars," whom the Dutch captain sold in exchange for supplies. These blacks had been baptized and therefore could not be sold as slaves. Nor, although interpretations were a bit murky, did

Mateaka als Rebecka daughter to the mighty Prince
Powhatan Emperour of Attanoughkomouck als virginia
converted and baptized in the Christian faith, and
wife to the wor:ᵍᵗ Mʳ Joh Rolff.
Pub.ᵈ Aug.10.1793. by W. Richardson, Castle Sᵗ Leicester Square.

FIGURE 6B
(New York Public Library.)

English common law recognize any such personal status as "slave." As a result, the first blacks to reach the English colonies were sold as servants for a set term of years rather than as slaves.

The third landmark occurrence of 1619 was the authorization by the London Company of a legislature to be elected by every adult male colonist of Virginia. The first meeting of the House of Burgesses, as this legislature was called, was held in the Jamestown church on July 30, 1619. It consisted of the governor, his six counsellors, and twenty-two elected members. Hot weather forced the adjournment of the session after six days, but the legislature passed laws (1) governing relations with, and conversion of, the Indians; (2) fostering agricultural diversification; (3) formalizing land and labor contracts; (4) requiring church attendance; and (5) regulating morals. The importance of this—the first representative assembly— in the English colonies can hardly be overestimated. It established the precedent that English colonists were to enjoy at least some degree of self-government.

The London Company had been £8,000 in debt in 1618, but the growing demand for Virginia tobacco and the events of 1619 seemed to indicate that its efforts were finally to prove remunerative. However, the increase and spread of Virginia's population threatened the Indians, whose counterattack led to the company's downfall. To understand the relations between the Indians and the settlers, it is necessary to go back to 1613, when the English kidnapped Pocahontas in order to blackmail Powhatan into supplying the colonists with corn and returning the Englishmen, guns, and tools which he had captured. Then, as already related, Rolfe and Pocahontas fell in love. Their proposed marriage raised immediate, and contradictory, objections. Some felt it degrading for an Englishman to marry an Indian; others felt that Rolfe, a commoner, was impertinent to aspire to the hand of a princess—even an Indian princess. Nevertheless, both these objections were ignored. Powhatan gave his blessing, and Pocahontas and Rolfe were married in 1614. Relations with the Indians then improved, but Pocahontas died in England in 1617 (at the age of twenty-two), just as she and Rolfe were about to return to Virginia.

VIRGINIA SURVIVES INDIAN ATTACKS

Powhatan, who had always opposed outright war with the English, died the following year. The new chief, Opechancanough, was justifiably upset by the continued seizure of Indian lands by the settlers. He believed that it was an either-or situation—the Indians must destroy the colony or themselves ultimately perish. He therefore organized all the surrounding tribes, and on Good Friday of 1622 attacked the white settlements in Virginia. Three hundred and forty-seven people (including John Rolfe) were killed, houses and fields were burned, and much cattle was destroyed. This attack was the proverbial last straw for the Virginia Company. The king terminated its charter in 1624, and although it remained in existence for a few more years, it finally expired with a debt of over £200,000.

Happily, the attack did not annihilate the Virginia colony, where 1,200 inhabitants survived and eventually repulsed the Indians. From 1624 until the end of the colonial period, Virginia was a royal colony under the control of the king. After some initial hesitation Charles I, in 1639, officially authorized the calling of an annual legislative assembly, thus confirming the principle of representative government for the colonies.

In 1644 encroachments of Indian lands and the knowledge that England was weakened by civil war induced the then-aged Opechancanough to lead another Indian uprising. Almost 500 colonists were killed in this assult, but its effects were not nearly as serious as those of the 1622 attack; by the 1640s Virginia was a well-established colony with a population of over 8,000. Sir William Berkeley, who had been appointed governor of Virginia in 1642, quickly took the offensive, defeated the Indians, and captured Opechancanough. Although the chief was unable to walk and almost blind, Berkeley intended to send him as a trophy of war to King Charles. However, as Robert Beverley recounted in his "The History and Present State of Virginia" (1705) one of the guards "resenting the calamities the colony had suffered by this prince's means" shot the old chief.

The power of the Virginia Indians was now broken. Berkeley forced them to ·withdraw from large areas of land—which they were no longer to enter without permission—and to have their choice of chiefs approved by him. In return, however, the Indians were promised that whites would be barred from the lands which were to be set aside as an Indian reservation. To guarantee that Indians and whites alike respected these decrees, a series of forts was built along the boundaries between their respective areas. However, as the white population increased, large parts of the supposed Indian reservation were opened for settlement. The Indians were now too weak to fight back effectively.

MARYLAND IS FOUNDED

While the founding of Maryland by George Calvert (Lord Baltimore) may remind us of the earlier individual attempts of Gilbert and Raleigh to found colonies, Baltimore's had a happy ending. The main reason for this difference was that techniques for founding colonies had improved through trial and error, so that the expenses were now within the means of a wealthy individual such as Lord Baltimore, who financed the colony almost completely out of his own pocket. In addition, he could also count on support from an established colony, Virginia, which was not available to Gilbert and Raleigh.

Lord Baltimore had served as a member of Parliament and as a royal official until his conversion to Catholicism ruined his political career. Since the beginning of the 1620s, he had been interested in acquiring land in the New World, where he might increase his own fortune and provide a haven for those of his coreligionists who desired to leave England. At first Lord Baltimore thought of colonizing New-foundland, but a winter spent there in 1628 convinced him that the climate and the French made successful colonization there unlikely.

In 1632 he obtained a charter from King Charles I making him the proprietor of a territory just north of Virginia and named Maryland—either in honor of Queen Henrietta Maria or for the Virgin Mary. Baltimore's charter was essentially a feudal document which granted him complete ownership of Maryland's soil, minerals, and fisheries. He could make land grants, impose taxes, regulate commerce, and create manors and towns. He had the right to establish courts, appoint judges, and pardon offenders. He could appoint all officials—civil and military. He had the sole power to initiate legislation, and although his suggestions were only to have the force of law with the consent of the freemen or their representatives, he also retained the veto power. For all this Baltimore had only to pay the king two Indian arrows a year plus one-fifth of all the gold and silver found in the colony. The Maryland Charter of 1632 also ordered Lord Baltimore to ensure that the laws he promulgated were not "repugnant" to the laws of England or in violation of the "privileges, franchises, and liberties" of Englishmen.

The first Lord Baltimore died just as the charter was being drafted, and the actual settlement of Maryland was left to his son Cecil. In 1634 two ships bearing over 200 passengers—mostly Protestant—arrived in America and founded the town of St. Mary's near the mouth of the Potomac River. The local Indians, under pressure from neighboring tribes, were already preparing to evacuate the area, so

Leonard Calvert (the second Lord Baltimore's brother, who acted as governor) purchased about thirty miles of territory for some "axes, hoes, and some yards of cloth." Father White, a Jesuit who accompanied the expedition, interpreted the Indian migration as a sign that God was with the colony.

Lord Baltimore was eager to attract settlers, for only through land sales could the colony be made profitable. He offered 1,000 acres at an annual charge, or quitrent, of twenty shillings to any settler who brought five (later twenty) adult males with him. Families received 100 acres for the husband, wife, and adult servants and 50 acres for each child under sixteen. However, it required more than cheap land to attract settlers to Maryland. In spite of the charter, the Maryland colonists insisted on the right to have a voice in the lawmaking process, as was enjoyed by their fellow colonists in Virginia. Lord Baltimore resisted at first, but again the desire to attract settlers forced him to relent after a few years, and he allowed the legislature to initiate laws. However, he maintained his right to veto any law at any time, even if it had already been approved by his governor.

Religion proved to be the most dangerous problem facing the proprietor. In spite of sporadic persecution of Catholics in England, far more Protestants than Catholics settled in Maryland. Lord Baltimore was constantly under pressure to protect his coreligionists without alienating the Protestant majority. This problem became even more severe when the Puritans came to power in England during the civil wars. For two years (1645-1646) a Protestant group ruled Maryland and forced Governor Calvert into exile in Virginia. However, in 1647 Lord Baltimore was able to reassert his authority by naming a Protestant governor and placing a majority of Protestants on the council. In order to protect the Catholic settlers, he proposed the Toleration Act, which was passed by the assembly in 1649. This act declared in part that

> . . . no person or persons . . . professing to believe in Jesus Christ shall from henceforth be any ways troubled, molested, or discountenanced for or in respect of his or her religion . . .

The Toleration Act was more of a symbolic than a real step toward religious freedom, since it did little in the long run to heal the ill feelings between Protestants and Catholics in Maryland.

THE ECONOMIC GROWTH OF THE TOBACCO COLONIES

The economy of both Virginia and Maryland was based primarily on the production of tobacco, although corn, wheat, fruit, and vegetables were also grown, and all types of livestock were raised. As the tobacco boom began to quiet in the 1620s, two interrelated "commodities" became more and more necessary to any planter who hoped to become prosperous—land and labor. Under the headright system land was relatively easy to come by. Some planters acquired thousands of acres, although in the seventeenth century they probably worked only a few hundred of them. Labor, however, even the unskilled labor which was all that tobacco cultivation required, was scarce; anyone who had the funds to transport himself to America was going to work his own land.

The seventeenth-century answer to the labor problem was indentured servitude. The London Company had paid the transportation to Virginia for those people who agreed to work for the company for seven years. Individual planters soon began to make similar arrangements. During this century most indentured servants came from England. They signed contracts before sailing which stipulated their term of service and their freedom dues. Skilled workers rarely had to indenture themselves for more than three years; most others agreed to four or five years; and seven was the usual maximum. Freedom dues included clothes, tools, a gun, and, during the first half of the seventeenth century, usually fifty acres of land. During this century about 1,500–2,000 indentured servants, male and female, arrived in Virginia each year.

Indentured servants who arrived in America during the eighteenth century tended to come from the continental nations rather than from England. They usually came as families rather than as individuals. These people were often called redemptioners because they placed themselves in the power of the merchant or sea captain who brought them to America. If no friend or relative redeemed them by paying the costs of the trip, the sea captain was authorized to sell them for the highest price he could obtain, which meant a longer period of indenture. The relative number of indentured servants in Virginia and Maryland declined during the eighteenth century because of the growth of black slavery.

Both in the seventeenth and eighteenth centuries, masters were required to feed, clothe, and house their indentured servants and to refrain from cruel or unusual punishment. Indentured servants were supposed to work faithfully, not to marry without their masters' permission, and, of course, not to run away. Articles of indenture were enforceable in the courts, but judges generally gave the benefit of the doubt to the master. On the other hand, the dire need for labor and the knowledge that if a colony acquired a bad reputation for mistreatment of its indentured servants, the supply of recruits would dry up, set limits on the exploitation of indentured servants. After their term of indenture was completed, most indentured servants graduated into the small-farmer class, by far the largest group in these two colonies. However, during the seventeenth century some became large planters and even served in the House of Burgesses.

The economies of Virginia and Maryland were also strongly influenced by the geography of the Chesapeake Bay, upon which both colonies were located. A ship arriving from England would enter the bay and then sail up one of the numerous navigable rivers which flowed into it. The leading landowners had plantations along these rivers. The ship would exchange furniture, clothing, tools, and other manufactured goods for the planter's tobacco as well as that of his smaller neighbors, which he usually purchased in advance. This scene would be reenacted at the other major plantations. This method of transacting business militated against the growth of towns and concentrated economic power in the hands of the large planters.

As a result, the large planters—though only a small minority of the population—began to accumulate the political power which was eventually to resemble that of the squire, or country gentleman, in the home country. Some of this power resulted from membership in the legislature; but perhaps to an even greater degree, it was based on their virtual domination of local government—the county courts and parishes.

By 1635 King Charles I had two prosperous colonies of which he could be proud. However, he also had some other, more northerly colonies, about which—by the time of his death—he must have had distinctly negative feelings.

BIBLIOGRAPHY

BARBOUR, PHILIP L. *The Three Worlds of Captain John Smith.* Boston, 1964.

BRIDENBAUGH, CARL. *Jamestown, 1544–1699.* New York, 1980.

CRAVEN, WESLEY FRANK. *The Southern Colonies in the Seventeenth Century, 1607–1689.* Baton Rouge, 1949.

CRAVEN, WESLEY FRANK. *White, Red and Black: The Seventeenth-Century Virginian.* Charlottesville, 1971.

LAND, AUBREY C. *Colonial Maryland: A History.* Millwood, N.Y., 1981.

MAIN, GLORIA L. *Tobacco Colony: Life in Early Maryland, 1650–1720.* Princeton, 1982.

MORTON, RICHARD L. *Colonial Virginia.* 2 vols. Chapel Hill, 1960.

SHEEHAN, BERNARD W. *Savagism & Civility: Indians and Englishmen in Colonial Virginia.* New York, 1980.

TATE, THAD W., and AMMERMAN, DAVID L., eds. *The Chesapeake in the Seventeenth Century: Essays on Anglo-American Society.* Chapel Hill, 1979.

7

The New England Colonies

No one can accuse the Pilgrims of being optimists. As William Bradford—their long-time leader—chronicled in his journal, *Of Plymouth Plantation* before they left Holland, they agreed that even if they were to raise the money to found a colony, and even if they should survive the voyage to America, they

> ... should be liable to famine, and nakedness ... sore sicknesses and grievous diseases. And also those which should escape or overcome these difficulties, should yet be in continual danger of the savage people, who are cruel, barbarous, and most treacherous. ...

THE FOUNDING OF THE PLYMOUTH COLONY

In England Separatists were punished by fines and imprisonment. The members of a small Separatist congregation at Scrooby in Yorkshire tired of being "clapt up in prison" and left England in 1608 for Holland and religious freedom. It was this congregation of ordinary farm workers—led by Bradford and their minister, John Robinson—whom we know as the Pilgrims. Although the Pilgrims found religious freedom in Holland, they faced difficult economic conditions, the assimilation of Dutch customs by their children, and the possibility of involvement in a war between Holland and Spain that threatened to break out in 1621. Therefore, a group of them decided—in spite of the perils enumerated above—to settle in the New World.

In 1620, after much negotiation, the London Company gave the Pilgrims permission to settle on its territory. To help with finances, a merchant named Thomas Weston formed a joint stock company which raised the funds necessary to transport them to America. Each colonist was given one share in the company and was expected to work for the company for seven years. At the end of that period, all the land and profits were to be divided between the colonists and the other investors in the company. Thirty-five Pilgrims (who called themselves saints) and sixty-seven other English men, women, and children (whom the Pilgrims called strangers) boarded the *Mayflower* when it set sail for America in September 1620.

The voyage lasted slightly over two months. Whether because storms blew them off course; or because the Pilgrims were attracted by John Smith's account of the furs, fish, and timber of New England; or because they felt they would be freer to worship as they pleased outside the jurisdiction of the London Company, the Pilgrims landed on Cape Cod (not Plymouth Rock) instead of Virginia. This created a problem: How, and by whom, were they to be ruled? The solution to this problem was the famous Mayflower Compact, in which forty-one of the adult males, both saints and strangers, agreed to

> . . . enact, constitute, and frame, such just and equal Laws, Ordinances, Acts, Constitutions, and Offices, from time to time, as shall be thought most meet and convenient for the general Good of the Colony; unto which we promise all due Submission and Obedience.

After a month of exploring the Cape Cod area (where they irritated the Indians by stealing their corn), the Pilgrims settled at Plymouth on Christmas Day. The Plymouth settlement was fortunate to survive that first winter. About half of the colonists died before spring. Probably all would have died if it had not been for the friendly attitude of the Indians of the immediate area, who had recently been decimated by illness—"the wonderful plague" King James called it. First Samoset walked into Plymouth and casually asked for beer. Then he brought Squanto, another English-speaking Indian, whom William Bradford called "a special instrument sent of God." Squanto had been kidnapped by English traders, brought to England, but allowed to return to America, where he found all the Indians of his village dead. Squanto himself only lived until 1622, but he helped provide the Pilgrims with food and taught them how the Indians raised corn.

Squanto also served as emissary to Massasoit, the chief of the Wampanoag Confederacy, who signed an offensive and defensive alliance with the Pilgrims. This treaty was honored by Massasoit until his death in 1662 and was not broken until King Philip's War of 1675. Although the Pilgrims executed three settlers for the murder of a Narragansett Indian and whipped another for stealing Indian corn, their treatment of Indians did not always reach this high level. Miles Standish, the fiery military leader of Plymouth (a stranger, not a saint) attacked neighboring Indians so frequently and on such slight pretexts that the Pilgrims' old minister, John Robinson—who had not come to America with them—chided him for his ferocity.

The harvest was so bountiful in 1621 that the Pilgrims invited Massasoit and ninety of his braves to a lavish three-day feast with deermeat and fowl (perhaps turkey) as the main dishes. Unfortunately, this first Thanksgiving proved premature. With the arrival of thirty-five new settlers in November 1621, the Pilgrims once again found themselves on short rations. However, conditions improved in 1623 when Governor Bradford decided, without asking the permission of the directors of the joint stock company, to divide the land among the settlers. By 1626 the company itself realized that no great profit was ever going to materialize from the enterprise and sold its ownership of the colony for £2,400. It took the Pilgrims seventeen years to pay this sum in full.

Plymouth never received a royal charter, but it remained an independent colony until 1691, when it was annexed by Massachusetts. The people of Plymouth and of the few small towns which grew up around it were primarily farmers, although they also did some fishing and fur trading with the Indians. True to their religious beliefs, each town had its own independent, self-supporting congregation. This congregational form of church government was to be followed by the Puritans when they arrived in America. Later, it became the accepted pattern all over New England.

The colony was ruled by a governor, seven counsellors, and representatives of each town. These representatives were elected annually by the adult males of "good character" (although later, voters were required to be church members who owned £20 worth of property), and they, in turn, elected the governor and his council. This simple form of government ideally suited the Pilgrims, whose main reason for coming to America was, as Bradford wrote in *Of Plymouth Plantation*

> . . . advancing the gospel of the kingdom of Christ in those remote parts of the world; yea, though they should be even as stepping-stones unto others for the performing of so great a work.

THE FOUNDING OF THE MASSACHUSETTS BAY COLONY

The "others" for whom the Pilgrims were the "stepping-stones" were the Puritans. In 1623 the Council of New England granted land to the Dorchester Company to plant a colony of fishermen in what is now Massachusetts. The experiment failed, but some of the settlers remained and settled the town of Salem. In 1628 a group of Puritan merchants formed the Company of New England and sent an additional group of settlers to Salem under the leadership of John Endecott. The following year the New England Company obtained a new charter from Charles I changing its name to the Massachusetts Bay Company and granting it the right to govern the territory under its jurisdiction. Several factors impelled the Puritans to take speedy advantage of this new charter. Archbishop Laud was insisting that Anglican practices be followed to the letter in every church, and ministers with Puritan leanings were being dismissed. In 1628 the king had just dissolved Parliament and had made it

FIGURE 7A
(New York Public Library.)

clear that he intended to rule the nation, levy taxes, and conduct what the Puritans considered a pro-Catholic foreign policy without any interference. Lastly, during the 1620s a depression in the cloth industry (in addition to the previously discussed enclosure movement and inflation) brought great economic distress to the southern and eastern counties of England, where the majority of Puritans lived.

The leader of the Massachusetts Bay Colony was John Winthrop. Winthrop received a legal education at Cambridge, held a royal judicial post, and was a substantial landowner in Suffolk County. However, by the end of the 1620s, he no longer held any office and was troubled by debt. Winthrop was well aware of the practical reasons for settling in America, but he had strong religious motivation as well. As he wrote in his *The History of New England from 1630 to 1649*, Winthrop was convinced that because of their sins, England and Europe were due to suffer "some heavy scourge and judgement" and that the Puritans "through a special overruling providence" had entered into a "covenant" with God, who had ordered them to "fly into the wilderness" and create a "City upon a Hill"—a holy commonwealth which would be the focus for "the eyes of all people."

In 1629, by the so-called Cambridge Agreement, the stockholders of the Massachusetts Bay Company who were not interested in settling in America agreed to sell their interest in the company to Winthrop and eleven other like-minded Puritans. They also agreed to allow them to take the company's charter with them to Massachusetts, where it was to serve as the colony's constitution. Before the end of 1630, Winthrop and over 2,000 Puritans—in family groups, not just men as in earlier colonies—left for Massachusetts. Because of sound preparation and help from the Pilgrims, Massachusetts grew within a dozen years to be a prosperous colony of several small towns with a population of 16,000 people—not all of whom were Puritans.

The rapid growth of the colony made it impossible to govern it according to the charter of the Massachusetts Bay Company. Like other joint stock companies, the Massachusetts Bay Company was to be governed by its freemen, or investors, meeting four times a year in a General Court. At one of these meetings, they were to elect a governor, deputy governor, and eighteen assistants. However, only Winthrop, Thomas Dudley, and eight other freemen met at the first General Court held in Massachusetts. They monopolized control of the colony for a year before admitting 118 other Puritan church members as freemen. Even then, for three more years Winthrop, Dudley—who served as deputy governor—and the eight other original freemen who acted as assistants (or as a council) enacted all the laws. In 1634, however, after complaints (including the Watertown Protest from the freemen of Watertown who objected to being taxed without their consent lest it result in "bondage"), lawmaking powers were transferred to a General Court which now included deputies elected by each town as well as the governor, deputy governor, and the assistants. For a measure to pass, however, it required a majority of the votes of both the deputies and the assistants.

Ten years later, a case came to the General Court (which also had judicial powers) concerning the ownership of a stray pig claimed by both Robert Keane, a rich merchant, and Mrs. Sherman, a widow. The deputies favored the widow; the assistants favored the merchant. So heated did the dispute between the two groups become that they agreed in the future to meet separately as a bicameral legislature. The members of the lower house chose their own speaker, developed their own procedures, and in spite of the assistants' veto power, gradually became the most influential element of the government. This trend was encouraged by the growth in the number of freemen. In spite of the fact that church membership and, later, a property qualification were required to be admitted as freemen, their number increased to about 300 by 1640 and 2,500 (about one-fifth of the adult male population) in 1675.

For the first decade of its existence, Massachusetts had no legal code. Winthrop always felt that justice would be better served if the assistants, who also acted as judges, had a great deal of discretion. He also feared that if the Massachusetts laws deviated too much from English law, its charter might be endangered. Yet, as he himself admitted, the deputies felt that the wide latitude allowed judges was potentially dangerous. In 1641 Nathaniel Ward—a minister with much legal experience—prepared a code based largely on English common law and called the Body of Liberties. However, ninety-seven out of the ninety-eight chapters of the Body of Liberties listed the civil and legal rights of freemen, women, children, servants, foreigners, the church, and even of the "brute creature." Only one section dealt with the eleven offenses for which Mosaic law demanded capital punishment plus "insurrection or public rebellion against our commonwealth," which the Puritans also considered deserving of the death penalty. It was not until 1648 that a more exhaustive code—called the Laws and Liberties of Massachusetts—based on Mosaic law, common law, and Massachusetts statutes, effectively circumscribed the powers of the magistrates.

A description of the form of government which developed in Massachusetts is best begun by indicating what it was not. For example, it was not a theocracy. Church and state were partners—ministers were asked for, and gave, advice but were barred from holding any civil office. The state saw to it that the church was supported financially and that attendance was compulsory. The state also punished heresy, using its own courts (unlike England, Massachusetts had no church courts) but only because a heretic was a menace to the civil order. In return, the ministers preached support of the civil government. A Puritan might be divested of his or her church membership, but that did not bar him (women were excluded from office in any case) if he was otherwise eligible, from voting and holding political office.

Further, Massachusetts was not a democracy, which the Puritans did not consider a fit government for church or commonwealth. As John Cotton, a leading Puritan minister rhetorically stated: "If the people be governors, who shall be governed?" The Puritan view was that the church members, as the least depraved part of the population, should carefully select their rulers from a restricted circle of men who could be trusted to carry out God's laws as interpreted by the Bible and the ministers. Winthrop described this form of government as a "mixed democracy"; Cotton characterized it as a "mixed aristocracy." When we note that the same few men were continuously elected to the highest offices and that only a quarter of the population had been admitted to church membership (and not all of that quarter had—though sometimes voluntarily—become freemen), Cotton's description sounds more accurate to the modern ear.

While still in England the Puritans remained part of the Anglican Church. However, upon their arrival in America, although they never officially separated, the Puritans adopted the Separatist theory that each individual church was to be organized by a voluntary covenant, or compact, of its members and was to be governed by them. The members chose their pastor, teacher, elders, and deacon. As already indicated, not everyone was accepted as a church member; candidates not only had to accept Puritan theology, but they had to testify (publicly, if male) to the actual spiritual experiences which had convinced them that they were among the elect who were deserving of church membership.

However, even under this congregational system, ministers met together informally and in synods to discuss theological matters. Although the conclusions reached at these meetings were not binding, when the ministers reached a consensus, the decision was usually implemented in the individual churches. The ministers usually agreed that no deviation from orthodox Puritan theology was to be tolerated. The Reverend Nathaniel Ward in his tract *The Simple Cobbler of Agawam* (1647) was only too eager "to proclaim to the world in the name of our colony, that all Familists, Antinomians, Anabaptists, and other Enthusiasts shall have free liberty to keep away from us."

OTHER NEW ENGLAND COLONIES

Not all Puritans, much less settlers of other denominations, agreed with the orthodox Puritan conceptions of church and state. The most famous of these dissenters
was Roger Williams. Williams, described by Bradford as "a man godly and zealous,
having many precious parts, but very unsettled in judgement," was–like most
Puritan ministers–a graduate of Cambridge. He arrived in Massachusetts in 1631,
turned down an offer from a Boston church because it had not officially separated
from the Church of England, moved to Plymouth, and then accepted a post with
the Salem church in 1634. For reasons far different from those of modern civil
libertarians, Williams preached separation of church and state and religious toleration. In his tract, *The Bloudy Tenet of Persecution* (1644), he contended that
"the civil magistrate's power extends only to the bodies and goods and outward
state of men," and that the church was profaned when it allowed the state to enforce religious tenets, church attendance, or financial support. Williams defended
toleration on the grounds that

> A false religion out of the church will not hurt the church, no more than
> weeds in a wilderness hurt the enclosed garden . . . and a false religion will
> not hurt the civil state in case the worshipper break no civil law.

Williams's religious views were anathema to the Puritan leaders, but his political views were even less acceptable. He had the temerity to deny that the king of
England had a right to grant any land in America. In a treatise written while he was
still living at Plymouth, he claimed: "James has no more right to give away or sell
Massasoit's lands . . . than Massasoit has to sell King James' kingdom." The Puritans
might have been amused by this contention if it had not thrown doubt on the legality of their charter, which was already under attack in England. When Williams refused to cease his religious and political attacks, the Puritan leaders ordered him
shipped back to England, where he might be liable to a charge of treason. Even
though it was already winter, Williams avoided this fate by taking refuge with the
Narragansett Indians, whose language he learned and whose land he purchased in
order to found the town of Providence in 1636.

Another celebrated dissenter from Orthodox Puritan doctrine was Anne
Hutchinson. Mrs. Hutchinson, the wife of a respected Boston merchant, held regular
biweekly meetings for her women friends (later men also attended) at which she
discussed the sermons of the previous Sunday. She insisted that some clergymen,
such as John Cotton, had more insight than others. They preached a covenant of
grace (that one knew when one was saved by means of an inner light, or feeling that
the Holy Spirit had blessed them) rather than a covenant of works (that an individual's good conduct was necessary for, and a sign of, his or her salvation).

Although no Puritan minister was actually preaching a covenant of works, the
controversy split the colony into warring factions, even dividing families. Orthodox
opinion felt that Anne Hutchinson's emphasis on individual conviction would under-

mine the authority of both church and state. Although in 1636 Mrs. Hutchinson's followers were strong enough to elect their candidate for governor, in the following year the orthodox Puritans, with Winthrop at their head, regained control of the government and Anne Hutchinson was tried for, in John Winthrop's words, "having troubled the peace of the commonwealth." Although she denied this allegation, Anne did admit at the trial to having an "immediate" (personal) revelation, which scandalized the court because most Puritans believed that revelation ended with the Bible. A sentence of banishment was pronounced against her, and in 1638 she and many of her followers left Massachusetts and founded the town of Portsmouth. Winthrop never forgave Mrs. Hutchinson for disturbing the peace of Massachusetts. He saw the hand of God in her death, which took place at the hands of the Indians of Long Island, where she had settled after leaving Portsmouth.

Two more towns—Newport in 1639 and Warwick in 1643—were founded by other dissident Puritans. In 1644 these four towns received a charter from Parliament (which was then ruling England) creating a new colony, Rhode Island and Providence Plantations. The settlers of Rhode Island established a "democratical" government in which all free, adult, white males were eligible to vote for representatives to a General Court and all groups, including Quakers—whom Roger Williams personally detested—were allowed to worship as they pleased. In 1663 King Charles II granted Rhode Island a royal charter which confirmed its right to virtual self-government. In spite of derogatory appellations such as Rogue's Island, Rhode Island grew into a prosperous colony of farmers, stock raisers, and merchants. By the late 1670s Edward Randolph, a royal official, described this colony in his report to the Lords of Trade as "the most profitable part of New England."

Connecticut also owes its origin, at least in part, to disagreement with the political beliefs of Massachusetts. The Reverend Thomas Hooker (the minister of the Cambridge church), though orthodox in religion, tended to be more democratic than his colleagues. He believed that the people should have the power not only to elect officials but also to guide their decisions. The people of his congregation were also interested in the fertile soil of the Connecticut River valley. For this combination of reasons, the congregation petitioned for, and after some hesitation received, permission from the General Court to emigrate from Massachusetts. A small group of settlers were already living at Wethersfield and Saybrook. Hooker's congregation founded Hartford in 1636. Within a few years Windsor and Springfield were also founded by settlers from Massachusetts.

By 1639 the desire for peace and union led to the drafting of the Fundamental Orders of Connecticut, the first American document that can truly be characterized as a constitution. This document made Connecticut a virtually self-governing colony in which all freemen (who did not have to be church members—although later a property qualification was added) elected the governor and his council as well as representatives to a General Court. In 1662 King Charles II granted Connecticut a charter which essentially confirmed the Fundamental Orders. New Haven, and a few other small towns on both sides of Long Island Sound, refused to join the new colony of Connecticut. The "extreme" Puritans (even Massa-

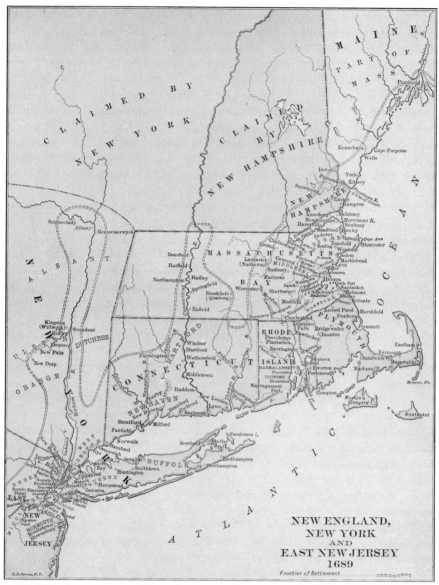

FIGURE 7B From *Colonial Self-Government (The American Nations Series, 1652–1689)* by Charles McLean Andrews. New York: Harper & Row, Publishers, Inc., p. 273. Reproduced by permission.

chusetts did not meet their strict standards) who founded these towns joined together in 1643 to form what has been termed a Biblical Commonwealth in which only church members could vote and where Mosaic law, rather than English common law, was followed. In 1662, however, when Connecticut received its royal charter, the New Haven Confederation was incorporated into it.

New Hampshire was also founded partly because of religious disagreements in Massachusetts. The town of Exeter was founded by the Reverend John Wheelwright, the brother-in-law and supporter of Anne Hutchinson. Other towns were later settled by orthodox Puritans and Anglicans. Massachusetts ruled the area until 1677, when New Hampsnire became a royal colony. The few small settlements in what is now the state of Maine, however, remained under the control of Massachusetts. Maine's progress was hampered largely because it was the scene of bitter fighting between England and France for almost the entire colonial period.

These "hivings out" did nothing to change the minds of the leaders of Massachusetts about religious toleration or democracy. In 1646, when a group of merchants presented a petition requesting that Anglicans and Presbyterians "not scandalous in their lives" be allowed to vote and hold office, the General Court not only rejected it but punished its signers. Two years later a church synod developed the Cambridge Platform, which continued the requirement of testimony to a religious experience before granting church membership and supported the partnership of church and state.

While Massachusetts was still ruled under its charter, only two modifications were made in the Cambridge Platform. In 1652 church membership was waived as a condition for voting in local elections. Also, in 1662 the Half Way Covenant made children of church members who lived blameless lives eligible to become church members without testifying to a religious experience. This made them eligible to vote and hold civil office but not to vote or hold church office.

INDIAN RELATIONS IN NEW ENGLAND

Indian relations were simplified for the Puritans of Massachusetts because of the terrible plagues which decimated the Indians just before, and just after, the Puritans first arrived. As Winthrop wrote in a letter to England in 1634: "They are near all dead of the smallpox, so the Lord hath cleared our title to what we possess." However, when the Lord failed to act, the colonists took matters into their own hands. As early as 1629, Winthrop refined a theory called *vacuum domicilium* (unoccupied land), or, in his words: "It was against the laws of God and nature, that so much land should be idle, while so many Christians wanted it to labor on and to raise bread."

The hunger for the Connecticut River valley lands was the basic cause of the Pequot War. In 1636, after the Pequots killed two Massachusetts merchants in Connecticut, the General Court sent John Endecott with nine men to punish the offenders. Endecott burned several Pequot villages, which only convinced Sassacus—the Pequot chief—that all whites must be driven from Connecticut. Fortunately for the settlers, Roger Williams persuaded the Narragansett Indians not to join the Pequots, or Sassacus might have succeeded. In 1637 John Mason of Massachusetts and John Underhill of Connecticut, with a combined army of ninety colonists plus several hundred Indian allies, surprised the main Pequot stronghold and killed 400 men, women, and children with a ferocity which appalled their Indian allies. However, Mason quoted the following Biblical verse: "It was the Lord's doings and it was marvellous in our eyes." The few surviving Pequots were handed over to Indian allies or sold as slaves in the West Indies.

Once the Pequot threat was removed, some New England ministers began to attempt what, according to the Massachusetts charter of 1629 was supposed to be the principal end of the colony: to "win and incite the Natives of the Country to . . . the Christian Faith." John Eliot, known as the apostle to the Indians, translated the Bible into the Algonquin language and was largely responsible for the establishment of fourteen "praying Indian" towns and 4,000 Christian Indians. A special college was established for Indians at Harvard, and most Indians who converted adopted English customs along with Christianity.

It was the murder of a "praying Indian" who had warned the authorities at Plymouth of an impending Indian attack that precipitated King Philip's War. Three Wampanoag Indians were executed for the crime, and their chief, Matacom—or King Philip—was outraged. An Indian attack may well have been brewing; King Philip had resented white authority ever since his brother (who had replaced Massasoit as chief in 1661) had died under mysterious circumstances after having been questioned by the Plymouth authorities about a possible Indian uprising at that time. King Philip also saw the suffering of his people as the fur trade declined in the New England area and as more and more of their land was occupied by colonists. The final insult came in 1671 when officials of Plymouth took him into custody and forced him to accept their authority over land sales and to surrender his tribe's weapons to the colony.

Therefore, in June 1675 Philip launched a full-scale Indian war. The Wampanoags were soon joined by the Narragansett and the Nipmunk Indians, who realized that their lands were also in danger of being confiscated by encroaching settlers from Massachusetts and Connecticut. For a time it seemed as if all of New England would be destroyed. Twelve towns were annihilated, and the Indians came within seventeen miles of Boston. One-tenth of all New England fighting men were killed, and thousands of others were wounded or captured. However, the Indians were outnumbered four to one. They were also disunited and short of food supplies and ammunition.

In August 1676 King Philip was killed by an Indian deserter (some say he was a "praying Indian"), and the war came to an end except in New Hampshire and Maine, where it lasted until 1678. Massachusetts and Connecticut executed many Indian warriors and—over Eliot's protests—sold hundreds of Indians, including Philip's wife and son, as slaves to the West Indies. They also confiscated Indian lands. Philip's head was placed on a pole and kept as a grisly token at Plymouth for over twenty years.

King Philip's War caused not only loss of life and property but a great deal of social dislocation. It left behind large numbers of widows, orphans, and disabled veterans. This gravely undermined the Puritan sense of mission. It was clear that God was punishing New England for its sins, and the numerous "days of prayer and humiliation" conducted throughout the area seemed fruitless. A synod held in 1679 still had the intellectual agility to be able to group New England's sins into twelve categories, but it lacked the confidence that these sins could be overcome. Perry Miller in *The New England Mind from Colony to Province* points out that the ministers did not surrender but they did begin to suspect that the people's sins were "incurable." Perhaps they might have regrouped their forces, but external political events were destined to destroy the church-state relationship which the Puritans considered indispensable for the maintenance of their wilderness Zion.

BIBLIOGRAPHY

BATTLE, EMERY. *Saints and Sectaries: Anne Hutchinson and the Antinomian Controversy in the Massachusetts Bay Colony.* Chapel Hill, 1962.

CLARK, CHARLES E. *The Eastern Frontier: The Settlement of Northern New England.* New York, 1970.

DANIELL, JERE E. *Colonial New Hampshire: A History.* Millwood, N.Y., 1981.

JAMES, SIDNEY V. *Colonial Rhode Island: A History.* New York, 1975.

JENNINGS, FRANCIS. *The Invasion of America: Indians, Colonialism, and the Cant of Conquest.* Chapel Hill, 1975.

LABAREE, BENJAMIN W. *Colonial Massachusetts: A History.* Millwood, N.Y., 1979.

LANGDON, GEORGE D. *Pilgrim Colony: A History of New Plymouth, 1620-1691.* New Haven, 1966.

LOCKRIDGE, KENNETH A. *A New England Town—The First Hundred Years: Dedham, Massachusetts, 1636-1736.* New York, 1970.

MILLER, PERRY. *Roger Williams: His Contribution to the American Tradition.* Indianapolis, 1953.

POWELL, SUMNER C. *Puritan Village: The Formation of a New England Town.* Middletown, Conn., 1963.

TAYLOR, ROBERT J. *Colonial Connecticut: A History.* Millwood, N.Y., 1979.

8

The Completion of Colonization

Lord Shaftesbury, one of the leading statesmen of the Restoration period—and a vigorous exponent of English colonization—advised King Charles II: "It is trade and commerce alone that draweth store of wealth along with it and the potency by sea by shipping which is not otherwise to be had." This statement is typical of the economic thinking of the second half of the seventeenth century, when the English government was making strenuous efforts to put the theories of mercantilism into practice. All English colonies, those already established and those still to be founded, were to feel the effects of these efforts.

THE COLONIES DURING
THE INTERREGNUM

The Puritan merchants who dominated the English government during the Commonwealth were ardent mercantilists who were eager to derive full advantage from the already-existing colonies. Specifically, they were determined to break the virtual monopoly of the maritime carrying trade which the Dutch, because of their lower freight rates, had developed. The Anglo-Dutch War of 1652–1654 was fought for this purpose. A more effective weapon against the Dutch monopoly was the Navigation Act of 1651. This act provided that all goods brought from Asia, Africa, or America to England, or to its possessions, had to be carried in English (including Irish and colonial) ships. Goods produced in European nations might be carried to the colonies in the ships of the nation which produced them as well as in English ships. The first Navigation Act had relatively little effect on the colonies, since the English government had not yet developed the machinery to enforce it. However, it served as a model for its successors.

During the period of the Interregnum, the colonies showed their economic independence in many other ways. Even New England (which, of course, sympathized with the English Puritan regime) placed its own interests first. Beginning in 1651 Massachusetts coined its own money, the famous pine tree shilling. New England fishermen took control of the American fishing waters when the English fishing industry was paralyzed by the civil war.

The most significant action of the New England colonies during this period was the formation of the United Colonies of New England, or—as it is usually called—the New England Confederation. This confederation was formed because the New England colonies felt that they could get no help from England to solve their problems: economic depression caused by the cessation of immigration; intercolonial boundary and commercial disputes; and the military threat posed by the French, Dutch, and Indians. The confederation included Massachusetts, Plymouth, Connecticut, and New Haven (Rhode Island was excluded because of its unorthodoxy)—each of which was represented by two commissioners. Each year the members elected a president, but his duties were limited to presiding over meetings.

The New England Confederation was the first example of American federalism. Each of the four colonies was to continue to govern its internal affairs, but military and Indian affairs were to be decided by a vote of six of the eight commissioners, and the admission of new members required a unanimous vote. Expenses were apportioned among its members on the basis of the number of males between sixteen and sixty in their population, but the expenditure had to be approved by each colonial legislature. The confederation lasted, in theory, until 1691; however, its *raison d'etre* and major achievements ended in the mid-1660s with the restoration of Charles II, the conquest of New Netherland, and the absorption of New Haven by Connecticut.

However, it had already defended the New England colonies from their enemies, settled boundary disputes between its members, signed a favorable treaty with the Dutch (which the English government later repudiated), facilitated the extradition of runaway servants and criminals, settled some religious questions, encouraged support for Harvard College, and encouraged missionary work among the Indians. It might have accomplished even more, but Massachusetts—which because of the size of its population had to bear the greatest burden of men and money— refused at times (particularly during the Dutch War of 1652-1654) to be bound by a vote of the other three colonies, thereby nullifying their decisions. Massachusetts was also responsible for the failure of the confederation to admit Maine, New Hampshire, and Rhode Island, because it had hopes of eventually annexing these colonies.

Virginia and Maryland tended to be royalist in sympathy during the English civil war, and many of the king's adherents settled in Virginia after his execution in 1649. However, under pressure from England both colonies ultimately acknowledged Parliamentary authority. William Berkeley, the royal governor of Virginia, was replaced, and twice (in 1645 and 1655) Maryland Protestants revolted against Lord Baltimore. On both occasions the proprietor's power was eventually reestablished. During this period the legislatures of both colonies became bicameral, with the elected house exercising powers it had never had in the past: In Virginia, it even elected the governor. The increase in and spread of population after the defeat of the Indians in 1644 led to an increase in the number and powers of county governments. Unlike the increase in the powers of the elected assembly, these proved to be permanent.

Significant economic changes took place in the West Indian colonies during the period of the Interregnum. The most important of these changes was the replacement of tobacco production by sugar production. This change required a large amount of capital and an increase in the number of workers. Small farmers were bought, or squeezed, out, leaving only a relatively small number of huge plantations worked by hundreds of slaves. On Barbados, for example, the slave population grew from 6,000 in the 1640s to 40,000 in the 1660s. The number of whites, on the other hand, decreased by 50 percent, and they were outnumbered four to one. The emphasis on the growth of sugar left the West Indies short of food and cattle, needs that were filled by the mainland colonies. Politically, the West Indies tended to be more amenable to the wishes of the mother country than the mainland colonies because of their more exposed position among the Spanish, French, and Dutch possessions in the immediate area.

COLONIAL POLICY
UNDER CHARLES II

The restoration of Charles II inaugurated a new and expanded era of English colonization. A number of contrasts set this period of colonization apart from the earlier one. With the development of industry in England, the fear of overpopulation disappeared and Parliament actually passed laws limiting emigration. This meant that many of the future settlers of the English colonies were to come from the continent or from earlier American colonies. With the exception of the Quakers, no significant religious group felt the necessity of leaving England during this period. While the political upheavals mentioned in an earlier chapter drove settlers to America, the primary motive for most of the settlers during this period was economic. Finally, King Charles returned to the system of founding proprietary colonies so that he could pay his many financial and political debts to those who had supported him during his exile.

One of the first steps taken by King Charles II upon his restoration in 1660 was to systematize colonial administration. Since the time of James I, the Privy Council had been in titular charge of the colonies. However, it had usually delegated this responsibility to a committee such as the Commission for Regulating

Plantations, which Charles I convened in 1634. Political turmoil prevented this body from carrying out its responsibilities.

In 1660 Charles II established two advisory bodies, the Council of Trade and the Council for Foreign Plantations, which were combined in 1672 into the Joint Council for Trade and Plantations. Three years later this group was replaced by the Committee of the Privy Council on Trade and Plantations (known commonly as the Lords of Trade). The Lords of Trade were all members of the Privy Council and therefore had the power to enforce their decisions.

In his letter of instruction to the Council for Foreign Plantations, written in 1660, the king specifically charged the council "to take especial care and enquire into the strict execution of the late Act of Parliament entitled An Act for the encouragement and increasing of Shipping and Navigation." This order referred to the Navigation Act of 1660, which revised and reenacted the Navigation Act of 1651. Like all acts passed by the Commonwealth, the earlier Navigation Act had been declared null and void, but mercantile sentiment forced its repassage. One provision of the Navigation Act of 1660 stated that goods from Asia, Africa, or America could be carried to England, Ireland, or any English colony only in an English ship, with an English captain, and with a crew that was three-quarters English. (The 1651 act made no mention of the captain and required that only half the crew be English.) Goods from Europe could be carried to England, Ireland, or the colonies in ships of the nation which produced the goods as well as in English ships.

The Navigation Act of 1660 also listed certain enumerated articles, goods or raw materials produced within the empire which could only be shipped to England or to another English colony. Included on the original list of enumerated articles were sugar, ginger, cotton, indigo, dyewoods, and tobacco. In 1673 Parliament passed the Staple Act, which required that all European goods pass through England before being shipped to the colonies. Only a few foreign imports such as salt, wine, and horses, which were virtual necessities in the colonies, were exempted from this requirement.

In 1673 Parliament passed the Plantation Duty Act, which required that colonial merchants pay a duty on enumerated articles shipped from one colony to another. Before this act was passed, no duty was charged on intercolonial trade, and merchants took advantage of this loophole by declaring that their goods were destined for another colonial port and then shipping them to Holland or France instead. The Plantation Duty Act also provided for customs collectors to be stationed in the colonies. This act, together with the Navigation Act of 1696, which provided for the establishment of (eventually twelve) admiralty courts with jurisdiction over violators of the Navigation Acts, essentially completed the enactments by which England expected to force its colonies to assume the role which mercantilist theory prescribed for them.

There is no doubt, however, that the English economy flourished after passage of the Navigation Acts. By the end of the seventeenth century, the English merchant marine doubled in size and overtook the Dutch. English merchants enjoyed new profits by reexporting colonial products to the other nations of Europe. English manufacturers were busy processing sugar, cotton, tobacco, and other enumerated articles carried to England. Further, the Crown benefited from the customs duties collected on enumerated articles as well as on foreign goods passing through England on their way to the colonies.

THE FOUNDING OF THE CAROLINAS

The first colony founded after the restoration was Carolina (present-day North Carolina, South Carolina, and Georgia), which Charles II granted to eight proprietors in 1663.* At first the proprietors promised settlers a representative government, religious toleration, and land grants with a quitrent of only half a penny an acre. However, in 1669 John Locke prepared a document called the Fundamental Constitutions of Carolina, which attempted to establish an essentially feudal regime for the colony.

Under Locke's plan all the land of the colony was to be divided in such a way that the proprietors and two subsidiary types of nobles—landgraves and caciques—were to control two-fifths of it, with the remaining three fifths to be divided among the common people. Even in this latter area, the document looked forward to the creation of large manors to be worked by virtual serfs. The government was to be equally aristocratic. All executive positions were reserved for the proprietors or lesser nobility, who also dominated a so-called Parliament in which a 500-acre property qualification was required, even of the representatives of the common people. Although the Fundamental Constitutions allowed religious toleration, its other provisions never proved satisfactory to the settlers. It was finally replaced by a more typical form of colonial government, which included a governor, council, and elected assembly.

What is now North Carolina became an area of small farms raising corn, hogs, and tobacco. By the end of the seventeenth century, it had about 3,000 settlers, most of whom had drifted down from Virginia. The lack of good harbors handicapped North Carolina economically, although later it became an important supplier of naval stores. When the proprietors realized that little profit was to be made from this section of their colony, they took no notice of it, and from 1691 on it had its own governor. After 1712 North Carolina was treated as a separate colony.

What became South Carolina received a great deal of attention from the proprietors because it had an excellent harbor at Charles Town (Charleston) and soil and climate suitable for growing subtropical products. By 1700 South Carolina had about 6,000 settlers—many from the West Indies, and others from England,

---

*The eight proprietors were Sir George Colleton; Anthony Ashley-Cooper (later the first earl of Shaftesbury); George Monck (the duke of Albemarle); Edward Hyde (the earl of Clarendon); Sir George Carteret; Sir William Berkeley; Lord John Berkeley; and the earl of Craven.

Scotland, Germany, and France (the Huguenots). Before long it had a prosperous economy based on the production of rice, and later, of indigo.

Perhaps because of its West Indian background, South Carolina had slaves from its inception; even before rice and indigo became staple crops, slaves made up from one-fourth to one-third of its population. In these pioneering years the slaves played a crucial role in the development of the colony. As Peter H. Wood points out in his volume *Black Majority,* slaves often knew more about hunting, fishing, and grazing than their owners—just as later they were more familiar with all phases of rice, indigo, and cotton cultivation. Wood describes this earlier period as one in which blacks lived in "forced intimacy and tenuous equality with Europeans." However, by 1720—when the white settlers became a minority in the colony and staple crops became more important—slavery in South Carolina became more onerous than in any other English mainland colony.

South Carolina expanded westward very rapidly and conducted a brisk trade in deerskins and furs with the Indians. The colony also engaged in another type of trade with the Indians—a slave trade. Perhaps because of their experiences in the West Indies, the idea of Indian slavery was not foreign to the early settlers of South Carolina. Traders used their Indian allies to capture the Indians of the interior and bring them to Charleston. From there most Indian slaves were sold to the West Indies. In 1708 South Carolina itself had about 1,400 Indian slaves. One of the reasons South Carolina sent troops to help North Carolina when that colony was attacked by the Tuscarora Indians in 1711 was the hope of capturing additional slaves.

For years the Yamasee Indians cooperated with the settlers of South Carolina. Nevertheless, in 1715—incited by the Spanish and/or by the encroachment of colonists on their hunting grounds—the Yamasees, the Creeks, and several other tribes attacked the South Carolina frontier. The proprietors failed to give South Carolina the military support it required; and 400 settlers were killed and much property was damaged. When the Yanasees and Creeks were finally defeated (with the help of the Cherokee Indians, and South Carolina slaves), the assembly requested that the English government make South Carolina a royal colony. The proprietors, however, refused to sell their rights to the colony. In 1719, when war threatened to break out between England and Spain, the assembly merely declared itself a royal colony and was accepted as such by the English authorities. Ten years later the proprietors sold their rights to the land of both South and North Carolina, and both settlements officially became royal colonies.

NEW YORK AND THE JERSIES

By the middle of the seventeenth century, the English government was unable to tolerate the presence of the Dutch in New Netherland. The Navigation Acts were impossible to enforce as long as the Dutch held territory on the coast of North America. In addition, in case of war New Netherland was a dangerous wedge separating New England from the English colonies in the South. Therefore, in 1664 the king granted New Netherland (and part of New England) to his brother—the duke of York—with orders to conquer the territory. The duke immediately outfitted a fleet of four ships. The Dutch, who were completely unprepared, were forced to surrender; and New Netherland (except for a brief period in 1673–1674 when it was reconquered by the Dutch) became an English province with the duke of York as proprietor.

The Dutch burghers were allowed a year and a half either to return home or else to remain as English subjects with the right to worship as they pleased. Practically all, including Peter Stuyvesant, the last Dutch governor, elected to remain. The so-called duke's laws—which were promulgated shortly after the English conquest—(first just for Long Island and later for the entire colony) allowed the colonists freedom of religion, the right to jury trial, and a greater voice in local government than they had been permitted under Dutch rule. However, the towns on Long Island which had been settled by New Englanders resented the fact that the duke's laws did not authorize a colonial assembly. Instead, laws were to be made by the governor and his council. The Long Islanders' repeated refusal to pay taxes to which they had not assented, and a desire to make the selection of a Catholic, Thomas Dongan, as governor more palatable to the Long Island towns, impelled the duke of York to call together an assembly of eighteen members in 1683. This assembly composed the Charter of Liberties and Privileges, which provided for the continuation of a popularly elected assembly as well as for freedom of religion. In 1684 the duke approved the charter, but when he became King James II in the following year, he invalidated the charter and transformed New York into a royal colony.

New York flourished under English rule—its population and economy both expanded. English merchants continued the practice of their Dutch colleagues and sold goods to the Indians more cheaply than did the French. This practice, and the Treaty of Albany (1684), in which the Iroquois Indians agreed to become allies of the English (as they had been of the Dutch), ensured the continued, and increasing, prosperity of the fur trade. Agriculture also thrived, and New York became an important exporter of grain and meat to the West Indies. Yet, New York could not be described as a completely contented colony. The Dutch population still feared that the English might attempt to extirpate their customs, and the New Englanders on Long Island were outraged at England's refusal to grant the colony a representative assembly.

The duke of York did not retain all the possessions which he had been granted by his brother. As early as 1664 he ceded what is now New Jersey to Sir George Carteret and Lord John Berkeley. At the time New Jersey contained only a few Dutch, Swedish, and Finnish settlers, and in order to attract additional colonists, the proprietors issued a document called the Concessions and Agreement. This document promised future settlers a representative assembly, religious freedom, and land grants which would not be subject to quitrents until 1670. New Englanders founded several towns in the colony, but their refusal to pay taxes and the claim of the duke of York (only relinquished in 1680) that he still had political control of New Jersey hampered the growth of the colony. In 1674, therefore, Berkeley sold his share of New Jersey, called West Jersey, to two English Quakers. Soon after, Quakers and other English citizens migrated to West Jersey, where they prospered by raising grain and cattle on comparatively large farms.

In East Jersey the refusal of the New Englanders to pay quitrent (which Carteret began charging after 1670) caused him to sell the province to William Penn and twenty-three other Quakers. East Jersey remained an area of small farms, and its capital and port, Perth Amboy, never proved a serious rival to New York City. In 1680 both Jerseys became part of the Dominion of New England, but they were later returned to their respective proprietors. In 1702, however, under pressure from the English government, the proprietors of both Jerseys surrendered their political rights (though not their property rights), and New Jersey became a royal colony.

THE FOUNDING OF PENNSYLVANIA

Long before the Jerseys' problems were settled, the main Quaker migration had shifted to Pennsylvania because of the efforts of William Penn. William was the son of Admiral Penn, who performed well for Cromwell and even better for Charles II, whose restoration he assisted with ships and loans amounting to £16,000. A great career was open to his son, who was—and remained—a personal friend of the king and the duke of York. However, William converted to the religion least palatable to the English authorities: Quakerism. Realizing that neither he nor his fellow Quakers had any future in England, Penn determined to found a colony and conduct a "holy experiment" in America.

The king agreed that England would be better off without the Quakers, and in 1681, in exchange for the cancellation of his debt to the admiral, he granted Penn a charter to Pennsylvania—the largest land grant ever made to one individual. (Later most of what is now Delaware was also added.) As with the other proprietary charters issued during this period, Penn received full rights to the land and almost full political control of his colony. However, as an indication of a trend toward more royal control, Penn's charter required that all laws passed in Pennsylvania be confirmed by the king who also had the right of disallowing them; that the Navigation Acts be enforced—by royal officials if necessary; and that an agent be maintained in London to represent the colony when called upon by the English authorities. In addition, appeals from Pennsylvania courts might be made to the Privy Council, and Parliament was expressly given the right to tax the colony.

Penn, like Roger Williams, realized that the Indians were the true owners of the land and that he would have to purchase the land from them before he could be the rightful owner of Pennsylvania. Therefore, in 1682 he began a series of cordial meetings with the Delaware Indians, who sold him much of their land because they needed English protection from the Iroquois Indians. Over the years white settlers forced the Delawares and other Indian tribes off the lands they still retained. However, it was not until the French and Indian War in the 1750s that they were in a position to obtain revenge.

William Penn had another motive for founding Pennsylvania in addition to providing a refuge for his Quaker brethren. He hoped to increase the family fortune by means of the sale of its land. The experience of earlier colonies had taught him that large numbers of settlers were only attracted to a colony if they could expect to enjoy cheap land, religious toleration, and a voice in the government. Land was no problem—quitrents were nominal, and a settler could buy 5,000 acres for £100 (which included 5 acres in Philadelphia) or 100 acres for £5. Indentured servants received 50 acres free at the expiration of their term of service. Nor did Penn have any qualms about religious liberty. His official policy as enunciated in his *Charter of Liberties* (1701) was that

> No person . . . who shall confess and acknowledge *One* almighty God . . . and profess him . . . shall be in any case molested or prejudiced . . . because of his . . . Persuasion or Practice.

However, in spite of all his good intentions, Penn found that setting up a government suitable for American conditions, satisfactory to the desires of the colonists, and still protective of his own interests was no simple task. His first "Frame of Government" (1682) provided for a council of 72 to initiate legislation and an assembly of 200 elected by the freemen (those who owned land or paid taxes) to approve or disapprove the laws exactly as they were drafted by the council. In addition, Penn retained the veto power for himself or for his governor. These unwieldy bodies were soon cut down to a council of 18 and an assembly of 54 (6 per county), which persistently fought first for the right to amend, and then for the right to initiate, legislation.

Penn was forced to return to England in 1684 to settle boundary disputes with Maryland and New York. (No action was taken at the time. The Maryland boundary was set by the Mason-Dixon Line of 1767, and the New York boundary was set only in 1787). There followed the Glorious Revolution, after which Penn's friendship with the late king was used as an excuse by the English authorities to take control of Pennsylvania away from him. In 1696, however, Penn's charter was confirmed, and his family retained possession of Pennsylvania until the American Revolution. From 1701 it was ruled under "A New Charter of Privileges." This provided for a governor, council, and—very atypically—a unicameral, or one-house, lawmaking body elected, for most of Pennsylvania's colonial history, by white males who owned fifty acres of land or £50 worth of personal property. The charter could be amended by a six-sevenths vote of the assembly and the consent of the proprietor, but the clause on religious liberty was to be guaranteed in perpetuity. The assembly remained under Quaker control until the middle of the eighteenth century, when (as we shall read) the exigencies of fighting a war made their presence a liability rather than an asset. Delaware had its own legislature, but the governor of Pennsylvania usually served as its governor as well.

Penn found only scattered Swedish and Dutch settlers in Pennsylvania, but he soon undertook a highly successful advertising campaign all over Europe. Of course, Quakers from England and Wales—on the whole a prosperous group—were attracted to the colony. In addition, Penn's promotional literature found many interested readers among the persecuted and the impoverished on the continent—particularly in Germany. Within a few years of its founding, the lure of cheap land and religious freedom had increased Pennsylvania's population to 12,000, and Philadelphia was an attractive and thriving capital city.

The location and well-planned development of Philadelphia were crucial factors in the success of the colony. It was carefully laid out, to Penn's specifications, in a checkerboard pattern and was located at the junction of the Delaware and Schuylkill rivers. The volume of Pennsylvania's imports and exports plus its large number of immigrants soon made it one of the most important and prosperous cities in the colonies.

THE FOUNDING OF GEORGIA

Although the founding of Georgia followed the establishment of the other colonies by at least half a century, its early history was so similar to that of many of its predecessors that it may be treated at this point in the narrative. Attempts at forming a colony between Florida and South Carolina had been made as early as 1717, but the true founder of Georgia proved to be James Edward Oglethorpe, a military man, philanthropist, and member of Parliament. General Oglethorpe combined a strategic interest in protecting South Carolina from a Spanish attack from Florida with a humanitarian desire to give a new start in life to those unfortunates condemned to debtors prison. In addition, Oglethorpe hoped that the colony would provide a refuge for persecuted European Protestants and serve as the base for a lucrative fur trade with the Indians. In 1732 the English government granted a charter for Georgia to twenty-one trustees who were to govern it—but not to own land in or profit from it. The king reserved the right to appoint the governor and approve all laws: after twenty-one years Georgia was to become a royal colony.

For the first year all landholding was communal. Thereafter, grants were to be limited to 500 acres. A treaty was signed with the Creek Indians, who agreed to be allies of the English. Much of the credit for this treaty and for Georgia's continuing good relations with the Indians belongs to Mary Musgrove, a half-Indian, half-English girl who became the wife of a Carolina trader. Slavery and the use of liquor were forbidden, and the fur trade was strictly regulated. All these provisions were designed to make Georgia a colony whose settlers would always be available for military duty. Obviously, this type of colony did not attract too many settlers, even though religious freedom was promised to all except Catholics.

Nevertheless, with Parliamentary and private support, the first group of settlers (former debtors who had cleared their accounts) arrived in 1733. They were followed by other immigrants from England, who founded the towns of Savannah and Augusta, and by a group of Germans, who called their settlement Ebenezer.

FIGURE 8A Map on page 285 from A HISTORY OF COLONIAL AMERICA. Third edition by Oliver Perry Chitwood. Copyright 1931, 1948 by Harper & Row, Publishers, Inc. Copyright © 1961 by Oliver Perry Chitwood. Reprinted by permission of the publishers.

Fighting did break out between England and Spain in 1739, but Oglethorpe was unable to conquer Florida. Conversely, the Spanish failed to occupy Georgia. After the war was over, the trustees removed all restrictions on landownership, slavery, and the consumption of alcoholic beverages and granted the settlers an assembly in which they might express their opinions but not pass laws. The settlers were still dissatisfied, and in 1751—two years before they were required to—the trustees turned the colony over to the Crown. Within the next decade the colony's population grew from 3,000 to 9,000 (including 3,000 slaves); rice and indigo became the staple crops, and the colonists were granted a representative assembly. Georgia was now following the pattern of its twelve mainland predecessors.

England had now completed planting a line of colonies along the Atlantic coast that extended from French Canada to Spanish Florida. These colonies were firmly established and were beginning to develop politically and economically. At the same time, England was inaugurating a policy of tighter economic and political control over these same colonies. As will be seen in the next chapter, this conflict of interests was to lead to dissension and open insurrection.

BIBLIOGRAPHY

COLEMAN, KENNETH. *Colonial Georgia: A History.* New York, 1976.

ILLICK, JOSEPH E. *Colonial Pennsylvania: A History.* New York, 1976.

KAMMEN, MICHAEL G. *Colonial New York: A History.* New York, 1975.

LEFLER, HUGH T., and POWELL, WILLIAM S. *Colonial North Carolina: A History.* New York, 1973.

MILLING, CHAPMAN JAMES. *Red Carolinians.* 2nd ed. Columbia, S. C., 1969.

MUNROE, JAMES A. *Colonial Delaware: A History.* Millwood, N.Y., 1978.

POMFRET, JOHN E. *Colonial New Jersey: A History.* New York, 1982.

SIRMANS, M. EUGENE. *Colonial South Carolina: A Political History, 1663-1763.* Chapel Hill, 1966.

SOSIN, JACK M. *English America and the Restoration Monarchy of Charles II: Transatlantic Politics, Commerce, and Kinship.* Lincoln, 1980.

TRELEASE, ALLEN W. *Indian Affairs in Colonial New York.* Ithaca, 1960.

9

Seventeenth-Century Revolts

The Colonies in Transition was the title Wesley Frank Craven felt appropriate for his volume describing the period from 1660 to 1713. Clarence L. Ver Steeg, in his book, *The Formative Years,* has a chapter roughly on the same period which he called "From Colonies to Provinces." The exact time it took place may be open to debate, but it is obvious that beginning in the late seventeenth century, the significant maturation which occurred in the English colonies was accompanied by severe growing pains.

THE EFFECTS OF THE NAVIGATION ACTS

One of the leading causes of colonial discomfort was the Navigation Acts. From the English point of view, the Navigation Acts were an unqualified success; however, colonial reactions to them varied according to place and time. New England's ship-building industry benefited from the monopoly granted English ships. Furthermore, none of its products was on the enumerated list. However, New England merchants resented the fact that some of their cargoes could only be sold in England and that they were not allowed to purchase goods directly from the nations of Europe. They were most vociferous against the Plantations Duty Act of 1673, which required that duties on enumerated articles being carried from one colonial port to another be paid in advance. This made it theoretically impossible to, for example, ship tobacco from Virginia to Boston and then to France without paying any customs duties. However, for over a century New England sea captains continued to evade this as well as other regulations of the Navigation Acts.

In Virginia the Navigation Acts were an unmitigated disaster. Even though the acts prohibited the importation of foreign tobacco into England (and even restrained the growing of tobacco in England), tobacco prices fell sharply during the 1670s. Overproduction was probably the main cause of this drop in tobacco prices, but the Virginia planters chose to blame it on the Navigation Acts, particularly the Plantations Duty Act. Virginians also resented the necessity of shipping their tobacco in English ships. Dutch vessels had charged lower rates and in general provided better service. Finally, Virginians found themselves paying higher prices for the goods which they imported from Europe because of the added freight charges and extra duties levied on the goods as they were transshipped through England. Robert Beverly, a Virginia planter, described the Navigation Acts as a "misfortune that cut with a double edge ... it reduced their staple tobacco to a very low price; and, secondly, it raised the value of European goods to what the merchants pleased to put upon them."

Although the Navigation Acts placed hardships on all Virginians, the large planters suffered least. They were the big businessmen of the period. Large planters had enough indentured servants or slaves to keep production costs down. They had established credit with the English merchants, and their plantations were often located on a river so that their tobacco crops could be easily transported. Very often their poorer neighbors farther inland were forced to sell them their tobacco at a very low price because they had no other way of marketing it.

BACON'S REBELLION

Another facet of Stuart policy—land grants to favorites—also adversely affected Virginia. Even before his restoration to the throne, Charles II granted a large area in Virginia known as the Northern Neck to several noblemen: and in 1673 the king granted Virginia to lords Culpeper and Arlington for thirty-one years. These men were to be the proprietors of Virginia with full power to collect quitrents, establish courts, and appoint local officials. The people of Virginia were alarmed at this threat to their political rights and land titles. They agreed to a special tax to finance the dispatching of three agents to London to fight the proprietary grant. Finally, Lord Culpeper bought out the other proprietors and sold all but the ungranted lands of the Northern Neck back to the Crown.

Resentment toward English policy was an important cause of the most famous colonial uprising, Bacon's Rebellion of 1676. However, local political grievances played an even greater role in the outbreak of the rebellion. Governor William Berkeley had been in Virginia since 1642. In line with Stewart policy, he had begun to build a local colonial oligarchy in Virginia. The election of 1661 produced a cooperative House of Burgesses which Berkeley kept proroguing, or adjourning, from year to year so that new elections could not be held.*

This assembly passed many laws favoring the large landowners in general and the supporters of Berkeley in particular. In 1670 the right to vote was taken away from freemen and restricted only to freeholders, those men who owned landed property. Taxes were increased, and Berkeley's assembly made the poll, or head, tax the basic tax of the colony. Even though the large planters paid for their servants and slaves, the poll tax—much like the modern sales tax—bore much more heavily on the poor than on the rich. The House of Burgesses resolutely refused to pass a land tax. While such a tax would have been more equitable, it would, of course, have been much more burdensome to the large landowner. The members of the governor's council were completely exempted from taxes. Other laws centralized power in the governor and the House of Burgesses, either by taking away power from the local government or by empowering the assembly to name local officials. Plural officeholding became common and served as a means by which the governor could reward his supporters.

Bacon's Rebellion may also be viewed as an east-west struggle. Certain elements in the colony—newcomers, land speculators, and former indentured servants (who often settled on the Virginia frontier)—hoped to see the colony expand westward. Berkeley and many of his associates tended to oppose, or at least to limit, this expansion. Ever since the Indian attack of 1644, Berkeley had attempted to solve the Indian problem by means of the reservation system. Western land was reserved for the Indians who accepted English rule, and a chain of forts was constructed to separate English-held land from Indian land.

The reservation system helped keep the peace for many years. However, in the 1670s, because of a shift in the fur trade, a southerly migration of Indians took place all along the eastern coast. The Senecas moved into Susquehannock lands, and the Susquehannocks moved onto the lands of the Doeg Indians, who lived along the Virginia frontier. The Doeg Indians were generally careful to observe the line of demarcation between white and Indian territory, but the Susquehannocks were either less aware of, or less concerned with, this arrangement. Nor were the white settlers of Virginia's frontier overly scrupulous about trespassing on Indian reservations and allowing their cattle and hogs to graze on the Indians' farm lands. For these reasons Indian attacks increased during 1675 with much loss of life on both sides.

The expansionists had long resented Governor Berkeley's policy of containment. They saw the recent Indian unrest as an opportunity to take over Indian lands, but the governor refused to sanction such a policy. Whether because of considerations of fairness, or because—as his enemies alleged—of his interest in the fur trade, Berkeley refused to commission any officers to wage an offensive war against the Indians. His solution was to reinforce the series of frontier forts. Virginians who lived along the frontier felt that these forts were not worth the taxes that were

---

*A possibility exists that an election was held in 1666, but this is uncertain.

levied to maintain them. They knew that it was simple for hostile Indians to infiltrate this immobile defense line and ravage the frontier.

The most outspoken opponent of the governor's policy was Nathaniel Bacon, a young Englishman of good family who had arrived in Virginia in 1674. According to Robert Beverley in his 1705 history, he was "young, bold, active of an inviting aspect and powerful elocution." As a cousin of Nathaniel Bacon, Sr., one of Berkeley's close associates, young Bacon was made a member of the governor's council. As it happened, Bacon's plantation was on the frontier, and his overseer was killed in one of the Indian attacks. In April 1676 Bacon—against the governor's express order—enrolled 300 volunteers, marched against the Indians (not those who participated in the attacks), and killed by his own account about 150 of them. Berkeley immediately removed Bacon from the council and declared that he and his followers were rebels. The governor also thought it wise to hold a new election for the House of Burgesses. When Bacon won a seat in the assembly, Berkeley returned him to the council and promised him a commission to fight the Indians. The governor felt that this arrangement was preferable to having Bacon serve in the assembly, where he might further inflame the people. Bacon, however, having little faith in Berkeley's promise of a commission, appeared in Jamestown with an army of about one hundred frontiersmen and virtually forced it from the governor at gunpoint.

Not surprisingly, after "General" Bacon collected a force of about 1,300 men, Berkeley again declared that he and his followers were rebels. This was too much for Bacon. Instead of attacking the Indians, he marched on Jamestown and took control of the colony. When Bacon later did march westward, Berkeley recaptured the capital. In September Bacon returned and regained control of Jamestown, but in the confusion it was destroyed by fire. At this time, as the royal commission that was later sent to investigate the rebellion reported, Bacon was extremely popular among the people. A month later, however, Bacon died, and his rebellion collapsed completely. By the end of 1676, even before the arrival of a thousand English troops, Berkeley was once again in control of Virginia and had executed over twenty of Bacon's followers. According to an account of the rebellion written by Thomas Mathew 30 years after the events, King Charles was supposed to complain: "That old fool has hanged more men in that naked country than I did for the murder of my father." Several women, too, were active in Bacon's behalf, and one, Sarah Grendon, was specifically excluded from the general pardon granted by the Virginia legislature in 1677.

No better evidence of the political grievances of the small Virginia planter may be found then the so-called Bacon's laws, passed by the House of Burgesses on June 23-25, 1676, just before it adjourned. Freemen were once again granted the vote, counsellors were no longer to be exempt from taxation, and plural officeholding was outlawed. The term of a sheriff was limited to one year, local taxes were to be levied and collected locally, and vestrymen (officials in charge of parishes) were to be elected rather than selected.

These laws were repealed after the collapse of the rebellion, but absolutism of the Stuart variety was not to prosper in Virginia anymore than in England. Though the governor's council remained the dominant branch of the Virginia legislature until about 1720, it never again attempted to monopolize such a huge amount of power. Virginia eventually developed a form of government in which a strong governor was kept in partial check by a group of well-to-do planters who, in the House of Burgesses and at the local-government level, represented the interests of their class primarily but not exclusively. The tradition of Bacon's Rebellion deserves at least partial credit for the "enlightenment" of the Virginia squirearchy.

Bacon's Rebellion did nothing to solve the economic grievances caused by the Navigation Acts. During the 1680s Virginians attempted to destroy their own crops in order to increase tobacco prices; but gradually, tobacco prices improved and the Virginia planters learned to live with, or avoid, the Navigation Acts. As so often happened in American history, the only complete losers in Bacon's Rebellion were the Indians. Berkeley's reservation system was discontinued. Rather than relying on a line of forts, a mobile scouting force was organized to contain the Indians. However, nothing was developed to contain the white settlers, and by the end of the seventeenth century, the Indians had been virtually driven out of the colony.

Bacon's Rebellion had repercussions, or served as an excuse for attempts to ameliorate local grievances, in both North Carolina and Maryland, but nothing definite was settled in either colony.

THE DOMINION OF NEW ENGLAND

Relations between the English government and Massachusetts had never been friendly. If not for the English civil war, the Massachusetts charter would certainly have been annulled by Charles I. Even the Puritan government of the Commonwealth period had been irked by Massachusetts's independent attitude. In 1660 Massachusetts at first declined to recognize Charles II as king and claimed the right to determine which English laws were to apply to the colony.

This stand induced a royal commission to warn the colony that their charter might be forfeited. More importantly, neither Massachusetts nor the other New England colonies fit into the mercantilist pattern, and they seemed to have no intention of complying with those aspects of the Navigation Acts which impaired their own economic interests. New England obviously could not supply England with any crop which required a warm climate, but it also largely failed to supply England with the timber and naval supplies with which it was so generously endowed. Its fishermen proved to be serious competitors to English fishermen, and its ships competed with English ships. Even New England's agricultural products were very much the same as those grown in the mother country. Further, during the seventeenth century New England, more than any other group of colonies, attempted to foster its own industry so as to minimize the need for English goods.

In 1676, therefore, the Lords of Trade sent Edward Randolph to Massachusetts to investigate the colony in general and its obedience to the Navigation Acts in particular. In his reports to the English authorities, Randolph not only documented his charge of smuggling but also accused Massachusetts of illegally ruling New Hampshire and Maine; of refusing to allow Anglicans to vote or even to worship; and of coining money in direct contradiction to royal instructions. All these charges were true, but the Massachusetts agents sent to England minimized them as "very inconsiderable things and easily answered."

Randolph's report was precisely what the Lords of Trade had wanted and expected. For several years they had been planning to strengthen royal control over the colonies. In their view such centralized authority was necessary if the Navigation Acts were to be enforced. The charters granted to the New England colonies were one of the major obstacles to their plan; so were the proprietary grants made to the king's favorites. The Lords of Trade failed to convince the king that he should annul the proprietary grants, but the recalcitrant attitude of Massachusetts made it easy to persuade him that the Massachusetts charter must be invalidated.

Therefore, legal proceedings began which resulted in the revocation of the Massachusetts charter in 1684. The power of the Puritan oligarchy was broken, and Massachusetts became a royal colony. This was only the first step in a long-range plan carried forward by Charles's successor, James II. The charters of Connecticut and Rhode Island were also vacated. These colonies—plus Maine, New Hampshire, Plymouth, Massachusetts, the Narragansett section of Rhode Island, as well as New York and New Jersey—were all combined into one administrative unit known as the Dominion of New England. Ultimately, James planned to group all of England's continental colonies into two or three such units.

An interim government under the leadership of Joseph Dudley of Massachusetts ruled the Dominion until the arrival of Sir Edmund Andros, the royal governor, in December 1686. Andros was empowered to make laws, assess taxes, and dispense justice. He was to be assisted by an appointed council, but no provision was made for an elected legislature. All future land grants were to be made in the king's name, and landowners were henceforth to pay a quitrent to the king of two shillings six pence per hundred acres. Andros and his council also levied an additional land tax and a tax on imported wine, rum, and brandy; and he saw to it that they, as well as the Navigation Acts, were enforced.

Andros reformed the courts to make them conform to English practice. He also built forts, trained militia units, and generally prepared New England for an expected attack by the French and Indians from Canada. In the area of religion, Andros insisted that Anglican church services be conducted. By 1688 Andros had accomplished much, but it had won him few friends in the Dominion. Landowners resented the quitrent and felt that their land titles were in danger. Merchants objected to the enforcement of the Navigation Acts. The Puritans abhorred the new policy of religious toleration. Further, most citizens were upset by the lack of representative government and by Andros's refusal to allow town meetings to be held more than once a year, and then only to elect town officials.

In April 1689 news arrived in Boston that William of Orange had landed in England and that he and his wife Mary were now ruling the nation. King William III instructed all colonial officials (except those who were Catholic) to remain in their positions, but this letter never arrived in Boston. Even if it had, it is unlikely that Andros could have retained power. Rumors were already circulating that he was a secret Catholic and that he planned to surrender all of New England to the French.

Andros, Randolph, and other members of the governor's council were quickly imprisoned. The Council of Safety was organized, which proclaimed William and Mary as rulers of England and attempted to return to the old charter form of government. However, the Council of Safety was not supported by the majority of the people of Massachusetts because they objected to being ruled by the Puritan oligarchy. Nor was it ever recognized by the English authorities. In 1690 the king ordered Andros to be returned to England. Connecticut and Rhode Island were allowed to return to their charter form of government. New Hampshire became a royal colony, and New Jersey was temporarily returned to its proprietors.

The Puritan leaders of Massachusetts struggled hard for the return of their old charter. After much negotiation, however, they were forced to compromise. The charter of 1691 transformed Massachusetts into a royal colony (including Maine and Plymouth) with a governor appointed by the king. The Massachusetts council, unlike the councils in other royal colonies, was to be selected jointly by the assembly and the council. The vote was no longer restricted to members of the Congregational Church but was granted to all property owners. All Protestants were allowed to worship as they pleased. All past land grants were confirmed, and quitrents were waived. Further, Massachusetts merchants continued (on the whole successfully) to evade the Navigation Acts for the duration of the colonial period.

THE GLORIOUS REVOLUTION
IN NEW YORK

The repercussions of the Glorious Revolution were also felt in New York, the colony which was ruled by Andros's lieutenant-governor, Francis Nicholson. Nicholson received news of the Glorious Revolution in March 1689 but took no steps to proclaim William and Mary as the new rulers. Nicholson's delay afforded an opportunity for disaffected groups within the colony to take matters into their own hands (and New York had many disaffected groups).

The largest such group was the Dutch. They resented the imposition on them of English laws and customs. They also resented English interference in their religious affairs, and the collection of quitrents on their lands. Most of all, they objected to the disruption of their trade with Holland caused by the enforcement of the Navigation Acts. The town government reconstituted under Dutch rule welcomed the Dutch reconquest of 1673 as a return to "their lawful and native sovereigns" and were unhappy at the return of English rule.

A second disaffected group was made up of New Englanders who had settled on Long Island. They, more than any other segment of New York's population, objected to the colony's lack of a representative assembly and to the assessment of quitrents. Also, the merchants of New York, like their counterparts in the other colonies, resented the Navigation Acts.

Moreover, a small group of mercantile and landowning families such as the Bayards, Livingstons, and Schuylers, in partnership with the governor, controlled the political and economic life of the colony. These men were responsible for the passage of laws controlling grain prices, granting Albany a monopoly of the fur trade, granting New York City a monopoly of flour milling, and making it the sole official port of the entire colony. Neither the small farmer nor the city worker benefited from, or appreciated, these regulations.

When Governor Nicholson delayed the proclamation of William and Mary, rumors began to circulate of a Catholic plot to surrender the colony to France. News of Andros's arrest encouraged those who disliked Nicholson's administration to take steps to replace it. The New York City militia companies seized the city's fort on May 31, 1689; soon after, Nicholson hurriedly departed from England. The leader of one of these militia companies—soon to be the leader of the new government in New York—was Jacob Leisler. Leisler was a German who had arrived in New Amsterdam in 1660 and had married a rich widow. While he became a leading merchant, he did not enter the mercantile aristocracy.

Once in power, Leisler ruled New York for almost two years. His first act was to proclaim William and Mary as lawful rulers of England. He then reorganized the court system. Later he convened a popularly elected legislature, which voted to remove the special privileges of the New York City and Albany merchants. Leisler also convened an intercolonial conference at Albany to plan for what turned out to be an ambitious, but unsuccessful, attack on Canada by land and sea. During his administration Leisler had the support of the Dutch inhabitants, the small farmers, the city workers, and even a few of the wealthy landowning families.

However, the leading merchants, whose economic interests had been badly damaged by Leisler, were able to convince the king that Leisler was a rebel. Leisler himself contributed to this impression by refusing to surrender the city's fort to the commander of the royal troops who arrived in New York in January 1691. When Henry Sloughter, the new governor, arrived in March, Leisler surrendered the fort to him, but it was already too late. Leisler and nine of his prominent followers were tried in the words of the grand jury charge of March 31, 1691, for "traitorously levying war against our Sovereign Lord and Lady the King and Queen." Eight were acquitted or later pardoned, but Leisler and his son-in-law, Jacob Milborne, were executed. Four years later, their convictions were reversed by Parliament.

Leisler's rebellion left an important legacy. Never again was New York to be ruled by a restricted mercantile-landed aristocarcy. Henceforth, the English authorities agreed to allow New Yorkers, like the citizens of all other English colonies, to be represented by an elected assembly. Until about 1715 this assembly was the scene of many battles between the supporters and opponents of Leisler and his ideas. On the whole, the Leislerians successfully supported the interests of the farmers and workers against mercantile monopolies. In so doing they developed the tradition of a democratic political party, which notion was never to die out in New York.

THE GLORIOUS REVOLUTION IN MARYLAND

Maryland was the third colony to experience a revolution in 1689. Lord Baltimore had done little to mitigate the political or economic grievances of the Maryland colonists. On the contrary, taxes and proprietary fees had been increased in spite of a deteriorating economic situation. Also, the highest offices in the colony were even more tightly restricted to the Catholic friends and relatives of the proprietor.

Therefore, when the Glorious Revolution took place and Lord Baltimore, who was in England, failed (because of the death of his messenger) to proclaim William and Mary as sovereigns of England, John Coode (and other opponents of the proprietor) saw their opportunity. They formed the Protestant Association and, following the example of dissidents in Massachusetts and New York, accused the proprietary regime in Maryland of plotting with the French and Indians to draw Protestants' blood. Despite the denials of any Papist Plot by the Maryland authorities, Coode raised a force of 700-800 men and bloodlessly took control of the colony. The Protestant Association continued to rule the colony in the name of William and Mary until 1692, when a royal governor arrived from England.

Coode's Rebellion was responsible for basic changes in the government of Maryland. Lord Baltimore's anachronistic powers were revoked. Although he retained his land ownership, he lost all vestiges of political control. Maryland temporarily became a royal province, and the Church of England became its established, or official, church. In 1716 a later Lord Baltimore converted to Anglicanism and Maryland again became a proprietary province. However, no attempt was ever made to return to the original feudal pattern of government. Maryland became a "normal" colony, in which the planters who dominated the assembly vied for power with the governor and his council—which represented English interests—whether proprietary or royal.

COMPARING AND CONTRASTING THE 1689 REVOLUTIONS IN AMERICA

As a whole, the colonial revolts of 1689 indicated that the colonists would not tolerate autocratic rule, whether imposed by England or developed locally by a provincial oligarchy. This is not to say that England would not tighten—at least in theory—the administration of its colonies during the eighteenth century. Nor does it mean that political power in the colonies was not wielded predominantly by large landowners, prominent merchants, or a combination of both. However, the Glorious Revolution led to an informal—but effective—compromise in which a balance between contending interests within each colony and between the colonies and the mother country was maintained until about 1763.

During the intervening years two related myths about the Glorious Revolution and its significance for the colonies developed in America. One was that the revolution won for the colonists the same rights gained by their compatriots who remained at home. However, every British monarch from William III to George III specifically denied this contention whenever it was advanced and considered his power over the colonies to be identical to that of the Stuarts, who ruled before 1688.

The collateral myth, or perhaps misperception, concerned the powers of Parliament after the Glorious Revolution. The colonists tended to ignore the subtle, but very definite, shift in power from king to Parliament, possibly because Parliament did not play an active or sustained role in colonial affairs until the 1760s. When this policy was reversed, colonial repercussions were immediate.

Finally, the Glorious Revolution—like the Puritan Revolution which preceded it—provided a body of political thought that was to serve the colonists well all during the eighteenth century, when they contended for a greater voice in their own government. Further, it was to become crucial in the era after 1763, when relations between colonists and the English government became increasingly strained.

BIBLIOGRAPHY

BARNES, VIOLA F. *The Dominion of New England.* New Haven, 1923.
CARR, LOIS GREEN, and JORDAN, DAVID WILLIAM. *Maryland's Revolution of Government, 1689-1692.* Ithaca, 1974.
CRAVEN, WESLEY FRANK. *The Colonies in Transition: 1660-1713.* New York, 1968.
HALL, MICHAEL G., et. al. *The Glorious Revolution in America.* Chapel Hill, 1964.
HARPER, LAWRENCE A. *The English Navigation Laws: A Seventeenth Century Experiment in Social Engineering.* New York, 1939.
JOHNSON, RICHARD R. *Adjustment to Empire: The New England Colonies in the Era of the Glorious Revolution, 1675-1715.* New Brunswick, 1981.
LEDER, LAWRENCE H. *Robert Livingston, 1654-1728, and the Politics of Colonial New York.* Chapel Hill, 1961.
LOVEJOY, DAVID S. *The Glorious Revolution in America.* New York, 1972.
REICH, JEROME R. *Leisler's Rebellion: A Study of Democracy in New York, 1664-1720.* Chicago, 1953.
SOSIN, JACK M. *English America and the Revolution of 1688: Royal Administration and the Structure of Provincial Government.* Lincoln, Neb., 1982.
WARD, HARRY M. *The United Colonies of New England, 1643-1690.* New York, 1961.
WASBURNE, WILCOMB E. *The Governor and the Rebel: The Story of Bacon's Rebellion and Its Leader.* Chapel Hill, 1957.

10
Colonial Government

In 1701 the Reunification Bill was introduced in Parliament, which would have transformed all of England's American colonies into royal colonies. The reason given for this bill was that other types of colonies had proved to be prejudicial to England's economic and commercial interests. William Penn, who assumed the leadership of the opposition to this bill, retorted that proprietary colonies were of more benefit to the Crown than royal colonies. Parliament, perhaps because it agreed with Penn that the power to govern was also a property right, refused to pass this bill or modified versions of it which were introduced in 1702 and 1706. In spite of Parliament's inaction, the Jerseys and the Carolinas did later become royal colonies. However, Maryland, Pennsylvania, Connecticut, and Rhode Island were able to avoid falling into the accepted pattern—the first two remaining proprietary colonies and the latter two remaining corporate colonies for the rest of the colonial period.

ENGLISH AGENCIES
OF COLONIAL GOVERNMENT

During the reign of the first three Stuart kings, the agencies of imperial rule were under the control of the king. Chief among these agencies was the Lords of Trade, which was made up of members of the Privy Council. The Glorious Revolution did not transfer power over colonial affairs from the king to Parliament nearly to the extent that it transferred power over domestic affairs. Even though there was an increase in Parliamentary legislation affecting the colonies, most of it was passed on the instigation of the Crown. In 1696 a new agency for colonial affairs, the Lords Commissioners of Trade and Plantations—better known as the Board of Trade—was established.

The Board of Trade was made up of sixteen members. Eight of them were members of the Privy Council, including the First Lord of the treasury; the Chancellor of the Exchequer; the First Lord of the Admiralty; the Lord High Admiral; and the Secretary of State for the Southern Department, who was the English official most closely concerned with colonial affairs until the post of Secretary of State for the Colonies was created in 1768. The other eight members were civil servants supposedly selected for their expertise in colonial and commercial affairs. In addition, at times the bishop of London joined the Board of Trade to guide it on religious matters; the Secretary at War advised it on military matters; and either the Attorney-General or Solicitor-General provided it with legal counsel.

The Board of Trade carried out many duties. It had a voice in the appointment of colonial governors and prepared the instructions for governors of royal colonies. It drafted laws affecting the colonies and submitted them to Parliament for passage. It supervised the financial, military, and naval affairs of the colonies. It attempted to enforce the laws regulating colonial trade. It (or the Privy Council directly) heard appeals from the highest colonial courts. Also, it reviewed all laws passed by the legislatures of the royal and proprietary colonies. If the Board of Trade felt that any of these laws were contrary to English common or statutory law, or contrary to the economic interests or privileges of the home country or another colony, it recommended to the Privy Council that they be disallowed, or annulled. Because of the diligence of the governors only 469 out of 8,563 laws reviewed by the Board of Trade—less than 6 percent—had to be disallowed. Nevertheless, even these few acts of royal disallowance were bitterly resented in the colonies affected.

Several other agencies joined with the Board of Trade to direct colonial affairs. Perhaps the most important of these was the Treasury Board. This board supervised all colonial financial affairs and included the commissioners of the customs, who were in charge of enforcing the Navigation Acts. Working closely with this group was the Admiralty, which sent naval ships to assist customs officials and appointed the members of the vice-admiralty courts, which tried violators of the acts. The War Office had jurisdiction over the regular English army in America, which grew larger as England became involved in a conflict with France for control of North America (see Chapter 24).

After 1675 the bishop of London was assigned the duty of supervising the Anglican churches in America. Opposition (by American Anglicans as well as by other Protestants) to the appointment of an Anglican bishop for America forced the bishop of London to rely on deputies, called commissaries, whom he sent to the colonies. Nevertheless, during the first part of the eighteenth century, the Anglican Church, which formerly had been the established, or official, church only in Virginia, grew influential enough to become the established church of the Carolinas, Maryland, and four counties of New York (later, also of Georgia).

On the whole, it may be said that the weight of the imperial governmental apparatus did not press heavily upon the colonies. The American point of view was continually presented to the Board of Trade by colonial agents representing the various colonial assemblies. Some of these colonial agents, such as Benjamin Franklin, were American; some such as Edmund Burke, were English; but all worked very much like present-day lobbyists. They met with officials of the Board of Trade and members of Parliament and tried to encourage legislation favorable to, and discourage legislation unfavorable to, the colony they represented. They were also heavily involved in the defense of colonial laws which were facing disallowance.

Still, American interests were even better protected by the weakness and inefficiency of the Board of Trade itself. Often men were appointed to the board for purely political reasons, being more interested in the salary than in colonial affairs. Even those members of the board who honestly attempted to carry out their duties were handicapped by a lack of knowledge of American conditions that not even the colonial agents could rectify. Sometimes contradictory orders were issued by different colonial agencies. Even clear and precise orders might take months or even years to reach the colonies, while others were captured by pirates or enemy ships.

Nor were these orders efficiently enforced if and when they did reach the colonies. Colonial officials were appointed on the basis of family or political connections—if not through sheer bribery. The colonial records include a letter from a man who offered an English official one thousand guineas if he would convince the Secretary of State for the Southern Department to appoint the writer's father to the governorship of New York. Often the appointee never left England but merely hired a poorly paid substitute to take his place in America. Whether the appointee or a substitute came to America, they both shared the same goal: to make as much money as they could as quickly as possible. This could only be done by accepting "gratuities" from colonial merchants and others who were interested in violating the very laws and regulations that the officials were sent to enforce. It should come as no surprise, therefore, that in the middle of the eighteenth century, the English government was spending more on the customs service than it was collecting in revenue.

GOVERNMENT IN THE AMERICAN COLONIES

The governmental system of their own colony affected the lives of the colonists much more than the imperial government. For example, the first colonial assemblies were modeled on the governing bodies of commercial companies. The House of Burgesses, the first representative assembly (which met in Jamestown in 1619), was modeled on the form of government established for the London Company by its revised charter of 1612. This charter gave the stockholders the right to determine company policy. It was a short, but significant, step from this to allowing the settlers of Virginia to have a voice in their own affairs. The governor of Virginia soon came to be comparable to the treasurer of the London Company (its chief executive officer) and his council came to resemble the company's board of directors.

This pattern of government continued in Virginia even after the London Company lost its charter in 1624 and the colony came under royal control. The basic difference was that the governor and his council were now appointed by the king. At first only when the governor felt it necessary did he convene an assembly. However, the value of frequent consultation with local leaders was soon established, and in 1639 King Charles I specifically granted Virginians the right to an annual assembly.

Political developments in the Massachusetts Bay Colony were another clear-cut example of the transformation of an English commercial company's charter into a pattern for colonial government. Once the Virginia and Massachusetts colonists established the precedent that representative government was one of the rights of Englishmen which not even migration to the New World could abrogate, it became necessary for every colony—whether royal, proprietary, or corporate—to offer its settlers some form of representative government. However, the early assemblies were limited in their rights and powers. One of their main weaknesses emerged from the custom which required them to meet together with the governor and his council as a unicameral legislature. This tended to reduce the assembly to a consultative body.

The so-called sow's case of 1642 had given the Massachusetts Bay Colony a bicameral legislature. Later in the seventeenth century, Virginia, Maryland, and the other colonies followed suit. By the beginning of the following century, all the mainland colonies except Pennsylvania had bicameral legislatures. (In that colony the council was not directly involved in the legislative process.) It should be remembered, however, that no bill could become a law until it was approved by both houses of the legislature as well as by the governor. This initiated a new struggle for power—one based on another English model: the two houses of Parliament and their relationship with the monarch. The colonial American viewed the governor as the representative of royal authority; the governor's council as the counterpart of the House of Lords; and the assembly as equivalent to the House of Commons. The tremendous spurt in the growth of the rights and powers of the House of Commons during the seventeenth and eighteenth centuries was a constant encouragement to the aspirations of the colonial assemblies.

In order to fully comprehend this struggle for power within the colonies, it is necessary to review the basic structure of colonial government as it existed toward the end of the seventeenth century. Every colony was headed by a governor. In a royal colony the governor was appointed by the king; in a proprietary colony, by the proprietor (usually with the approval of the king); and in a corporate colony, the governor was elected, directly or indirectly, by the qualified voters.

Whatever the type of colony, the power of the governor was apparently overwhelming. Except in the corporate colonies, he called the legislature together and dismissed it at his discretion. In addition, he had the power to veto any and all acts passed by the legislature and no formal procedure existed by which this veto could be overruled. (However, influential Englishmen might be persuaded to appeal to the authorities on behalf of a colony.) The governor was commander-in-chief of the military and naval forces of the colony, with full authority to appoint subordinate officers. He sat as a member of the highest court of the colony and had the power to grant pardons or reprieves to convicted criminals. He appointed and had the power to dismiss judges, justices of the peace, and many other types of officials. The governor granted lands, regulated his colony's trade, and conducted its "diplomatic affairs" with other colonies, the Indians, and sometimes even with foreign nations. Lastly, he had supervisory power over religious affairs.

Bernard Bailyn points out, however, that the governors' powers were not as great in practice as they were in theory. The commissions and the detailed instructions which royal governors received from the Board of Trade allowed them little scope for political flexibility in dealing with their legislatures, and the transfer of their appointive powers to English authorities left them without the patronage necessary to influence the legislatures. In addition, the shortness of their terms (the average term of a royal governor was five years) militated against their effectiveness. As Cadwallader Colden, a veteran royal official in New York, lamented to the authorities in England, a governor "without Friends or any Natural Interest" is never in a position to "exert Arbitrary Powers."

The governor was advised by a council consisting of from seven to twelve members. Once again, depending upon the type of colony, councillors were appointed by the king or the proprietor (usually upon the advice of the governor); in the corporate colonies they were elected. The council had executive, legislative, and judicial powers. As an executive body it had to concur in important decisions of the governor such as calling an assembly or appointing a judge. As a legislative body it served as the upper house of the colonial legislature, and its consent was necessary for the passage of any bill. As a judicial body it sat as the supreme court of the colony. Members of the council were generally wealthy and influential men whose economic ties to England would tend to encourage, though not guarantee their support of the governor's policies. As Governor Glen of South Carolina wrote when recommending a man for a seat on the council to the Board of Trade, he "is a Gentleman well acquainted with the Constitution, for supporting the King's Prerogative and Government, and is not of the levelling principles that prevail too much here."

The assembly was the popularly elected branch of the colonial legislature. As might be expected, the assemblies, almost from the start, modeled their procedures on those of the House of Commons. A speaker presided over each assembly. Bills were considered by standing committees. The assembly often met as a committee of the whole house to discuss matters informally. Also, a bill went through three readings before being passed.

However, the members of the colonial assemblies were not satisfied with merely following the procedures of the House of Commons; they also wanted the rights and privileges of the House of Commons—particularly those won as a result of the Glorious Revolution. Most, but not all, of these rights were gained in different colonies and in varying degrees. Members of the assembly soon won the right of freedom of discussion on the floor of the legislature and immunity from arrest while the legislature was in session. Next they won the right to make their own rules, settle contested elections, and—after much struggle—elect their own speaker. Most importantly, the assemblies won the "power of the purse," the exclusive right to initiate all money bills. (In many colonies the council even lost the power to amend money bills.)

This power of the purse was to be the instrument that made it possible for the assembly to challenge, often successfully, the authority of the governor. The British government insisted that each colony had to levy taxes to support its governor. This meant that, except in a few colonies where permanent taxes were levied for the purpose, the governor was dependent on the assembly (often on a year-to-year basis) for his salary. By either decreasing or postponing the governor's salary, or by showing their generosity when the governor cooperated with them, most assemblies eventually won a voice in the appointment of colonial officials, the expenditure of public funds, and the conduct of military and Indian affairs. Though colonial assemblies had not won all the rights of the House of Commons (as we shall see below), by the middle of the eighteenth century, they had far eclipsed the governor's council and were a powerful counterbalance to the authority of the governor himself.

While the colonial assemblies were often referred to by contemporaries as the "democratical" element of colonial government, this does not imply that they were democratic in the modern sense of the term. First, the franchise was restricted. Essentially, only free, white, natural-born or naturalized British Protestant males, generally over the age of twenty-one, who owned land or personal property (the exact value differed from colony to colony) were eligible to vote. This, of course, disqualified propertyless laborers, indentured servants, and slaves. It was the rare free black man who was allowed to vote, and the records contain the names of few women—for example, Margaret Brent of Maryland, Deborah Moody of Long Island, and some wealthy widows—who voted or attempted to vote. Also, by custom, if not by statute, Indians were excluded from the franchise in every colony. Nevertheless, it is now estimated that 50 to 80 percent of the adult white male population was eligible to vote. Generally, the percentage was higher in New England and in those colonies where land was relatively easy and cheap to obtain.

Actually, getting out the vote was a problem. Distance, bad weather, and poor roads discouraged large numbers of voters. Often the choice of a candidate was settled in advance, and the election was a mere formality. Non-English-speaking groups suffered from a lack of communication and/or lacked a tradition of political participation in their homelands. If no issue touched voters' particular concerns, and if the incumbent officeholders had not ignored or betrayed their trust, voters were apt to remain at home on election day. All these factors were compounded by the absence of organized political parties, which help to publicize issues and candidates. Perhaps the low level of participation explains why for example, it was alleged in one South Carolina election that servants, foreigners, and other ineligible people were allowed to vote.

Officeholders had to meet even more stringent property (and other) qualifications than ordinary voters. However, in most colonies members of the assembly tended to own far more land or personal property than was required. A pattern emerged which indicates that more than strict legal qualifications were necessary for a man to be successful in colonial politics. A political career was usually reserved for members of the highest social class—those who were considered to have the greatest stake in the community and, therefore, the greatest concern for its welfare. Voters were accustomed to give their deference and their political support to those men who were entitled to add "Esquire" or "Gentleman" to their names. Outside of New England, and not too often even there, a man of lesser status who merely met the legal qualifications seldom considered running for office. If and when he did, his neighbors tended not to vote for him (which may have been a blessing in disguise because the expenses of running for, and holding office, far exceeded the allotment most colonies paid their legislators).

No matter how aristocratic the officeholder, he did represent the people of the distinct geographical district in which he resided (or at least owned property in)—people to whom he had to return for reelection every one or two years. Deference could carry him only so far. Lavish outlays for food and drink could help only so much. Unless the voters were convinced that their representative was looking after their interests as well as his own, there was always another candidate soliciting their votes. Voting was conducted publicly in about half the colonies, with each voter naming the candidate of his choice, usually in the presence of the candidates and all other voters. Paper ballots were utilized in the other colonies, but they still were not necessarily secret.

The colonial court system was a simplified version of the English judicial system. Justices of the peace had jurisdiction over the least important civil and criminal cases. County courts (composed of justices of the peace) dealt with civil cases involving more substantial amounts of money and with those felony cases not involving loss of life or property. Superior courts evolved during the eighteenth century to hear the most serious felony cases and those civil cases in which extremely large sums of money were involved. Either the governor's council or a specially constituted supreme court served as the highest colonial court of appeals, although appeals in civil cases involving more than £500 might be, but rarely were, appealed to the Privy Council.

Colonial courts generally followed English common law but did not hesitate to modify it. For example, unlike England, many colonies allowed a person accused of a felony to be defended by counsel. Until the 1750s colonial judges were appointed by the governor of their colony for life (dependent on good behavior). In the years following they served only at the king's pleasure. Americans viewed this change (and the insistence of the English authorities that only the governor could

create and abolish courts) as royal attempts to dominate the colonial judicial
system.

A FEDERAL EMPIRE?

In essence, what had developed, albeit haphazardly, was a federal system of government in which power was divided between the organs of the central government—
the Privy Council and Parliament—and the colonial legislatures—the organs of local
government. The Privy Council and Parliament dealt with problems common to the
entire empire: regulation of trade, regulation of coinage and currency, naturalization, postal services, military and naval defense, and the conduct of foreign affairs.
The colonial legislatures concerned themselves with all aspects of colonial life: care
of the poor, marriage and divorce, roads and bridges, and, most importantly, taxation. Essentially, with the exception of taxation, this resembled the division of
powers between the federal government and state governments as later established
by the United States Constitution.

Other analogies may be drawn between the British imperial form of government and the present American system of government. Remember that among those
who sat on the Board of Trade and advised the king on American affairs were a
secretary of state, the First Lord of the Treasury, the First Lord of the Admiralty,
and—at times—the Attorney-General and the Secretary at War. It was no accident,
therefore, that when President Washington formed a cabinet, it consisted of a
secretary of state, a secretary of the treasury, a secretary of war, and an attorney-
general (and the first addition to the cabinet was a secretary of the navy).

Finally, a comparison can be made between the authority of the Privy Council
to disallow colonial laws and to hear appeals from colonial courts and the United
States Supreme Court's power of judicial review and its appellate jurisdiction over
state courts (and lower federal courts).

Even though the British Empire was a "federal empire," this fact was never
recognized by British authorities, who believed that it was a unitary empire with all
power residing in the king and/or Parliament. To British officialdom the colonial
legislatures were far inferior to Parliament, having no more authority—or legal
status—than the ruling body of a craftguild or of an English borough (town). As Sir
William Keith, a governor of Pennsylvania, wrote to the Board of Trade in 1726,
the colonial legislatures were "corporations . . . with the Ability to make temporary
By Laws for themselves agreeable to their Respective Situations & Climates but no
ways interfering with the Legal Prerogative of the Crown or the true Legislative
Power of the Mother State."

This view of the empire helps explain why the British government was so
steadfastly opposed to granting the colonial assemblies the rights that the House of
Commons won as a result of the Glorious Revolution. In England no royal officer
was allowed to sit in the House of Commons; when colonial assemblies passed laws

to exclude the governor's appointees, these laws were disallowed. In England the king virtually lost the power to veto acts of Parliament, but the governor's and the Privy Council's absolute veto power over acts passed by colonial legislatures was rigorously maintained. In England Parliament created new electoral districts and allotted each its proper number of representatives; attempts by colonial legislatures to assert this privilege were all disallowed. In England judges held office during good behavior, and the king could no longer control them by removing them at will; when colonial laws attempted to limit the governor's power to dismiss judges at will, the laws were disallowed. In England a law was passed requiring that Parliamentary elections be held every three (later seven) years; colonial laws to this effect were always disallowed.

The English claim that the colonial legislatures were subordinate to Parliament and that Parliament could, at any time it pleased, legislate on any matter affecting the colonies was completely unacceptable to the American colonists. If, as they insisted, the British Empire was a federal empire, then logically each colonial legislature must have essentially the same powers in and over that colony as Parliament had within England proper. Prior to 1763 Parliament was acknowledged to have the power to deal with imperial affairs, but local colonial affairs were firmly believed to be completely and exclusively within the jurisdiction of the colonial legislatures. Also, while British and American theories about the nature of the empire were diametrically opposed, no concrete challenge had arisen to test the degree of commitment which each party had to its theories. After 1763, however, this situation changed radically and culminated in the American Revolution.

LOCAL GOVERNMENT

It may be anticlimactic—though nevertheless accurate—to add that voter turnout indicates that the average colonist was much more concerned about local government than about wider colonial affairs. The taxes a person paid, the price one was charged at the tavern, the time to be spent drilling with the militia, and disputes over the boundary of a farm were all generally determined at the local level.

In New England the unit of local government was the town. The governing body was the town meeting, which selected a wide variety of town officials, elected the town's delegates to the colonial assembly, set the tax rate, and passed whatever ordinances were necessary to meet local problems. All residents of the town were allowed to speak at the town meeting; however, contrary to popular belief, property and religious qualifications restricted the number of those who were eligible to vote at the town meeting. Still, the New England town meeting was the closest approach to representative democracy found in colonial America.

Outside of New England the county was the usual unit of local government. The county court or individual justices of the peace made administrative and judicial decisions, which were recorded by the county clerk and enforced by the county sheriff. In most of the southern colonies, the parish was a political subdivision of the county as well as a unit of church government. The parish was governed by a group of vestrymen who held their offices virtually for life. If a vestryman resigned or died, some colonies authorized the other members of the vestry to select his replacement; in others the voters of the parish made the choice. The vestrymen supervised relief for the poor and were charged with the duty of referring violators of religious or moral practices to the appropriate authorities. They were assisted in these responsibilities by churchwardens and constables.

TAXATION

The American colonists were blessed with a light tax load. It is presently believed that the burden of the Navigation Acts did not exceed 1 to 2 percent of total annual colonial income. Although the colonies and their local subdivisions levied a wide variety of taxes, they came to no more than 5 percent of per capita income, even in the towns where taxes tended to be highest. Compare this rate with that in England, where national taxes alone comprised 5 to 7.5 percent of per capita income.

Paradoxically, these low taxes may have been an important cause of the American Revolution. Having enjoyed such a light tax burden for so long a period, even the relatively modest taxes which the English government levied (or attempted to levy) beginning in 1764 aroused sufficient resentment to impel the colonists to review and question the legitimacy of parliamentary taxation of the American colonies.

BIBLIOGRAPHY

BARROW, THOMAS C. *The British Customs Service in Colonial America, 1660–1775.* Cambridge, 1967.
BROWN, ROBERT E. *Middle-Class Democracy and the Revolution in Massachusetts, 1691–1780.* Ithaca, 1955.
BROWN, ROBERT E., and BROWN, B. KATHERINE. *Virginia, 1705–1786: Democracy or Aristocracy?* East Lansing, 1964.
DINKIN, ROBERT J. *Voting in Provincial America: A Study of Elections in the Thirteen Colonies, 1689–1776.* Westport, Conn., 1977.
GREENE, JACK P. *The Quest for Power: The Lower Houses of Assembly in the Southern Royal Colonies, 1689–1776.* Chapel Hill, 1963.
KAMMEN, MICHAEL G. *A Rope of Sand: Colonial Agents, British Politics, and the American Revolution.* Ithaca, 1968.
LABAREE, LEONARD W. *Royal Government in America: A Study of the British Colonial System before 1783.* New Haven, 1930.
LEDER, LAWRENCE. *Liberty and Authority: Early American Political Ideology, 1689–1763.* Chicago, 1968.
PORTER, ALBERT O. *County Government in Virginia.* New York, 1947.

SMITH, JOSEPH HENRY. *Appeals to the Privy Council from the American Plantations.* New York, 1950.
SYDNOR, CHARLES. *Gentlemen Freeholders: Political Practices in Washington's Virginia.* Chapel Hill, 1952.
WILLIAMSON, CHILTON. *American Suffrage from Property to Democracy.* Princeton, 1960.
ZUCKERMAN, MICHAEL. *Peaceable Kingdoms: New England Towns in the Eighteenth Century.* New York, 1970.

II

Blacks in the English Colonies

The Negroes . . . , though they be naturally of a barbarous and cruel temper, yet are they kept under by severe discipline upon occasion, and by good laws are prevented from running away, injuring the English, or neglecting their business. Their work . . . is not very laborious; their greatest hardship consisting in that they and their posterity are not at their own liberty or disposal, but are the property of their owners. . . .

So wrote Hugh Jones, an Anglican minister who assumed the post of professor of mathematics at William and Mary College in 1717. Shortly after, he published a volume *Present State of Virginia* (1724), describing life in Virginia. We shall now look at how these "barbarous and cruel" Negroes came to Virginia and how accurate Jones's picture of their life there really was.

THE SLAVE TRADE

English traders had little contact with Africa until the middle of the sixteenth century; even then most of them did not—or, more accurately, were not allowed by Spain or Portugal to—participate in the slave trade. The earliest violator of this rule was John Hawkins, who between 1562 and 1567 made three slave-trading voyages from Africa to the Spanish West Indies (barely escaping with his life from the third). Although the English government made several attempts to organize slave-trading companies, the Dutch controlled the slave trade for most of the seventeenth century. In 1672, however, the Royal African Company was granted a monopoly of the

English slave trade, which it held until 1698. During this period the company took the first of several steps which ultimately were to win for England the dubious distinction of being the largest slave-trading nation in the world. This domination was reinforced after the company's monopoly was broken: In 1713 England was granted the Asiento, or privilege of importing about 4,800 slaves annually into Spanish America for thirty years.

Relatively small numbers of African slaves were imported into Portugal and Spain. It was only the demand for labor in the New World that triggered the modern slave trade that was eventually to bring an estimated 10 million Africans to the Americas. (It is estimated that of this group, only about 350,000 or about 5 percent, came to England's mainland colonies.) Most of these slaves were captured by African rulers who sent their troops into the interior on slave-hunting expeditions.

European nations established forts, or "factories," along the west coast of Africa, where they held the slaves they purchased from the local rulers. Sometimes slaves were purchased for cash, but more often they were exchanged for textiles, tools, guns, beads, or liquor. Often a slave trader had to make several stops along the African coast to secure a full cargo of slaves and the supplies necessary for the voyage to America—the infamous middle passage. With almost no attention paid to sanitation, it was inevitable that smallpox and other diseases would wipe out large numbers of slaves—and crew members as well. Other slaves jumped overboard, starved themselves, strangled themselves with their chains, and, in spite of their lack of seamanship, attempted to take over the vessel and sail to freedom.

Many slaves were brought first to the West Indies for "seasoning." The death rate during this three- to four-year-period often ran as high as 30 percent because of disease, change of climate, lack of proper food, maltreatment, and suicide. After the seasoning period some of the survivors were shipped to the continental colonies, where they were preferred over slaves brought fresh from Africa. Other slaves were brought directly from Africa to the mainland colonies and seasoned there. In either case the purpose of the seasoning period was to produce hard-working, yet docile, slaves.

THE DEVELOPMENT OF SLAVERY

To understand the development of slavery in the mainland colonies, it is necessary to review the institution of indentured servitude which, as we have seen, was the main source of labor for Virginia and Maryland (as well as other colonies) during the entire seventeenth century. From the point of view of the planter, however, indentured servitude had many drawbacks. Indentured servants with, for example, four-year terms barely became proficient in their duties before they had to be freed. Indentured servants could not be worked past a certain point for fear of violating local laws or discouraging the emigration of other indentured servants. Being indistinguishable from the rest of the population, indentured servants had the opportunity—which they often exercised—of running away from their owners, moving elsewhere, and becoming lost in the general population. Once freed, indentured servants typically received a suit of clothes, a barrel of corn, an ax, a hoe, and a parcel of land which made them potential competitors of their former owners. Gradually, the planters of Virginia and Maryland began to realize that black slavery would have few, if any, of these drawbacks.

In contrast to white indentured servants, Africans came to the New World involuntarily. They were forcibly uprooted from their homes and transported to America for the sole purpose of having their labor exploited. The planters were well aware of the existence of slavery in Latin America and were all too eager to take advantage of the Africans' skin color and lack of Christianity to place them in a similarly degraded status in the English colonies. Economically, the price of a slave was not much higher than that of an indentured servant, and the cost of maintaining a slave was far less. Most slave owners possessed fewer than five slaves, but it is estimated that three to four slaves could double their owners' income.

The first Africans arrived at Jamestown in 1619. Others must have followed them, since in 1649, 300 blacks were listed among Virginia's population of about 15,000. The status of these blacks varied. Anthony Johnson, one of the original twenty, was free and owned servants of his own. Some blacks served short terms as indentured servants and received land at the expiration of their terms of service; gradually, however, blacks began serving longer terms than whites and were discriminated against in other ways as well.

Even if free, blacks were not allowed to bear arms. Female black indentured servants were put to work in the fields but not female white indentured servants. Also, opposition to sexual relations or marriage between the races became institutionalized. This contrasts sharply with Latin America, where—perhaps because of the small number of female settlers and the influence of the Catholic Church—intermarriage was always practiced. In 1630 a white man was whipped in the words of the court for "defiling his body in lying with a negro," but we are not sure whether this was because of a breach of racial etiquette or a case of homosexuality. In 1662 Virginia passed a law levying a stiff fine for interracial sexual relations, and in 1664 Maryland banned "shameful Matches," or interracial marriages. Yet, marriage between blacks and whites still took place occasionally until finally banned by Virginia in 1691.

The greatest distinction made between the races was in the length and conditions of their servitude. In 1640 a Virginia court added several years to the terms of two runaway white servants but sentenced a black man who ran away with them to servitude for the rest of his life. The higher prices paid for black indentured servants indicates that life servitude became common for them during the 1640s and 1650s and often for their progeny, as well.

A Virginia law of 1661 demonstrates that by that time, most blacks were servants for life, if not full slaves. It declared that white indentured servants who ran away with blacks were to have not only their own missed time added to the term of their indenture but also the blacks' time, because as the statute states, blacks "are incapable of making satisfaction by addition of time." In 1662 another Virginia law declared that a child born of a black woman was to be a slave even if the father was white. In 1664 Maryland attempted to make all the blacks residing in that colony slaves by proclaiming that all blacks already in, or later imported into, Maryland were to serve for life. (Later, however, this law was modified so that it was possible to be both black and free in Maryland.) Further, Locke's Fundamental Constitutions of Carolina (1662) contained a clause stating that every freeman had absolute power and authority over his Negro slaves.

One of the major obstacles to the development of full-fledged slavery was the commonly held belief that only heathens might be enslaved and that Christianity freed one from bondage. As already noted, that may have been one of the reasons why the first blacks to arrive in Jamestown were not sold as slaves. Instances where slaves were freed because they were Christians indicate that this theory was actually put into practice. In 1667, however, the legislature of Virginia decreed that "the conferring of baptisme doth not alter the condition of the person as to his bondage or freedome." Maryland followed with a similar law in 1671, and other colonies gradually came to the same conclusion. Ministers who hoped to win converts and owners who hoped that Christian slaves might prove more tractable welcomed this change of attitude.

As the religious rationale for slavery declined, the racial rationale was emphasized. The alleged "savagery" or "barbarism" of the black race was cited to justify the enslavement of anyone of that color. This helps explain why in the mainland colonies, unlike the West Indies or Latin America, mulattoes were considered to be the same as full-blooded blacks. Winthrop Jordan in *White Over Black* sums up this transformation by pointing out that *Christian* was the term by which the colonists distinguished themselves from blacks during the first half of the seventeenth century. As time went on this term was replaced first by *English*, then by *free*, and, finally, by *white*.

THE BLACK POPULATION

By the eighteenth century, once slavery was legally recognized and the Royal African Company and other English and American slave traders gained experience, the importation of Africans into the English colonies increased greatly. The figures (though admittedly inexact) are illuminating. In 1671 Virginia had a population of about 40,000 which included 6,000 white indentured servants and only 2,000 slaves. By 1708 the number of slaves in Virginia reached 12,000; by 1715, 23,000; and by 1756, 120,000 as compared to 173,000 whites. At the middle of the century, Maryland had 40,000 slaves, compared to 100,000 whites. In the Carolinas slavery was encouraged from the start by promises of land grants for every slave imported into the colony. By 1708 the black and white populations of South Carolina were about equal at 4,000, but by the middle of the century slaves outnumbered whites by more than two to one (70,000 to 30,000). At that latter date North Carolina, where small farms still predominated, only had 19,000 slaves, as compared to 60,000 whites.

Slavery, as you may recall, was first banned in Georgia. Even after the ban was lifted in 1750, restrictions on the importation of slaves were supposedly maintained. However, by the 1760s, Georgia's population included 8,000 slaves, as compared to 10,000 whites. The importation of slaves swelled after 1763 so that by the end of the colonial period, the slave population of the mainland colonies totaled about 500,000. This increase in the importation of slaves took place in spite of the fact that slave prices rose from approximately £25 for a male field hand in 1700 to £75 three-quarters of a century later.

BLACK OPPOSITION TO SLAVERY

As the number of slaves multiplied during the eighteenth century, the degree to which they accepted their servitude became an important—literally a vital—matter. The purpose of the seasoning process was to produce hard-working, yet docile, slaves. Although slaves were worked hard, they tended not to be hard workers; contrary to the Sambo stereotype, significant numbers of slaves were far from docile. Nor does Stanley Elkin's theory (formulated in *Slavery: An American Institution*) that the plantation system infantilized the slaves and made them completely dependent on their masters (much as the concentration camp system operated on its inmates) hold up under close scrutiny. True, some slaves did act obsequiously, but often this was merely an example of "puttin' on massa," or of slaves playing the role which they believed their owners expected from them.

The best evidence of the slaves' lack of docility is the innumerable accounts of their malingering, running away (particularly at busy seasons), injuring themselves, infanticide and suicide, assaulting or poisoning overseers or owners, breaking tools, pilfering, burning barns, and—most terrifying of all—slave revolts. The choice of these protest tactics depended somewhat on the slaves' status. Plantations had three types of slaves: skilled workers, house servants, and field hands. Carpenters, bricklayers, blacksmiths, tailors, and coopers were all needed on a plantation. The slaves who performed these tasks were more valuable and tended to be better treated than the unskilled laborers. Sometimes they were rented out to other whites; sometimes they were allowed off the plantation to purchase needed supplies. In either case they had an opportunity, which they often seized, of running away and,

FIGURE 11A   (New York Public Library.)

RUNAWAY.—$200 REWARD will be given if taken in the state, and $500 if taken out of the state.
Run away, my negro boy JOE, sometimes called JOE WINSTON; about 23 years old, a little over 5 feet high, rather stout-built, dark ginger-bread color, small moustache, stammers badly when confused or spoken to; took along two or three suits of clothes, one a blue dress coat with brass buttons, black pants, and patent leather shoes, white hat, silver watch with gold chain; was last seen in this city on Tuesday last, had a pass to Hanover county, and supposed to be making his way towards York River, for the purpose of getting on board some coasting vessel.

SAMUEL ELLIS.

if successful, practicing their much-needed trades as free men in some other area—often with the aid of free blacks or even of whites.

House servants such as cooks, maids, nurses, butlers, and coachmen were also better fed, clothed, and housed than the agricultural workers. House servants who were well treated were much more likely to identify with their owners than were other groups of slaves. However, house servants were constantly under the direct supervision, and more exposed to the cruelty, of whites than were other groups of slaves. In addition, they often felt isolated from their fellow slaves. Their discontent was often manifested through malingering, stealing, stammering, and drunkenness.

The largest group of slaves was the field hands who did the clearing, planting, cultivating, and harvesting of the tobacco, rice, indigo, or whatever else was grown on the plantation. Field hands might work from sunrise to sunset (and even longer during the harvest season) with only a short time off for lunch. The staple slave diet was corn meal, salt pork, and fish (supplemented by an occasional rabbit or opossum) and vegetables, if the owner allowed the slaves some time to tend their gardens. Clothes were made of the cheapest and coarsest cloth, and shoes were worn only in the winter. During the colonial period slave quarters were usually cabins with dirt floors and no windows. Air and light—and rain and cold—came in through the chinks between the logs. As might be expected, the field hands were the most discontented group of slaves.

The slave revolt was the most alarming method of demonstrating this discontent. Slave revolts are virtually as old as slavery itself. In 1663 a group of Virginia slaves and white indentured servants planned an uprising, but the plot was uncovered and quashed. Virginia experienced many slave insurrections—one of the most serious occurring in 1730, when slaves in the vicinity of Williamsburg heard a rumor that the king had issued an order freeing all slaves who were baptized. Ten years later a large group of Maryland slaves attempted to capture Annapolis, but the plotters failed.

However, the revolts that involved the largest number of slaves took place in South Carolina, where the percentage of slaves in the population was higher than in any other colony. South Carolina slaves may also have been more discontented than other slaves because in the early years of South Carolina's settlement—before the development of rice as a staple crop—they had enjoyed more freedom than the slaves of the Chesapeake area. In 1720 an uprising in South Carolina resulted in the death of two whites and the execution of three slaves. In 1730 another plot was discovered in Charleston, and its leaders were put to death. Several revolts took place in South Carolina in 1739 when war broke out between England and Spain. A group of Charleston slaves attempted to reach Florida (where the Spanish had promised them refuge) but failed. Later the same year about 100 slaves under a leader named Cato made the same attempt. They were turned back after fighting several battles with the militia. Forty-four blacks and 21 whites were killed. The following year about 200 slaves in Charleston planned a revolt, but it was crushed in its incipient stage, and 50 slaves were executed. No major outbreak took place again in South Carolina until 1765, when over 100 slaves attempted to fight their way to freedom on the frontier.

WHITE REACTION
TO SLAVE DISCONTENT

Although no slave insurrection of the colonial period ever reached the proportions of Nat Turner's Rebellion or other nineteenth-century revolts, southerners of the eighteenth century lived in continuous fear of slave wars. Here again a brief comparison with Latin American slavery is in order. It is not surprising that Latin American revolts were on a larger scale than North American revolts—Latin America had a much larger slave population. Numbers also help explain why fewer North American slaves ran away to the Indians (although additional factors come into play here). By the eighteenth century contacts between Indians and slaves were limited in New England, the middle colonies, and the Chesapeake area. However, in South Carolina, in spite of a policy of turning the Indians against slaves, and vice versa, by using slaves to fight Indians and Indians to put down slave revolts, significant numbers of slaves sought refuge with the Tuscaroras, Yamasees, Creeks, and Cherokees. Some were returned to their owners; some were enslaved by the Indians; but most were peacefully absorbed into the Indian tribes.

Fear of slave uprisings caused many colonies to pass laws discouraging the increase in the number of slaves. Usually these laws placed heavy duties on slaves imported into the colony. During the eighteenth century every southern colony, at one time or another, enacted such laws. South Carolina, for example, fearing that troublesome slaves might be "dumped" within its border, imposed a tax of £50 on slaves imported from other mainland colonies (and lower taxes on slaves imported from Africa or the West Indies). Pennsylvania, New Jersey, and North Carolina, all of which had large Quaker populations, had similar laws, but for more humanitarian reasons. It is worthy of note, however, that in almost every case these laws were disallowed by the Privy Council on the grounds that they adversely affected the economic interests of English slave traders.

Another reaction to slave revolts—as well as to the other manifestations of black resistance to slavery—may be seen in the increasingly harsh slave codes promulgated during the eighteenth century. The beginnings of slave codes might be traced back to a statute passed by the Bermuda legislature in 1623 which attempted to curb so-called "insolencies of the Negroes." Certainly, by the last quarter of the seventeenth century, when slaves far outnumbered whites, elaborate and brutal slave codes had been developed in the West Indies. Slaves were not allowed to leave the plantation without a pass or to possess weapons, engage in trade, meet together, strike a white person even in self-defense, drink alcoholic beverages, or learn to read or write. Penalties for the violation of any of these provisions included whipping, branding, cropping the ears or slitting the nose, breaking bones or cutting the hamstring muscle, and castration. White men formed special slave patrols to enforce these regulations. It was not considered murder to kill a slave who was undergoing punishment or resisting a slave patrol.

During most of the seventeenth century, the mainland colonies did without any formal slave codes, utilizing the body of law governing indentured servants whenever necessary. Virginia was the first colony to draft a slave code (1682). However, as might be expected from its West Indian antecedents and the high percentage of slaves in its population, by 1712 South Carolina had developed the harshest code of any of the mainland colonies (though gradually, other colonies copied many of its features). The premise of the South Carolina Slave Code of 1712 was simple, its preamble taking for granted that slaves were:

> ... of barbarous, wild savage natures, and such as renders them wholly unqualified to be governed by the laws, customs, and practices of this Province; but that it is absolutely necessary, that other such constitutions, laws and orders, should in this Province be made and enacted ... as may restrain the disorders, rapines and inhumanity to which they are naturally prone and inclined. . . .

FAMILY AND RELIGIOUS LIFE

The slave codes reduced slaves to the level of chattels, or inanimate property. This was a lower status than that of Latin American slaves who, under the protection of the Catholic Church and Roman law, were considered human beings with immortal souls and human rights. Yet, in North America, even if they were not legally recognized as such, blacks remained living human beings with a rich cultural heritage. It is true that the devastating effects of being wrenched from their homeland and forced to work under brutal conditions disrupted African cultural patterns. This process was intensified by plantation owners who refused to allow their slaves to use drums or perform African dances lest they promote group solidarity and resistance to slavery. However, even with the work schedule of the plantation, slaves had the opportunity—at least on Sundays—to meet together and have (particularly in South Carolina and Georgia) the many newly arrived slaves from Africa refresh their memories and their ties with their homeland. Children who were too young to work in the fields were usually taken care of by elderly women who might pass on bits and pieces of African lore and customs to them.

Christianization of slaves proceeded slowly, even after it had been established that baptism did not free them. As Morgan Godwyn, a minister interested in slave conversion, complained in a 1681 tract, owners still feared that baptism might make their slaves expect more "merciful usage." Unconverted slaves still held to their African religious beliefs and taboos, and witch doctors practiced their arts all during the colonial period. Even after the Great Awakening of the 1740s, when large numbers of slaves were converted to revivalistic Protestantism, they shaped their religious experience to fit their own needs. Rather than allow religion to shift their focus from "this world to a world after death where the weary would find rest" (as the sociologist Franklin Frazier expressed it in *The Negro Family in the United States*) the slaves used religion to keep alive their own self-respect and hopes for freedom. Nowhere is this better illustrated than in black spirituals, which, using African rythms, reminded the slaves how an earlier group of slaves, the Hebrews, had escaped from bondage in Egypt.

The other institution around which slave life revolved was the family. True, unlike Latin American slave codes, the codes in the English colonies did not recognize the validity of slave marriages: A husband could be separated from wife and children at their owner's discretion. The best that might be expected was that a mother and her extremely young children would be kept together. Another deterrent to stable family life was the surplus of male over female slaves, which lasted until the 1750s. Most destructive to normal family relations was the realization by the black husband that he could neither provide for his family nor protect his wife and children from physical, or even sexual, assault by white males. Marriages had to be approved by the owner. The ceremony often consisted of having the couple jump over a broomstick together. Even after marriage, promiscuity among slaves was tolerated, if not encouraged, by slave owners. Nevertheless, close monogamous relationships were formed between slaves. Unlike wives in most white families, the slave wife was equal to her husband because she worked beside him in the fields as well as in the cabin. Therefore, the husband was no longer the absolute ruler of the family as he had been in Africa. Still, he assumed the responsibility for disciplining the children. As the colonial period came to a close, more planters were beginning to encourage slave marriages, realizing that slaves were less likely to run away or cause trouble if they were part of a family unit.

SLAVERY IN THE NORTHERN COLONIES

Although the form of slavery that developed in the southern colonies became almost standard, it is still of value to survey the development of slavery in the northern colonies. Slavery in New England (outside of the large farms in Rhode Island) was largely an urban institution. Slaves worked in lumberyards and shipyards, on the docks and aboard ship, and as servants for wealthy merchants. Often it was to their owner's advantage to teach them to read and write. Cotton Mather in a work called *The Negro Christianized* claimed that slaves had souls "as white and pure as those of other Nations," and many were admitted to membership in the Congregational Church. Although all New England colonies drafted slave codes in the eighteenth century, they were much more moderate than southern slave codes and recognized slave marriages and the integrity of slave families.

Slavery was opposed by the Quakers and, therefore, never played a crucial role in the economies of Pennsylvania, Delaware, and New Jersey. However, by the end of the colonial period, New York had the highest percentage of slaves (14 percent) of any colony outside the south. Many slaves had been imported into the colony by the Dutch East India Company before 1664, and the English settlers continued the practice. Some New York slaves worked on the huge estates along the Hudson River, but most worked in New York City, where slaves made up about 20 percent of the population. Most of these urban slaves were household servants, teamsters, porters, gardeners, and semiskilled laborers in shipyards. It is ironic, but not surprising, that the relative freedom they enjoyed helped lead to the most serious slave revolts which ever took place in the colonies.

In April 1712 a group of about twenty slaves in New York City deliberately set fire to a house and then lay in wait for any whites who might come to put it out. Nine white men were killed and nine others wounded before the militia put down this revolt. Eight slaves were killed in the fighting, six committed suicide, and eighteen more were executed—three were burnt, thirteen hanged, one broke on the wheel, and one hanged alive in chains. In spite of the harshness of these punishments and the slave code which was drawn up after these events, in 1741 New York City was again plagued by a series of fires and thefts, and the fear of a slave conspiracy was revived. Two slaves were executed, though they denied any knowledge of a conspiracy. Afterwards a white tavern owner, his wife, and a female indentured servant (who had made the accusations of a slave conspiracy in the first place) were executed in spite of their denials of complicity in the plot. Even this did not allay the general panic, and during the next few months over 150 slaves and twenty-five whites were arrested. Under threat of, or actual, torture, sixty-seven confessions were elicited. Finally, eighteen slaves and four whites (including two women) were hanged; thirteen slaves were burned at the stake; and seventy others were transported to the West Indies in what the black historian, John Hope Franklin, called in his volume *From Slavery to Freedom* "the greatest orgy of Negro persecution that appeared anywhere during the colonial period."

White opposition to slavery was relatively rare for most of the colonial period. The first recorded protest was that presented by Francis (or Franz) Daniel Pastorius to a Quaker meeting in 1688. The signers of this so-called Germantown Protest stated that they felt it unchristian "to bring men hither, or to rob and sell them against their will" merely because they were black. No action was taken on this petition, but the seed had been planted. Much later, in 1755, the Quakers decided to expel any of their members who imported slaves, and three years later they recommended that all Quakers who owned slaves should free them.

George Fox, the founder of the Society of Friends, opposed slavery, but the man most responsible for developing antislavery sentiment among the Quakers (and others) was John Woolman. Woolman preached in *Some Considerations on the Keeping of Negroes* (1754) that "liberty was the natural right of all men equally" and that slavery fostered "misery on both [races]" because it not only oppressed blacks but gave whites a false sense of pride and power. Another Quaker, Anthony Benezet, influenced by Woolman, opened a school for black children to prove that the alleged mental inferiority of blacks was founded only on white ignorance and prejudice.

One of the few non-Quaker opponents of slavery was Judge Samuel Sewall, a stern Boston Puritan. In 1700 Sewall wrote a tract entitled "The Selling of Joseph," which denied that the curse on the descendants of Ham (Genesis IX, 25-27) or the doctrine of captives in a just war justified black slavery. Sewall, however, was no believer in racial equality and warned his readers that slavery could only adversely affect the prosperity and security of New England—"as many Negro Men as there are among us, so many empty places are there in our Train Bands (militia) and the places taken up by men that might make husbands for our Daughters." Interestingly enough, the only rebuttal to Sewall's pamphlet, and—according to Winthrop Jordan—the "only forthright defense of slavery in the continental colonies until the time of the Revolution" came from the pen of John Saffin, a fellow townsman of Sewall's. Saffin defended slavery on the dual bases of the Africans' paganism as well as their alleged innate inferiority.

FREE BLACKS

Some blacks were free in all colonies, although their lives were not easy. The very fact that they were free was felt to be a bad example for slaves. Free blacks were frequently accused of dealing in goods stolen by slaves, helping them to escape, and even of fomenting slave revolts. Some colonies ordered newly freed slaves to leave the colony; other colonies passed laws which made it difficult for owners to free their slaves. This contrasts with Latin American slavery in which manumission was encouraged.

Free blacks suffered from a wide variety of legal disabilities. In the southern colonies they were not allowed to testify against whites, to move about freely, to own real estate, to marry whites, and (except in North Carolina) to vote. In many colonies they were barred from service on juries or in the militia and were kept out of certain occupations. Most free blacks owned small farms, although even during the colonial period, many moved to towns. There they worked as domestics, barbers, skilled and unskilled laborers, sailors, and in numerous other occupations. Overall, the number of free blacks continued to grow by means of manumission, purchase of a slave's freedom by the slave or by a free black, running away, and natural increase. It is estimated that free blacks made up about 7 percent of the total black population by the end of the colonial period.

BIBLIOGRAPHY

BREEN, T. H., and INNES, STEPHEN. *"Myne Owne Ground": Race and Freedom on Virginia's Eastern Shore, 1640-1676.* New York, 1980.
CURTIN, PHILIP. *The Atlantic Slave Trade: A Census.* Madison, 1969.
GALENSON, DAVID. *White Servitude in Colonial America.* New York, 1981.
GREENE, LORENZO J. *The Negro in Colonial New England, 1620-1776.* New York, 1942.

HIGGINBOTHAM, A. LEON, JR. *In the Matter of Color: Race and the American Legal Process, the Colonial Period.* New York, 1978.

JORDAN, WINTHROP. *White Over Black: American Attitudes toward the Negro, 1550-1812.* Chapel Hill, 1968.

KLEIN, HERBERT S. *The Middle Passage: Comparative Studies in the Atlantic Slave Trade.* Princeton, 1978.

LITTLEFIELD, DANIEL C. *Rice and Slaves: Ethnicity and the Slave Trade in Colonial South Carolina.* Baton Rouge, 1981.

McMANUS, EDGAR J. *Black Bondage in the North.* Syracuse, 1973.

MORGAN, EDMUND S. *American Slavery American Freedom: The Ordeal of Colonial Virginia.* New York, 1975.

MULLEN, GERALD W. *Flight and Rebellion: Slave Resistance in Eighteenth-Century Virginia.* London, England, 1972.

SCHERER, LESTER B. *Slavery and the Church in Early America, 1619-1819.* Grand Rapids, 1975.

SMITH, ABBOT E. *Colonists in Bondage: White Servitude and Convict Labor in America, 1607-1776.* Chapel Hill, 1947.

TATE, THAD W. *The Negro in Eighteenth Century Williamsburg.* Charlottesville, 1965.

WOOD, PAUL H. *Black Majority: Negroes in Colonial South Carolina from 1670 through the Stono Rebellion.* New York, 1974.

12
Immigration

We have referred again and again to the English colonies; but how "English" were they by population? In spite of the fact that after the middle of the seventeenth century, the English government discouraged the emigration of its own citizens (with the exception of convicts and political prisoners), for most of the remainder of the century, the majority of America's settlers continued to come from England. Even in 1790, when our first census was taken, it was estimated that 60 percent of the population was of English origin. Nevertheless, the fact that 40 percent of the population was non-English in origin was a sharp departure from the policy of other European empires in the New World and proved to have a significant impact on the development of the English colonies.

PUSH AND PULL FACTORS

Immigrants, no matter where they come from, are influenced by what are called push and pull factors. Push factors are those reasons why people wish to leave their homeland: war, depression, overpopulation, and political or religious persecution. Pull factors, the reasons why settlers want to come to a certain country, are, in a sense, the converse of push factors. They include the possibility of making a good living, of enjoying religious and political freedom, and of obtaining free, or at least cheap, land. All these advantages might be publicized by letters from satisfied immigrants or by grossly exaggerated pamphlets published by landed or shipping interests who would gain from increased immigration.

The immigrants were influenced by a wide variety of push and pull factors. However, they all shared one experience—the harrowing and hazardous voyage across the Atlantic Ocean. The trip from a German port could take from six weeks to six months. Supplies of food and water often ran out, and storms caused accidents and even shipwrecks in which all aboard lost their lives. Cooking was done on deck. As for the food, here is a description by Jaspar Dankers and Peter Sluyter who sailed to New York in 1679:

> I do not know how long it was we had nothing to eat except heads of salt fish, and those spoiled for the most part. Most of the time we had white peas, which our cook was too lazy to clean, or were boiled in stinking water, and . . . we had to throw them away. The meat was old and tainted, . . . and the bread was mouldy or wormy.

Immigrants were not packed together as tightly as slaves, but they were still crammed below decks into a space no more than six feet high with two tiers of wooden shelves along the sides for sleeping. Under these conditions it is not surprising that scurvy, smallpox, and dysentery were common among the passengers. If anyone boarded the ship with a contagious disease, an epidemic often developed. On one voyage to New York in 1710, 773 out of about 3,000 German immigrants died of fever. Toward the end of the colonial period, some colonies, particularly Pennsylvania—which received the largest number of immigrants—passed laws requiring immigrant ships to provide decent food, adequate space, and proper sanitation. However, these laws were poorly enforced, and conditions on immigrant ships continued to be deplorable.

THE HUGUENOTS

Outside of the Dutch in New York and a few Finns and Swedes in Delaware, the first non-English group to arrive in the colonies in any significant numbers were the Huguenots, or French Protestants. The Huguenots were literally pushed out of France by the thousands when, in 1685, Louis XIV revoked the Edict of Nantes, which had granted them religious toleration. About 15,000 of these well-educated and relatively prosperous people reached the English colonies in America. They tended to settle in the towns—Boston, New York, Philadelphia, and Charleston— where they became prosperous merchants or skilled artisans. The Huguenots were relatively few in number, but their descendants—such as Paul Revere, John Jay, and Henry Laurens—played important roles in the American Revolution.

THE GERMANS

The next group to arrive in the colonies was made up of Germans and German-speaking Swiss. No one suffered from as many push factors as the Germans. Politically, Germany was divided into a myriad of petty principalities whose rulers were mainly interested in the taxes they could exact from their subjects or, particularly in the Swiss cantons, in the possibility of hiring their subjects out as mercenaries. It was also expected that all the inhabitants of each state would practice the religion of their ruler (*cuis regio, eius religio*). Those who refused to conform were subject to vicious persecution. The worst sufferers were the members of the numerous Pietistic sects—the Mennonites, Amish, and Dunkers—who were harassed by both Catholic and Lutheran rulers.

As with most immigrants, Germans came to America primarily for economic reasons. The Thirty Years' War (1618-1648) devastated the German economy. Farms were often ruined beyond repair, and trade and industry came to a standstill. Further, a succession of later wars and invasions prevented any substantial recovery. No wonder then that when merchants, land companies, and shippers began to encourage Germans to come to America, they met with an enthusiastic response. Particularly successful were the well-dressed travel agents called "newlanders" who masqueraded as Germans who had become wealthy in America and wanted their fellow countrymen to come share in their prosperity.

A few Germans had come to Jamestown as early as 1607, and others had helped the Puritans construct the town of Boston, but the real beginning of German settlement in the English colonies was made by Francis (Franz) Daniel Pastorius in 1683. Pastorius settled a group of Pietists at Germantown about six miles from Philadelphia. Others soon joined them in Quakerthal, as Pennsylvania became known in Germany. Additional settlement was delayed by the outbreak of the War of the League of Augsburg in 1687 and the War of the Spanish Succession in 1701.

Early in that latter war, however, the Palatine (on the Rhine River) was ravaged by the French armies and about 15,000 German refugees were admitted into England. The English economy was unable to absorb a group this size, so the Palatines were encouraged to sail for America. A small group of Palatines founded Newburgh, New York, in 1708. Another group arrived in New York two years later to found a settlement which would produce naval stores. This project soon failed because of governmental callousness and mismanagement, and the settlers eventually moved either to the Mohawk Valley in upper New York or to Pennsylvania. Another group of about 700, led by Baron Christopher de Graffenreid, founded a settlement at New Bern, North Carolina, but it was soon crushed by Indian attacks.

Other German settlements were started in New Jersey and Maryland, but Pennsylvania continued to be the most attractive colony to German immigrants because of its religious toleration and cheap land policy. Mennonites and Moravians, who—like Quakers—refused to take oaths or bear arms, felt particularly comfortable in Pennsylvania. The Moravians were very successful in converting the Indians to their beliefs. However, the majority of Germans who settled in Pennsylvania were members of either the Lutheran or the German Reformed churches who arrived during the eighteenth century. They were happy just to be able to farm the fertile soil of the colony. By the end of the colonial period, more than 100,000 Germans lived in Pennsylvania, and they made up about one-third of the population.

However, by this time many Germans had already left Pennsylvania. As early as the 1720s, they had begun to take the Great Philadelphia Wagon Road south to the Shenandoah Valley of Virginia. From there they gradually migrated to the back country of the Carolinas. At about the time Georgia was founded, all Protestants were expelled from Salzburg in Germany. General Oglethorpe was happy to welcome a group of them to Georgia, where they founded the town of Ebenezer about twenty-five miles from Savannah. Later they moved to New Ebenezer where, with the help of some German Swiss, they developed a thriving silk industry. However, when war broke out between England and Spain in 1739, most of them left Georgia for Pennsylvania.

Wherever they settled, Germans proved to be good farmers—the best of the colonial period. Many of them also were skilled artisans. They tended to settle as church groups and retain their language and customs. This worked to limit the political influence to which their numbers entitled them and retarded their absorption into American life. Toward the end of the colonial period, however, the Germans—particularly in Pennsylvania—played a more active role in politics and continued to do so during the period of the Revolution. During this latter period their prosperous farms and pretty daughters were irresistible pull factors which induced thousands of Hessian mercenaries to desert the British army and remain in America.

THE SCOTCH-IRISH AND SCOTS

The next, and largest, group (about one-quarter of a million or about 14 percent of non-English immigrants in the population in 1790) to arrive in America was the Scotch-Irish.* The Scotch-Irish were lowland Scots or their descendants, Presbyterian in religion, who settled in Ulster (Northern Ireland) during the seventeenth century. After the restoration of Charles II, they prospered through the sale of their woolen goods all over Europe. In 1699, however, under English pressure the Irish Parliament passed the Woolen Act, which limited the sale of Irish woolen cloth and wool to England and Wales—and even there they had to pay enormous duties.

Another push factor to Scotch-Irish emigration was the passage of the Test Act in 1704, which took the right to vote and to hold any but the most insignificant political offices away from all non-Anglicans. Presbyterian ministers were also forbidden to conduct services, solemnize weddings and funerals, and teach school. Beginning in 1714 drought and frost wrecked the crops. Finally (and most importantly), in 1717 the thirty-one year lease on many of their farms expired, and their absentee landlords would only renew them at double or triple the previous rents.

By this date the general prosperity of the American colonies served as a pull factor to the Scotch-Irish. They were familiar with the success of the settlers of New England and with the liberal religious and land policies of Pennsylvania. In 1717 alone, therefore, because of religious persecution and deepening poverty,

*Often misleadingly called Irish during the colonial period.

about 5,000 Scotch-Irish migrated to America. At first they settled in the New England frontiers in Maine, New Hampshire, and western Massachusetts. However, although both were Calvinist in theology, the Congregational churches did not welcome the establishment of Presbyterian churches in their midst.

Some Scotch-Irish settled in New York and New Jersey, but most turned their attention to Pennsylvania. Additional waves of Scotch-Irish immigration took place in 1725-1729, 1740-1741, 1754-1755, and 1771-1775. Depressions served as the main push factor, but pull factors such as the many agents who traversed Ulster in search of indentured servants and the success of earlier settlers reinforced the decision to migrate. Letters referring to the cheapness and fertility of the land and claiming that Pennsylvania was the "best country for working folk & tradesmen of any in the world" proved to be potent advertisements.

Because they lacked the ability and/or the inclination to purchase lands, the Scotch-Irish squatted on vacant frontier lands and steadfastly refused to pay any quitrents to the Penn family. Like the Germans, the Scotch-Irish also took to traveling the Great Philadelphia Wagon Road through the Shenandoah Valley into the back country of all the southern colonies as far south as Georgia. As frontier settlers they tended to have the most contact, and conflict, with the Indians. They acted on, if they did not actually coin the expression, "The only good Indian is a dead Indian." James Logan, one of the leading proprietary officials of Pennsylvania, who tried hard to maintain peace on the frontier, complained that

> the Indians themselves are alarmed at the swarm of strangers, and we are afraid of a breach between them—for the (Scotch) Irish are very rough to them.

Two other groups of Scots also came to America. One was made up of lowland Scots who arrived in small numbers all during the seventeenth and eighteenth centuries. The other, and larger, group, was made up of highland Scots, most of whom were exiled to America because of the two abortive attempts (1715 and 1745) to restore the Stuart dynasty to the throne of England. So congenial did they find the colonies, particularly North Carolina—which granted them a ten-year tax exemption—that 25,000 additional highland Scots emigrated to America after 1763 when Scotland was hard hit by depression. The highlanders were clannish in the literal sense of the word and remained faithful to their Catholic religion, their Gaelic tongue, and—during the Revolution—to King George III.

THE IRISH AND THE JEWS

Irish Catholics came to America only in small numbers during the colonial period. This hesitancy was because of the religious and political disabilities they faced in virtually all the colonies. A majority of those who did emigrate from Ireland came to America as indentured servants and settled either in Pennsylvania or Maryland.

Another religious minority which settled in America was the Jews. The first twenty-three Jewish settlers arrived in New Amsterdam in 1654 as refugees from a

Dutch colony in Brazil which had just been recaptured by the Portuguese. At first almost all the Jews who settled in the English colonies were Sephardim (descendants of Spanish or Portuguese Jews), but by the time of the Revolution, at least half of the approximately 1,500 Jews in the colonies were Ashkenazim of northern European origin. Jews were found primarily in Newport, New York, Philadelphia, Charleston, and Savannah—the leading commercial towns of those colonies which allowed them to worship as they pleased. They made their living as merchants and artisans and, largely because of their small numbers, were able to enjoy more political rights than their coreligionists in any other part of the world at the time.

THE NATURALIZATION PROCESS

In eighteenth century Europe naturalization of foreigners was difficult if not impossible. The English government, however, did on occasion grant citizenship to a foreigner or group of foreigners, but this citizenship was often temporary or limited. The colonies, however, enacted naturalization laws of their own. Most of these laws attempted to encourage immigration. Massachusetts made it possible to become a citizen after a residence of only one year; South Carolina granted a tax exemption to any foreigner who settled in the colony; and Virginia and Maryland gave settlers a five-year grace period during which they could not be sued for debts incurred prior to their settlement. The problem with these laws, however, was that a person naturalized in one colony was not recognized as a citizen in any other colony. Finally, in 1740 Parliament—in one of the few noncommercial laws it passed affecting the colonies—provided that foreigners might become British citizens after a residence of seven years in any colony if they took the oath of allegiance and worshiped in a Protestant church. Quakers and Jews were exempted from the latter requirement. Such foreigners would then enjoy full citizenship rights in the colonies but not in England (although their descendants could).

IMMIGRANTS ON THE FRONTIER

As noted, most immigrants settled on the Pennsylvania frontier and the back country of the southern colonies. We have seen how religious intolerance barred even the Calvinist Scotch-Irish from New England. Other factors which kept that area almost 95 percent English were the lack of good farm land in the already-settled towns and the threat of Indian attack on the frontiers. New York's mishandling of the Palatines was widely publicized in Germany, and that colony was avoided by Germans for the rest of the century. In addition, the semifeudal tenant system in force on many of the large estates along the Hudson River, and the Iroquois threat in the northern part of the colony, discouraged other possible immigrants from settling in New York.

The eastern parts of the southern colonies were also unattractive to most eighteenth-century immigrants. Ports of entry were few; land was no longer available in the tidewater area along the coast; and the planters there were turning increasingly to slave labor. Crèvecoeur, a young Frenchman who settled in New York in the 1750s, was essentially correct when he described the inhabitants of the east in his *Letters from an American Farmer* as "being the unmixed descendants of Englishmen."

In contrast, immigrants found land on the frontier to be available at little or no cost. It was in this area—between the fall line of the rivers and the Appalachian Mountains—that they settled and created settlements which had much more in common with one another than they had with the eastern parts of their respective colonies. Much more than nationality and distance set off the back-country people from the inhabitants of the east. Their way of life was different—life in the west tended to recapitulate that of Jamestown or Plymouth when they were first settled.

William Byrd was exaggerating when he claimed in his *History of the Dividing Line* (1728) that the North Carolina frontiersman, "just like the Indians, impose all the work upon the poor women." Nevertheless, it is true that the pioneer women worked and—if necessary—fought, beside their husbands as well as doing the ordinary tasks reserved for women in colonial America: cooking, washing, cleaning, spinning, weaving, and making necessities such as soap and candles.

The lack of sharp division of labor between the sexes on the frontier greatly elevated the status of the pioneer woman. In no other section did she enjoy the prestige and freedom that she had earned by undergoing the hardships of frontier life. Women and the church were the two civilizing forces on the frontier. If a book was to be found in these log cabins, it was almost certain to be a Bible. Also, a few circuit-riding preachers held services and performed (often overdue) weddings and baptisms.

It should be understood that the frontier, even in the eighteenth century, was constantly moving and developing. The small farms which at first barely sufficed to feed the frontier family were enlarged and diversified until a cash crop and/or enough cattle were raised to justify taking them north to Philadelphia or east to Charleston for sale. Many settlers were able to improve their log cabins, and a few were eventually successful enough to replace them with the same type of homes which were found back east. These were the homes of the frontier aristocracy.

However, even on the older frontiers, most of the farmers raised just enough crops to meet their needs and buy a few additional tools, utensils, or livestock. On the western edge of the frontier, the cycle was beginning again. In this area lived not only hard-working pioneer families but those who, in Byrd's words, had "a thorough aversion to labor," as well as large numbers of outlaws who preyed unmercifully upon their neighbors.

EAST-WEST FRICTION

While colonial governors and legislatures approved the establishment of counties in the older sections of the back country, they were always careful to limit the number of these counties so that control of the assembly remained in the hands of the east.

Many of these western counties were so large in area (one in Virginia was ninety miles in length) that a trip to attend a session of the county court (when a farmer was involved in a legal matter or wanted to complain about taxes) was difficult, if not impossible. The large size of the counties also made protection from the depredations of cattle thieves and outlaws a nearly hopeless task.

In addition, the colonial governors, who had the power to appoint county sheriffs and justices of the peace, tended to name easterners, or sons of prominent easterners who had settled in the west, to government positions. Numerous grievances grew out of this political domination of the west by the east. Not only did most colonial assemblies not reduce the taxes to which westerners were opposed, they refused to levy the taxes which westerners felt were needed for their economic well-being, if not for their actual safety. For example, assemblies failed to vote the taxes to build roads and bridges so badly needed by frontier farmers to transport their crops to market. Nor would they vote the money to provide the necessary men and supplies to defend the frontier against Indian attacks.

Several taxes were particularly disliked by westerners. One of these was the poll tax, which they tried unsuccessfully to have replaced by a land tax; they felt the latter would rightfully transfer the tax burden to the large landowners of the east. The Scotch-Irish, Scots, and Germans who predominated in the west were not Anglicans and, therefore, strongly opposed the collection of the tax which was levied in all the southern colonies to support the Anglican Church. Westerners also attempted, and again failed, to persuade the assemblies to reduce the often-excessive charges collected by sheriffs and other local officials.

Nor were western grievances limited to purely political issues. Frontier settlers refused to pay what they considered unfair land prices or quitrents to proprietors or land speculators. As debtors, they wanted to pay their debts in cheap paper money, but most colonial assemblies—partly because of English opposition—refused to adopt a soft-money policy.

For years westerners tried, usually without success, to secure redress of their political and economic grievances. Finally, their sheer growth in numbers and the severe hardships they underwent during the French and Indian War (1754-1763) impelled them to use force. Violence broke out first in Pennsylvania, where Quakers held twenty-eight out of the thirty-six seats in the assembly and were determined to maintain their power by refusing to create new counties on the frontier. In addition, partly because of Quaker pacifism and partly because the assembly was trying to limit the prerogative of the proprietor, very little money was voted for critically needed frontier defense. To show their displeasure, a group of frontiersmen called the Paxton Boys (because they lived in the vicinity of the town of Paxton) first massacred about twenty innocent Christian Indians and then returned to kill fourteen more. Although cries of protest arose, no frontier jury was willing to find them guilty.

In June 1764, 600 frontier settlers marched on Philadelphia demanding protection from the Indians, the removal of all Indians from the settled parts of Pennsylvania, better roads, and a redistribution of seats in the assembly. Benjamin

Franklin persuaded them to return home by promising that the assembly would seriously consider their grievances. Although the Quakers retired from the assembly, the basic grievances of the westerners were not redressed before the Revolution. However, the conclusion of the French and Indian War brought relative quiet to the frontier, and no further violent action took place in Pennsylvania.

Violence did erupt, however, in the Carolinas. South Carolina frontier settlers had more complaints against the east than those of any other colony. Not only were they underrepresented in the legislature, but they had no local courts. They were forced to make the long trek to Charleston to handle their legal affairs. Not only did they suffer from unfair taxation and lack of decent roads, but they had received no protection against the organized bands of outlaws which had been plundering their farms all during the 1760s. Finally, in 1767 western leaders formed an association to "regulate" conditions on the South Carolina frontier. Regulators used vigilante methods to bring peace to the area. They also persuaded the South Carolina legislature to pass the Circuit Court Act in 1769, which established six back-country judicial districts. Although the Regulation movement failed to secure equitable representation for the west in the South Carolina lesiglature, it was satisfied enough with its other gains to disband in 1770.

In North Carolina, however, the Regulation movement was more violent. Although they were not as badly off as their fellow westerners in South Carolina, North Carolina frontier inhabitants also suffered from unfair representation, unjust taxation, the uncertainty of land titles, the exactions of nonresident county officials, and lack of protection against Indians and outlaws. "Regulation Advertisement Number 1," protesting these grievances, was drafted in August 1766. However, the legislature took no notice of it or of similar protests which followed. In 1768, therefore, a Regulation movement was formally organized, and westerners agreed to withhold their taxes until such impositions were more equitably levied and expended.

Although Governor William Tryon (whose £15,000 "palace"—a residence built at public expense—had helped exasperate the Regulators) tried to limit fees for local officials, he dissolved the legislature before it could consider other western grievances. Riots then broke out in several western counties, in which some local officials were roughed up and the windows of their homes broken. When a few Regulator leaders were arrested for inciting these riots, their followers raided the jails and freed them. These actions convinced the governor that the Regulators were rebels who must be subdued by force. In 1771 he raised about 1,500 militiamen from the eastern counties and marched against the Regulators. The militia met about 2,000 Regulators at Great Alamance Creek in May 1771 and defeated them in a two-hour battle in which nine men were killed on each side. Six other Regulators were hanged, but the remainder were all pardoned. Nevertheless, many of them preferred to leave North Carolina for what was later to become Tennessee.

It is interesting to note the attitude of the former Regulators during the American Revolution (which broke out relatively soon after their movement had been quashed). At first historians thought that hatred of easterners was still so strong among the Regulators that they must have supported the English. However, recent research indicates that with few exceptions, former Regulators either supported the American cause or, like so many of those who lived on the very edge of the frontier, virtually ignored the entire affair.

No Regulation movement developed in Virginia or Maryland, although the people living on their frontiers also voiced the common frontier complaints. In both these colonies, however, it was in the interests of eastern land speculators to keep western grievances to a minimum. Even in Pennsylvania and the Carolinas, violence was brief and sporadic. Westerners were interested in reforming, not overthrowing, their colonial governments. In spite of east-west tensions, religious and nationality differences, and intercolonial rivalries, Crèvecoeur was correct in his perception that from a mixture of the varied people who had settled in the English colonies, a new "race now called Americans" had developed.

BIBLIOGRAPHY

BROWN, MAXWELL. *South Carolina Regulators*. Cambridge, 1963.

De JONG, GERALD F. *The Dutch in America*. Boston, 1975.

DICKSON, R. J. *Ulster Emigration to Colonial America, 1718-1775*. London, England, 1966.

DOUGLAS, DONALD. *The Huguenot: The Story of the Huguenot Emigrations Particularly to New England*. New York, 1954.

FAUST, ALBERT B. *The German Element in the United States*. 2 vols. New York, 1909.

GOODMAN, ABRAM VOSSEN. *American Overture: Jewish Rights in Colonial Times*. Philadelphia, 1947.

GRAHAM, IAN C. C. *Colonists from Scotland: Emigration to North America, 1707-1783*. Ithaca, 1956.

JACOBS, W. R. *Dispossessing the American Indian: Indians and Whites on the Colonial Frontier*. New York, 1972.

KETTNER, JAMES H. *The Development of American Citizenship, 1608-1870*. Chapel Hill, 1978.

KLEES, FREDERICK. *The Pennsylvania Dutch*. New York, 1950.

LEHMANN, WILLIAM C. *Scottish and Scotch-Irish Contributions to Early American Life and Culture*. Port Washington, N.Y., 1978.

LEYBURN, JAMES G. *The Scotch-Irish: A Social History*. Chapel Hill, 1962.

MARCUS, JACOB RADER. *The Colonial American Jew, 1492-1776*. 3 vols. Detroit, 1970.

POWELL, WILLIAM S. *The Regulators in North Carolina: A Documentary History, 1759-1776*. Raleigh, 1971.

ROBINSON, W. STITT. *The Southern Colonial Frontier, 1607-1763*. Albuquerque, 1979.

13
Colonial Agriculture

Benjamin Franklin wrote in his *Positions to be Examined, Concerning National Wealth:*

> There seems to be three ways for a nation to acquire wealth. The first is by *war....* The second is by *commerce....* The third by *agriculture,* the only *honest way,* wherein man receives a real increase of the seed thrown into the ground, in a kind of continual miracle, wrought by the hand of God in his favor, as a reward for his innocent life and his virtuous industry.

If Franklin was correct, then America should have been one of the wealthiest nations of the world; at no time during the colonial period did less than 90 percent of the population gain its livelihood from farming. However, it was not easy to make a success of farming under the unfamiliar conditions which faced most colonists in the New World.

THE BEGINNINGS

Most of the first settlers of Jamestown were townspeople, not farmers, and they were unable to raise enough food to keep themselves alive. It was the food they obtained by trade or force from the Indians that saved the lives of some of them. Even the later settlers, who had been farmers in England, soon learned that European crops and methods of agriculture were not necessarily successful in the New World. Fortunately, the Indians taught the settlers how to grow corn, which became the staple crop in all the early colonies. Corn provided man with food and drink and also served as fodder for the livestock. New "American" words (most of them borrowings from Indian languages) such as hominy, mush, succotash, and pone illustrate the many ways in which corn was consumed.

Other Indian food crops which the colonists borrowed were potatoes (both sweet and white), beans, pumpkins, and squash. The Indians also taught the colonists how to dry fruits and vegetables and how to preserve them in honey or maple syrup. Still, a great deal of experimentation had to be done before the colonial farmer could determine which crop was best suited for a particular area. New Englanders attempted unsuccessfully to grow cotton, rice, and indigo. In spite of encouragement from the English government, southern farmers failed in their experiments with wine and silk culture and the growing of olives, figs, and spices.

Fortunately, as time went on, European crops such as wheat, rye, oats, and barley were grown successfully in America. Also, cattle, sheep, hogs, horses, and other livestock previously unknown on this continent proved able to adapt to the climate in all thirteen colonies. Not only crops but also farming methods were transported to America, where local conditions often modified or completely changed them. In America farm land was—at first—exceedingly scarce. The eastern seacoast was thickly forested, and the soil had not been plowed. Only here and there had the Indians cleared the ground to plant their crops. Thus, at first crops such as wheat, which required deep plowing, could not be successfully grown on American soil. This lack was overcome by the growth of corn. Corn was planted Indian fashion by digging holes about four feet apart with a pointed stick or simple hoe. If the corn was carefully tended and kept free of weeds, the crop was usually good. Corn also had the advantage of being easy to harvest because it did not require threshing or winnowing.

At first settlers merely appropriated Indian clearings to plant their crops. Later, when more land was required, they copied the Indian method of clearing land by "girdling," or cutting a ring around each tree, removing the bark, and—by cutting off the flow of sap—allowing the tree to die. Crops were planted between these trees until they either fell or were chopped down. The trunks and branches were then burned and their ashes used as fertilizer. Only later were oxen or horses available to pull out tree stumps. At this point, when clearings became larger, it finally became possible to plow the land more thoroughly and to grow wheat.

The story of early American agriculture continued to be one of trial and error. However, after the early years of settlement, American agriculture became extensive in nature. This was largely because of the easy, and virtually free, supply of good land and the scarcity of capital and labor. Rather than utilize more scientific rotation of crops and better methods of fertilization, American farmers merely cultivated new fields. Peter Kalm, an eighteenth-century Swedish botanist described the process, in his *Travels into North America* (1771).

[American farmers] sow uncultivated grounds, as long as they will provide a crop without manuring, but . . . turn them into pastures as soon as they can bear no more, and . . . take in hand new spots of ground . . .

It might well be said that American farmers practiced field rotation rather than crop rotation. The only significant amount of intensive agriculture in colonial America was found among German farmers, who used manure and lime as fertilizers and practiced crop rotation.

FARM IMPLEMENTS

Farm implements were few and simple. No settler of Plymouth owned a plow until the early 1630s. It is estimated that even in the 1760s, only one American farmer out of five owned a plow. The plow that was in use during the seventeenth and eighteenth centuries was made of wood and was tipped with an iron plowshare. This plow was not efficient; a farmer was lucky to plow one acre a day with it. After plowing, farmers used a harrow with wooden teeth to crush the clods of earth. Other tools, such as hoes, spades, scythes, flails, rakes, and pitchforks, were also usually made of wood. A two-wheeled cart, usually pulled by oxen (as was the plow), took care of the transportation of the farmers, their families, and their crops.

Sowing was done by hand, with crops scattered widely in broadcast fashion. Scythes, or sickles, were used to cut the grain at a rate of, perhaps, three-fourths of an acre a day. Only the introduction of the cradle scythe in about 1750 increased the amount a person could harvest. The grain was tied into bundles which were dried out and then taken to the threshing floor. There they were beaten with flails made of a two-foot striker attached by a leather thong to a four-foot handle. Using this tool, a person was able to thresh six bushels a day. Later, however, horses or cattle were driven onto the threshing floor to thresh the grain. To separate the grain from the chaff, farmers dropped the grain from the top of a barn on a windy day. These inefficient tools and methods helped make farming a tedious occupation. So too did crop diseases and all types of predators, including bears, foxes, rabbits, crows, and wild pigeons. Nevertheless, one worker was usually able to produce eighty to a hundred bushels of corn a year, which was sufficient to feed an entire family.

AGRICULTURE IN THE
NEW ENGLAND COLONIES

It is instructive to investigate the effects of soil and climate on the agriculture of each section of the new country. New England had the least promising conditions for agriculture. Here the coastal plain was only fifty to eighty miles wide, the soil (with the exception of the Connecticut River valley) was thin and rocky, summers were short, and winters were long and severe. Only hardy crops—corn, oats, rye, barley, cabbages, peas, turnips, onions, beans, squash, pumpkins, apples, pears, berries, and, after the middle of the eighteenth century, the white potato—could be grown under these conditions. New England farming was largely subsistence farming. Most of the work was done by farmers and their families, and the region imported more food than it exported.

Farms in seventeenth-century New England most closely resembled those of the mother country. The legislature granted each town an area six miles square. The town, in turn, allotted its freemen a small (three- to five-acre) "home lot" near the village, where they could grow fruits and vegetables. The towns also included woodland where the farmers could obtain firewood for their homes, stones for their fences, and meadows to pasture their livestock. Each freeman also received a portion of land outside the village. The size of this allotment depended on the freeman's economic and social status as well as family size. Because various tracts of land were put into cultivation at different times, every freeman eventually owned a number of scattered parcels of land. Because each parcel was so small, farmers would usually agree to plant the same crop on each tract of land. Farmers were responsible for working their own parcel of the tract, although cooperation during planting and harvesting seasons was a necessity.

This land system was obviously inefficient. Farmers lost a great deal of time going from one parcel of their land to another. The smallness of the parcels made it difficult to rotate crops or to fertilize them properly. By the eighteenth century, therefore, a noticeable trend toward consolidation and absentee ownership was seen in all New England towns. These trends were furthered by arranged marriages, exchanges, and sales. Still, most New England farms ranged between 50 and 150 acres.

Scientific stockbreeding was also impossible when all cattle shared the same fields. Cattle did very poorly until the last years of the seventeenth century because hay, and other feed, was not grown in America. Only when various types of clovers were imported from England did American cattle begin to improve. Even in the eighteenth century, however, Peter Kalm reported that "their cattle are harassed by labour, and each generation decreases in goodness and size by being kept short of food." Sheep also found the New England climate difficult and, all during the colonial period, produced less wool there than they did in England.

On the other hand, hogs flourished in New England as they did in all sections of colonial America. After being fattened all summer and fall, the hogs were slaughtered in the winter. Very little of the animal was wasted. The lean meat was ground into sausage. Intestines were eaten as "chitterlings." The fat was converted into lard and the remainder of the meat was either cured or salted. Salt pork remained edible almost indefinitely, and large amounts were exported to the West Indies.

Horses were also an important New England export to the West Indies. The best horses were the "Narragansett Pacers" from Rhode Island. This Narragansett section of Rhode Island differed greatly from the rest of New England in that it had estates—similar to southern plantations, even including slaves—on which horses and cattle were bred, using the most scientific techniques known at the period.

AGRICULTURE IN THE MIDDLE COLONIES

The soil and climate of the middle colonies as well as a broad coastal plain (over a hundred miles wide) were much more favorable to agriculture than the conditions in New England. The crops grown in the middle colonies were similar to those grown in New England, although wheat, rather than corn, became the principal crop. A typical farmer could grow five to twelve bushels an acre, and so much wheat and flour was exported from Philadelphia and New York (mostly to the West Indies but also to the southern colonies and southern Europe) that the middle colonies became known as the Bread or Breadbasket Colonies.

In these colonies the cattle and hogs were fed on corn and then exported to the West Indies. Sheep (valued more for their wool than for their meat) also did well in the middle colonies, but fewer horses were bred than in New England. The agriculture of the middle colonies may best be described as mixed. Much of the crop grown here was consumed by farmers and their families. However, a significant surplus—perhaps as much as 40 percent after 1750—remained, which was exported to the areas already mentioned and brought in return many articles which were not produced domestically.

Because the middle colonies began as proprietary colonies, the earliest grants of land within their boundaries tended to be large and subject to a quitrent. However, the necessity of attracting immigrants soon led to the sale of smaller parcels of land at reasonable prices and with reduced quitrents. Only in the Hudson River valley of New York did large semifeudal estates—such as Rensselaerswyck with its 700,000 acres, and other large grants—survive. In the rest of the section, the typical farm consisted of about 200 acres and was held by its owner in fee simple. Probably less than half was under cultivation; the rest served as pasture or remained forested. Quitrents were low, two to four shillings per hundred acres, and usually payable in produce; yet the Penn family collected barely one-third of the rents due it. Middle colony farms usually required some supplemental labor. On most farms this need was supplied by indentured servants and a smaller number of hired hands.

AGRICULTURE IN THE SOUTHERN COLONIES

The southern colonies were ideally suited for agriculture. The coastal plain was approximately 200 miles wide, the soil was generally rich, and the climate was mild. The most important crop of the upper south (Maryland, Virginia, and North Carolina) was tobacco. Even at the beginning of the seventeenth century, England was importing about £200,000 worth of tobacco—mainly from the Spanish empire. Between 1612 and 1616 John Rolfe learned from the Indians how to cure tobacco, and the success of the crop on the English market was assured. The English government banned the growing of tobacco at home and forbid the importation of foreign tobacco. Twenty thousand pounds of tobacco were sent to England from America in 1618; 500,000, in 1629; 28 million, by 1688; and 105 million, in the years just before the Revolution.

As you will recall, land in Virginia was originally owned by the Virginia company, and in Maryland, by the Calvert family. Private ownership soon developed, but quitrents continued to be collected in both colonies. The headright system, under which those who imported indentured servants were granted additional lands, led to a rapid increase in the size of estates, though they tended to be limited by the shortage of labor to about 600 acres for most of the seventeenth century. With the large scale importation of slaves in the eighteenth century, however, the lid was removed. William Byrd II was the owner of almost 180,000 acres, and Robert "King" Carter ruled over 300,000 acres and 1,000 slaves.

However, only a small portion of a plantation was under cultivation at any one time. This was partly due to the fact that plantation owners kept using the same fields until they were exhausted (which with tobacco usually occurred within seven years) and then deserted them and opened up new fields. The second reason for limiting acreage under cultivation was the high cost of production. Gray, in his history of southern agriculture, estimated that it cost almost £1,900 to keep 2,000 acres of tobacco under cultivation and even more to grow rice or indigo. Many planters, discouraged by the falling prices for tobacco during most of the eighteenth century, switched to the production of winter wheat, which was planted in the fall after the tobacco was harvested and did not ripen until June or July, after the tobacco plants were transplanted. By 1770 Virginia and Maryland were exporting over 1 million bushels of grain. Other planters rented or sold their excess land and earned a larger income from land speculation than from farming.

The two staple crops of the lower south (South Carolina and Georgia) came to be rice and indigo. Rice was introduced into South Carolina during the 1660s, but its cultivation did not succeed until a more hearty variety from Madagascar was imported by John Thurber, a sea captain, in the 1690s. Rice grew best in the swampy, mosquito-infested fields along the coast. Rice cultivation proved to be extremely profitable. Rice sold for £2 a barrel, and over 150,000 barrels were being exported from Charleston just prior to the Revolution.

Indigo, the source of a valuable blue dye, was introduced into South Carolina in 1741 by Eliza Lucas (later Mrs. Charles Pinckney), whose father had been a governor in the West Indies. It proved to be an ideal supplement to rice cultivation because it grew in the uplands and needed care at different periods of the year than rice did. Indigo was in such demand that the English government paid producers a bounty of four pence a pound. This raised prices to as much as five shillings a pound, and South Carolina and Georgia were producing well over 1 million pounds a year during the early 1770s. After independence, when the bounty no longer existed, American indigo could not compete in the English market and was no longer produced.

The cultivation of rice and indigo was more intensive than that of tobacco, and plantations in the lower south rarely exceeded 300 acres. Because of the danger, arduousness, and unpleasantness of the labor involved in both rice and indigo cultivation, all work was done by slaves—usually thirty or forty to a plantation. Actually, in the rice plantations owners probably learned the production techniques from their slaves, who were familiar with West African methods of growing rice.

While the production of staple crops for market is called commercial agriculture, two points should be kept in mind in studying southern agriculture. Corn (whose acreage exceeded that of tobacco), wheat, and a wide variety of fruits and vegetables were grown in all parts of the south largely for home consumption. Many of these crops were grown on fields that could no longer produce tobacco. Cotton was also grown in the colonial south, but the difficulty of separating the seeds from the lint limited its commercial possibilities. Lastly, the vast majority of southerners did not live on plantations but on farms of about 300 acres—only slightly larger than those of the middle colonies. They had difficulty in competing with the large planters (who were able to cut production costs) and therefore grew more corn and wheat than tobacco, which usually had to be sold to their richer neighbors. Still, it is estimated that over half of all southern crops were exported overseas.

Cattle raising was also important to the southern farmer. The livestock industry of the southern colonies, particularly the Carolinas, had many of the characteristics which we usually associate with the post-Civil War west. Cattle were allowed to run loose on the open range to forage. Periodic roundups took place, in which the cattle were enclosed in cow pens, or corrals, branded, and then driven to coastal towns—usually Charleston. There they were sold for their meat, hides, and fat, which was used for candles. Sheep and horses were also raised and, as in the other sections, hogs did exceptionally well. Some southern beef and pork was exported to the West Indies, yet in other parts of the south where planters concentrated strictly on the production of a staple crop, these same products had to be imported from the middle colonies.

Colonial farmers have been accused of being stodgy and conservative in their methods. Yet, the handicaps under which they labored—primitive tools, high labor costs, poor transportation, lack of a sound currency, and the trial-and-error process of adapting European crops and methods to American conditions—must have seemed almost insurmountable. Still, these problems were surmounted, and American farmers supplied the products needed not only for themselves and their families but also for fellow colonists on the mainland and in the West Indies and for innumerable Europeans of whose existence these farmers were only dimly aware.

BIBLIOGRAPHY

BIDWELL, PERCY W., and FALCONER, JOHN I. *History of Agriculture in the Northern United States, 1620-1860.* Washington, D.C., 1925.

CLOWSE, CONVERSE D. *Economic Beginnings in Colonial South Carolina, 1670-1730.* Columbia, S.C., 1971.

CLEMONS, PAUL G. E. *The Atlantic Economy and Colonial Maryland's Eastern Shore: From Tobacco to Grain.* Ithaca, 1980.

DOAR, DAVID. *Rice and Rice Planting in the South Carolina Low Country.* Charleston, 1936.

GRAY, LEWIS C. *A History of Agriculture in the Southern United States.* 2 vols. Washington, D.C., 1933.

KIM, SUNG BOK. *Landlord and Tenant in Colonial New York: Manorial Society, 1664-1775.* Chapel Hill, 1978.

RUTMAN, DARETT B. *Husbandmen of Plymouth: Farms and Villages in the Old Colony, 1620–1692.* Boston, 1967.
SAKOLSKI, AARON M. *Land Tenure and Land Taxation in America.* New York, 1957.

14
Colonial Commerce

The basic rule of mercantilism as expressed by Thomas Mun in his tract, *England's Treasure by Forraign Trade*, (1664) was "to sell more to strangers yearly than we consume of theirs in value." Colonies were founded to help achieve this goal. The role of the colonies was to supply the mother country with raw materials, purchase its manufactured goods, and serve as the outlet for surplus capital.

Almost from their beginnings colonists refused to accept this role and contested all English attempts to regulate their economy. For example, Massachusetts officials told an investigating royal commission that the Navigation Acts were "an invasion of the rights, liberties, and properties of the subjects of his Majesty in the colony." Even Sir William Berkeley, the governor of Virginia, wrote the English authorities that their effects were "destructive" to the economy of Virginia.

THE COLONIES AS SUPPLIERS
AND MARKETS

Nevertheless, the colonies did fall into the expected pattern of providing raw materials for the mother country. Even before the colonies were founded, Europeans were obtaining fish, furs, and timber from the North American continent. Later, tobacco, rice, indigo, and sugar were added to the list of colonial staples. On the other hand, the colonists depended on England for much of their manufactured and capital goods.

Even the poorest family might own an English-made knife or gun. Farmers and artisans hoped to acquire English tools and implements. Housewives needed pots, pans, and other household utensils. Also, as some families became wealthy, they bought their best clothes, furniture, silver, and tableware from England. Capital goods obtained from the mother country included machinery and Indian trading goods. Obviously, then, overseas trade was of mutual benefit to both colonies and mother country.

During the first part of the seventeenth century, the trade between England and its colonies was relatively unimportant. This may be explained in part by the small number of colonists and their low standard of living. It may also be explained by the English civil war of the period. However, it was primarily due to the fact that much of the trade that the Navigation Acts were later to channel to England was still conducted with Holland. Even in 1697-1700 (when fairly accurate records began to be kept) exports from the colonies to England had an average annual value of £289,081. The annual value of English goods imported into the colonies for the same period was £336,545. By 1771, the peak year for colonial imports before political difficulties caused them to decline, exports from the colonies grew to £1.452,476 and imports to £4,202,472. Note that by this date the colonies were much more important as markets for English goods than they were as suppliers of raw materials. Colonial trade now constituted about one-third of English trade (up from one-sixth in 1700), but this percentage was destined to decline in the 1770s because the English government failed to take this economic change into consideration.

Regional specialization in production developed in the colonies largely as a result of climatic differences. New England specialized from the first in fish (America's fourth most valuable export), timber, and furs. The middle colonies specialized in cattle, grain, flour (America's second most valuable export), and furs. The most important products of the upper south were tobacco (America's most valuable export) and naval stores. The lower south came to concentrate on deerskins, rice, and indigo (America's third and fifth most valuable exports).

These import and export figures may be analyzed in many different ways. For example, where did the products come from and where were they sold? Overall, in terms of value, Britain purchased 55 percent of all colonial exports with four-fifths of the products coming from the upper and lower south. The West Indies purchased just over a quarter of colonial exports—primarily products from New England and the middle colonies. Southern Europe purchased between 14-18 percent of colonial exports—one-third from the middle colonies and the rest divided fairly evenly between the other three sections. Africa, which purchased only 1 percent of colonial exports, obtained almost all of them from New England.

In return, southern Europe sold the colonies salt, wine, and spices, which were valued at the end of the colonial period at slightly under £100,000. West Indian sugar, rum, molasses, and cotton sales to the mainland colonies exceeded £800,000 in value. Africa supplied gold dust, ivory, and after 1715—when the monopoly of the Royal African Company was broken—slaves. Yet, even though profits from the

THE INCONVENIENCIES

THAT HAVE HAPPENED TO SOME PER-
SONS WHICH HAVE TRANSPORTED THEMSELVES

from *England* to *Virginia*, vvithout prouisions necessary to sustaine themselues, hath
greatly hindred the Progresse of that noble Plantation: For preuention of the like disorders
heereafter, that no man suffer, either through ignorance or misinformation; it is thought requisite to publish this short declaration: wherein is contained a particular of such neces-
saries, as either priuate families or single persons shall haue cause to furnish themselues with, for their better
support at their first landing in Virginia; whereby also greater numbers may receiue in part,
directions how to prouide themselues.

Apparrell.	li.	s.	d.
One Monmouth Cap	00	01	10
Three falling bands	—	01	03
Three shirts	—	07	06
One waste coate	—	02	02
One suite of Canuase	—	07	06
One suite of Frize	—	10	00
One suite of Cloth	—	15	00
Three paire of Irish stockins	—	04	—
Foure paire of shooes	—	08	08
One paire of garters	—	00	10
One doozen of points	—	00	03
One paire of Canuase sheets	—	08	00
Seuen ells of Canuase, to make a bed and boulster, to be filled in Virginia 8.s.	—	08	00
One Rug for a bed 8.s. which with the bed seruing for two men, halfe is			
Fiue ells coorse Canuase, to make a bed at Sea for two men, to be filled with straw, iiij.s	—	05	00
One coorse Rug at Sea for two men, will cost vj.s. is for one	04	00	00

Apparrell for one man, and so after the rate for more.

Victuall.			
Eight bushels of Meale	02	00	00
Two bushels of pease at 3.s.	—	06	00
Two bushels of Oatemeale 4.s. 6.d.	—	09	00
One gallon of Aquauitæ	—	02	06
One gallon of Oyle	—	03	06
Two gallons of Vineger 1. s.	—	02	00
	03	03	00

For a whole yeere for one man, and so for more after the rate.

Armes.			
One Armour compleat, light	—	17	00
One long Peece fiue foot or fiue and a halfe, neere Musket bore	01	02	—
One sword	—	05	—
One belt	—	01	—
One bandaleere	—	01	06
Twenty pound of powder	—	18	00
Sixty pound of shot or lead, Pistoll and Goose shot	—	05	00
	03	09	06

For one man, but if halfe of your men haue armour it is sufficient so that all haue Peeces and swords.

Tooles.	li.	s.	d.
Fiue broad howes at 2.s. a piece	—	10	—
Fiue narrow howes at 16.d. a piece	—	06	08
Two broad Axes at 3.s. 8.d. a piece	—	07	04
Fiue felling Axes at 18.d. a piece	—	07	06
Two steele hand sawes at 16.d. a piece	—	02	08
Two two-hand sawes at 5.s. a piece	—	10	—
One whip-saw, set and filed with box, file, and wrest	—	10	—
Two hammers 12.d. a piece	—	02	00
Three shouels 18.d. a piece	—	04	06
Two spades at 18.d. a piece	—	03	—
Two augers 6.d. a piece	—	01	00
Sixe chissels 6.d. a piece	—	03	00
Two percers stocked 4.d. a piece	—	00	08
Three gimlets 2.d. a piece	—	00	06
Two hatchets 21.d. a piece	—	03	06
Two frowes to cleaue pale 18.d.	—	03	00
Two hand bills 20. a piece	—	03	04
One grindlestone 4.s.	—	04	00
Nailes of all sorts to the value of	02	00	—
Two Pickaxes	—	03	—
	06	02	08

For a family of 6. persons and so after the rate for more.

Houshold Implements.			
One Iron Pot	—	07	—
One kettle	—	06	—
One large frying pan	—	02	06
One gridiron	—	01	06
Two skillets	—	05	—
One spit	—	02	—
Platters, dishes, spoones of wood	—	04	—
	01	08	00

For a family of 6. persons, and so for more or lesse after the rate.

For Sugar, Spice, and fruit, and at Sea for 6.men—	00	12	06
So the full charge of Apparrell, Victuall, Armes, Tooles, and houshold stuffe, and after this rate for each person, will amount vnto about the summe of	12	10	—
The passage of each man is	06	00	—
The fraight of these prouisions for a man, will bee about halfe a Tun, which is	01	10	—
So the whole charge will amount to about	20	00	00

Nets, hookes, lines, and a tent must be added, if the number of people be greater, as also some kine.

And this is the usuall proportion that the Virginia Company doe bestow vpon their Tenants which they send.

Whosoeuer transports himselfe or any other at his owne charge vnto *Virginia*, shall for each person so transported before Midsummer 1625. haue to him and his heires for euer fifty Acres of Land vpon a first, and fifty Acres vpon a second diuision.

Imprinted at London by FELIX KYNGSTON. 1622.

FIGURE 14A   (Library of Congress.)

slave trade rarely fell below 33 percent, merchants from Boston, Salem, Newport, and New York together sent out only about seventy slave ships a year to Africa.

The remainder of colonial imports—almost 90 percent—came from England. About 65 percent of these imports were textiles, and 15 percent were metal goods.

It was largely because of the high value of these imports that the colonies had an unfavorable balance of payments. However, this phenomenon, too, needs regional analysis. The two southern sections generally had a slightly favorable balance: In the years between 1768 and 1772, it averaged £99,000 (according to the calculations of J. F. Shepherd and G. M. Walton in their volume, *Shipping, Maritime Trade, and the Economic Development of Colonial North America*. During the same period, though, the New England and middle colonies had an average deficit of £1,220,000.

TRIANGULAR TRADE ROUTES

The colonies had several so-called triangular trade routes. The most famous one was the voyage from New England to Africa, where rum was traded for slaves who were carried to the West Indies. The slaves were exchanged for sugar and molasses which were brought back to New England to be distilled into more rum. A second triangular route went from New England or the middle colonies to the West Indies: Food, horses, lumber, and fish were exchanged for sugar, which was taken to England. There it was traded for manufactured goods which were then brought back to the mainland colonies. The third triangular route went from New England or the middle colonies with fish, food, furs, or timber to southern Europe, where they were exchanged for wine, silk, spices, or fruit. These were traded for manufactured goods in England which were then brought back to America.

Yet, in spite of all the attention triangular trade routes have received in the past, recent studies by Walton and Shepherd (*The Economic Rise of Early America*) indicate that at least the first two were virtually nonexistent. It has already been pointed out that the African trade comprised at most 1 percent of colonial commerce. The second route (to England—after leaving the West Indies) also seems to be mythical: The vast majority of the ships which sailed to the West Indies returned to American ports. Evidence about the third alleged triangular route to southern Europe is less certain; on the whole, it seems clear that most colonial ships tended to restrict themselves to fairly regular routes between a limited number of ports.

ANGLO-AMERICAN TRADE RELATIONS

No matter what the shape of their routes, American traders were able to sell their goods at highly inflated prices, particularly in the West Indies, and thereby they made up a great deal of their trade deficit with England. New England's trade with the West Indies posed serious problems for the English government because so much of it was conducted with the non-English West Indian islands. As far as New Englanders were concerned, their economy required that they be able to sell their excess products to the non-English West Indies, where they tended to get higher prices for their merchandise while paying less for sugar and molasses than they did in the English West Indies.

In 1733, after a long campaign by the English West Indian planters, Parliament passed the Molasses Act. This act placed a duty of nine pence a gallon on foreign rum, six pence a gallon on foreign molasses, and five shillings per hundredweight on foreign sugar. These duties were—and were meant to be—prohibitive. If the Molasses Act had been enforced, it would have ruined the New England economy. Fortunately for New Englanders, no serious step in this direction was taken for almost thirty years.

The northern colonies' unfavorable balance of payments with England was decreased not only by their lucrative trade with the West Indies and southern Europe, but also by what economists call invisible earnings. These colonies had the vast majority of merchant ships. Owners of these vessels regained much of this deficit through their shipping charges, insurance and interest fees, and the sale of ships to England. By 1772 these invisible earnings were estimated at £740,000. Further, the money spent by the English government in the colonies (as much as £800,000 a year between 1757 and 1767)—mainly for military purposes but also for civil administration—further reduced the deficit.

On the other hand, the slight apparent balance of payments in favor of the southern colonies was canceled out by insurance and freight rates, and the commissions paid to their factors, or agents. When the amount spent for the importation of slaves (which was not counted in the official trade statistics) is included, the southern colonies actually had an unfavorable balance of payments with England. The West Indian favorable balance of trade was also largely erased by the annual importation of £200,000 worth of slaves.

English merchants used the consignment system in trading with the southern planters. Under this system the planter retained ownership of the crop, and the merchant sold the tobacco, rice, or indigo on commission—also, for a fee, purchasing the English goods which the planters ordered. Often the latter amount exceeded what planters earned for their crops; it was almost impossible for the planter to know in advance what the crop would bring. Very often these merchants sent agents to the colonies to see that the tobacco they were purchasing was properly packed and labeled, and also hopefully to collect any debts the planters might owe them. The planters often viewed these English factors as competitors; many of the planters also acted as merchants by purchasing the tobacco of their smaller neighbors and selling them goods in return.

Often a hostile relationship developed between the English merchants and the planters they represented. The planters complained about the high price of (often inferior) English goods, which often cost three times as much as they did at home. They also resented the high shipping rates (£9 a ton in peacetime and £16 a ton in wartime), the high insurance rates, the high storage and inspection fees, the high commission, the high interest rate, and the high import duties which they were forced to pay. In return, they received low prices for their crops. There is no doubt that the sellers of the relatively bulky, low-cost colonial products had their profits sharply cut by these kinds of expenses, which accounted for three-fourths of the gross sales price of tobacco. This only added to the resentment of the planters who knew, or at least suspected, that English merchants made a profit of £400,000 a year on the tobacco that they reexported to the continent.

On the other hand, planters relied on these merchants for their business advice and for the credit they extended. The merchants resented planters' attempts to foist poorer grade tobacco on them, and they did not like the planters' attempts, always quashed by the English government, to pay their debts in devalued colonial currency. The amount of these debts has been highly exaggerated. Just prior to the Revolution, some 35,000 Virginians owed a total of £2,000,000 to English merchants, with most owing less than £100.

Between 1740 and 1770 the English merchants' control of the tobacco trade was largely broken by Scottish merchants. These merchants operated stores along the rivers of Virginia and Maryland and purchased tobacco with either goods or cash. The Scottish merchants paid relatively high prices for the tobacco, making the bulk of their profit on the sale of European goods to the planters. Many of the planters, especially the smaller ones, preferred receiving a sure and fair price for their crops rather than gambling on the price they might receive in London when their tobacco arrived. In addition, Scottish merchants, like their English competitors, were generous with credit.

DOMESTIC TRADE

New England and the middle colonies were under a severe handicap in their trade with England. Parliament had forbidden the importation of colonial meat, flour, wheat, and fish—all products which were then plentiful in England—into the mother country. This left only timber, furs, and the products of the whaling industry for New England and the middle colonies to exchange for the English manufactured goods which their people demanded.

The merchants of Boston, New York, and Philadelphia, however, built up a thriving trade with their hinterlands. One branch of this domestic trade was the collection (by small boat) of products such as grain, potash, and naval stores, which were then brought back to the home port and transshipped overseas. Conversely, ships from the major ports would distribute throughout the thirteen colonies the foreign goods which they had imported.

New England ships (particularly in the winter, when ocean crossings were most dangerous and few fishing expeditions were underway) went south with foreign and domestically manufactured goods; these they traded for tobacco, rice, and naval stores. Ships from the middle colonies carried bread, flour, paper, and iron products both to the south and to New England. These goods were marketed in either general or country stores; at markets and fairs which were held regularly in the northern colonies; or by peddlers, or hawkers, as they were called in the eighteenth century, who visited the isolated communities on the frontier. All in all, domestic commerce was probably greater in volume (312 of the 509 ships that left Boston were involved in this trade), though less in value, than foreign commerce. Further, this trade was under virtually complete colonial control, and the balance of payments was overwhelmingly in favor of the northern merchants.

By the middle of the eighteenth century, the merchants of New England and the middle colonies operated much like English merchants, though still on a smaller scale. Some of their trade was carried on by means of barter, but much was transacted through an intricate system of letters of credit, insurance charges, freight charges, commissions, and loans to their local customers as well as to southern and West Indian planters. In a time when communications were poor, these merchants relied heavily on the ship captains or other agents whom they placed on their ships. It was they who had to decide what price to accept for the cargo, what to buy as a new cargo, and where to take it for sale.

Most northern merchants did not feel themselves bound by the Navigation Acts and regularly smuggled goods in and out of France, Spain, Holland, and England itself. It is impossible to determine the exact extent of this illegal traffic, but some experts have estimated it to be as high as 30 percent of all northern commerce. It was also common practice for foreign vessels—usually Dutch—to smuggle cargoes into the colonies. The most telling comment on this illegal trade is that in 1750 the English authorities collected only £1,500 in duties in the colonies—at a cost of from £7,000 to £8,000. When Benjamin Franklin described gaining wealth from commerce as "cheating," he could not have been far wrong.

PIRACY

One of the great hindrances to colonial commerce was piracy. Pirates dominated the Caribbean during the last third of the seventeenth century, when the decline of Spanish naval power created a power vacuum in the region. After this area was brought under control, primarily by the English navy, the pirates shifted their base of operations to the Red Sea and Indian Ocean, where they could prey on East Indian commerce. At first most colonial towns welcomed these pirates because they spent freely—in hard money, which was particularly valued—and sold their stolen goods at bargain prices. Merchants, and even royal governors, helped finance or provision these expeditions and entertained pirate leaders in their homes. Charleston and New York were the two main pirate havens at the turn of the eighteenth century.

The pirates soon wore out their welcome in colonial towns when they took to capturing ships of the very towns which harbored them. In 1700 Parliament authorized the establishment of special courts to try pirates without juries, and the English navy was ordered to clear the American coast of piracy. Then, in 1717 the English government offered amnesty to all pirates who surrendered, and many took advantage of this offer. With the execution of Steve Bonnet and the shooting of Edward

Teach ("Blackbeard" as he was more commonly called) by a South Carolina expedition in 1718, piracy was largely wiped out along the American coast and in the Caribbean.

When the Atlantic trade routes became safer, it became possible for colonial shippers to make use of the Dutch flyboat (or flute). This ship was long and narrow and lacked the guns, gun platform, and reinforced planking which had formerly been necessary for defense. The flyboat was therefore much speedier as well as cheaper to build, simpler to rig, and easier to man than the type of ship built in English and American shipyards when piracy was still a menace. The use of the flyboat lowered freight rates and ushered in a new era of prosperity for British shippers.

LAND TRANSPORTATION
AND COMMUNICATION

As already mentioned, the intercolonial trade was of considerable significance. Most of this trade was carried on by water—either on the numerous rivers which ran inland or on the Atlantic Ocean. Even though sea transportation was slow and dangerous because of storms, pirates, and lack of navigational aids, it was preferred to land transportation. In the seventeenth century particularly, colonists avoided travel by land if at all possible. The first roads were Indian trails not nearly wide enough for a horse or wagon. The woods were so thick that it was difficult to keep one's sense of direction. The colonists learned to blaze, or cut a piece of bark from, the trees along the road to keep them on the proper path. Snowshoes were a great convenience in the winter, but nothing helped to overcome the dust and mud that clogged roads at other times of the year. Bridges and inns were few and far between, and ferries were rare and unreliable.

As in most other areas, great improvements in transportation were made during the eighteenth century. Ships became larger and faster, and improved charts and lighthouses made water transportation much safer. The major improvements, however, were made in land transportation. Roads between the large towns were widened, bridges were built, inns improved in quantity (if not always in quality), and, after 1760, stagecoach lines began to operate on regular schedules. The trip from New York to Philadelphia (about ninety miles) was being made at the end of the colonial period by these "flying machines," as express coaches were called, in two days at a cost of about three pence a mile.

Even during the eighteenth century, inns were small—many having just one room for men and one for women. When they became crowded, travelers were forced to roll up in a blanket on the floor of the parlor. A few larger inns did have several rooms (often with alluring names such as the Azure Chamber or the Sun Chamber) and a commodious lounge where travelers could eat and drink. Inns were less frequently found in the south, where planters often preferred to welcome travelers into their own homes.

Much of the improvement in land transportation was connected with the growth of a mail service. The English government did not institute any formal mail service in the colonies until 1691, and even then it was under private auspices. Before that time ship captains carried letters to and from Europe for a fee, and local letters were delivered if and when someone happened to be going to the vicinity of the addressee. Several colonies attempted to establish some form of postal service, but without any success. In the early eighteenth century, under the leadership of Andrew Hamilton—the deputy postmaster in the colonies—mail deliveries began to be made on a regular basis between the towns of the north, but Maryland, Virginia, and the Carolinas were completely neglected. Even in 1711, when Parliament placed the postal system under government control, this omission was not rectified. Only after 1753, when Benjamin Franklin and William Hunter of Virginia became joint deputy postmaster generals, was postal service extended to all thirteen colonies. Franklin's system of post roads and post riders who rode day and night cut the time for the delivery of and reply to a letter between Boston and Philadelphia from three weeks to six days. However, it still took ten weeks for a letter from Charleston to reach a northern town.*

Even transportation between the frontier and the seacoast improved during the eighteenth century. At first goods were transported on pack horses tethered together in long trains. Two men could handle a train of fifteen horses, with one man guiding the lead horse and the other bringing up the rear. By the end of the eighteenth century, the most popular vehicle on the frontier was the Conestoga wagon. These wagons had high, broad wheels and roomy bodies which could carry four to six tons. The wagon body was painted in blue and red and was covered with heavy white cloth supported by six to eight arched bows. These wagons were pulled by four to six horses, depending on the load. They often traveled in trains of up to one hundred wagons. Yet, in spite of the improvements in land travel, costs were still high, and most merchants preferred to ship their goods by sea.

THE FUR TRADE

The fur trade depended on both land and sea transportation. The demand for furs both in Europe and in the colonies ensured the profitability of this trade. The English authorities officially took cognizance of this in 1722 when they placed furs on the list of enumerated articles. Furs could be purchased cheaply from the Indians in exchange for axes, knives, blankets, beads, guns, and rum (though the latter two were illegal). England had a great advantage over France in the fur trade because the price of its trade goods was so much lower. Nevertheless, the French remained competitive because their traders went directly to the Indians, while the English encouraged the Indians to come to the main trading centers such as Albany or Phila-

---

*During the colonial period postage was paid by the person who received the letter.

delphia. The most valuable northern fur was the beaver, followed by otter, raccoon, mink, fox, and bear. The southern fur trade centered largely on the deerskin, although fox, raccoon, and beaver were also trapped.

During the seventeenth century (but not the eighteenth) New England was an important fur trading area along with New York, Pennsylvania, and the back country of Virginia, South Carolina, and, later, Georgia. By the eighteenth century, as the fur trade moved westward, it became more and more controlled by the merchants of Albany, Philadelphia, and Charleston. This was a result of the large amount of capital—about £1,000—needed to buy trade goods and the length of time—often several years—before profits could be realized. By this time the English were following the French method and sending traders directly to the Indians. Although the wait was long, the ultimate profits were substantial, running to approximately £700,000 by 1770.

In summary, colonial trade was economically significant and varied. One need not wade through a morass of trade figures to realize that large merchants and planters (the wealthiest colonists) profited directly, and countless other colonists profited indirectly, from the far-flung foreign and extensive domestic trade. It is therefore not surprising that commercial interests were a major concern in colonial politics.

BIBLIOGRAPHY

BAILYN, BERNARD, and BAILYN, LOTTE. *Massachusetts Shipping, 1697–1714: A Statistical Study.* Cambridge, 1959.

BRUCHEY, STUART, ed. *The Colonial Merchant: Sources and Readings.* New York, 1966.

BRUCHEY, STUART. *The Roots of American Economic Growth, 1607–1861.* New York, 1965.

CLOWSE, CONVERSE D. *Measuring Charleston's Overseas Commerce, 1717–1767: Statistics from the Port's Naval Lists.* Washington, D.C., 1981.

JENSEN, ARTHUR L. *The Maritime Commerce of Colonial Philadelphia.* Madison, 1963.

KARRAKER, CYRUS H. *Piracy Was A Business.* Rindge, N.H., 1953.

MARTIN, CALVIN. *Keepers of the Game: Indian-Animal Relationships and the Fur Trade.* Berkeley, 1978.

MIDDLETON, ARTHUR P. *Tobacco Coast: A Maritime History of Chesapeake Bay in the Colonial Era.* Newport News, Va., 1953.

NORTON, THOMAS ELLIOT. *The Fur Trade in Colonial New York, 1686–1776.* Madison, 1974.

PARES, RICHARD. *Yankees and Creoles: The Trade Between North America and the West Indies before the American Revolution.* London, England, 1956.

PHILLIPS, PAUL C. *The Fur Trade.* 2 vols. Norman, Okla., 1961.

SHEPHERD, JAMES F., and WALTON, GARY M. *Shipping, Maritime Trade, and the Economic Development of Colonial North America.* Cambridge, 1972.

WALTON, GARY M., and SHEPHERD, JAMES F. *The Economic Rise of Early America.* Cambridge, 1979.

I5
Colonial Industry

As an agrarian philosopher, Benjamin Franklin deprecated the importance of manufacturing. As he wrote in *Positions to be Examined, Concerning National Wealth,* "manufacturers were only *another shape* into which so much provision and subsistence are turned, as were equal in value to the manufactures produced." It is true that colonial industry must be classified as extractive, or primary, in that it consisted of relatively simple processing of the products of the forest, the sea, or the earth. Yet, by 1732 the Board of Trade was complaining:

> More trades [are] carried on and more manufacturers set up in the provinces on the continent of America to the northward of Virginia, prejudicial to the trade and manufactures of Great Britain, particularly in New England, than in any of the British colonies.

Although the search for raw materials was the primary motive for colonization, the English government also hoped to develop in the colonies certain industries which were not found in the mother country. Artisans were sent to Jamestown from its inception, and the Virginia Company had plans for an ironworks, a naval stores industry, and the manufacture of glass. None of these plans materialized, however, partly because of the profitability of tobacco growing.

OBSTACLES TO THE GROWTH
OF INDUSTRY

Later colonies offered bounties to encourage the establishment of some of the industries mentioned above; but in spite of these subsidies, America never became industrialized, even as the word was understood at the time. One reason for this was the lack of capital—either working capital or capital goods.* The lack of financial institutions which might loan money made it extremely difficult to acquire either type of capital. Thus, the few individuals who did have money to lend were able to charge high rates of interest. This forced manufacturers (and others) to plow back profits into their businesses in order to expand. Further complicating this entire process was the lack of a stable medium of exchange.

A combination of other factors also helped deter industrialization in colonial America. Skilled workers were scarce, and the high wages they commanded increased the costs of production and lessened the ability of colonial manufacturers to compete with their English counterparts. In spite of their high wages, many artisans preferred the independence and prestige they could obtain by purchasing land and becoming farmers. Other problems were poor transportation, high freight rates, a relatively small (for most of the period) and scattered population, and—most importantly—the lack of ready money in the hands of potential consumers. The average farmer received little, or no, cash when selling a crop. What cash the farmers might obtain went only for those few articles which could not be made at home.

All food was grown and processed at home. Grain was ground into flour and baked into bread and biscuits. Milk was churned into butter and cheese. Cattle were slaughtered and preserved by smoking or pickling. Beer, cider, and brandy were distilled at home. Farmers fashioned their own furniture and most of their tools. Men, women, and children cooperated in preparing, spinning, and weaving woolen, linen, and leather clothing. Candles and soap were also made by the family. Thus, home industry, or household manufacturing—as it was also called—severely impeded the growth of large-scale commercial industry in colonial America.

Further, English policy tended, on the whole, to be inimical to the growth of colonial industry. While shipbuilding and the production of naval stores were encouraged, English manufacturers were vehemently opposed to anything which appeared to challenge their interests (as shown by the Woolens, Hat, and Iron Acts, which will be discussed later in this chapter). In addition, colonial acts to encourage industries that might compete with English industries, whether by bounties or tariffs on English goods, were either vetoed by colonial governors or disallowed by the Privy Council. Lastly, England prohibited the emigration of skilled workers and the export of machinery.

Yet, in spite of all these obstacles, industry did develop in colonial America. One type of industry that developed may be described as domestic industry (not to be confused with household industry). In this type of industry (which was also common in Europe at the time), merchants brought raw materials such as wool or flax to the farmers and their families, and the latter would turn them into cloth. Leather making was another important domestic industry.

---

*Working capital is the ready cash necessary to pay workers, buy materials, and cover the other costs of conducting a business. Capital goods are the tools and relatively simple machines necessary to produce goods.

FOREST-BASED INDUSTRIES

Still more crucial were the commercial industries which developed in the colonies. Even before the colonies were founded, fish, furs, and timber were in great demand in western and southern Europe. England was in dire need of wood for shipbuilding and for charcoal, which was basic to the smelting of iron. However, England obtained much less timber than it hoped from the colonies because American oak, pine, and maple trees were in great demand in the colonies themselves for construction of homes, ships, furniture, tools, and household implements. Coopers, or barrelmakers, also consumed a tremendous amount of wood because barrels were used to contain tobacco, sugar, wine, rice, fish, meat, naval stores, and all the other products which today are packed in cardboard, tin, or plastic containers.

Maine had a sawmill as early as 1623; New Hampshire built one in 1635. These and the many later mills were powered either by water or wind. Most of the planks, shingles, and clapboards produced by these mills were consumed locally, but when in 1722 England abolished its import duty on American lumber (and later actually placed it on the list of enumerated articles), large amounts went to the mother country. However, as was the case with other enumerated articles, a significant quantity continued to be exported to other nations, particularly Spain and Portugal. By the time of the Revolution, the colonies exported 40 million board feet of lumber; 15,000 tons of timber; and 20 million barrel staves.

Shipbuilding was another early colonial industry. Attempts to build ships were made at Jamestown; the Dutch built a ship on Manhattan Island in 1614; two ships were built at Plymouth in 1624; and the thirty ton *Blessing of the Bay* was built for John Winthrop in 1631. Later, after the passage of the Navigation Acts, thousands of ships were constructed in the colonies—two-thirds of them in New England and the rest in the middle colonies and upper south. The cheap price of colonial timber overcame the high cost of labor and made it possible for colonial ships to be built for about £2 to £4 a ton, about 40 percent less than a similar ship could be built in England. As a result, by the end of the colonial period, about 200,000 tons, or one-third of all British ships, were made in the colonies. An average of £40,000 worth of ships was sold annually to English merchants by the New England colonies alone. Yet, most colonial ships remained under American ownership, and New England possessed a fleet of almost 2,000 merchant ships and a greater number of smaller fishing vessels. It is estimated that 33,000 seamen manned American ships—the largest single group of workers in the colonies.

The size of colony-made ships varied greatly—from 10 tons for fishing sloops to 500 tons for "topsail" ships for the Atlantic trade; the average was about 60 tons. These smaller ships, often constructed at Newport, were preferred because they could sail into shallow waters to pick up cargoes and because maritime risks were so great, particularly in wartime, that merchants preferred to own several small ships rather than one large one. Not only was shipbuilding important in itself, but ancillary industries—sail lofts, rope yards, foundries for ships' hardware, and chandleries to provide them with supplies—created thousands of jobs for colonial workers.

One complaint of American shipbuilders was that the tallest pines (at least seventy-two feet in height and twenty-four to thirty-six inches in diameter), which made the best masts, were reserved for the royal navy. Although owners were compensated when such a tree was cut, anyone who illegally cut down a tree marked with the king's "broad arrow" was liable to a fine of up to £100. However, enforcement of this statute was lax, and although many masts were shipped to England, American ships never lacked adequate masts.

Closely allied to the shipping industry was the naval stores industry—the manufacture of pitch, tar, hemp, turpentine, and resin. Pitch, tar, and resin were necessary to protect a ship's planks and rigging. So crucial were these supplies for the English navy (which had previously depended largely on Swedish sources) that in 1705 naval stores were placed on the list of enumerated articles. Generous bounties (originally £6 a ton for hemp, £4 a ton for pitch and tar, and £3 a ton for resin and turpentine) were paid for their production. With certain modifications, these bounties were paid for most of the remainder of the colonial period. The naval stores industry boomed, particularly in North Carolina, South Carolina, and Virginia, where farmers made it an important supplement to their income. By the end of the colonial period, almost £200,000 worth of naval stores was being exported from the American colonies.

Another forest-based industry was the production of potash, which was used in England and in the colonies to make soap, glass, and fertilizers, and as a bleach in the woolen industry. Potash was a thick brown salt produced by taking the ash from hardwood trees such as the oak or birch and boiling it with water in huge kettles. Potash might then be placed in hot ovens and cooked until the carbon was burned out and it yielded a more refined product, called pearl ash. Many colonies paid bounties for the manufacture of potash or pearl ash, although the English government did not place them on the list of enumerated articles until 1764. Farmers in New England and the middle colonies were enthusiastic producers of about £50,000 worth of these products; the farmers had to clear their lands anyway, and the profits from potash production were greater than those made from the sale of raw timber.

The last of the industries we might call forest based was hat making. The making of beaver hats centered in New York, Pennsylvania, and Rhode Island. These hats were very popular in Spain, Portugal, and the West Indies as well as in the mainland colonies. When American exports reached about 10,000 a year, English hat makers, the Company of Feltmakers, felt threatened. A Parliamentary inquiry supported their contention, and the Hat Act of 1732 banned the export of hats from any colony, limited colonial hat makers to two apprentices, and lengthened the period of apprenticeship to a full seven years. Although the Hat Act largely deprived colonial hat makers of their overseas markets, the domestic market continued to grow. Further, colonial hat makers also began making much cheaper hats of wool and other fabrics, which were bought by plantation owners for their slaves.

SEA-BASED INDUSTRIES

Two very profitable industries stemmed from the products of the sea. The most important of these industries was fishing. Although fishing was good all along the Atlantic coast, the area off Newfoundland, the Grand Banks, was one of the world's premier fishing grounds—abounding in cod, mackerel, salmon, and herring. Fishermen from several European nations reached the Grand Banks by 1500, if not before. There they fought each other for fishing stations where they could dry and salt their catches. By the end of the seventeenth century, however, English and colonial fishermen dominated the area.

Fishermen caught cod with hand lines and nets, using mackerel as bait. As soon as they were caught, the fish were cleaned and preserved either in salt or brine. The heads were used to feed hogs, the livers were saved for their oil (which was used to soften leather), and the tongues were considered a gourmet's delight. The remainder of the fish was divided into three grades. The best grade, the "merchantable," was sold in southern Europe and Ireland. The "middlings," or middle grade, was consumed in large quantities in every colony. The poorest grade, the "refuse," was sold at about half the price of the "merchantable" to the West Indian planters who used it to feed their slaves.

New England's own teeming waters, its proximity to the Grand Banks, its many good harbors, and its poor soil combined to make its people the leading commercial fishermen of the colonial period. It required little capital to go into the fishing business. All that was required was a small boat and a crew of eight to ten men and boys. Often these crews were made up of farmers who went to sea during their "off" season. Each fisherman worked "on his own hook"; that is, he was paid on the basis of what he caught. Even on large fishing ships, one-third of the profits was divided among the crew; one-third was spent on food, salt, nets, and other equipment; and the final third went to the ship's owner(s). By the time of the Revolution, Gloucester, Marblehead, and the other New England fishing ports were sending out over 10,000 fishermen, who brought in a catch worth £2 million, accounting for over half of New England's exports. No wonder a gilded codfish still hangs over the desk of the speaker of the Massachusetts House of Representatives.

Whaling was the second of the maritime industries. It, too, was largely limited to New England. During the seventeenth century only offshore whaling was practiced. Whales who wandered into shallow water or drifted onto beaches and became stranded were the main victims. By the eighteenth century, as whales became more rare in the north Atlantic, larger ships—outfitted in Nantucket, Marblehead, or New Bedford—began to venture into the Arctic and south Atlantic oceans. These ships were equipped with iron pots to melt down blubber and casks in which to store the resulting oil.

In addition to oil (which was used for illumination and lubrication), whales were prized for baleen (the strainers often called whalebone) in their throat, used for women's corsets; a secretion called ambergris, used as a base for perfume; and spermaceti, or head matter, used for candles. By 1750, 300 ships (150 from Nantucket alone) employing about 4,000 men were engaged in the whaling industry. Like fishing, whaling was a cooperative venture in which every member of the crew received a share of the profits, depending on his rank.

EARTH-BASED INDUSTRIES

The processing of products grown on the surface of, or under, the earth led to the development of several other colonial industries. Lack of money and the Navigation-Act's ban on the importation of relatively cheap Dutch products forced the colonists to manufacture their own clothing. As already noted, cloth making was a prime example of domestic manufacturing. Attempts at fostering commercial textile manufacturing were also made in all the northern colonies. Although costs in the colonial textile industry were so high that it presented no threat to the English, the Irish textile industry was competitive. When the Woolens Act of 1699 banned the export of woolens from Ireland, it also prohibited their export from the American colonies. Yet, only a handful of Americans could afford English-made textiles, and most continued to make or buy domestic products.

Leather making was another industry which had both domestic and commercial aspects. Almost every home made clothes, shoes, belts, and numerous other articles out of the hides of their cattle and sheep, or from the skins of other animals they were able to trap. More skilled workers made and sold the saddles, harnesses, and other paraphernalia necessary in that horse-drawn society. Shoemaking also became an important industry in Massachusetts. Most shoes were ultimately sold to the owners of slaves in the southern colonies and the West Indies.

Brewing was important as both a household and a commercial industry. Alcoholic beverages made from barley, wheat, rye, and corn (as well as a variety of fruits) were all produced and consumed in the average home. The distilling of rum, however, was a large-scale commercial enterprise: New England alone had more than 150 distilleries. Toward the end of the colonial period, about 4 million gallons of molasses were being imported from the West Indies, and each gallon of molasses was converted into a gallon of rum. Much of this rum was consumed in American homes and inns. The surplus served as a crucial item in the slave trade with Africa and the fur trade with the Indians.

The milling industry was extremely important in colonial America. Cornmeal was made at home, but wheat had to be ground into flour at grist mills. To encourage the construction of mills, local governments often granted mill owners exemption from taxes and from militia duty. In addition, they were allowed to keep from one-sixteenth to one-sixth (depending on the locality) of the flour or meal as their fee. Most mills were run by water power, although a few were operated by the wind. As the eighteenth century progressed, mills around New York and Philadelphia increased in size and widened their operations. They milled flour for the export trade and baked ships' biscuits, which were in great demand. Still later these large commercial millers had to be closely regulated because they attempted to hold grain off the market or otherwise increase the price of their bread.

The first colonists had busied themselves in a frantic search for gold and silver, but none was found. A profitable mining industry did develop in America, but it was based on a much less glamorous metal—iron. Bog iron, a brownish liquid that could be dug up from the bottom of swamps and ponds and made into useful utensils, was plentiful in every colony. Iron ore was also found in most colonies. With the need for iron implements so great and the cost of importing them so high, it is not surprising that Virginians attempted to forge their own iron as early as 1620. However, the Indian war of 1622 aborted this experiment. John Winthrop, Jr., was smelting iron in Massachusetts in 1644, and more sophisticated forges were soon built there and in other colonies. However, the largest number of ironworks was located in Pennsylvania. By the time of the Revolution, ironworks had become very large. It is significant, however, that the two largest ironworks—the Principio works in Maryland and the Hasenclaver works in New Jersey—were financed by English and German capitalists respectively.

The iron industry was divided into two branches. The first branch took the ore and converted it into pig and bar iron. The second produced finished wrought-iron articles such as farm tools, kitchen utensils, and stoves. Both branches flourished in colonial America during the eighteenth century. English manufacturers of pig and bar iron became so concerned that they requested that Parliament ban all colonial iron from England. The English manufacturers of finished iron products, however, wanted the colonial pig iron, which tended to be of higher quality than the English product. On the other hand, they did not want competition from finished American iron products. Parliament solved both their problems with the passage of the Iron Act of 1750. This act prohibited the erection of any new plating forges (for sheet iron), steel furnaces (to make tools), and slitting mills (for nails) in the colonies; forbade the export of finished iron products from any colony; but continued to allow the import of pig iron and bar iron into England duty free. The outbreak of the French and Indian War nullified any possibility, or reason, to enforce this law. By 1770 America was producing 27,600 tons of iron and exporting about 8,000 tons of it. This was about 15 percent of the entire world's production and was more than England was producing at the time.

OTHER COLONIAL INDUSTRIES

Attempts were made to develop numerous other industries in colonial America. Paper making became an important commercial industry, requiring complex machinery and skilled (usually German) labor. Philadelphia was the center of the paper-making industry, and Benjamin Franklin was the leading supplier of the linen rags which were used in the manufacture of paper. Colonial paper mills virtually monopolized the American market because their lower shipping costs made it possible for them to undersell their English competitors.

A glass furnace was built at Jamestown as early as 1608, and a few years later a group of Italian workers were imported to produce glassware. That attempt (as like most later efforts at fine colonial glassmaking) failed because of English competition. The most famous—temporary—exception was the factory built by "Baron" Stiegel with German capital near Lancaster, Pennsylvania. Stiegel prospered for several years before finally going bankrupt in 1774 because of his own extravagance. However, Caspar Wistar, a manufacturer of brass buttons, opened a successful glass factory in New Jersey, which was managed after his death by his son Richard. The Wistars' main source of income came from window glass, but they also manufactured jars, canisters, and tubing for some of Franklin's scientific experiments.

A variety of other industries were started, many of which prospered in eighteenth-century America. Brick and tile works were founded in all colonies to build houses and provide them with the necessary fireplaces, chimneys, and roofs. In the 1760s several of the leading merchants of Newport formed the United Company of Spermaceti Candlers, which developed a monopoly of the manufacture and sale of spermaceti candles. Also, two peculiarly "western" industries developed around Lancaster, Pennsylvania. One was the manufacture of what were later called Kentucky rifles. In 1721 Peter Leman, a Swiss gunsmith, is believed to have made a long-barreled, small-bore rifle. Other gunsmiths improved the weapon until it was faster to load and had greater accuracy than any other rifle of its time. The Conestoga wagon was also developed in the Lancaster area. This wagon, the progenitor of the covered wagon, was built to keep the load in the center of the wagon. It had extremely high wheels to help traverse rough roads, it was covered with canvas, and it was usually pulled by six horses. The Conestoga wagon, together with the Kentucky rifle, helped open up the west.

WORKERS AND WAGES

As can be seen, a wide variety of artisans were found in the colonies. Estimates vary, but it is thought that they made up about 18 percent of the colonial population. Artisans, encouraged by the high wages paid in the colonies, came from England, Scotland, Ireland, and France (the Huguenots). Many were skilled specialists who could compete successfully with their English counterparts. Nowhere is this more obvious than in the furniture industry. In the 1760s, 2 million Americans were buying less furniture from England than 200,000 Americans had bought at the beginning of the century. The upper classes also provided a market for other colonial luxury products such as silverware, wallpaper, and coaches.

Other artisans supplied their fellow colonists with shoes, hats, clothes, wigs, bread, beer, books, and newspapers. While most of these artisans were men, a surprisingly large number of women are noted in the records. Female dressmakers, milliners, hairdressers, and flower makers were common, but women were also active as shoemakers, as tinsmiths, and in other traditionally male occupations. Most women engaged in the retail trade; some also specialized in laying out the dead. Some of these women had helped their husbands while the latter were alive and then carried on the family trade when they were widowed.

No matter what the trade or craft, the standard method of learning it was similar, but not identical, to that followed in Europe at the time. The first step was apprenticeship. The apprentice agreed to work for a set number of years—usually four to seven years, but not past age eighteen for girls and twenty-one for men. Apprentices also agreed to serve their masters faithfully and not to marry during the term of service. The master promised to teach the apprentice the "art and mystery" of the craft; to provide the apprentice with the necessities of life; and perhaps to give the apprentice a set of tools at the completion of the apprenticeship. In addition, the master was usually expected to teach the apprentice reading, writing, and some arithmetic.

Ideally, the apprentice was treated as one of the family and might eventually marry into it. On the other hand, some masters cruelly exploited their apprentices, not giving them the proper training or even the proper food. This was more often true of compulsory apprentices—orphans or illegitimate children who were bound out as apprentices by the local authorities. Although supposedly protected by law, most apprentices preferred to solve their problems by running away—often to sea. Poor girls were also apprenticed out to learn sewing, spinning, weaving, fancy needlework, cooking, or baking. They usually served until they were married.

In the highly skilled trades, masters often charged a fee for taking an apprentice. This was done primarily to limit the number of apprentices and thus reduce future competition. However, in some crafts the lack of candidates for apprenticeship was so severe that masters in these trades often paid parents to apprentice their children to them and promised to teach their trade to these young people in three or four years rather than the more usual seven. This problem arose more commonly in the rural districts than in the towns. Since there were no formal schools for most of the colonial period, even professions such as law and medicine trained new practitioners by means of the apprenticeship system.

Once the period of apprenticeship was completed, the young man* became a journeyman and hired himself out to a master craftsman. If he had the necessary skill and had saved enough money, he might become a master craftsman himself. Unlike in Europe, no guilds existed to regulate the trades and limit individual initiative. However, a few relatively feeble attempts were made to create trade associations. In 1724 ten master carpenters formed the Carpenters Company of the City and County of Philadelphia to set prices and regulate wages in their industry. In the same year thirty-two Boston barbers organized to increase the prices for shaves and for making wigs. Other trade groups tried to form similar associations, but none was strong enough to carry out its purposes over any length of time.

Journeymen's associations were virtually nonexistent, and the only known strike during the colonial period took place in New York in 1758, when journeymen tailors walked off their jobs. Wages seem to have been the issue here, although modern workers would certainly also have protested the twelve-hour—and longer—days put in by colonial artisans. However, the work pace was slower during the colonial period, and breaks for food and liquid refreshment were frequent and lengthy.

It is difficult to generalize about wages during the colonial period. Certainly, they were higher (some allege that they were two to three times higher) than wages

---

*Rarely did a young woman go through this formal process to become a master.

for comparable crafts in England. Farm workers received the lowest wages (about £10 to £15 a year just before the Revolution), but if they were hired for a month or more, they usually also received room and board. Billy G. Smith in an article, "The Material Lives of Laboring Philadelphians," has estimated that in the late colonial period in Philadelphia, a family needed about £60 a year on which to live. In families headed by sailors and unskilled laborers whose wages were about £50 *if* they worked steadily all year, it is obvious that the wife, and probably the children, had to supplement the family income. Skilled workers such as shoemakers and tailors did earn slightly over £60, and masons, carpenters, tanners, and blacksmiths often made even more. Ship's captains earned only slightly more than skilled workers, but they had the opportunity to do some trading on their own.

Thus, despite its status as a nonindustrialized area, eighteenth-century America had a wide variety of enterprises which provided generous wages for its workers, met the needs of its own consumers, and produced 40 percent of that produced by Great Britain, with only one-third of the latter's population.

BIBLIOGRAPHY

BINING, ARTHUR C. *Pennsylvania Iron Manufacture in the Eighteenth Century.* Harrisburg, 1938.

BRIDENBAUGH, CARL. *The Colonial Craftsman.* New York, 1950.

BROWN, M. L. *Firearms in Colonial America: The Impact of History and Technology, 1492–1792.* Washington, D.C., 1980.

CLARK, VICTOR S. *History of Manufactures in the United States.* 3 vols. New York, 1929.

ELLSWORTH, LUCIUS F. *Technology in Early America.* Chapel Hill, 1966.

GOLDENBERG, JOSEPH A. *Shipbuilding in Colonial America.* Charlottesville, 1976.

INNES, HAROLD A. *The Cod Fisheries: The History of an International Economy.* New Haven, 1940.

MALONE, JOSEPH J. *Pine Trees and Politics: The Naval Stores and Forest Policy in Colonial New England, 1691–1775.* Seattle, 1964.

MORRIS, RICHARD B. *Government and Labor in Early America.* New York, 1946.

SMITH, PHILIP CHADWICK. *Seafaring in Colonial Massachusetts.* Charlottesville, 1981.

16
Money
and Social Status

In 1748 Cadwallader Colden, Lieutenant Governor of New York, complained in a letter about New York society that among the colonists, "the only principle of life propagated among the young people is to get money, and men are only esteemed according to what they are worth." Colden may have been correct, but his contemporaries might have muttered under their breath, "What kind of money?"; for one of the problems which most bedeviled the colonists was the lack of a suitable medium of exchange.

HARD MONEY

A few colonists were hard-money supporters who believed that silver and—to a lesser degree—gold should be the only media of exchange. They felt that any other forms of money would lead to inflation and instability. Most colonial Americans, however, if the actions of colonial assemblies are taken as representative of colonists' financial thinking, accepted Benjamin Franklin's contention in *A Modest Inquiry into the Nature and Necessity of a Paper Currency* (1729) that paper money was necessary to strengthen American "settlements, numbers, buildings, improvements, agriculture, shipping, and commerce" as well as to increase the "vent and demand for [English] commodities." Even some of the English governors such as William Burnet of New York, agreed in a 1724 letter to the Board of Trade that paper money "occasions much more trade and business than would be without it, and that more specie is exported to England."

However, the battle was not merely between the proponents of specie and of paper money. From the very beginning of the colonial period, the colonists used ingenuity and sometimes disingenuousness to solve this problem, but they satisfied neither themselves nor the English government.

In spite of a frantic search, no gold or silver was found in the British North American colonies. In line with prevalent mercantilist theory, the English government forbade the export of gold and silver coins from the country. This regulation, and virtually all future English monetary policy, was designed to minimize the supply of specie in the colonies and thus stifle the development of colonial industry and commerce.

The colonies tried to maintain a supply of hard money in two ways. One was to forbid the export of money. In the seventeenth century Massachusetts even had special officials to check ships before they sailed to make sure that no money was being smuggled out of the colony. The English government, however, soon forbade this practice.

The second method, overvaluing foreign coins to attract them into the colony, was more common and more effective. The most popular coin in colonial America was the Spanish silver dollar (or piece of eight reals), whose official value was four shillings six pence. As early as 1652 Massachusetts valued it at slightly under six shillings. Virginia responded by raising it to slightly over six shillings, New York went to six shillings nine pence, Pennsylvania paid seven shillings six pence, and in some colonies it was valued as high as eight shillings. The same thing happened to Portuguese "Joes" and the French pistole. This overvaluation made it possible for the planters of the southern colonies to pay their debts to the merchants and their taxes to the king in inflated currency. In addition, the increased number of coins in the hands of northern merchants made the latter more dangerous competitors of English merchants.

For all these reasons the English government made an attempt to halt this price war by proclaiming in 1704 that the maximum value of a Spanish dollar was six shillings. Even when penalties of six months in prison or a fine of £10 were added four years later, the edict proved difficult to enforce. Further, in spite of numerous and stringent laws against the practice, counterfeiting was common, and sweating (chemically removing part of a coin's metallic content) or clipping (shaving off the edges of a coin to lower its metallic value) were often practiced in the colonies (as they were in the mother country as well).

The only colony that ever dared coin money of its own (a royal prerogative) was Massachusetts, during the period from 1652 to 1684. These famous "pine tree shillings" contained less silver (seventy-two versus ninety-three grams) than English shillings; for this reason the Massachusetts government thought they would circulate only in the colony. However, English merchants raised their prices when their goods were to be paid for in pine tree shillings, and these coins, too, began to flow to England. In 1654 Massachusetts banned their export. In the same year the English government banned their production altogether, but the Massachusetts authorities circumvented this edict by stamping 1654 on all the coins they issued for the next thirty years.

MONETARY EXPERIMENTS

The lack of gold and silver coins forced the colonists to experiment with a wide variety of often exotic media of exchange. In the seventeenth century several of the northern colonies attempted to make wampum serve their purpose. (Hence the expression "shell out.") However, wampum varied in value too much to serve as legal tender. Its use died out by the eighteenth century. The same disadvantage also held for "country pay," or commodity money, which—depending on the colony—included commodities such as tobacco, wheat, rye, rice, corn, rum, cattle, sheep, and furs. Yet, all during the colonial period, one or more of these articles was accepted in payment of taxes, rents, school fees, and ordinary debts. However, these commodities fluctuated in value and were bulky and difficult to transport and store. In addition, most people tried to buy goods with the poorest quality of "country money."

Among themselves, merchants utilized bills of exchange—written orders to pay a set sum of money to a certain person or firm. Suppose that a New York merchant early in the eighteenth century bought goods worth £200 sterling from a London merchant. In order to pay the London merchant, the colonist would buy a bill of exchange from a mercantile firm that had an agent in London. The original merchant then sent the bill of exchange to the London merchant who had sold the goods, and the London merchant collected payment from the agent of the other firm. The price that the New York merchant had to pay for the bill of exchange was based on several factors. Probably the most important was the relative value of New York currency to the pound sterling. In the early part of the eighteenth century, about £150 of New York currency was worth £100 sterling. Thus, the price of the bill of exchange would have been about £300 in New York money.

However, because a bill of exchange from New York was usually not payable in London for thirty to forty days after issuance, the purchaser of a bill of exchange was usually allowed a small discount for the month or so that the seller of the bill had the money before actually disbursing it. On the other hand, a purchaser of a bill of exchange might sometimes be willing to pay a bit more for it in order to buy it from a firm which had a solid record of making good on its payments. (Some firms refused to honor a bill of exchange, and then its purchaser had to go through tedious and costly legal procedures.) Finally, supply and demand influenced the price of bills of exchange. If the colonial balance of payments became extremely unfavorable, bills became more costly, and the colonial buyer would choose to pay the London merchant with goods or (more rarely) with gold or silver, rather than purchase a bill at an exorbitant rate.

PAPER MONEY AND LAND BANKS

None of these forms of legal tender was satisfactory, however, and beginning in 1690 paper money was printed. The first paper money in the colonies, £7,000 worth, was issued by Massachusetts to pay the expenses of an expedition against Quebec in 1690. This early issue of paper money was limited in amount and duration, and because it was made legal tender for the payment of provincial taxes, it depreciated only slightly in value. However, during Queen Anne's War Massachusetts and the other New England colonies, New York, New Jersey, and the Carolinas printed large amounts of paper money which, although also legal tender for public obligations, gradually declined in value.

At first, because these issues of paper money were used to help finance military expeditions, England did not object to their issuance. Even when they were later used for the support of ordinary government projects, the English government remained neutral. Some colonies—Pennsylvania, Delaware, New Jersey, and Maryland—maintained a conservative fiscal policy. They issued only a limited amount of paper money, specified the purpose for which the money was to be used, and assessed taxes for its ultimate redemption. In these colonies the paper money circulated at, or close to, face value and proved an economic boon to the entire community. The creditor class—rich merchants and large landowners—even such staunch defenders of English interest as Governor William Keith of Pennsylvania and Thomas Pownall of Massachusetts, supported this type of paper-money policy.

In other parts of New England and in the southern colonies, these safeguards were not observed. While large amounts of money were printed, no provision was made for its redemption, and it was made legal tender. Thus, it had to be accepted in payment of debts. This led to rapid and extreme depreciation. (In Rhode Island paper money at one time was worth one–twenty-third of its face value.) Under these circumstances royal officials and the creditor class bitterly opposed the use of paper money, while small farmers and other debtors supported it just as vehemently.

If the struggle had remained purely domestic, the soft-money advocates would probably have triumphed. However, English merchants, who resented being paid in depreciated colonial currency, appealed to the English government. As early as 1706 the Board of Trade ordered royal governors to veto any paper issues which were declared to be legal tender or which were not to be redeemed by taxes within a set period of time. In 1740 the Board of Trade forbade governors to assent to the issuance of paper money unless the act clearly stipulated that it would not go into effect until approved by the king.

This law was difficult to enforce, even in the royal colonies; in New England it was completely ignored. In 1751, therefore, Parliament passed an act forbidding anyone from accepting as legal tender any paper money issued by the New England colonies. However, the New England colonies could still issue paper money for military or other governmental purposes, as long as it was redeemed within two years.

Because of the French and Indian War, the 1751 act was never enforced. On the contrary, military needs and the disruption of the economy led to the widespread printing of paper money, which was made legal tender in virtually every colony. As this money depreciated (which it did rapidly), merchants both in England and America once again sent their remonstrances to Parliament. In 1764 the Colonial Currency Act extended the 1751 New England regulations to all colonies. The English government viewed the problem so seriously that it even refused to allow paper money to be used for governmental purposes, as it had in New England. (This provision, however, was repealed in 1773 after continuous pressure from the colonists.) In addition, Parliament decreed that any governor who signed a law violating the Currency Act was liable to a fine of £1,000 and permanent displacement from office. To the colonists, on the other hand, the Currency Act seemed a grave threat to their economy (particularly since it came in the same year as the Sugar Act, which disrupted their trade with the West Indies).

A final experiment aimed at widening credit facilities was the land bank. In the eighteenth century all colonies except Virginia experimented with this institution. Pennsylvania organized a public loan office in 1722 which loaned up to £200 for eight years at 5 percent interest to any landowners willing to mortgage their property as security. Pennsylvania's land bank was a financial success along with those in Delaware and New Jersey. The most notorious land bank was chartered in Massachusetts. The plan of its founders was eventually to issue £150,000 in bills which were to be loaned to farmers willing to mortgage their lands. The farmers would then pay 3 percent interest a year over twenty years. In 1740, its first year of operation, the land bank issued a little less than £50,000 in bills to about 1,000 farmers, but the merchants absolutely refused to accept any of these bills in payment of their debts. The farmers were so incensed that in 1741 they marched on Boston and won control of the assembly. Since the assembly nominated the members of the governor's council, this body, too, became sympathetic to the "soft-money" policy. Governor Belcher, however, dissolved the assembly and refused to accept the new councillors; together with the merchants, he appealed for aid from England against the farmers. Parliament responded enthusiastically—not only did it apply, retroactively, the Bubble Act (a 1720 law outlawing joint stock companies not approved by Parliament) to the colonies, but it also stretched the act to include land banks as well. This ended the brief career of the Massachusetts land bank and ruined many of its backers, including the father of Samuel Adams.

WEALTH AND SOCIAL CLASS

Money and social class were related in the colonial period, even as it is now. Just as certain of Franklin's writings reflected most Americans' views on paper money, other of his writings exemplify American faith in the self-made man. In *Poor Richard's Almanac* Franklin popularized "Early to bed and early to rise . . .",

"Wide strokes fell great oaks," and similar sayings stressing industry and frugality. Franklin believed that these two attributes were the "means of procuring wealth, and thereby securing virtue."

This meshed very closely with the Puritan belief that God rewarded the elect in this world as well as the next, and both philosophies admirably suited conditions in a new land where opportunity for all (with the significant exception of slaves) far exceeded anything dreamed of in the Old World.

Although America was a land of opportunity, it was anything but a classless society. The European heritage was far too strong for colonial Americans to abandon the concept of social classes. John Winthrop advanced the "religious" argument in the *Modell of Christian Charity* (1630) that "God Almighty . . . hath so disposed of the condition of mankinde, as in all times, some may be rich, some poore, some high and eminent in power and dignitie; others meane and in subjection." Others defended social stratification for purely secular reasons.

However, the class structure of colonial America differed from the European pattern in two ways. Although originally planned for in Maryland and the Carolinas, the colonies lacked a hereditary nobility at the top, and it had a large (approximately 20 percent of the population at the time of the Revolution) slave class at the bottom. In addition, social mobility was so much greater in all the American colonies that European travelers commented on the confidence that most Americans had of rising in the social scale. While the rate of social mobility was never as high as this statement indicated, American social classes were not nearly as fixed as those in England. Americans tended to divide themselves loosely into three groups: the "better sort," or rich; the "middling sort," or yeomanry; and the "lower sort," or poor.

By the eighteenth century one may discern more precise gradations. The highest social class was made up of large landowners and/or wealthy merchants. These two groups may be combined: In the south the large planters carried on numerous mercantile activities; in the north the wealthy merchants often had widespread landed interests. During their term in America, royal governors headed—and the holders of other high royal offices were included in—the aristocracy. Below the aristocracy came the ordinary businesspersons, professionals, and wealthier farmers. The professions which merited this status varied by time and place. In seventeenth-century New England the clergy were certainly included in this group; in the south they rarely were included at any time during the colonial period. During the seventeenth century doctors and lawyers were conspicuously absent from this category. This attitude can be better understood when one notes that in 1690 no Boston physician had a medical degree and, of the seven lawyers in New York in 1700, two were ex-convicts and one had been a dancing master. However, between 1750 and 1775, although most lawyers still learned their craft by serving as apprentices to established lawyers, over 150 Americans had received formal training at the Inns of Court in London. Even those who remained in the colonies had Blackstone's *Commentaries* and other standard law books from which to study. The earliest bar association was organized in New York in 1729, and gradually most—but not all—

colonies began requiring that prospective lawyers pass an examination. With this improvement in their training, and their active participation in colonial politics (over half the delegates to the Albany, Stamp Act, and Continental congresses were lawyers), lawyers began to acquire a noticeably higher social status.

The bulk of the middle class was made up of small farmers. Probably half of all white Americans fell into this category. Skilled artisans were also respected members of the middle class. The lower class was composed of landless laborers. Most of these people worked only temporarily as tenant farmers or farm laborers; others filled the unskilled jobs in the towns or went to sea as sailors. At the bottom of the social ladder were the indentured servants (who made up only 2 percent of the population at the end of the colonial period) and, finally, the slaves.

The percentages of people who fell into these social classes also varied with time and place. At all times and places, however, class distinctions were least noticeable on the frontier. There almost all settlers owned the same-sized farms and had to spend their meager incomes on stock and tools and on otherwise improving their holdings. When artisans or a minister settled on the frontier, they usually combined their trade or profession with farming. Where land was free or inexpensive, it was rare to find landless workers; and under frontier conditions it was almost impossible to acquire large estates.

Even when the frontier stage passed, most of New England had what has been described as subsistence agriculture. In this type of agriculture, farm families raised enough to support themselves, with just enough surplus to purchase the few necessities which they could not produce. Typically, about 70 percent of the population owned their own farms, about 20 percent were farm workers or tenant farmers, and the remaining 10 percent were divided between a business and professional group (clergy, shopkeepers, tavern keepers, and millers) and necessary artisans such as blacksmiths or gunsmiths. Depending on the quality of the soil and the access to markets, inequality developed even in a society characterized by subsistence agriculture, but the differences in size and value of farms were not extreme, and the vast majority remained in the small-farmer class.

Subsistence agriculture was also found in the middle colonies and the south (particularly in North Carolina), but most parts of these two areas engaged in commercial agriculture, where crops were grown primarily for the wider market. This type of agriculture was generally practiced on large farms, causing wider deviations in wealth and social class, usually accompanied by a higher percentage of business and professional persons and more landless laborers. Yet, even in the southern colonies during the eighteenth century, where commercial agriculture was most developed, about 40 percent of the white population fell into the small-farmer category, members of which owned few, if any, slaves. The southern colonies differed from the middle colonies in having more tenant farmers and far fewer artisans (because many slaves fulfilled the latter function). Wealth and power were even more concentrated in the planter class of the south than in the aristocracies of the other two sections.

Yet, in many respects class distinctions were most extreme in urban areas, particularly in the northern towns. A group of wealthy merchants, who usually also had large landed interests, dominated these towns economically, socially, and politically. About 25 percent of a town's population was made up of shopkeepers and small traders; 30 percent (Charleston) to 50 percent (in the northern towns), of artisans; 3 percent, of professional men; and the remainder, of unskilled laborers, indentured servants, and slaves.

During the colonial period one was supposed to dress and conduct oneself in a manner suitable to one's station in life. Anyone dressed in silks and satins and wearing a huge powdered wig was telling the world that he or she was an aristocrat who did not have to perform any kind of work. Most colonies passed laws forbidding the wearing of such finery by those of lower status. For example, in the middle of the seventeenth century, Massachusetts forbade anyone whose estate was valued at less than £200 to wear "gold or silver lace," or other such ornaments. This law, as well as similar laws passed in other colonies, failed to prevent extravagant dress on the part of workers and even slaves. And in most cases—such as that of Ruth Hemenway who was tried in the Suffolk (Massachusetts) County Court in 1676 for "exceeding her ranke in her apparrell"—the defendant was found not guilty.

Various forms of address were connected with social class. Normally, aristocrats were referred to by the title "esquire" and the wives as "madam." Upper middle-class couples were "ladies" and "gentlemen," and those just below them were "mister" and "mistress." Even the small farmer and his wife were addressed as "goodman" and "goodwife," but no one below this level was accorded any title. Seating in church—"dooming the seats" as the Puritans termed it—or one's place in a class at Harvard College was determined by social class. Even punishment might vary depending on social class: The aristocrat never had to suffer corporal punishment.

SOCIAL MOBILITY

As noted, the effects of social stratification in colonial America were mitigated by social mobility. Here again time, place, and type of agriculture played an important role. Indentured servants had much more opportunity to improve their status in the seventeenth century than in the eighteenth century. Forty-three percent of the members of the Virginia House of Burgesses in 1670 were former indentured servants. Yet, even in the eighteenth century, Charles Thomson, secretary of the Continental Congress, and two signers of the Declaration of Independence began their American careers as indentured servants.

Upward mobility was more difficult in the more settled areas and where commercial rather than subsistence agriculture was practiced. However, the chances of a landless person acquiring a small plot of less fertile land remained fairly good. An immigrant with any type of skill had a much better chance of advancement than one who did not. At any time skilled workers could go into business for themselves and eventually utilize their savings to buy a farm. Prestige attached to landownership, while artisans and shopkeepers though not poor were often included among the "inferior orders of people."

By the eighteenth century it was extremely difficult for a self-made colonist to amass a large estate. Most of the Virginia aristocrats were descended from immigrants who arrived during the last half of the seventeenth century. Some, like the Randolphs and the Washingtons, came from the English country gentleman class or were younger sons of peers; however, most, like the Carters and Byrds, came from the middle class. Still, the availability of cheap or free land, the general economic expansion of the colonies, and the lack of social or legal restrictions on whites led to a high rate of social mobility. One's standing in the colonies depended on wealth and property rather than on one's inherited status.

Social class and material wealth became more and more closely related as the colonial period progressed. Alice Hanson Jones in her work, *Wealth of a Nation To Be,* estimated that the colonies in 1774 were "very nearly on a par in per capita income with England, but somewhat lower in wealth." (The average per capita wealth of free persons was £38 in New England, £46 in the middle colonies, and £93—including £31 worth of servants and slaves—in the south.) Jones also showed that by this date the wealthiest 10 percent of the colonial population owned 51 percent of the total wealth, while the bottom 10 percent owned less than 0.5 percent of the wealth. A similar study "Economic Development and Social Structure in Colonial Boston" by James A. Henretta for Boston shows that in 1771 the upper 15 percent of society controlled 66 percent of the assessable wealth (a significant increase from the 52 percent they controlled in 1687, the earliest year covered by this study). A study of Chester County, Pennsylvania, "The Distribution of Wealth in Eighteenth-Century America" by Lemon and Nash describes how the share of the assessed wealth of the lowest 10 percent of society declined from 5.8 percent to 0.7 percent from 1693 to 1760, while the share of the top 10 percent increased from 23.8 percent to 29.9 percent during the same period.

The fact that their social status was based on wealth—often recently acquired wealth—rather than on feudal title or longstanding inherited wealth, somewhat diminished the prestige enjoyed by colonial aristocrats. "A man who has money here, no matter how he came by it, he is everything," said a Rhode Island sea captain. William Byrd of Virginia was the son of a goldsmith; the Livingston family of New York descended from a Scottish parson. The entry into the aristocracy of merchants such as Thomas Hancock of Boston or Henry Laurens of Charleston (whose father was a saddler) was ever more rapid. Nevertheless, they did expect—and usually received—the deference of ordinary folk. Much of this respect was earned by service in their local governments, colonial legislatures, or in military or church offices. Even though the aristocrats tended to monopolize the more important of these offices, they found it necessary to heed the voice of the people. A Pennsylvania newspaper stated that "the meanest among them [the ordinary people] thinks he has a right to civility from the greatest," and it is therefore not surprising that two-thirds of the colonial aristocracy supported the Revolution. As Richard Hofstadter notes, colonial America was a "middle class world."

BIBLIOGRAPHY

BILLIAS, GEORGE A. *The Massachusetts Land Bankers of 1740.* Orono, Me., 1959.

BOCK, LESLIE. *The Currency System of the American Colonies, 1700–1764.* New York, 1975.

BRIDENBAUGH, CARL. *Myths and Realities: Societies of the Colonial South.* Baton Rouge, 1952.

ERNST, JOSEPH. *Money and Politics in America, 1755–1775: A Study in the Currency Act of 1764 and the Political Economy of Revolution.* Chapel Hill, 1973.

HENRETTA, JAMES. *The Evolution of American Society, 1700–1815.* Lexington, 1973.

JERNEGAN, MARCUS W. *Laboring and Dependent Classes in Colonial America.* Chicago, 1931.

JONES, ALICE HANSON. *Wealth of a Nation To Be: The American Colonies on the Eve of the Revolution.* New York, 1980.

LESTER, RICHARD A. *Monetary Experiments.* Princeton, 1939.

MAIN, JACKSON T. *The Social Structure of Revolutionary America.* Princeton, 1965.

McCUSKER, JOHN J. *Money and Exchange in Europe and America, 1600–1775: A Handbook.* Chapel Hill, 1978.

NASH, GARY B. *Class and Society in Early America.* Englewood Cliffs, N.J., 1970.

NETTELS, CURTIS P. *The Money Supply of the American Colonies before 1720.* Madison, 1934.

NEWMAN, ERIC P. *The Early Paper Money of America.* Racine, 1967.

PERKINS, EDWIN J. *The Economy of Colonial America.* New York, 1980.

PRICE, JACOB M. *Capital and Credit in British Overseas Trade: The View from the Chesapeake, 1700–1776.* Cambridge, 1980.

17
The Colonial Town

Although towns may have contained no more than 9 percent of the colonial population at their peak, (and only 4 to 5 percent by the end of the colonial period), they were important enough—economically, culturally, and politically—to merit a chapter of their own. In fact, Carl Bridenbaugh, the leading student of colonial urban life, maintained in the conclusion of his volume, *Cities in Revolt,* that colonial towns developed an urban character and came to dominate the rest of colonial society. He also states that "the culture of the late colonial period was of urban origin."

CHARACTERISTICS
OF COLONIAL TOWNS

Location was the crucial factor in the growth and success of colonial towns. In an era when commerce was the major source of wealth, the definition of a good location automatically included a good harbor and a clear water route to the interior. New York at the mouth of the Hudson River; Boston at the mouth of the Charles River; Philadelphia between the Schuylkill and Delaware rivers; and Charleston between the Ashley and Cooper rivers all met these twin criteria. Newport, the fifth leading colonial town, had a fine harbor but lacked the easy access to the interior. Boston, too, had a relatively small hinterland. Perhaps that is why, in addition to their proximity to each other, both towns declined in relative importance as seaports during the final years of the colonial period.

One should not confuse the colonial town with a modern city. Almost every home had a large yard in which vegetables were grown, and families kept a milk cow, poultry, and perhaps a pig (when the latter were not wandering the streets). Most houses were built of wood, though brick houses became more common in the eighteenth century. For example, in 1722 Boston had about 3,000 houses, of which one-third were built of brick.

Boston was the largest town for most of the colonial period, but after the 1740s its growth ceased. By the end of the colonial period, both Philadelphia and New York far exceeded it in population.

	1690	1720	1743	1775
Boston	7,000	12,000	16,000	16,000
Philadelphia	4,000	10,000	13,000	40,000
New York	3,900	7,000	11,000	25,000
Newport	2,600	3,800	6,200	11,000
Charleston	1,100	3,500	6,800	12,000

The governments of these towns varied greatly. Boston and Newport enjoyed the most autonomy, possessing the town-meeting form of government. In Boston every male whose estate was valued at £20 for tax purposes was eligible to vote. By the end of the eighteenth century, 212 town officials were elected at Boston and 188 at Newport. The most important of these offices—those of selectmen, town clerk, moderator (of the town meeting), and overseers of the poor—were generally in the hands of the merchant class. Lesser offices were held by the middle class. All offices were unpaid, and citizens often preferred to pay a fine rather than accept office.

New York and Philadelphia had governments modeled after the medieval English borough, or town. Each was ruled by a chartered corporation consisting of a mayor, recorder, aldermen, and councilmen. At first the aldermen and councilmen were self-perpetuating groups, but after 1731 the freemen of New York (but not Philadelphia) were able to vote for both. However, during most of the eighteenth century, freemen of Philadelphia who possessed taxable estates worth £50 were empowered by the Pennsylvania assembly to elect a variety of boards to work with (or later, in place of) the corporation in financing and supervising services for the town. These groups rarely worked harmoniously with each other or with the corporation, and therefore municipal services were somewhat limited both in quantity and quality.

Charlestonians tried till the very end of the colonial period to convince the South Carolina assembly to issue them a municipal charter, but they never did receive one. The South Carolina legislature governed the town directly, and before 1712 commissioners appointed by the assembly supervised the enforcement of these acts. The only taste of self-government enjoyed by some Charlestonians was through the parish, where male Anglicans with an estate valued at £60 (proclamation money) were allowed to vote for churchwardens, vestrymen, and officials dealing with markets, weights, measures, roads, poor relief, and police and fire protection. This helps explain why Charleston generally provided its citizens with fewer and poorer services than any of the other towns.

Whatever the form of colonial government, colonial towns all voiced a complaint that is still heard today. The towns felt that their colonial assemblies were forcing them to pay an unfair proportion of their colony's taxes without giving them adequate representation in the legislature. In the middle of the eighteenth century, New York City, which had one-fifth of the population of the colony, was assessed one-third of the colony's taxes. Philadelphia which paid 43 percent of Pennsylvania's property taxes, had only four representatives out of twenty-seven in the provincial council and two representatives in the assembly; on the basis of population, it was entitled to four, and on the basis of taxes paid to almost eight. This underrepresentation meant that towns tended to receive far less money from the legislature than their contributions or needs dictated.

Another characteristic typical of American towns during the colonial period (as of towns today) was heterogeneity. New York exhibited this trait most strongly. Eighteen different languages were spoken there as early as 1643. Philadelphia, too, included Dutch, Swedish, Welsh, Irish, Scotch-Irish, Swiss, and German inhabitants within a few years of its founding. Charleston had the largest Huguenot population, although some Huguenots were found in all colonial towns. Boston and Newport were more homogeneous, although the latter, because of Rhode Island's religious tolerance, had the largest Jewish community in the colonies. Blacks were found in all towns, making up in the early 1750s about 40 percent of Charleston's population; 16 percent of New York's and of Newport's population; 8 percent of Boston's; and 4 percent of Philadelphia's.

The earliest towns grew up haphazardly, but Charleston and Philadelphia were carefully planned. Both were organized in a checkerboard pattern with wide straight streets laid out before any buildings were erected. Peter Kalm in his *Travels into North America* described Philadelphia's streets as "regular, pretty . . . and fifty feet . . . broad." In contrast, streets in the other three towns tended to be narrow and crooked, although many were widened in the eighteenth century. A few streets in Boston and New York had cobblestones, but at the end of the seventeenth century, most streets in all five towns (Boston, Philadelphia, New York, Newport, and Charleston) were unpaved. This condition greatly improved, however, by 1720. By that time most of Boston's main streets were paved. By the end of the colonial period, the main streets in all five towns (with some exceptions in Charleston) were well paved. By this time, too, raised sidewalks were found in most towns, and all towns had named their streets and numbered their houses. These improvements were carried out by means of special tax assessments or by requiring that each householder work a few days a year on road improvement (or hire someone as a substitute).

URBAN PROBLEMS

Keeping the streets clean was a serious problem. In spite of possible fines, town dwellers threw refuse and rubbish out of their doors and windows indiscriminately. At first householders were held responsible for cleaning the street in front of their homes. When this system failed, scavengers were hired to do this work. Probably the most efficient scavengers were the innumerable hogs who wandered the streets. However, the hogs interfered with traffic, and most towns tried—with varying degrees of success—to force their owners to keep them penned up. For a brief period in the early eighteenth century, Boston employed the services of eight scavengers, but the selectmen decided that the expense was too great. However, the return to the old system proved disastrous, and Boston (and eventually the other towns) returned to the use of paid scavengers.

Sewage disposal was, to put it mildly, inefficient. Most sewage was deposited in the closest body of water. Early in the eighteenth century, however, Boston and New York began to build underground sewers, and the other towns gradually followed. By the end of the colonial period, cities were utilizing both public and private funds to construct a system of conduits and sewers to dispose of waste materials.

Traffic problems developed as early as the seventeenth century and only increased in the eighteenth. Livestock and cattle clogged the streets. Not until the 1740s did most towns pass laws such as Charleston's, which ordered that all livestock found at large should be seized and either slaughtered or donated to the poor. Fortunately, at this early period few people could afford to own coaches, but hackney (public) coaches were already becoming available. Porters, packhorses, wheelbarrows, and, in the winter, sleighs—but, above all, carts—tied up traffic all over colonial towns. Carters were licensed and regulated by the town governments, but they typically ignored traffic rules—particularly those limiting the size and weight of carts. Traffic accidents, some fatal, were frequent, and the noise in the busy streets was deafening. Fines were levied for "galloping" or "irregular riding" through the streets but did little to solve the problem.

Streets were doubly hazardous at night. Not only were pedestrians in danger of being run over, but they also faced the possibility of being robbed. Better street lighting was viewed as a possible solution to both these problems. Even before the end of the seventeenth century, New York ordered its citizens to hang a lantern on a pole outside every seventh house (all seven householders to share the expense). Other towns tried similar measures, but it was not until the middle of the eighteenth century that the citizens of Philadelphia made a realistic attempt to light their streets. In 1749 a large number of them voluntarily agreed to put lamps in front of their houses and to pay a lamplighter to tend them. The following year the Pennsylvania legislature voted to tax the people of Philadelphia for a municipal lighting system. In 1751 the first whale-oil lamps were placed in the streets of Philadelphia, and within fifteen years the town could boast of 320 such lamps and an ordinance fining anyone who broke one of them £20. Other towns followed a similar pattern.

Private citizens voluntarily supplied their streets with lamps until laws were passed giving municipal authorities the power to tax for street lighting. By the time of the Revolution, only Newport retained the system of private street lighting.

Even with better street lighting, maintaining the peace remained a problem in all colonial towns. All able-bodied male freemen were expected to serve a term as constable, but many preferred to pay an (often stiff) fine rather than serve. Constables were on duty in the daytime. Citizens were even more reluctant to serve at night, and most towns were forced to hire watchmen for this duty. These watchmen carried a long staff, a lantern, and a rattle to frighten away thieves (hence the name "rattle watch"). They enforced the curfew which was designed to keep the streets clear at night. During the wars of the eighteenth century, it often became necessary for troops to reinforce the ordinary watch.

During the seventeenth century most crimes were what one would expect in a seaport. Sailors were often drunk or disorderly, petty theft was common, and prostitutes plied a busy trade. Waterfront areas were particularly notorious, and even Philadelphia had a section known as "Hell Town." During the eighteenth century criminals became more sophisticated and more commercial. Housebreaking, robbery, and counterfeiting were complained of in every town.

American law codes tended to be somewhat more humane than the laws in effect in England during the same period. Burglary, robbery, and other crimes against property—which were punishable by death in England—were considered much less serious in the colonies. Usually offenders were expected to make restitution and to suffer some form of public humiliation; this was supposed to punish them and deter spectators from committing similar crimes. If the culprit was unable to make restitution, he or she might be bound out as a servant—often to the victim of the crime.

Prison terms were rare because the colonists saw no reason to support anyone in idleness. Prisoners had to pay for their own meals, and three convicts died of starvation in Philadelphia as late as 1772. Prisons—although cold, damp, and unclean—had the advantage, for most of the colonial period, of being rather ramshackle, and offenders were able to escape from them easily. Even the Philadelphia prison, the most substantial such institution in the colonies, suffered fifteen successful jailbreaks in three years. One group of prisoners who fled the Newport jail in 1737 mocked their former jailer by leaving behind a poem.

The only group of prisoners who might look forward to lengthy jail terms were debtors. This was done primarily to prevent them from leaving town without paying their debts. About fifty of these unfortunates were confined in Philadelphia's prison just prior to the Revolution, and the other towns each had their quota. It was only at this late period that debtors were separated from other prisoners.

Whipping was the most common form of punishment during the colonial period, followed by the use of the stocks and pillory. (One sat in the stocks and stood in the pillory.) Women who were convicted as common scolds might be punished in the seventeenth century by means of the ducking stool, although husbands might save them by paying a fine. The practice of forcing a convicted criminal to wear a letter designating his or her crime—"D" for drunkard, "T" for thief—was common, and repetition of the crime might result in the branding of the letter on the person's forehead. Other criminals were punished by having one or both ears cut off, having their tongue bored, or having their nose slit. Those who were eligible to plead benefit of clergy (which by the eighteenth century included almost anyone who could read) were merely branded on the thumb for the first offense. (This was the punishment for those English soldiers convicted for their participation in the Boston Massacre.)

At different times and in different colonies, the number of offenses punishable by death varied. The Massachusetts Body of Liberties included twelve capital crimes. This number doubled before the end of the seventeenth century and then declined again during the eighteenth. Pennsylvania began with only one capital crime and gradually increased the list to eighteen. Connecticut had fifteen; New York, sixteen; and Delaware, twenty.

Yet, typically, the death penalty was rarely invoked except for murder or piracy. Even a slave who attempted to incite his fellows to revolt—a crime which certainly would have been punishable by death in the nineteenth century—"escaped" with several floggings and the wearing of an iron collar for life. Probably, the shortage of labor helps explain this "leniency." Hanging was by far the most popular form of capital punishment in colonial America. Hangings were gala events attended by all classes and ages of citizens. Over 5,000 people attended the last hangings for piracy in the colonies—at Newport in 1760.

Concerned as colonial Americans were about crime, they worried much more about the danger of fire. Most houses were built of wood and built close together. All types of laws were passed to diminish the danger of fire. Roofs made with straw or thatch were declared illegal. Fire wardens checked chimneys and flues regularly. Yet, even in the eighteenth century, more fires were blamed on sooty chimneys than on any other factor. Homeowners were expected to put out—or, at least, cover up—their fires at night. They were also required to keep a bucket and ladder ready in case of fire. After a series of disastrous fires, the Massachusetts legislature decreed that all houses must be built of stone or brick; however, the law was not enforced.

Boston had a fire engine as early as 1679. It was pumped by hand and had to be filled with buckets. In that same year the town was divided into quarters—each under the supervision of a militia officer. This officer was in charge of ladders, buckets, hooks, axes, and gunpowder (used to destroy houses to stop the spread of fires). If a fire broke out, the men under his control were expected to form a double line between the burning building and the nearest source of water. One line passed full buckets from the water to the fire; the other passed them in the reverse direction to be refilled.

Other towns followed Boston's lead. Nevertheless, serious fires broke out in all of them. One of the worst—in Boston in 1711—destroyed over a hundred homes. As a result of this fire, the Boston Fire Society was organized in 1717, the first volunteer firefighting company in the colonies. Within twenty-five years seven more companies were organized in Boston, including 102 men in all. The first company reaching the scene of a fire received a bonus of £5. Yet, in spite of all their efforts, in 1760 the worst fire in Boston's history destroyed over 400 buildings.

Benjamin Franklin organized Philadelphia's first firefighting company, the Union Fire Company, in 1736, and sixteen more were organized there by the time of the Revolution. As Franklin wrote in his *Autobiography* the members of his company met monthly for social purposes and to exchange "such ideas as occurred to us on the subject of fires." Similar groups were formed in all the other towns except Charleston. That city tragically suffered from its lack of fire fighting personnel when, in 1740, it was struck by the most severe fire of the entire colonial period. Over 300 dwellings, as well as stores and warehouses, were destroyed, at an estimated loss of over £200,000. Fire insurance companies were organized in the northern towns, but they tended to be ephemeral. The first successful company was organized by Franklin and the members of the Union Fire Company.

Obviously, a plentiful water supply was necessary for more reasons than just putting out fires (though serving as a beverage was not high on the list). During the seventeenth century springs and wells—both public and private—furnished an adequate water supply for all five towns. As time went on, more wells were dug by public agencies, and officials were appointed to see that these wells were kept in good condition and fitted with pumps if necessary. By the middle of the eighteenth century, the citizens of New York and Charleston were complaining of brackish water, but the other towns still had no real problems except when the pumps froze in the winter. New York was in the process of constructing public waterworks at the time of the Revolution. The plan was to supply water to the entire town from a central reservoir by means of hollow log pipes.

THE URBAN ECONOMY

By modern standards the population of colonial towns was miniscule. Yet, in 1690, when Boston had a population of 7,000, only four cities in England had a population over 10,000. In 1775 Philadelphia's population of 40,000 made it larger than any English city except London.

Therefore, colonial towns were substantial concentrations of people. This, in turn, led to the development of a wide variety of businesses and industries. Four towns (again Charleston was a temporary exception) immediately established one or more market days where, at a set location, farmers could sell their produce to the townspeople. As towns spread out, additional markets were opened. Some of these markets sold only specific goods—for example, only fish, meat, or vegetables. Boston, New York, and Philadelphia also sponsored fairs where cattle and other merchandise could be purchased. Town authorities carefully policed these markets and fairs as well as other local businesses. In New England laws were passed regulating prices and wages, weights and measures, standards of quality, and rates of interest. Unfair business practices such as forestalling (selling before the market officially opened) or engrossing (buying large amounts of a product in order to increase its price) were sternly punished.

The most commonly regulated item, both in price and quality, was bread; but bricks, casks, leather goods, and numerous other items were also subject to inspection in most towns. If a particular product—usually food—was scarce, its exportation would be forbidden. More often increased production of a commodity was encouraged by bounties, exemption from taxation, or even by granting a monopoly.

Numerous other businesses and industries grew up in every town. (These have been covered in an earlier chapter.) One business, however, was typically—though far from exclusively—urban. Taverns served townspeople as social, political, and economic centers. Here colonists enjoyed food, drink, games of cards, backgammon, billiards, and sociability. Business deals were discussed, electioneering took place, and captains signed on their crews. These taverns varied in quality from the bawdy waterfront taverns to the staid taverns where the members of the General Court dined. Coffee houses and restaurants (where take-out food was also available) were also well patronized. All towns required that their taverns obtain a license; these could be revoked if liquor was sold on Sunday or after hours, if prices were excessive, or if standard services were not available.

In the seventeenth century colonial towns, like their European models, limited the right to do business or work in them to legal residents—those who had received the freedom of the town. This practice was relaxed in the following century, but towns still "warned out" those people whom they feared might become public charges. However, the large numbers of immigrants who arrived by sea and the large number of refugees from Indian attacks (resulting from the Anglo-French wars) who arrived from the frontier created a severe problem for colonial towns. The number of indigents was further increased by the depressions that followed most of these wars, ruining many previously prosperous townspeople.

Church and private groups were active in this area, but public support was badly needed. As would be expected, the colonists relied on English precedents. Taxes were levied to shelter the sick or aged poor, at first in private homes, and later in poorhouses. The able-bodied poor were sent to a workhouse, which in seventeenth-century Boston was also the town jail. Orphans were bound out as apprentices until they came of age. The extent of the poverty problem toward the end of the colonial period may be judged from the fact that in 1760 Boston had 230 people in the workhouse; 40 in the poorhouse; and still others receiving some relief. To cover the expenses involved, the tax rate had to be 80 percent higher in the period between 1760 and 1764 than it had been a decade earlier (though later it was reduced to the 1750s level). Philadelphia's tax rate increased 250 percent over the same period (and was not reduced); yet, in 1776 the wardens of the poorhouse were quoted in the *Pennsylvania Gazette* of May 29th, as stating that many of their inmates were "naked and helpless, and emaciated with Poverty and Disease to such a Degree that some have died in a few days after their Admission."

One of the problems which troubled all townspeople, but the poor most of all, was the shortage of fuel. This shortage was not serious in the seventeenth century, when the areas surrounding the towns were still well forested. However, by the beginning of the eighteenth century in Boston (and later in the other towns), this was no longer true. The price of wood rose rapidly, especially if the winter was long and cold. Inspectors were appointed in an effort to ensure that wood sellers gave their customers a full bundle of wood; however, this had no effect on the constantly rising prices. At times such as these, towns had to appropriate special funds to buy wood for their poor. The use of coal was no solution to this problem because coal came mainly from England or Wales and was much more expensive than wood.

Towns began as European outposts on American soil; but unhampered by the traditions that bound their European counterparts, they developed a uniquely American character. Until about the middle of the eighteenth century, these towns developed a sense of civic responsibility, which is illustrated by the cooperative and innovative methods by which they tried to solve their problems. In spite of undoubted social stratification, most townspeople shared a unity of purpose and values—a much more sophisticated and cosmopolitan outlook on life than that held by rural Americans.

However, perhaps as early as the 1740s (according to Carl Bridenbaugh, in his *Cities in Revolt*) wars, depressions, and their attendant dislocations disturbed the urban consensus. Gary B. Nash in *The Urban Crucible* points specifically to the poverty and rising taxes caused by the French and Indian War as crucial causes of the discontent of city artisans and laborers. This situation was exacerbated by the laws passed by the English government to control colonial trade, which laws fell particularly heavily on the towns. Already a separate entity from the tidewater and the frontier, colonial towns became the most anti-English part of America. As Bridenbaugh wrote, "Revolt would never have succeeded—nay, it would hardly have been attempted" without the presence of colonial towns.

URBAN CULTURE

Much of this chapter has dealt with urban problems. Nevertheless, town life had many compensations. Towns imported European ideas and tastes as well as European goods. As with the goods, towns dispersed these new ideas to their hinterlands. Most of the colonial intellectual, cultural, and artistic achievements were produced in the towns. Townspeople typically had the money and leisure to read books, magazines, and newspapers. Also, their sheer numbers made possible the presentation of plays, concerts, and exhibitions. One must agree with the statement of Governor Francis Bernard of Massachusetts who wrote to Lord Barrington in 1760 that when he was in the country, he missed the "refined conversation and the amusements that arise from letters, arts, and sciences" which were only available in town.

The advantages—economic, cultural, and social—of town life were such that by the time of the Revolution, the original five urban centers were joined by fifteen other towns with populations of from 3,000 to 8,000 people. When one adds

FIGURE 17A   (Library of Congress.)

General Thomas Gage's economic assessment written to Lord Barrington in August 1772 that "[American] cities flourish and increase by extensive Trade" the significance of towns in colonial America begins to be appreciated.

BIBLIOGRAPHY

ALEXANDER, JOHN K. *Render Them Submissive: Responses to Poverty in Philadelphia, 1760-1800.* Amherst, 1980.

ARCHDEACON, THOMAS J. *New York City, 1664-1710: Conquest and Change.* Ithaca, 1976.

BRIDENBAUGH, CARL. *Cities in Revolt: Urban Life in America, 1743-1776.* New York, 1955.

BRIDENBAUGH, CARL, and BRIDENBAUGH, JESSICA. *Rebels and Gentlemen: Philadelphia in the Age of Franklin.* New York, 1942.

GREENBERG, DOUGLAS. *Crime and Law Enforcement in Colonial New York, 1691-1776.* Ithaca, 1976.

REPS, JOHN W. *The Making of Urban America: A History of City Planning in the United States.* Princeton, 1965.

WERTENBAKER, THOMAS J. *The Golden Age of Colonial Culture.* New York, 1942.

18

The Colonial Family

In the colonial period the family was the basic unit of social, economic, and (often) political life: the "sacred cement" (as Franklin called it) of human society. The development of stable family life was a high priority of the early colonies. This is evidenced by the importation of wives into Virginia by the London Company in 1619. Later, colonies encouraged men to marry by both positive and negative means. Some New England towns, for example, promised free land, a very attractive incentive, to any male upon marriage. Maryland and Pennsylvania, on the other hand, placed a special tax on bachelors, while seventeenth-century Connecticut refused to allow them to live alone.

MARRIAGE

Few women remained unmarried because until late in the colonial period, men outnumbered women by about three to two. To remain unwed was considered to be a disgrace for a woman. William Byrd called his own twenty-year-old daughter Evelyn, an "antique virgin" in a letter to his friend the Earl of Orrery and commented on a sister-in-law of a friend who often "bewail'd her fate as an unmarried woman." It was a great shock to an eighteenth-century Bostonian to meet a thirty-year-old spinster who maintained that she remained unwed by choice not necessity. If a marriage was broken by death, the surviving partner usually lost no time in choosing another mate. Edward Winslow of Plymouth was a widower of seven weeks when he married Susanna White, a widow of twelve weeks.

By custom (and by law in many colonies) parental consent was necessary for marriage unless the man involved was over twenty-one and the woman over sixteen. The Plymouth colony punished any attempt to marry without parental consent by "fine or corporal punishment or both." Plymouth records indicate that in 1678 one John Lorin was convicted "of making love to Mary Willis without her parents consent" and fined £5. Nevertheless, a father usually asked his daughter's opinion of her suitor. Eliza Lucas (later Pinckney) wrote her father in 1740 when she was not yet eighteen rejecting a suggested match with the heated words:

> ... that the riches of Chile and Peru put together, if he had them, could not purchase a sufficient Esteem for him to make him my husband.

In a similar vein Judge Samuel Sewall of Boston wrote his daughter Elizabeth in 1699 recommending a suitor to her but adding:

> If you find in yourself an imovable incurable Aversion from him [a suitor], and cannot love, and honour, and obey him, I shall say no more, nor give you any further trouble in this matter.

In cases where a father disapproved of a girl's choice of a husband, the girls did not always give in. Toward the end of the colonial period, three of the four daughters of Philip Schuyler, later a general in the Revolutionary War, married without his permission.

If all agreed to the marriage, however, the two fathers then worked out the financial arrangements so important in upper- and middle-class marriages. These arrangements differed greatly depending on the wealth and position of the parents, but generally, the young man's parents were expected to be the most generous, providing land, a house, cattle, and tools. The bride's parents contributed clothing, furniture, linens, and money. When all financial arrangements were settled, the banns were read, and the couple was officially considered to be engaged.

Often the custom of bundling was practiced during the period between engagement and marriage. Bundling permitted the couple to bed together for the night. This custom probably arose because it was almost impossible for the couple to have both privacy and warmth in the small, freezing homes of New England and the middle colonies. Although they were supposed to keep their clothes on and to abstain from sexual relations, one finds a significant number of early babies among the firstborn children of these couples. Often they were forced to confess their sin publicly in church before their baby could be baptized. Yet, as late as 1761 so stern a moralist as John Adams stated in a letter to his two young nieces, "I cannot wholly disapprove of bundling." Not until the time of the Revolutionary War, when our French allies misunderstood the rules of the game, did the practice of bundling come to an end in most areas of the United States.

As noted, banns were read in church on several consecutive Sundays—as well as publicly posted—to announce an upcoming wedding. This was necessary because, all too often, one of the partners to the marriage had been married previously either in Europe or in some other part of America. Even the reading of banns was not fool-proof. One woman was granted a divorce in Plymouth because her husband was found to have one wife in England, one in the West Indies, and one in Boston.

During the seventeenth century marriage in New England was viewed as a purely civil matter, and marriage ceremonies were performed by a magistrate. After 1686, however, Massachusetts followed the custom of most of the other colonies, and marriages were performed by a minister. Quaker marriages took place at the meeting without the presence of clergy. No matter what type of ceremony was performed, it was almost impossible to dissolve a marriage by legal means. In the New England colonies and Pennsylvania, divorce was permissible for adultery or desertion. Impotence, a previous marriage, or marriage between close relatives were causes for annulment.

Sometimes a legal separation was possible, but this solution did not work out too well for one of Judge Sewall's sons, whose wife scandalized the community by having a child during the third year of their separation. More often, at least among the "common folk," the husband or the wife merely ran away. If they remained in the vicinity, a court might order the couple to reunite. However, if one partner disappeared completely, the remaining mate was allowed to remarry after a delay of from one to seven years. For example, Benjamin Franklin's wife had been deserted by her first husband, but, as Franklin noted in his *Autobiography* (1730), "there were no great objections to our union."

PREMARITAL AND EXTRAMARITAL AFFAIRS

Premarital sex relations were frowned upon. Fines and floggings were utilized to discourage both partners in these affairs. It was the woman, however, who suffered most if an illegitimate child resulted from these unions. Judge Sewall records several cases in which women were executed for murdering their illegitimate children. In seventeenth century New England, however, the man named as the father by the mother was required to support the child. Apparently, some women lied about the person responsible, as one New England woman wrote to her lover that she would either kill her child or accuse another man of being its father.

Sexual relations outside of marriage, as well as rape and sodomy, were found among all classes but most commonly among indentured servants, who were forbidden to marry without the permission of their master. This consent was practically never given, even if both were servants of the same master, because of the possibility of pregnancy and the resulting loss of the female's labor. Yet, since both male and female indentured servants often slept in the same room, little impediment stood in the way of sexual intercourse. Female indentured servants were often taken advantage of by their master or by male members of his family. In a case in Virginia in 1639, the master involved in such a case was ordered to appear in church in a white sheet, but the woman was still whipped. It is not surprising, then, that the birth rate of illegitimate children among female indentured servants was much higher than that found among free women. In seventeenth-century Virginia the penalty for a female indentured servant having an illegitimate child was an extension of service for two years or a fine of 2,000 pounds of tobacco. If the child was fathered by a black man—as one-fourth to one-third of them were—the penalty was a public whipping and another full term of indentured servitude. In New England, however, the court records indicate that female indentured servants were given the benefit of the doubt, and several masters were punished for forcing their attention on them.

Adultery was considered a serious offense all during the colonial period. It was legally punishable by death in seventeenth-century New England, and John Winthrop records a case in 1643 in which both the man and woman were condemned to die. However, even during the seventeenth century and certainly later, the guilty parties were only symbolically executed by having to stand on the gallows with a rope around their necks. Actually, they were punished by a whipping, a fine, or having to wear (or be branded with) the letter "A." In the eighteenth century the male involved in an adulterous affair could be prosecuted for abduction; a wife was not considered to have the power to consent—even to illicit sexual relations.

CHARACTERISTICS OF THE FAMILY

Contrary to earlier belief, the colonial family was closer to the modern nuclear family than to the extended family—consisting of several generations—which was more traditional in Europe at the time. Although a widowed grandparent or an unmarried aunt might live with the family, the relative abundance of land in America encouraged the married children to leave the parental home. It is difficult to generalize on the ages of men and women at marriage. Most estimates suggest that women usually married while still in their teens. Men tended to marry in their early twenties. However, recent studies of New England towns in the seventeenth century indicate that women did not marry until about age twenty-two and men not until age twenty-four to twenty-seven. These somewhat later ages may be partly explained by the shortage of good land in New England at this period. (Yet, this was still earlier than in western Europe, where at that period marriage partners tended to be in their late twenties.)

Early marriage, the primitive state of birth control, and the shortage of labor in the colonies resulted in large families. Sir William Phips, a governor of Massachusetts at the end of the seventeenth century, had twenty-five brothers and sisters—all born of one mother. Benjamin Franklin's father sired seventeen children by two wives, and Paul Revere was the father of sixteen children. However, a high rate of infant mortality kept most families from reaching this size. Estimates vary, but disease, poor diet, and lack of—or poor—medical care killed approximately one out of every six infants during the seventeenth century (a lower rate than that of western Europe at the time). However, some families were unusually hard hit. Only five of Samuel Sewall's fourteen children lived to the age of thirty, and only three of them survived him. One woman was so proud that all fourteen of the children born to her lived to adulthood that she had the fact carved on her tombstone. Hard figures are difficult to come by, but it is estimated that the colonial birthrate was forty-five to fifty births per thousand women compared to twenty-eight per thousand in western Europe at the time. The colonial figure indicates almost seven births per fertile marriage for whites and between seven and eight for blacks.

Giving birth to children at regular two-year intervals (breast-feeding for a full year helps explain this gap) took a heavy toll on colonial women. Death in, or because of, childbirth was common. Most of the large colonial families were produced by two or more mothers. However, if a woman did survive the childbearing years, she could look forward to a long life.

In spite of (or because of?) the fact that many marriages were arranged, a deep love and respect often developed between husbands and wives. When Eliza Lucas did marry, she reported that she was "the happiest mortal upon Earth!" Anne Bradstreet, the seventeenth-century Puritan poetess wrote a poem "To My Dear and Loving Husband" beginning with the words:

> If ever two were one, then surely we;
> If ever man were loved by wife, then thee;
> If ever wife was happy in a man,
> Compare with me, ye women, if you can.*

Numerous husbands were happy to utilize their wives' business skills as well as their domestic skills. Before leaving for England in 1757, Franklin wrote to his wife that he was able to undertake the journey only because "I can rely on your Prudence in the Management of my Affairs, and education of my dear Child." The wife of the Reverend John Davenport managed the extensive business interests of John Winthrop the Younger when he was away in England. Further, the first Mrs. Frederick Philipse of New York organized the earliest regular shipping service between Europe and New York and helped her husband amass a huge landed estate.

Other women ran shops and inns; worked as cooks, bakers, seamstresses, tailors, laundresses, midwives, and teachers; and, in the south, managed large plantations. The most outstanding of this latter group was Eliza Lucas Pinckney. At the age of seventeen, she managed three plantations in the absence of her father and was largely responsible for the introduction of indigo culture into South Carolina. After the death of her husband in 1758, she successfully managed his extensive estates until her own death in 1793. Typically, however, a colonial woman's time was more occupied with a wide variety of rather pedestrian tasks. Not only did she

*From *The Complete Works of Anne Bradstreet* by McElrath & Robb. Reprinted by permission of Twayne Publishers.

bear and rear her children, but she also did the cooking, cleaning, washing, and milking and made most of her family's clothing as well as its butter, cheese, candles, soap, cider, beer, and other necessities. She might even, though this was considered unseemly for white women, work in the fields alongside her menfolk. Fortunately, in the performance of these domestic duties, the housewife might have the assistance of her children, her—and her husband's—unmarried sisters, and, possibly, of servants.

THE LEGAL STATUS OF WOMEN

In the early colonial period, a married woman had no legal status. According to English common law, her legal existence was incorporated and consolidated into that of her husband. She could own nothing and even lost control of her dowry, which might be seized to satisfy her husband's creditors. If she worked outside the home, her earnings belonged to her husband. She could not sue or be sued. Her husband was (except in Connecticut) the sole guardian of the children. Further, he had just as much right to use physical force to control his wife as he had to discipline his children. The Massachusetts Body of Liberties (1641) was several centuries ahead of its time when it ruled that "Everie marryd woeman shall be free from bodilie correction or stripes by her husband, unlesse it be in his owne defence upon her assalt." That the latter clause was more than hypothetical may be seen from the case of Joan Miller, found in the Plymouth Colony Records for 1655, who was accused of

> ... beating and reviling her husband, and egging her children to healp her, bidding them knock him in the head, and wishing his victuals might choake him.

Wives were not treated as servants, and colonial laws attempted to limit, to some extent at least, the amount of force a husband could use against his wife. One statute, for example, forbade a husband to chastise his wife with a rod larger than a finger in diameter. A wife had the right to appeal to the courts if her husband's abuse was threatening her life or health. A man in Plymouth was whipped for kicking his wife from "a stoole into the fier," but the records indicate that in most cases the husband usually escaped by paying a small fine or posting a bond for future good behavior.

During the eighteenth century (and in Plymouth during the later seventeenth century) the legal status of married women improved. In some colonies they were able to sue or be sued if they engaged in a business. In others they were guaranteed one-third of their husbands' estate if they had not been properly provided for in the will. Connecticut made it mandatory for a husband to obtain his wife's consent before selling any property which she had inherited. In addition, the consent of the mother was required when children were "put out" into foster families. Quakers and Moravians accepted women as full church members and allowed them to assume positions of religious leadership. On the whole, however, during the colonial period husbands expected, in the words of John Robinson, the Pilgrims' pastor, in his tract, "Of Marriage" "a reverend subjection" from their wives.

The legal status of spinsters and widows was somewhat better than that of married women. They were able to sue and be sued, administer their own estates, inherit and will property, buy and sell, and keep the earnings from their employment. If a widow remarried, she might insist on a prenuptial agreement recognizing her control of her own property and that of her children. "Mistresse Margarett Brent, Spinster," as she was officially listed in Maryland records, was probably more active in commercial and public affairs than any other woman of the early colonial period. She owned thousands of acres of land in her own name, conducted courts on these estates, sued on her own behalf and on behalf of friends and relatives, and served as executrix of the will of Governor Leonard Calvert. In this latter capacity she demanded a seat—and a vote—in the Maryland assembly, but was refused. Nevertheless, this same assembly wrote to Lord Baltimore that she deserved "favour and thanks" from him for the effective manner in which she had protected proprietary interests following his brother's death.

The reluctance to grant women any political rights was characteristic of the entire colonial period. Even the docile poetess, Anne Bradstreet, chided the male sex in a poem dedicated to the memory of Queen Elizabeth:

Let such as say our sex is void of reason
Know 'tis a slander now but once was treason.*

Yet, in 1788 Thomas Jefferson was still writing to Angelica Church, one of the "emancipated" daughters of General Schuyler, that "the tender breasts of ladies were not formed for political convulsion."

THE CONCEPT OF CHILDHOOD

At the time of the Revolution, half of the colonial population was under the age of fifteen—children or early teenagers by today's standards. After weaning their children, most parents accepted the advice of John Robinson, who warned in his tract, "Of Children and Their Education" (1625), that all children were characterized by "a stubbornness and stoutness of mind rising from natural pride" that had to be "broken and beaten down" before they could be properly educated. Discipline, therefore, though it obviously differed from family to family, tended to be very strict. Parents also began the education of their children very early. Charles C. Pinckney, one of South Carolina's delegates to the Constitutional Convention, began

*From *The Complete Works of Anne Bradstreet* by McElrath & Robb. Reprinted by permission of Twayne Publishers.

reading when he was only two. And Jane Colman Turell, the daughter of one of Harvard's presidents, could read and recite the catechism and many psalms at the age of three.

In the seventeenth century childhood ended at the age of six or seven. Children were thereafter thought of as miniature adults. This was indicated by their change of dress. Before this age children of both sexes wore a long, loose robe, but now they began to dress just as their parents did. On formal occasions among the aristocracy, young boys wore knee britches and wigs; girls wore full skirts, stiff stays, gloves, and high-heeled shoes. Children of most colonists, however, wore the hand-me-downs of their parents or older siblings. Both boys and girls were apprenticed out at the age of six or seven. Whether in their own homes or in those of their masters, they had numerous chores to do. Here is a diary entry of Abigail Foote of Colchester, Connecticut made in 1775:

> Fix'd gown . . . Mend Mothers Riding Hood, Spun short thread, Spun linen . . . Pleated and ironed . . . Milked the cows . . . Made a Broom . . . Set a Red dye . . . carded two pounds of white wool . . . Scoured the pewter . . . *

A typical boy's day on the farm or in the shop was just as busy.

During the eighteenth century, however, conceptions of childhood began to change. Much of this change was influenced by John Locke's *Thoughts on Education* (1693), which denied that children were depraved or that they should be treated as miniature adults. It became more common for children to attend school at least part of the year. Some churches held special children's services with appropriate sermons. Children's books appeared, at first with formidable titles such as *A Token for Children, Being an Exact Account of the Conversion, Holy and Exemplary Lives and Joyful Deaths of Several Young Children.* By the middle of the eighteenth century, some parents were allowing their children to read expurgated versions of *Robinson Crusoe, Gulliver's Travels, Tom Jones,* and other English novels. By this time, too, books specially written for children—such as *Mother Goose's Melodies*—were sold in the colonies by John Newberry, the famous English publisher and bookseller.

It had never been literally "all work and no play" for the colonial child. Even in the seventeenth century, girls played with dolls, boys went hunting and fishing, and children of both sexes played games such as blind man's bluff, hopscotch, marbles, top spinning, and leap frog. Eighteenth-century newspapers carried numerous advertisements for "play-books" and such elaborate toys as hobbyhorses and battledores and shuttlecocks. Just before the Revolution special children's clothing began to come into fashion in the more well-to-do families. Still, the concept of "teenager" was completely unknown. Adulthood for young men began at age sixteen, when they became eligible for militia duty; for young ladies it began when they were old enough to marry.

---

*From *Home Life in Colonial Days* by Alice Morse Earle, 1898. Reprinted by permission of the Macmillan Publishing Co., Inc.

All in all, the colonial family, because of the numerous functions which it performed, was a close-knit unit; the father's *de jure* authority was diluted by the obvious contributions made by each member of the family.

BIBLIOGRAPHY

DEMOS, JOHN. *A Little Commonwealth: Family Life in Plymouth Colony.* New York, 1970.

DEXTER, ELIZABETH. *Colonial Women of Affairs: Women in Business and the Professions in America before 1776.* Boston, 1931.

FROST, J. WILLIAM. *The Quaker Family in America: A Portrait of the Society of Friends.* New York, 1973.

GLUBOCK, SHIRLEY, ed. *Home and Child Life in Colonial Days.* (Abridged and edited from *Home Life in Colonial Days* and *Child Life in Colonial Days* by Alice Morse Earle) London, England, 1969.

GREVEN, PHILIP J. *Four Generations: Population, Land, and Family in Colonial Andover, Massachusetts.* Ithaca, 1970.

GREVEN, PHILIP J. *The Protestant Temperament: Patterns of Child-Rearing, Religious Experience, and the Self in Early America.* New York, 1977.

KOEHLER, LYLE. *A Search for Power: The "Weaker Sex" in Seventeenth-Century New England.* Urbana, 1980.

MORGAN, EDMUND S. *The Puritan Family: Religion and Domestic Relations in Seventeenth Century New England.* New York, 1966.

MORGAN, EDMUND S. *Virginians at Home: Family Life in the Eighteenth Century.* Williamsburg, 1952.

SLATER, PETER GREGG. *Children in the New England Mind: In Death and in Life.* Hamden, Conn., 1977.

SMITH, DANIEL BLAKE. *Inside the Great House: Planter Family Life in Eighteenth-Century Chesapeake Society.* Ithaca, 1980.

SPRUILL, JULIA C. *Women's Life and Work in the Southern Colonies.* Chapel Hill, 1938.

THOMPSON, ROGER. *Women in Stuart England and America: A Comparative Study.* London, England, 1974.

ULRICH, LAUREL THATCHER. *Good Wives: Image and Reality in the Lives of Women in Northern New England, 1650-1750.* New York, 1982.

WOLF, STEPHANEE GRAUMEN. *Urban Village: Population, Community, and Family Structure in Germantown, Pennsylvania, 1683-1800.* Princeton, 1976.

19

Religion in Colonial America

Richard Hakluyt's *A Discourse on Western Planting* (1584) advocated the spread of "the true and sincere religion" to the New World by means of settlement rather than scattered missionary efforts. The English people followed his advice. However, it is doubtful whether Hakluyt, who was an Anglican clergyman, would have been satisfied with religious conditions as they developed in the thirteen colonies. He would, however, have been pleased at the fulfillment of his hope that America would "provide a safe and a sure place to receive people from all parts of the world that are forced to flee for the truth of God's word." (*A Discourse on Western Planting*)

THE ANGLICAN CHURCH

Hakluyt's own denomination was the first to reach the English colonies in America. Robert Hunt, chaplain of the Virginia colony, conducted services under "an old saile" at Jamestown shortly after the colony was founded. In 1619 the first House of Burgesses made the Anglican Church the established, or official, church of the colony. However, establishment of the Anglican Church came much later, if at all, in the other colonies (in four counties of New York in 1693 and in Maryland, South Carolina, North Carolina, and Georgia only in the eighteenth century). Yet, even in these colonies the majority of the people belonged to other denominations. Only in Virginia and Maryland were tax revenues at all adequate to support the Anglican clergy.

In the other southern colonies, the Society for the Propogation of the Gospel in Foreign Parts, usually called the SPG, or the Venerable Society, had to subsidize the salaries of Anglican clergymen, missionaries, and schoolteachers. The SPG and the Society for Promoting Christian Knowledge (the SPCK) were both founded by Dr. Thomas Bray, who served as the commissary, or personal representative, of the bishop of London in Maryland. Bray was also responsible for the founding of over fifty lending libraries in America and the sending of 34,000 books and religious tracts to stock them. Between 1702 and 1783 the SPG sent 309 missionaries to America to convert the Indians and the slaves to Christianity. It enjoyed practically no success with the Indians and little more with the slaves. As its secretary reported in 1730, most slave owners continued to insist that blacks had no souls.

The bishop of London was the titular head of the Anglican Church in America, but his control was minimal. Even when he sent able commissaries such as Bray or James Blair to America, they lacked the authority to ordain new, or discipline erring, clergymen. If an American wished to become an Anglican clergyman, he was required to make the long, expensive, and often dangerous journey to England. This deterred all but the most sincere candidates, left many parishes without a clergyman, and forced the Anglican Church in America to rely on many clergymen who had already proven themselves failures in England. Nevertheless, to balance the scales, many Anglican clergymen ministered faithfully to their congregations under the most difficult circumstances.

The appointment of a resident bishop in America might have alleviated some of the problems of the Anglican Church. However, Parliament refused to sanction such a position—partly out of its indifference to religious matters; partly because of the opposition of non-Anglicans in America who feared the loss of religious toleration; and partly because of the hostility of Anglican lay leaders, particularly in the southern colonies, who realized that a resident bishop would diminish their control of the church.

The collection of the tithe to support Anglican clergymen was always unpopular and difficult especially because it was levied on members of all denominations. This resulted in meager clerical stipends, usually paid in tobacco, whose poor quality and fluctuations in price further restricted a clergyman's standard of living. Fortunately for them, however, every Anglican minister in Virginia and Maryland was given a farm of 200 acres upon which he, and his family, could raise tobacco and other crops to supplement their income.

Geography was also an enemy of the Anglican Church. Because of the nature of settlement in the south, parishes were large in extent but thinly settled. It was impossible for a minister, who was often responsible for more than one of these huge parishes, to be present for all services, christenings, weddings, or funerals. John Blair, an SPG missionary, wrote that it took him from ten to twelve weeks to cover his parish and that the people refused to ride more than five miles to come to church. Many of these religious ceremonies were performed at home by lay members. Most plantations had their own cemetery, and many of those who lay there had been buried without benefit of clergy.

During the eighteenth century a new, "natural" philosophy of religion called Deism developed, largely within the Anglican Church. Deism was strongly influenced by the scientific theories of Sir Isaac Newton. Deists agreed with Newton that God had created the universe and laid down the laws which governed it. From observation of nature it seemed obvious to them that only a benevolent and omniscient God could have created the world. Through their rational powers alone, human beings could come to understand the moral law which governed human conduct much as the law of gravity governed physical objects. Revelation, therefore, was thought to be unnecessary, and the Bible was not considered to be the literal word of God.

Deists felt that God no longer "interfered" in the affairs of men. Man had been created naturally good and was blessed with the moral insight to know what was good and then to perform it. Anyone who lived a moral life was ensured a happy life in this world as well as the next. As Franklin wrote, in a letter to his father, "We shall not be examined [by] what we thought but what we did" on the day of judgment. Deists did not organize separate churches. Most, like Thomas Jefferson and Benjamin Franklin, continued to attend Anglican services. Deism attracted only a small circle of intellectuals. Its lack of emotion and its disinterest in a better life in a future world made it unpalatable to the average person.

In spite of all its problems, however, the Anglican Church was the most prestigious denomination in the English colonies. By the middle of the eighteenth century, the aristocratic class outside of New England, and to a growing extent even in New England itself, felt that Anglicanism was the only respectable church. It is estimated that by the time of the Revolution, the Anglican Church had about half a million members in 480 churches, the second largest denomination in America.

THE CONGREGATIONAL CHURCH

The Congregational Church, with about 575,000 members in 658 churches at the time of the Revolution, was the largest denomination in the thirteen colonies. As you may recall, the Puritans came to America to create a true church—a church that would set an example and lead to the regeneration of the Church of England. The attempt may have been sincere, but it was doomed to failure. Even when the Puritans who remained in England overthrew the monarchy, they chose not to attempt to reform the Church of England along the lines suggested by their brethren in New England.

The New England Puritans, therefore, created a new denomination—the Congregational Church. John Cotton, one of the leading clergymen of Boston, spelled out the differences between the Congregational and Anglican churches: The local congregation, not a bishop, was the highest ecclesiastical authority; the Book of Common Prayer, the Anglican prayerbook, was discarded; the Congregational Church was formed by means of a covenant among the "visible saints," only those who had given evidence of being consciously redeemed by the saving grace of God.

This distinction between people was based on the Calvinist doctrine that people were totally depraved and that neither faith nor good works could commute their sentence to hell. However, a few fortunate individuals had been elected by God for salvation. Only these saints were capable of joining with God in the formation of a church.

In 1646 the General Court of Massachusetts requested that the churches meet together in a synod to discuss religious matters. Two years later this synod, made up of clergymen from all the New England colonies except Rhode Island, produced the Cambridge Platform, which has been called the Great Charter of Congregationalism. The Cambridge Platform reemphasized the autonomy of each individual congregation but also advised voluntary church-communion, or fellowship between churches. Church councils, or synods, were called on occasion, but their decisions were not binding on the individual congregations and could not be enforced. The Cambridge Platform of 1648 continued the strict requirements for church membership. All candidates had to be examined so that the congregants could be sure of their "knowledge in the principles of religion, and of their experience in the ways of grace."

Puritans preferred calling their place of worship a meetinghouse rather than a church, which had a popish ring to it. In the seventeenth century the meetinghouse was a square structure without a steeple. Later, bell towers were added, which evolved into steeples. Men sat on one side of the church, women on the other. Both sat on backless benches. The meetinghouse was unheated; in winter the worshipers had to wear their coats and warm their feet with "foot stoves" full of live coals. When these stoves caused numerous fires, the congregants had to be satisfied with hot bricks wrapped in quilts. Only in the eighteenth century did family pews and heating come into general use in Congregational churches.

Prayers, during which the entire congregation stood, might last an hour. Bible readings and sermons might take another two hours or more. To see that no one fell asleep during the sermon, a special church official circulated through the church carrying a long rod with a foxtail attached to one end. If women or children fell asleep, he would wake them with that end of the rod; the men he would tap firmly with the wooden end. All church officials—which also included the pastor, teacher, elders, and deacons—were elected by the church members.

The Puritan sabbath, or Lord's day, began at sundown on Saturday. No work or amusements were permitted from then to the conclusion of the sabbath on Sunday evening. So many people violated the sabbath that in 1653 the Massachusetts General Court passed a series of laws against actions which "tended much to the dishonor of God, the reproach of religion, and the prophanation of his holy Sabbath." Violators of these so-called blue laws might be fined or put into the stocks. The classic case involved the captain who was punished for kissing his wife on the sabbath after returning from three years at sea. In all fairness, however, it should be remembered that blue laws were passed in Virginia and in other colonies outside New England. Nor was idleness proper on the Lord's day. When not in church, Puritans of all ages were expected to join in family prayers and meditation.

Not everyone, even in New England, wanted to—or was able to—live up to the Puritan ideal. Very early in Massachusetts history, a long-winded minister was reminded that, although many settlers came for religious reasons, the fisheries were almost as great an attraction. A very clear signal of the loss in momentum of the Congregational Church was the adoption, after years of discussion, of the Half Way Covenant by a Massachusetts synod in 1662. The Half Way Covenant was an attempt to solve a double dilemma. By the 1650s children of the first generation "saints" who had been accepted as church members had children of their own who were eligible for membership. The question arose as to whether the second generation should be allowed to participate in the sacrament of the Lord's Supper and whether their children should be admitted as church members and/or be allowed to participate in the sacrament. The Half Way Covenant admitted both generations to church membership and thus entitled them to political rights; but it refused to allow either of them to participate in the Lord's Supper or to vote in church affairs. The admission to church membership of any person "not scandalous in life" indicated that the Puritan ideal of a fellowship of saints was not going to be realized.

Nevertheless, even the Half Way Covenant could not stem the loss of interest in religion. The havoc of King Philip's War, the challenge to the Massachusetts charter, and a serious smallpox epidemic led to the calling of the Reforming Synod in 1679–1680. The members of this synod cataloged the sins which they felt had precipitated these disasters. Included among them were

An excess of pride	Profanity and irreverence
Sabbath-breaking	Lack of community concern
Dishonesty	Intemperance and drunkenness

Although the ministers preached moving "jeremiads" based upon the findings of this synod, the reform was only temporary. Before the end of the century, it was again reported that New England was suffering from religious laxity.

One of the reasons for the final collapse of Puritan fervor was the reaction to the Salem witchcraft trials. In January 1692 several girls between the ages of nine and twenty—including the daughter and niece of the Reverend Samuel Parris—in Salem Village began to act strangely. They suffered from convulsive fits; temporary loss of hearing, speech, and sight; and horrible hallucinations. Both doctors and the Reverend Deodat Lawson, another minister at Salem Village agreed on the diagnosis: "The sovereign and Holy God was pleased to permit Satan and his Instruments to affright and afflict these poor mortals."

This finding was not surprising. In Europe and America few doubted the existence of witches and witchcraft, and during the 1600s more witches were executed in Europe than in any previous, or later, century. When questioned, the Salem girls accused Tituba, an Indian slave owned by Reverend Parris, and two elderly women, Sarah Good and Sarah Osburn, of bewitching them. The two old women denied the accusation, but Tituba readily confessed being a witch, implicated the two others, and added that still other witches, unknown to her, were practicing in Salem. Her testimony, and the fact that the girls suffered seizures which they claimed were caused by the "specters" of the accused women, led the two Salem magistrates to commit all three women to prison in March. Soon after, Martha Corey and Rebecca Nurse, members in good standing of the Salem church, were also accused of witchcraft.

Not everyone believed these accusations. John Proctor, a farmer whose servant, Mary Warren, was one of the afflicted girls, warned that the girls' testimony could not be relied upon. However, the tide was not to be stemmed. Soon the outspoken Proctor, Martha Corey's husband, and several women were accused of witchcraft. Before the hysteria was over, hundreds of suspects, including a minister, were crowding the jails. Of this number, about fifty offered elaborate, detailed confessions, often implicating numerous other people. Some of these confessions may have been sincere; but, more likely, they were intended as a means—usually successful— of saving their lives.

In spite of such writings as *The Wonders of the Invisible World* (1692), Cotton Mather fought against the witchcraft hysteria. On June 15, 1692, he and eleven other ministers from the Boston area drew up a statement which specifically warned the court that was to try the accused witches not to

> . . . lay more stress upon pure specter testimony than it will bear. . . . It is very certain that the Devils have sometimes represented the shapes of persons not only innocent but very virtuous. . . .

The court, however, insisted that the devil could not take a person's likeness without his or her consent and therefore accepted spectral evidence. It is not surprising, then, that thirteen women and six men were eventually hanged. Giles Cory, probably hoping to save his property from confiscation, refused to plead to his indictment and, according to English practice, was pressed to death by weights placed upon him.

Finally, on October 3, 1692, Increase Mather delivered a paper to a conference of ministers in Cambridge, *Cases of Conscience,* in which he stated flatly, "It were better that ten suspected witches should escape than that one innocent person should be condemned." The new governor of Massachusetts, Sir William Phips, a protégé of Mather, temporarily suspended further proceedings in October 1692, and when the court next met in June 1693, it no longer accepted spectral evidence. Of the fifty-two people brought before the court, only three were now convicted and sentenced to death, and they were saved by the governor's pardon. In January 1697 the Massachusetts General Court proclaimed a day of fasting and penitence for the "late tragedy raised among us by Satan." Later, Judge Samuel Sewall publicly apologized for his part in the trials. Finally, in 1711 the heirs of those who had been executed received compensation from the General Court.

Numerous theses have been developed to explain the Salem witchcraft episode. Was it the result of petty village quarrels over land, livestock, or the payment of the minister's salary? Was it the attempt of young women to throw off the authority of their elders? Was an economic transformation then taking place in the Salem area? Was it due to Puritan "repression"? Perhaps it was in response to the dangers to the colony posed by the Dominion of New England, the refusal of the English authorities to restore the old charter, and the outbreak of King William's War, which led to attacks by the French and Indians and threatened a papist conquest of New England.

No matter what their cause, the Salem witchcraft trials caused a crisis in the Congregational Church. In the last years of the seventeenth century, a prosperous group of Boston merchants, many of whom had opposed the trials, organized the Brattle Street church. In this church all professed Christians were eligible for baptism, and all contributors—women as well as men—were allowed a voice in its government. It only remained for the Reverend Solomon Stoddard who recommended in his treatise, *The Doctrine of Instituted Churches* (1700) that anyone who shall "profess faith in and obedience to Christ" should be allowed to participate in the Lord's Supper. The select fellowship of the saints was now open to all.

Other Congregationalists became convinced that only the adoption of a presbyterian system of church organization, in which synods and councils would have ultimate authority over individual churches, could save their Church. In 1708, by the Saybrook Platform, the Congregational churches of Connecticut formed councils which set church doctrine and appointed ministers to the individual churches. Even though Cotton Mather supported a similar form of church government in Massachusetts, it was never adopted. The leading opponent of the presbyterian form of church government was the Reverend John Wise. Wise insisted that a synod form of church government would be oppressive and in violation of the covenant theory, by which a group of individuals voluntarily form a church and share in its governance. Wise's democratic ideas were directed toward church government, but they were resurrected half a century later and used to support the American Revolution.

RELIGIOUS GROUPS IN THE MIDDLE COLONIES

The middle colonies were the most heterogeneous in religion as well as in nationality. In 1628 the Reverend Jonas Michaelis arrived in New Amsterdam, and in the following year the Dutch Reformed Church was officially established in New Netherland, where it held sway until the English conquest of 1664. In that year New Amsterdam alone had thirteen Dutch Reformed churches and eight ministers. For most of the remainder of the colonial period, Dutch remained the language of services and sermons, and the Classis of Amsterdam retained the sole right to ordain ministers. Only in 1771 did Dr. John Henry Livingston conclude the Plan of Union with the Classis which gave the Dutch Reformed Church in America the right to train and ordain ministers while still maintaining ties with the mother church. By this time, too, English had replaced Dutch in the services.

Pennsylvania was first settled by the Quakers, whose early history has already been discussed. George Fox, the founder of Quakerism, believed that there was a seed or light in every soul which enables human beings to experience direct revelation from God. Obviously, all people would thus be equal in the sight of God. From this it followed that they were equal in the sight of man and need show no special deference to any human being. Nor would Quakers take oaths, perform military duties, or pay taxes (which might be used for military purposes).

The Quakers felt no need for ministers. By the eighteenth century their First Day meetings, or religious services, were pervaded by a spirit of quietism in which no one spoke unless he or she (Quaker women enjoyed religious equality) felt moved to it by God. At monthly meetings the congregation conducted its business, admitted new members, and disciplined backsliders. In spite of the loss of their original enthusiasm, Quakers pioneered in the abolition of slavery and other humane reforms. At the time of the Revolution, the 295 Quaker meetings scattered throughout Pennsylvania, New Jersey, Rhode Island, and North Carolina were organized into regional associations called Yearly Meetings.

William Penn's tolerant religious principles encouraged the settlement of many German religious denominations in Pennsylvania. You have already read about the Mennonites. They were followed by Dunkards, the German Reformed, and Moravians. Moravian settlement in America began under the sponsorship of Count Nicholaus Ludwig von Zinzendorf. The first permanent Moravian settlement in America was made in Bethlehem, Pennsylvania, in 1741. Later other settlements were made in Pennsylvania and in Salem (now Winston-Salem), North Carolina. Moravian communities never lost their missionary impulse and proved more successful in converting the Indians than any other religious group.

Lutherans had arrived in America even before the establishment of Pennsylvania. They were among the first settlers of the Swedish colony along the Delaware River in 1637. A few years later a group of Lutherans arrived in New Amsterdam, but Peter Stuyvesant refused to allow them to organize a church. Therefore, most Lutherans settled in Pennsylvania and Georgia. The Lutheran Church in America was officially organized by Heinrich Melchior Muhlenberg, the patriarch of the Lutheran Church in America. He organized the first Lutheran synod of America in 1748 and went on to found churches, train and ordain ministers, and produce an American edition of the hymnal. By the time of the Revolution, the Lutherans had 151 churches in America, mainly in Pennsylvania and along the southern frontier.

THE PRESBYTERIAN CHURCH

The Presbyterian Church was the third largest denomination in the colonies in number of members (over 400,000) and second largest in number of churches (543).* Presbyterians came to the English colonies almost from the latter's inception, but

---

*Presbyterians followed the teachings of Calvin but differed from Congregationalists in believing that ultimate control of their churches should be in the hands of church federations called presbyteries, or even larger groupings called synods.

by the end of the seventeenth century, only twelve Presbyterian churches were functioning in the colonies.

The major growth of the Presbyterian Church came only in the eighteenth century with the migration of the Scotch-Irish to America. In the early years of the century, the Reverend Francis Makemie, the father of American Presbyterianism, founded the first American presbytery. By 1716 the Presbytery of Philadelphia had grown so large that it divided into four presbyteries, which formed one synod. When the Scotch-Irish migrated from Pennsylvania to the frontier of the southern colonies, they founded new churches and formed additional presbyteries. In 1735, to supply ministers for these new churches, William Tennent established Log College. Most of these ministers were native-born Americans, and many of them were to become leaders of the Great Awakening.

Very few Baptists were found in America for most of the colonial period. Roger Williams is often credited with founding the first Baptist church in America in 1639, but others claim that John Clark, also of Rhode Island, preceded him. For most of the seventeenth century, Baptists were persecuted in New England and elsewhere largely because of their opposition to infant baptism and their demand for separation of church and state. Like other persecuted groups, Baptists settled in Pennsylvania, where the first association of Baptist churches was formed in 1707. Only with the Great Awakening did Baptist congregations spread to all the colonies.

THE GREAT AWAKENING
AND ITS RESULTS

In spite of the multiplicity of denominations, church membership—never high even in the seventeenth century—declined in the eighteenth century, and the vast majority (an estimated seven out of eight in New England, fourteen of fifteen in the middle colonies, and nineteen of twenty in the south) of Americans had no formal religious affiliation. Among the reasons for this phenomenon were the struggle of new immigrants to establish themselves, the isolation of frontier life, the formalized, sterile doctrines preached in many of the churches, and the churches' rigid admission requirements. On the other hand, the intermittent eighteenth-century wars, the economic dislocation which accompanied them, and the numerous epidemics and other natural disasters of the first half of the century created a need for an acceptable outlet for psychological tension. Religious leaders met the challenges of this situation in various ways. Some contented themselves with warnings of doom for their flocks unless they speedily repented. Others, however, began to search for an approach that would meet the spiritual and emotional needs of the average colonist.

One of these clergymen was Theodore Frelinghuyson, who began preaching in the Dutch Reformed Church in the Raritan Valley of New Jersey in 1720. Frelinghuyson, like other leaders of what was to develop into the Great Awakening, was influenced by such pietistic ideas as personal reform, public penance, and the performance of good deeds. Frelinghuyson's emotional approach was followed in

FIGURE 19A
(Library of Congress.)

the Presbyterian Church by William Tennent's sons—Gilbert, John, and William Jr.—who preached that all persons might win salvation by their own repentance and upright lives.

The next step toward the Great Awakening was taken in Connecticut under the leadership of the outstanding Congregational minister Jonathan Edwards. Edwards was the grandson of the Reverend Solomon Stoddard, who had admitted all persons of good reputation to full membership in his church. Edwards, however, refused to follow his grandfather's open membership policy. He believed that the emotions as well as the intellect must be engaged if people were to heighten the quality of their religious experience. He felt that the members of a congregation needed to have their hearts touched to be converted, so that their lives could be changed.

Edward's revival began in Northhampton in 1734, but his most famous effort to accomplish this was a sermon preached in 1741 called "Sinners in the Hands of an Angry God." So graphic and horrifying was his description of the fate of unrepentant sinners that his hearers broke down in an agony of terror and hysteria even before the sermon was concluded. In essence, Jonathan Edwards frightened his congregation with the terrors of hell in order to win them over to the kingdom of heaven.

The men already mentioned were only precursors: The Great Awakening truly began with the arrival in America of George Whitefield. Whitefield visited Georgia briefly in 1738 and then returned to America, where he preached his way up and down the Atlantic coast from New England to Georgia between 1739 and 1741. Wherever he preached—in churches of all denominations (he was ordained in the Anglican Church) or in the open to audiences as large as 30,000 people—his audience was moved by his message of penitence and pardon. Though Whitefield, unlike most later revivalists, did not attempt to terrify his listeners, they fell to the ground in paroxysms of grief, confessed their sins, and promised to live better lives in the future.

Benjamin Franklin has left one of the best accounts of Whitefield's effectiveness. Franklin attended one of Whitefield's prayer meetings but had determined not to contribute anything to the collection which followed. Yet, as he recounted in his *Autobiography,* he

> . . . began to soften, and concluded to give the coppers. Another stroke of his oratory made me ashamed of that; and determined me to give the silver; and he finished so admirably that I emptied my pocket wholly into the collector's dish, gold and all.

Whitefield made seven trips to America, preached more than 18,000 sermons, and died here in 1770.

To many of those affected by the Great Awakening, the older ministers were looked down upon as "dead men"—men who had not been saved or touched by God's grace. And, as Whitefield rhetorically asked in his Journals, "How can dead men beget living Children?" Surely, it would be better for these unfortunate congregants to leave these "dead men" and find a more worthy minister. Those who followed this doctrine turned to the many volunteer preachers who emerged in all colonies. These exhorters screamed, shouted, and frightened their hearers into convulsions and fits.

These excesses, and the challenge to established church authority, led to splits in the Congregational and Presbyterian churches between Old Lights and New Lights, or Old Sides and New Sides. The Presbyterian Church reunited in 1758, but the Congregationalists remained split. Many of the Old Lights complained about the lack of knowledge of the self-appointed ministers in the New Light churches. They also feared that New Light congregants were mistaking overheated imagination for true religion. Some of the conservative clergymen—both Presbyterian and Congregational—were so incensed at the innovations in their churches that they became Anglicans.

Three churches gained the most members as a result of the Great Awakening. The Presbyterians under the leadership of Samuel Davies made most of their converts in the southern colonies. The Baptists, in spite of harsh persecution, won followers among former Congregationalists in New England and former Anglicans and the unchurched in the south. By the time of the Revolution, the Baptists had 498 churches—the third highest number in the colonies.

The third group was the Methodists, which began in England as a reform movement within the Anglican Church. In 1735 John and Charles Wesley, the founders of Methodism, went to Georgia to do missionary work among the settlers and Indians. Although the mission failed, John was deeply impressed by the teachings of the Moravians with whom he came into contact in Georgia.

Methodism, with its belief in human perfectibility and the possibility of salvation for all, spread rapidly in the colonies. Several Methodists were preaching in America during the 1760s, and in 1771 Francis Asbury, who was to become the creator of American Methodism, arrived in the colonies. Before his death in 1816, Asbury had traveled 270,000 miles, preached 16,000 times, and enrolled 200,000 members in the Methodist Church.

The exact number of new members of the Congregational Church is impossible to determine, although a typical estimate for the revival years of the early 1740s is 27,000. However, Bumsted and Van de Wetering, in their study of the Great Awakening, point out that it was not mere numbers that proved significant but the fact that younger people and a higher proportion of males than belonged formerly joined this church within a very short period of time. These people—in the Congregational Church as well as in other churches—shared the emotional conversion experience and believed that they were responsible for their own conduct and for the welfare of others. Religion, therefore, became a greater influence in colonial society than it had ever been outside of early New England.

Another result of the Great Awakening was an increase of religious freedom in the colonies. Prior to the Awakening only Rhode Island and Pennsylvania accepted the idea of religious freedom. Nevertheless, Americans enjoyed more freedom than did the English even after the passage of the Toleration Act of 1689. This was partly due to the disinterest in religion in the colonies during the first portion of the eighteenth century. Paradoxically, however, the surge of interest in religion caused by the Great Awakening had the same effect. Groups such as the Baptists and Presbyterians fought, on the whole successfully, against established churches in the south and in New England. Public opinion supported them because the Great Awakening had stressed conduct over creed: The way one lived one's life was more important than the cathechism one repeated.

In 1727 the English government ordered the colonies of Massachusetts and Connecticut to use the church tax paid by dissenters to support their own, rather than the Congregational, church. In 1747, when the governor of Virginia attempted to impede the flow of converts to the Presbyterian Church by ordering the arrest of all itinerant preachers, he was overruled by the English authorities. Thus, Presbyterian ministers were allowed to continue their preaching. However, in spite of the efforts of Isaac Backus, a New England Baptist leader who fought for religious freedom in Virginia, Baptist ministers were still arrested on charges of disturbing the peace.

The two religious groups which found least acceptance in the colonies were Catholics and Jews. Because of the traditional emnity between Protestants and Catholics, and because England's two main enemies, France and Spain, were Catholic nations, Catholics suffered from discrimination even more than Jews, who were few in number and economically self-sustaining. In 1740 Parliament forbade the colonies to naturalize Catholics. No colony allowed a Catholic to vote or hold office. The same was true of Jews, although they were allowed to vote in South Carolina. However, in spite of their political disabilities, Catholics and Jews were allowed to worship as they pleased and to engage in all types of economic activities. At the time of the Revolution, about 25,000 Catholics were worshiping in fifty churches, and congregations in Newport, New York, Charleston, and Savannah were meeting the needs of the, perhaps, 2,000 Jews in the colonies.

The New Lights were very sensitive to the charge that their ministers were not properly trained. This led to the founding of several new colleges, which were originally intended to train ministers, but which also functioned as liberal arts colleges. (These will be treated in more detail in the following chapter.) Lawrence Cremin, in *American Education: The Colonial Experience,* wrote that one of the results of the Great Awakening was "to enhance the educative influence of the church . . . in the everyday life of the colonists." Another result of the Great Awakening was a renewed interest in reform movements such as improvement of orphanages and conversion and more humane treatment of Indians and blacks (but not the abolition of slavery). This grew out of the emphasis on good works by the new group of preachers.

Lastly, in a very general sense, the Great Awakening may be said to have promoted democracy in America. Its message that all people (including, according to Whitefield, slaves) had the possibility of winning salvation meant that all people were equal before God. As a result, the ordinary church member won a far greater voice in the management of church affairs, even including the selection of the minister. It was not long before these same churchgoers began wondering why so much inequality existed in secular affairs and why the "lesser orders" had so little influence in political matters. The two great mass movements in colonial history were the Great Awakening and the American Revolution: Both challenged "establishments"—either religious or political—and both used similar strategies and tactics.

BIBLIOGRAPHY

BOYER, PAUL, and NISSENBAUM, STEPHEN. *Salem Possessed: The Social Origins of Witchcraft.* Cambridge, 1974.

BUMSTED, J. M., and VAN DE WETERING, JOHN D. *What Must I Do To Be Saved? The Great Awakening in Colonial America.* Hinsdale, Ill., 1976.

DEMOS, JOHN PUTNAM. *Entertaining Satan: Witchcraft and the Culture of Early New England.* New York, 1982.

ELLIS, JOHN TRACY. *Catholics in Colonial America.* Baltimore, 1965.

GAUSTAD, EDWIN S. *The Great Awakening in New England.* New York, 1957.

GEWEHR, WESLEY M. *The Great Awakening in Virginia, 1740-1790.* Durham, 1930.

HEIMART, ALAN. *Religion and the American Mind from the Great Awakening to the Revolution.* Cambridge, 1966.

ISAAC, RHYS. *The Transformation of Virginia, 1740-1790.* Chapel Hill: University of North Carolina Press, 1982.

JAMES, SIDNEY V. *A People Among Peoples: Quaker Benevolence in Eighteenth Century America.* Cambridge, 1963.

MILLER, PERRY. *The New England Mind: The Seventeenth Century.* New York, 1939.

MILLS, FREDERIC V., SR. *Bishops by Ballot: An Eighteenth Century Ecclesiastical Revolution.* New York, 1978.

MORAIS, M. *Deism in Eighteenth-Century America.* New York, 1934.

SOLBERG, WINTON U. *Redeem the Time: The Puritan Sabbath in Early America.* Cambridge, 1977.

TRINTERUD, L. J. *The Formation of an American Tradition: A Re-examination of Colonial Presbyterianism.* Philadelphia, 1949.

WORRALL, ARTHUR J. *Quakers in the Colonial Northeast.* Hanover, N.H., 1980.

ZIFF, LARZAR. *Puritanism in America: New Culture in a New World.* New York, 1973.

20

Education in Colonial America

Crèvecoeur opened his letter on "Customary Education and Employment of the Inhabitants of Nantucket" by advising his readers that the best way of understanding any group of people "is to examine what sort of education they give their children, how they treat them at home, and what they are taught in their places of public worship."* It appears that in this passage Crèvecoeur meant education to be synonymous with schooling; he describes family life and religious life and then states that in the schools of Nantucket, "They [the children] learn to read and write a good hand."** Modern educational historians would differ sharply. Lawrence A. Cremin, for example, defines colonial education as the combined influence of the home, the church, the various types of literature to which the colonists were exposed, as well as whatever formal schooling they received.

Because earlier chapters have dealt with apprenticeship and the educational functions of the family and church, and since the following chapter surveys colonial literature, this chapter will concentrate only on formal schooling. As Bernard Bailyn pointed out in *Education and the Forming of American Society*, the unfamiliar problems of the frontier environment weakened the influence of parents and ministers and transferred their educational functions "to formal institutions . . . for the most part schools."

Letters from An American Farmer.
**Ibid.*

However, in spite of the gradual—and it was very gradual and never complete—transfer of the responsibility for education, the influence of the Renaissance and Reformation on the goals of education was as pervasive in the colonies as it was in England. As Cremin has pointed out, piety, civility (including social graces), and learning were the three major purposes of education. Only in the eighteenth century did a more utilitarian approach to education become more common.

EDUCATION IN THE SOUTHERN COLONIES

As noted, in the English tradition education was considered the responsibility primarily of the family and secondarily of the church. The southern colonies followed this pattern most closely. As Governor Berkeley reported in 1670 when asked who was responsible for education in Virginia, "Every man according to his ability [is] instructing his children." It was not that the southern colonists felt the need for schools less than their fellow settlers farther north, but the scattered population pattern in the south severely handicapped the development of educational institutions. Poor children usually received a smattering of education if they were apprenticed out; but, as we have seen, the amount of general education masters were forced to provide their apprentices was generally more modest than in England. If they were not apprenticed out, they might, at least in the eighteenth century, attend one of the charity schools supported by the SPG, or the schools of other denominations which also accepted a few nonpaying students.

If the parents were small farmers, they usually organized what came to be known as "old field schools." These schools were usually log cabins erected in an abandoned tobacco field. There, often under the supervision of the local clergyman, the children would learn reading and writing in the months of April to September, the off-season for tobacco growing. Those who were slightly better off sent their children to endowed schools or strictly private schools. Students in endowed schools, practically all of which were on the elementary level, paid lower tuition (and a few paid nothing at all) than those at private schools. This was made possible through the generosity of such benefactors as Benjamin Symmes or Thomas Eaton who bequeathed land and cattle to help support these institutions.

Private schools gave instruction on both the elementary and secondary levels. By the middle of the eighteenth century, secondary schools in the south and, as we shall see, in other colonies as well, were giving their male students courses in mathematics, geography, surveying, navigation, and bookkeeping as well as the more traditional Latin and Greek. Private schools for girls instructed them in the basic subjects and then concentrated on music, dancing, drawing, needlework, and French. The children of the planter class received their education from tutors or governesses. These tutors were often divinity students or educated indentured servants. Some planters sent their sons or daughters (such as Ursula Byrd, who was sent as early as age four) to England to be educated.

EDUCATION IN THE MIDDLE COLONIES

Education also remained a family and church responsibility in the middle colonies. Here all attempts at public education were thwarted by the tremendous variety of religious and national groups which had settled the area. The Dutch children of New York continued to attend schools sponsored by the Dutch Reformed Church. There Calvinist doctrine and the Dutch language were taught, just as these subjects had been taught while the Dutch ruled the colony. English children in New York attended either the charity schools of the SPG or the many private schools which were open both to boys and girls.

Penn's Frame of Government for Pennsylvania stipulated that children were to be taught the "3 Rs" until the age of twelve, when they were to learn some useful trade or skill. However, although the Friends' Public School (now known as the William Penn Charter School) was established in 1689, it operated strictly as a private school for Quakers, and no system of public schools ever developed in Pennsylvania. Most Quaker meetings were satisfied to establish schools which were supported by tuition fees and contributions. All the numerous other religious groups in Pennsylvania maintained similar systems of parochial schools.

The middle colonies were famous for the quality of their private schools—particularly those located in Philadelphia. These schools pioneered in the teaching of the more utilitarian subjects, which have already been mentioned in connection with the private schools of the south. This trend away from the classical curriculum may best be seen from the 1750 prospectus of the Philadelphia Academy, which offered its students

> Latin, Greek, English, French and German Languages, together with History, Geography, Chronology, Logic, and Rhetoric; also Writing, Arithmetic, Merchants Accounts, Geometry, Algebra, Surveying, Gauging, Navigation, Astronomy, Drawing in Perspective, and other mathematical Sciences; with natural and mechanical philosophy, . . .

The Philadelphia Academy set the example that was to be followed by secondary schools for the remainder of the colonial period. Many of these secondary schools became known as academies rather than as Latin grammar schools (the older term for secondary schools) in order to underscore the changes in their curriculum. Academies for girls—or female seminaries, as they were later called—taught needlework, music, dancing, etiquette, and French. Most cities also had low-cost private schools which met in the evening so that working people of both sexes might take many of the same courses offered by the academies. By the time of the Revolution, education was more accessible in the colonies than in any nation of western Europe.

EDUCATION IN THE NEW ENGLAND COLONIES

In New England a combination of factors facilitated the transition from old English educational tradition to the American emphasis on formal schooling. The religious zeal of the first generation of Puritans was more intense than that of any other major group of settlers. The number of college graduates among this group was higher than in any other time or place during the colonial period. This plus the facts that church and state worked together routinely and that the population was concentrated in small towns helps explain why the beginnings of the American public school system developed in New England.

In 1642 the Massachusetts General Court passed a law (amended slightly in 1648) which berated parents and masters of apprentices for neglecting the "training of their children in learning and labor" and ordered them to teach their children a trade and sufficient reading to understand "the principles of religion and the capital laws of the country." The selectmen of each town were empowered to take children from the parents or masters and apprentice them to others if parents and masters failed to obey the law. This Massachusetts law was copied, with only minor variations, in Connecticut, New Haven, and Plymouth. Of all the New England colonies, only Rhode Island failed to pass a compulsory education law.

It should be noted, however, that none of these laws made any reference to compulsory school attendance. In 1647 only eleven towns in Massachusetts were maintaining schools. In that year, therefore, the General Court passed the "Old Deluder Act," so called from its preamble:

> It being one chief project of that old deluder, Satan, to keep men from the knowledge of the Scriptures . . .

This act required that every town of 50 householders establish schools to teach reading and writing and that towns of 100 householders establish a grammar (secondary) school. A fine of £5 was to be levied on any town which violated this enactment. Later educational laws increased the fine and ordered towns of 500 householders to maintain two elementary and two secondary schools. Once again, all the New England colonies—with the sole exception of Rhode Island—imitated the Massachusetts law. Even many towns in Rhode Island voluntarily maintained schools.

These schools were tax supported (though a modest tuition fee was charged) and were open to all. This system of state-supported, compulsory education was a sharp break with tradition. Neither in England nor elsewhere on the American

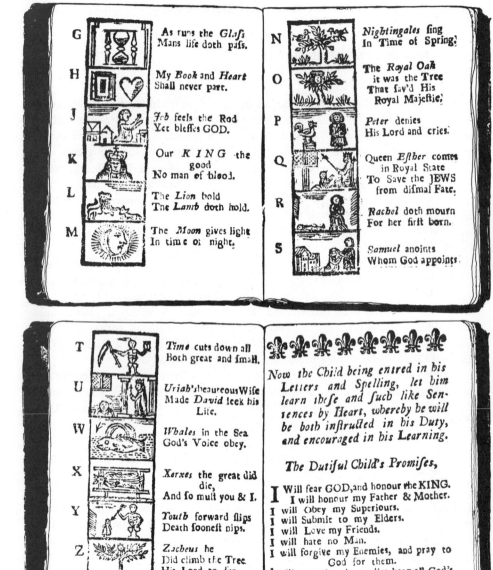

G As runs the *Glafs* Mans life doth pafs.

H My *Book* and *Heart* Shall never part.

J *Job* feels the Rod Yet blefses GOD.

K Our *K I N G* the good No man of blood.

L The *Lion* bold The *Lamb* doth hold.

M The *Moon* gives light In time of night.

N *Nightingales* fing In Time of Spring.

O The *Royal Oak* it was the Tree That fav'd His Royal Majeftie.

P *Peter* denies His Lord and cries.

Q Queen *Efther* comes in Royal State To Save the JEWS from difmal Fate.

R *Rachel* doth mourn For her firft born.

S *Samuel* anoints Whom God appoints.

T *Time* cuts down all Both great and fmall.

U *Uriah's* beauteous Wife Made *David* feek his Life.

W *Whales* in the Sea God's Voice obey.

X *Xerxes* the great did die, And fo muft you & I.

Y *Youth* forward flips Death fooneft nips.

Z *Zacheus* he Did climb the Tree His Lord to fee.

Now the Child being entred in his Letters and Spelling, let him learn thefe and fuch like Sentences by Heart, whereby he will be both inftructed in his Duty, and encouraged in his Learning.

The Dutiful Child's Promifes,

I Will fear GOD, and honour the KING. I will honour my Father & Mother. I will Obey my Superiours. I will Submit to my Elders. I will Love my Friends. I will hate no Man. I will forgive my Enemies, and pray to God for them. I will as much as in me lies keep all God's Holy Commandments.

FIGURE 20A (Library of Congress.)

continent had education been considered a public function. However, even in New England the degree of compliance with these laws is a matter for debate. For about twenty years after their passage, the laws seem to have been enforced. However, with the outbreak of King Philip's War, the crisis caused by the formation of the Dominion of New England, and the general decline in religious fervor, the enforcement policy broke down.

In the eighteenth century, as towns became larger and their population more dispersed, it became impossible for all children to attend one town school. The first solution was the moving school—a school which moved to a different part of town every few months. This meant, however, that if the school spent time in four locations, the children would not attend for more than one quarter of the school year. By the end of the colonial period, therefore, the New England colonies authorized their towns to divide themselves into school districts, each of which would have the taxing power to support a school of its own.

These New England laws did not establish a system of free public education in the modern sense of the concept. However, they did set two important precedents: Education should be compulsory, and public funds should be used to support education.

In the seventeenth century most New England children first learned their letters at a dame school—so called because they were conducted by a woman who charged a small fee to educate children in her own home. In addition to their "A, B, Cs," the children began learning to read. Often girls also learned sewing, knitting, and perhaps a little writing and arithmetic; the dame school was usually the only one they ever attended. In the seventeenth century less than 50 percent of the women who were involved in signing deeds or other legal documents were able to sign their names as compared with 90 percent of the men. (In Virginia the comparable figures were 55 percent of the men and 25 percent of the women.)

Even in the eighteenth century, Abigail Adams complained in a 1778 letter to her husband, about "the trifling narrow contracted" education—usually limited to writing and arithmetic and perhaps, music and dancing—which females received. Yet, Abigail and a few other women did manage to overcome these educational obstacles. Eliza Pinckney of South Carolina reports reading Locke and Virgil and learning shorthand. She confessed that she had enough legal knowledge to "convey by will, Estates, Real and Personal." All this was in addition to her expertise in agriculture.

Boys went on to the town school which, until the very end of the colonial period, was always taught by a man. Reading instruction continued in a hornbook—a sheet of paper attached to a board and covered with transparent horn.* Beginning in 1690 generations of New England students began using *The New England Primer.* The most famous feature of the primer was the rhymed alphabet with its messages to the learner:

---

*Taken from the horn of an animal, scraped thin so that it could be seen through.

A—In Adam's Fall
We Sinned All

I—The Idle Fool
Is whipt at School

X—Xerxes the Great did Die
And so must you and I

The New England Primer also contained the Lord's Prayer, the Ten Commandments, the Shorter Catechism, and other bits of rhymed advice such as

He who ne'er learns his A, B, C
Forever will a Blockhead be;
But he who learns his Letters fair
Shall have a Coach to take the Air.*

Because children were tainted by original sin, "spare the rod and spoil the child" was a favorite maxim of colonial schoolmasters. However, Puritan schoolmasters, most of whom were college graduates waiting to fill a ministerial position, added insult to injury by forcing their students to kiss the rod which punished them. Other forms of punishment included being forced to balance oneself on a one-legged stool with a dunce cap on, or having one's nose inserted in a split stick of wood. The students sat on rough benches; those who paid the least sat farthest from the fire in the cold weather. Birchbark was used instead of paper, which was scarce and expensive. Lead pencils were almost unknown, and writing was done with home-made ink and a goose quill. Schoolbooks were prized, and a familiar warning was found in many of them:

Steal not this Book for if you Do
The Devil will be after you.**

The older boys from more affluent families attended the Latin grammar school. The Boston Latin School, the earliest secondary school in the English colonies, was founded in 1636. There, and in other grammar schools, boys spent seven years learning Latin and Greek. In the grammar schools of New England, the introductory text was Ezekiel Cheever's *Accidence,* written by the master of the Boston Latin School, who served for over seventy years. They then studied classical authors such as Ovid, Cicero, Horace, and Virgil in Latin and Homer and Hesiod in Greek. Even in New England, however, before the end of the colonial period, secondary schools began introducing modern languages, mathematics, science, history, and commercial subjects.

*Excerpts from the *New England Primer,* 1897, edited by Paul L. Ford. Reprinted by permission of Dodd, Mead & Company.
**As quoted in *Old-Time Schools and School-Books* by Clifton Johnson (New York: The Macmillan Company, 1904), p. 154. By permission.

HIGHER EDUCATION

Graduation from a grammar school was required for admission to college. In 1636 the Massachusetts General Court, concerned about what might happen when in the words of a pamphlet called *New England's First Fruits,** "our present Ministers shall lie in the Dust," allocated £400 for the establishment of a college at Newton (soon to be renamed Cambridge). The first group of students was admitted in 1638, and in the same year John Harvard left half his estate (valued between £700 and £800) and his entire library to the institution, which gratefully took his name.

However, Harvard was not to be merely a theological seminary. Its charter, drawn up in 1650, specifically charged it with "the advancement of all good literature, arts and sciences." Harvard grew rather slowly. It had no permanent faculty until the 1680s, and by 1700 it had only graduated 465 students (out of the somewhat less than 600 who enrolled). According to the author of *New England's First Fruits,* to be admitted to Harvard, a student had to be able

> . . . to read Tully or such like classical author *ex tempore,* and make and speak Latin in Verse and Prose . . . and decline perfectly the Paradims of Nouns and Verbs in the Greek tongue. . . .

Once in Harvard the students continued learning Latin, Greek, and Hebrew and studied the Trivium (grammar, rhetoric, and logic) and Quadrivium (arithmetic, geometry, music, and astronomy). This had been the traditional curriculum in English universities and was to remain the standard curriculum in all colonial colleges until the middle of the eighteenth century.

A Harvard student's life was quite spartan. He lived in a dormitory on campus and arose at dawn for prayers and "bevers," a breakfast of bread and beer. The day was spent attending lectures and working with his tutor. Lunch was served at 11:00 A.M. and dinner at 7:30 P.M. He was then required to study, attend evening prayers, and retire early. Harvard expected proper dress and decorum from its students at all times. In spite of, or perhaps because of, the multitude of college regulations, students felt the need of letting off steam. Commencement Day was the traditional time for hijinks, but they might break out at any time of the school year. One of the most famous student "rebellions" took place in 1766 over the quality of butter served to them.

If plans had gone through as hoped, Virginia, not Massachusetts, would have had the first college in the English colonies. In 1619 King James I ordered the Anglican Church to raise money for a college to be located at Henrico, Virginia—a short distance from Jamestown. He believed that the Indians were "children of light" and should be taught the Christian religion. The Virginia Company set aside land and also appropriated money for this college, and thirty Indian children were forced into attending it. However, the Indian uprising of 1622 convinced the colo-

---

*Its author is believed to be Henry Dunster, the first president of Harvard College.

nists that the Indians were "children of the devil," suitable more for extermination than for education, and nothing more was heard of Henrico College.

Seventy years later the glaring need to train young American men for the Anglican ministry led to the founding of William and Mary College. In 1693 the king granted William and Mary College a charter which directed the college to train ministers for the Anglican Church, to foster the liberal arts, and to christianize the Indians. William and Mary's first classes were only on the secondary level, but by 1729 it had a faculty of six professors who were teaching respectable college courses. Its location at Williamsburg, Virginia's capital, provided its students close contact with the political and social leaders of Virginia and prepared them to play similar roles. No Indian ever voluntarily attended William and Mary, but the Virginia authorities forced the chiefs of tributary tribes to send their sons there as hostages for the tribes' good behavior.

The third colonial college was founded at the beginning of the eighteenth century when the people of Connecticut decided that they needed a college closer to home which would be less liberal in religious outlook than they thought Harvard had become. Yet, though the ministers of Connecticut founded the future Yale College to produce ministers, they also expected it to prepare its students in the liberal arts. The Collegiate School opened in Saybrook in 1701; moved to New Haven in 1716; and, in 1718, changed its name to Yale in gratitude for a gift by Elihu Yale of £500 worth of goods, some books, and a picture of George I.

The other colleges founded during the colonial period (with the exception of the College of Philadelphia) originated partly to meet the new demand for ministers caused by the Great Awakening, and partly in response to the need for more professionals caused by the growth of wealth and population in the colonies. In 1746 some of the alumni of the Log Cabin College, feeling the need for a Presbyterian institution of higher learning, established the College of New Jersey—later Princeton. Although founded primarily to train Presbyterian clergymen, Princeton admitted students of other denominations as well and pledged to educate them in the liberal arts and sciences.

William and Mary, the only Anglican college in the colonies, did not attract many students from the northern colonies. In 1754, therefore, King George II granted a charter for a college in New York, first called King's College and later, Columbia. Its president and a majority of its trustees had to be Anglican. However, because of pressure from Presbyterians in New York, Columbia, too, followed the policy of accepting all qualified students regardless of religious affiliation.

No one was more sensitive to the educational problems of colonial America than Benjamin Franklin. He realized that the social change and social mobility characteristic of the colonies required a new educational outlook—not one based solely on the traditional classical curriculum. In 1749 Franklin published *Proposals Relating to the Education of Youth in Pennsylvania,* in which he stressed the need for a nonsectarian college that would teach more useful subjects than Latin and Greek. This publication led, two years later, to the foundation of the Academy and

Charitable School of Philadelphia, which was supported by a combination of private and public funds. In 1755 this school began to offer higher level courses and became known as the College of Philadelphia. The college began as a nondenominational institution but later came under Anglican control. Under the leadership of William Smith, the College of Philadelphia deviated from the traditional curriculum more than any other colonial college. One-third of its courses were in the classics; one-third in ethics and metaphysics; and, most radical, one-third of the courses were in advanced mathematics, physics, chemistry, and other sciences. This college opened the first department of medicine in a colonial college in 1765 and later became the University of Pennsylvania.

The College of Rhode Island, later Brown, was established in 1764 to train Baptist ministers. It, too, however, expected its students to master the liberal arts and sciences. Although a Baptist institution, Brown's charter waived all religious requirements for admission and promised all students full liberty of conscience. Roger Williams would have been proud.

The Dutch Reformed Church also felt the need of a college. Theodore Freling-huysen requested that church authorities in Amsterdam approve a school to train Americans for the ministry. In 1766 Queen's College was approved and in 1771 it began instruction in New Brunswick, New Jersey. The outbreak of the Revolution almost destroyed Queen's College, but it reopened early in the nineteenth century as Rutgers.

In the 1760s the Reverend Eleazer Wheelock conducted a school for Indians in Connecticut. Knowing that certain wealthy Englishmen were interested in the education of Indians, he sent one of his students, Samson Occom to England to raise money for an Indian college. Occom raised over £11,000, including a generous contribution from Lord Dartmouth. New Hampshire then granted Wheelock land on which to erect a college. Dartmouth College received its charter in 1769, but in spite of the protests of Occom and others, it was an almost completely white school from its inception.

As with so many other institutions, American colleges differed from those in England. There a college was an integral part of a university and was governed by its professors. However, beginning with Harvard, American colleges were placed under the control of nonacademic boards. These boards—made up of laymen and minis-ters—appointed professors and presidents, determined curriculum, and regulated student life. The power of the board and the weakness of the faculty resulted in an increase in the authority of the president, the agent of the board. During the coloni-al period these presidents were always clergymen (as were most of the faculty mem-bers).

Colonial colleges were small. At the time of the Revolution, Harvard, the largest, had an enrollment of 180; most had less than 100; and the total number of college students was about 750. Although tuition was modest—four hogs a year at seventeenth-century Harvard—most of the students came from upper-class families. Scholarships, however, were available, and working one's way through college by waiting on tables or doing other chores around school was not uncommon. However, for most of the eighteenth century, one's rank in class was determined by social status rather than academic standing.

The fees levied for tuition, room, and board were never sufficient to support a college. Six colleges—including Harvard, Yale, and William and Mary—received support from their colonial legislatures. Yet, even they had to depend on funds raised by lotteries or private contributions. Fortunately, benefactors were found, mostly from the thirteen colonies themselves but also from England and the West Indies. David Garrick, the famous English actor, gave a benefit performance for the College of Philadelphia, and in 1757 Joseph Murray, a New York lawyer, left £5,555 to King's College, the largest gift to a college of the entire colonial period.

The colleges formed as a result of the Great Awakening served two important purposes. They provided American churches with relatively well-trained clergymen, so that they were no longer dependent on European clergymen. Secondly, these colleges served to unite the colonies. They attracted students from all colonies, not merely from their own locality. James Madison, for example, attended the College of New Jersey; almost half of the students at the College of Philadelphia were from outside the colony; and Baptists from every colony attended Brown.

In 1762 King George III, in urging contributions for King's College and the College of Philadelphia, had predicted that they would give their students a "common Education" and prepare them for "the just use of rational Liberty." Within a few years he must have been dismayed to realize just how successful these two (and the other colonial colleges) had been in these undertakings. Probably five-sixths of the approximately 3,000 living graduates of colonial colleges chose in 1776 to support—and lead—the American Revolution; and 22 of the 56 signers of the Declaration of Independence had graduated from colonial colleges.

Thus, by the middle of the eighteenth century, most white Americans had a wide variety of relatively accessible schools through which they could prepare themselves for participation in the thriving economic, cultural, and political life of the colonies.

BIBLIOGRAPHY

AXTELL, JAMES. *The School Upon a Hill: Education and Society in Colonial New England.* New Haven, 1974.

BAILYN, BERNARD. *Education in the Forming of American Society: Needs and Opportunity for Study.* Chapel Hill, 1960.

CREMIN, LAWRENCE A. *American Education: The Colonial Experience, 1607–1783.* New York, 1970.

HUMPHREY, DAVID C. *From King's College to Columbia, 1746–1800.* New York, 1976.

LOCKRIDGE, KENNETH A. *Literacy in Colonial New England: An Enquiry into the Social Context of Literacy in the Early Modern West.* New York, 1974.

MIDDLEKAUFF, ROBERT. *Ancients and Axioms: Secondary Education in Eighteenth-Century New England.* New Haven, 1963.
MILLER, HOWARD. *The Revolutionary College: American Presbyterian Higher Education, 1707–1837.* New York, 1976.
MORISON, SAMUEL E. *The Founding of Harvard College.* Cambridge, 1935.
WARCH, RICHARD. *School of the Prophets: Yale College, 1701–1740.* New Haven, 1973.

21
Language
and Literature

The English colonies served as a refuge for a wide variety of ethnic and religious groups. Yet, as Daniel J. Boorstin pointed out, one area of colonial life showed a startling degree of uniformity: That area was language. Unlike England and the other nations of Europe at the time—and for a long time after—regional and social differences in speech were relatively slight during the colonial period. Wherever they settled in the colonies, English people who came from London, the Midlands, or southern England all spoke with something very much like our contemporary southern accent. Non-English-speaking newcomers, with the exception of those Germans who settled together in groups, also tended, like later immigrants, to adopt English as the sign of their Americanization.

THE GROWTH OF AMERICAN ENGLISH

Just as religion, education, and other institutions changed to fit the new American environment, the English language itself began to change. Many factors influenced the growth of what we now call American English. One of these factors was the necessity of finding names for the many new plants, animals, and birds which the colonists found in the New World. Sometimes an English word was misapplied to meet this need. Thus, the American bison was called a *buffalo*; maize was called *corn*; and the red-breasted thrush was called a *robin*. More often plants or animals were named by combining two descriptive words, such as *bluebird, groundhog, eggplant, catfish,* or *bullfrog.*

A wide variety of words such as *tomahawk, squaw, papoose, canoe, toboggan, moccasin,* and *succotash* were borrowed from the Indians. By the eighteenth century American English was further enriched by an infusion of foreign words. The Dutch contributed *sleigh, yacht,* and *boss.* The Germans supplied *sauerkraut, dollar,* and *pretzel.* The French added *chowder, portage, cafe,* and *prairie.* Divergence between American English and the language spoken in the mother country increased as words such as *deft, ornate,* and *bub* (for *boy*) died out in England but were retained in the colonies. Also, English words such as *cliff, pond,* and *creek* acquired new meanings in America. Nor would Americanisms—a term coined by John Witherspoon (a president of the College of New Jersey)—such as *handy, chunky, fall* (for *autumn*), or *schooner,* have been understood in England. Yet, in spite of all these modifications, it should be remembered that American English differed less from standard English than the English spoken in most of the rural English counties.

THE DEVELOPMENT
OF AMERICAN LITERATURE

Throughout the long years during which American English was developing, colonial men and women produced an enormous, varied, practical and—on the whole—sophisticated, literature. For example, a good deal of early colonial writing was promotional in nature. In 1608 John Smith wrote *A True Relation of . . . Virginia,* and in 1613 the Virginia Company published the Reverend Alexander Whitaker's *Good News from Virginia,* both of which urged settlement and/or investment in that colony. John Smith also wrote the first promotional tract for New England, *A Description of New England* (1616).

In 1622 William Bradford and Edward Winslow advertised the Plymouth colony, and later the Reverend Francis Higginson and William Wood did the same for the Massachusetts Bay colony. Charles Hammond and George Alsop wrote about the Chesapeake colonies with much enthusiasm. William Penn himself composed one of the many tracts proclaiming the advantages of Pennsylvania. Many similar pamphlets written in German proved effective in attracting immigrants from that part of Europe. Likewise, the proprietors of the Carolinas reprinted John Lawson's account of his adventures among the Indians of North Carolina just a few years before the latter terminated his career by burning him at the stake.

Some literature was produced to counteract the exaggerated picture of America found in this promotional literature. One of the most humorous and satirical of these rebuttals was written by Ebenezer Cook, who spent a few unhappy years in Maryland. In 1708 he wrote a mock-heroic poem called the *Sot-Weed Factor,* lambasting every aspect of Maryland life. Later, Gottfried Mittelberger, a German immigrant, penned a more serious response to the propaganda aimed at his fellow countrymen. He described the horrors of the voyage across the Atlantic; the hardships suffered by redemptioners; and the difficulty of adjusting to American life. Finally, in 1741 *A True and Historical Narrative of the Colony of Georgia* satirized Oglethorpe's rule of that colony.

Another genre of writing was that produced by leaders who were concerned about recording the events in which they participated. John Smith, for example, in his *True Relation* and *The General History of Virginia* (1621), had no hesitation in placing himself center stage in the history of early Virginia. In contrast, William Bradford's chronicle *Of Plymouth Plantation* minimized his own role in the success of the colony and gave full credit to the Almighty. John Winthrop's *The History of New England from 1630 to 1649* (originally, his *Journal*) also stressed the role of God in the establishment of Massachusetts. In a similar vein Edward Johnson wrote *Wonder-Working Providence of Sion's Savior in New England* (1654), triumphantly recording the divine support which had enabled the New England saints to prosper. The last of the truly Puritan historians was Cotton Mather. His *Magnalia Christi Americana* (1702) was a curious mixture of biographies of lay and religious leaders; church history; and "remarkable providences"—all designed to convince his readers that unless they mended their ways and once again followed in the footsteps of their illustrious predecessor, they were doomed to perdition.

By the eighteenth century most American historians were recording history with a rational, secular, and almost patriotic approach. In 1705 Robert Beverley, a Virginia landowner, completed *The History and Present State of Virginia,* a study which generally praised the colony but which also noted its shortcomings. Beverley's brother-in-law, William Byrd II, also wrote three graphic descriptions of southern life: *The History of the Dividing Line, A Journey to the Land of Eden,* and *A Progress to the Mines.* In 1724 Hugh Jones, a professor at William and Mary College, wrote *The Present State of Virginia,* but the most valuable work on colonial Virginia, at least for its early years, was William Smith's *History of the First Discovery and Settlement of Virginia* (1747), which made extensive use of early Virginia records.

William Smith wrote *History of the Province of New York* (1757), and Thomas Prince attempted a history of New England; however, his passion for detail prevented him from progressing beyond 1633. Fortunately, New England's history was dealt with in Thomas Hutchinson's *History of the Colony of Massachusetts,* by modern standards the outstanding historical work of the colonial period. However, in many ways the most interesting historical work of the period was Dr. William Douglass's uncompleted general history of the colonies, written between 1747 and 1752. This work showed a realization that an American entity, rather than thirteen disconnected colonies, was already in existence.

Colonial writers did not confine themselves to prose. Contrary to popular belief, the Puritans did not hesitate to use poetry if it glorified God or propagated their creed. The *Bay Psalm Book* (1640) was an attempt to render the Psalms of David into English verse. The Twenty-third Psalm read:

> The Lord to mee a shepheard is,
>   want therefore shall not I
> Hee in the fold of tender-grasse,
>   doth cause mee downe to lie*

*From *The Bay Psalm Book—A Facsimile Reprint of the 1640 First Edition.* Reprinted by permission of Zoltan Haraszti.

This may seem to be a forced version of the psalm to modern ears, but it—and the other psalms in the *Bay Psalm Book*—went through twenty-seven editions by 1750.

The most famous exposition of Puritan theology in verse form was Michael Wigglesworth's *Day of Doom* (1662). This poem portrays the fate of the wicked in a lake of brimstone:

> Where day and night, without respite,
>   they wail, and cry, and howl
> For tort'ring pain, which they sustain,
>   in Body and in Soul.[1]

Even those relatively innocent infants who died before baptism fared only slightly better:

> A Crime it is, therefore in bliss you
>   may not hope to dwell
> But unto you I shall allow the easiest
>   room in Hell.[2]

The Reverend Edward Taylor composed a series of "Meditations" over a period of forty years, which interpreted Puritan theology and his own personal acceptance and reaction to it. His work is considered to be the best in the Puritan poetic tradition.

The earliest American woman poet was Anne Bradstreet, a seventeenth-century Puritan housewife and mother of eight children. Although much of her poetry was religiously motivated, she also wrote charmingly of earthly love and the beauties of nature.

> The trees all richly clad, yet void of pride,
> Were gilded o're by his rich golden head.
> Their leaves & fruits seem'd painted, but was true
> Of green, of red, of yellow, mixed hew,
> Rapt were my sences at this delectable view.*

Another poetess of the later colonial period was Phillis Wheatley. Phillis was brought to Boston as a slave in 1761 while still a young child. Her intellectual ability was so obvious to her owner, John Wheatley, that he allowed his daughters to educate her; encouraged her to write verse; and in 1773 freed her completely. Her poetry was published in a volume entitled *Poems on Various Subjects, Religious and Moral*. After her emancipation Phillis continued to write poems—the most famous of which is a celebration of the appointment of George Washington as commander-

[1] From "Day of Doom" by Wigglesworth. *In Puritan Pronaos* by S. E. Morison. New York: New York University Press, 1936, p. 209. By permission.

[2] *Ibid.*

*From *The Complete Works of Anne Bradstreet* by McElrath & Robb. Reprinted by permission of Twayne Publishers.

222   Language and Literature

in-chief of the Continental army. Unfortunately, the Wheatleys died; Phillis had an unhappy marriage; and she died in childbirth in 1784. Phillis Wheatley was not the only, or even the first, black poet in the colonies. Jupiter Hammon, a New York slave, had his earliest work published in 1760 and continued writing both poetry and prose dealing primarily with religious topics for over twenty years.

Americans also expressed their thoughts in diaries. Samuel Sewall, a Boston merchant and magistrate, kept a diary from 1674 to 1729. In it he detailed his religious and personal problems and commented on family and community life. Cotton Mather also kept a diary from 1681 to 1708, which described his version of the struggle between God and Satan for his soul and for the soul of all of New England. However, not only Puritans kept diaries. In his *Secret Diary* William Byrd II wrote gracefully of life in Virginia and England with a maximum of wit and a minimum of moral judgment.

Both the *Journal* of the Quaker leader John Woolman and the more famous *Autobiography* of Benjamin Franklin closely resemble diaries. The latter was written in three installments between 1771 and 1788 but was never completed. This work, too, was completely secular, and its clear and pithy style and the moral of its rags-to-riches plot still influence American life and literature. Franklin was also the author of many short works dealing perceptively, and often drolly, with the economic and social problems and foibles of his era.

The two most typically American types of literature were the almanac and the Indian captivity narratives. The almanac was a compendium containing monthly calendars; information about the weather, the tides, and farming methods; recipes; and advice aimed at farmers, seafarers, and housewives—all spiced with poems, sayings, and other amusing tidbits. The earliest almanac appeared in Massachusetts in 1639, and by the eighteenth century almanacs were second only to the Bible in volume of sales. *Poor Richard's Almanack,* because it was published by Benjamin Franklin, is best known to us. However, the almanacs put out by Nathaniel Ames, Sr. and Jr., sold 60,000 copies a year—far more than Franklin's product. In any case, both almanacs stressed self-reliance, industry, and frugality, which were to become known as typically American virtues.

Close behind almanacs in popularity were the many tales of suffering and escape from Indian captivity, which remained a realistic possibility for some Americans all through the colonial period. The earliest, and most popular, of these books was Mary Rowlandson's *Captivity and Restoration* (1682), which recounted her capture by, and eventual redemption with the help of God from, the Indians. Other Americans wrote more serious accounts of Indian life. A few, such as John Eliot and Daniel Gookin, praised the Indians' attempts to defend their lands and way of life. Most, however, such as William Hubbard and both Mathers, viewed the Indians as "hounds of hell" who must either be converted or destroyed. However, the best colonial work on Indian life was Cadwallader Colden's *History of the Five Indian Nations* (1727).

Still other Americans helped to inform both their fellow Americans and Europeans by writing about their travels throughout the colonies. Sarah Kemble Knight of Massachusetts, Dr. Alexander Hamilton of Maryland, and John Bartram, the Pennsylvania botanist, all left valuable and lively accounts of the people and places they visited on their journeys. The popularity of these accounts indicates an interest by Americans in regions outside their own immediate vicinity.

Plays were very much an eighteenth-century colonial phenomenon. Thomas Godfrey of Philadelphia, who wrote much poetry, is better remembered as the author of a play called the *Prince of Parthia* (1758). This oriental tragedy, produced in 1767—four years after its author's death—was the first full-length verse play by an American to be produced professionally in America. Earlier, in 1714, Robert Hunter (the governor of New York) wrote the first play in the English colonies. However, this play, which attacked his political enemies, was only performed privately. Major Robert Rogers wrote a play based on the life of Pontiac in 1766, but it was produced in London—not in the colonies. Many plays were written in the 1770s to attack English policy toward the colonies. Most of these plays, however, such as Mercy Otis Warren's *The Adulateur* and *The Group*, were propaganda pieces designed to be read rather than performed.

LITERARY TASTES
OF COLONIAL AMERICANS

One of the reasons why the colonists produced so few works of a purely literary nature was that they could—and did, particularly in the eighteenth century—import such works from England. Library lists tell us a great deal about the reading interests of colonial Americans. Some private colonial libraries were large by any standard: Cotton Mather owned 4,000 books; William Byrd owned 3,600; and James Logan of Pennsylvania owned over 3,000, including many scientific works. Harvard had the largest colonial library, almost 5,000 volumes, before the collection was destroyed by fire in 1764. Puritans, southern planters, and merchants in the middle colonies all had many volumes of theology and sermons on their library shelves. The classics, both in the original and in translation, were also found in libraries in all the colonies. So too were books on history and government along with a wide variety of how-to books on law, medicine, farming, and surveying—particularly in the south.

One of the most popular books of the seventeenth century was Pierre de La Prémaudaye's *The French Academy,* an encyclopedic work on natural and moral science. Sir Walter Raleigh's *History of the World* was also found in many colonial libraries. The most-read religious books (with the exception of the Bible) were John Foxe's *The Book of Martyrs* and John Bunyon's *Pilgrims Progress.* The former volume's depiction of Catholic persecution of Protestants did much to preserve anti-Catholic sentiment in the colonies. Fictional works, although not unknown, were not plentiful on the shelves of seventeenth-century libraries. This changed markedly in the eighteenth century, in conformity with a similar trend in the mother country. Although nonfiction works by Montaigne, Descartes, Locke, and others predominated, the writings of English authors such as Swift, Sterne, Pope, Steele, Richardson, and Addison were read in all the colonies (although they were somewhat more popular in the colonies south of New England).

During this century most colonial towns organized public, or semipublic, libraries. A Bostonian bequeathed books to the townspeople of Boston as early as 1656, although this did not develop into a full-fledged public library. The South Carolina legislature voted funds for a library in 1698, and New York City organized one in 1730. However, both these libraries contained few books and were housed in very poor facilities. Later the Library Company of Philadelphia (1731), the Redwood Library of Newport (1747), and the New York Society Library (1754) proved to be more successful. Most towns also had circulating libraries, which levied a small charge for borrowing books. Here the utilitarian view of literature prevailed, and books on mathematics, physics, astronomy, history, and travel outnumbered classics, religious works, and English novels. This probably reflected the interests of the patrons of these libraries—the "middling" group of townspeople. Towns also had numerous booksellers.

NEWSPAPERS AND MAGAZINES

Toward the end of the seventeenth century, the colonies were mature enough economically and intellectually to feel the need for newspapers. The first colonial newspaper was *Public Occurrences,* which published one issue at Boston in 1690 and was immediately shut down by the authorities. The first successful newspaper, *The Boston News-Letter,* did not appear until 1704. By 1732 Philadelphia, New York, Newport, and Charleston (as well as Boston) all had at least one newspaper. By 1763 the colonies could boast of twenty-three newspapers, a number which grew to thirty-seven by the time of the Revolution. To us the most interesting material found in these newspapers is the advertisements for goods, medicines, land, and runaway slaves and wives. The rest of the space was occupied with European news, governmental edicts, notices of ship sailings and arrivals, and essays, stories, and poems copied from European journals or produced locally. Papers, at least until the hectic days of the 1760s and 1770s, were four pages in size and came out once a week. Illustrations and cartoons were rare—the most famous of the latter was Franklin's cut-up snake representing the colonies, with the caption "Join, or Die" (1754). Newspapers were probably second only to almanacs in their readership and proved extremely important in developing colonial self-consciousness and unity.

At first most colonial newspapers tended to be conservative because their publishers were usually the local colonial postmasters, who were allowed to distribute their papers through the mails. Therefore, they could not afford to irritate governmental leaders. However, this precedent was broken by James Franklin (Benjamin's older halfbrother) in Boston and William Bradford in Philadelphia, who did not hesitate to criticize the authorities. The most significant controversy of the colonial period centered on John Peter Zenger, the publisher of the *New York Weekly Journal.* His continued attacks on Governor William Cosby led to his arrest

225 Language and Literature

for seditious libel in 1734. At his trial ten months later, Zenger was defended by Andrew Hamilton of Philadelphia, one of the leading lawyers of the period. Hitherto in such cases the jury's sole duty was to decide if the offending articles had in fact been printed. The judge (or judges) then decided if the articles were libelous. According to *A Brief Narrative of the Case and Trial of John Peter Zenger* by James Alexander (1736), in his arguments Hamilton stressed the press's need for "the liberty both of exposing and opposing arbitrary Power . . . by speaking and writing Truth." He convinced the jury that it, and not the judges, should study Zenger's articles: If it found them to be accurate, it should acquit him. The jury agreed with Hamilton's contention that truth is a defense and freed Zenger. Other colonies gradually followed this new practice of allowing juries to decide libel cases. However, the Zenger case was more of a symbol than a precedent. Colonial newspapers still did not enjoy full freedom of the press. In a few trials the old procedure was followed, and, even more often—and more threatening—colonial assemblies did not hesitate to shut down newspapers or fine publishers who dared to criticize them. Nevertheless, the Zenger case did encourage other newspapers to censure political leaders when they felt it necessary and made these leaders less likely to use prior restraint or to bring legal action against the papers.

Americans were not ready to support a magazine during the colonial period. Three attempts, one by Benjamin Franklin, were made to publish magazines in the 1740s, but all failed within a year or less. *The American Magazine and Monthly Chronicle* (published in Philadelphia) lasted a year (1757), in spite of printing a wide variety of scientific articles and contributions from Thomas Godfrey and Francis Hopkinson. The latter was later to win fame as a poet, composer, and signer of the Declaration of Independence. Apparently, those Americans interested in magazines preferred to read the already-established English publications rather than colonial imitations.

No American of the colonial period may properly be described as a professional writer. Most books still came from England and/or followed English literary conventions. Nevertheless, as this chapter has attempted to indicate, a great deal of worthwhile writing was done; by the end of the period, a literature that was distinctly American in theme and outlook had been produced. Much of it—an estimated 1,200 titles a year—was printed on the twenty-four presses at work in the colonies. By the end of the colonial period, common experiences—as expressed in its literature—had laid the foundations for American cultural autonomy.

BIBLIOGRAPHY

BOWES, FREDERICK. *The Culture of Early Charleston.* Chapel Hill, 1942.
BRIGHAM, C. S. *Journals and Journeymen: A Contribution to the History of Early American Newspapers.* Westport, Conn., 1971. (Reprint of 1950 ed.).

DAVIS, HAROLD E. *The Fledgling Province: Social and Cultural Life in Colonial Georgia*. Chapel Hill, 1976.

DAVIS, RICHARD BEALE. *Intellectual Life in the Colonial South, 1585-1763*. 3 vols. Knoxville, 1978.

KOBRE, SIDNEY. *The Development of the Colonial Newspaper*. Pittsburgh, 1944.

LEVY, LEONARD W. *Legacy of Suppression: Freedom of Speech and Press in Early American History*. Cambridge, 1960.

MAY, HENRY F. *The Enlightenment in America*. New York, 1978.

MORISON, SAMUEL E. *The Intellectual Life of Colonial New England*. New York, 1956.

MURDOCK, KENNETH B. *Literature and Theology in Colonial New England*. New York, 1949.

NYE, RUSSELL B. *American Literary History, 1607-1830*. New York, 1970.

RICHARDSON, LYON N. *A History of Early American Magazines*. New York, 1931.

TOLLES, FREDERICK. *Meeting House and Counting House: The Quaker Merchants of Colonial Philadelphia, 1682-1763*. New York, 1948.

WRIGHT, LOUIS B. *The Cultural Life of the American Colonies, 1607-1763*. New York, 1957.

WRIGHT, LOUIS B. *The First Gentlemen of Virginia*. San Marino, Ca., 1940.

WROTH, LAWRENCE C. *An American Bookshelf*. Philadelphia, 1934.

22
Colonial Arts and Sciences

"America has not yet produced one good poet, one able mathematician, one man of genius in a single art, or a single science." So wrote the French scholar Abbé Raynal in his *History of European Colonies and Commerce* (1770). Was he correct? Was he "fair"? One might question whether a provincial society (such as the colonies) can be expected to shine in the arts and sciences. At any rate, we must first examine the state of European scientific development before surveying colonial developments.

AMERICAN SCIENTISTS

As Max Savelle has pointed out, during the seventeenth century, when the English colonies were being founded, scientists such as Kepler, Galileo, Bacon, Harvey, Boyle, Descartes, Leibnitz, and Newton were laying the foundations of modern physics, astronomy, chemistry, and mathematics. Thus, the colonists were aware of the latest scientific discoveries almost as soon as they were made and were in a position to react to, make use of, and build upon them as far as their abilities and desires allowed. Fortunately, the American environment was open to new ideas, and unlike the situation in parts of Europe, clerical opposition to science was minimal. The Mathers (and clergymen of other denominations) tended to welcome science as a new and additional way of comprehending the greatness of God; even the more skeptical clergymen never made an issue of their doubts and questions.

Newton was, by far, the most influential European scientist. His view that a benevolent God had created the universe and laid down the immutable laws which were to govern it had a profound influence upon every aspect of eighteenth-century life in America. This outlook characterized what is known as the Enlightenment, or the Age of Reason. The Age of Reason was one in which the dignity and rationality of people was stressed. Through reason people could discover and comprehend the natural laws which governed every phase of life. By using moral and ethical sense, people would live in conformity with these natural laws and ultimately reach a stage of perfection that would result in a virtual "golden age." Nowhere were these ideas more accepted than in America, where the absence of feudal vestiges and the abundance of free land seemed to offer an ideal laboratory for the experimentation necessary to verify the Rationalist hypotheses.

From the beginning of settlement, America proved hospitable to science and scientists.* Thomas Hariot, an astronomer and mathematician, was a member of the first Roanoke colony. In 1588 he wrote an account of his observations in the New World. In early Jamestown Dr. Lawrence Bohun made a study of the herbs and plants growing in the area and particularly recommended the medicinal properties of sassafras. (Later botanists found many other therapeutic plants in the colonies.) John Winthrop, Jr., was the outstanding scientist of the early colonial period. In 1663 he imported a telescope through which he saw a fifth satellite of Jupiter (which was not confirmed until 1892). Winthrop embraced and taught the Copernican system of astronomy long before it was accepted in most European nations. He was also an expert in metallurgy and was elected a fellow of the Royal Society, the most select group of English scientists, only a year after it was founded.

A later Winthrop, John Winthrop IV, held the position of Hollis Professor of Mathematics and Natural Philosophy at Harvard between 1738 and 1779. He taught astronomy, chemistry, physics, and geology in addition to introducing the calculus to his students. Winthrop was also the author of many learned papers on eclipses and other astronomical phenomena. Americans were also active in what might be called applied science. Thomas Godfrey of Philadelphia improved the quadrant in 1730, and Edward Bromfield, a New Englander, improved the microscope during the 1740s. Toward the end of the colonial period, David Rittenhouse, a self-taught Pennsylvania clockmaker who became a professor of science at the College of Philadelphia, made improvements on the telescope and constructed models of the solar system which faithfully mirrored the state of knowledge of the time.

The abundance of natural resources led to an emphasis on natural history. Linnaeus's classification of plants and animals made during the eighteenth century only increased interest in American plants. William Byrd II had earlier written a paper on the healthful effects of tobacco and ginseng. John Bartram, a Pennsylvania Quaker, designed a botanical garden which had the largest collection of American

---

*Natural philosophy was one of the two branches of science at that period. It included physics, chemistry, astronomy, and mathematics. The other branch, natural history, included botany, zoology, and geology. However, the boundaries between these two branches were hazy and people engaged in both.

plants and flowers up to that time. Bartram had the honor of being appointed the royal botanist for the American colonies by George III. Other outstanding botanists were Dr. Samuel Garden of South Carolina (who is commemorated by the gardenia); Cadwallader Colden of New York (who also excelled in physics, math, and medicine); and John Mitchell and John Clayton of Virginia.

With an abundance of free land, most colonial farmers were inefficient. Still, a few Americans did pioneer in the development of scientific agriculture. Paul Dudley, a New Englander, sent the Royal Society numerous papers on the scientific growing of corn, pumpkins, and squash as well as on the production of maple syrup. The best studies of scientific agriculture, however, were written by Jared Elliot, a Connecticut clergyman. He advocated proper fertilization, crop rotation, stock-breeding, and the use of more advanced agricultural implements.

In all, eighteen Americans—including both Increase and Cotton Mather—were elected to the Royal Society. Still, the most renowned scientist was Benjamin Franklin. Franklin combined the instincts of a pure researcher with those of a practical man of affairs. His studies of electricity led to the lightning rod; his studies of optics led to bifocal glasses; and his studies of heat led to the "Franklin stove." Franklin's research on electricity was translated into French, German, and Italian, and he did more than anyone else to popularize science. The Library Company of Philadelphia—which he organized—had the largest collection of scientific books in the English colonies. *Poor Richard's Almanack* did much to disseminate scientific information. Most importantly, in 1769—after a quarter of a century of effort—Franklin managed to activate the American Philosophical Society. By the time of the Revo-

FIGURE 22A
(New York Public Library.)

lution, the Society had members from eleven colonies, the West Indies, England, and several other European nations.

MEDICINE

Health care was a perennial problem for colonial Americans. Immigrants literally took their lives in their hands when they journeyed to America. The danger came not from Indian attacks, as many of them feared, but from disease. Immigrants were most vulnerable to disease after the long ocean voyage which brought them to these shores. Among the leading killers were smallpox, yellow fever, dysentery, typhoid fever, malaria, diphtheria, cholera, whooping cough, scarlet fever, measles, and influenza.

The physicians, whether colonial or European, could be as deadly as the diseases they attempted to treat. A distorted version of Galen's medical theory (still prevalent in the early colonial period) maintained that in order to be healthy, the human body had to have the proper balance of humors: heat, dryness, moistness, and cold. A disease that resulted from coldness was to be treated with heat; one that resulted from moistness was to be dried up. Therefore, patients were blistered by heat and bled, only too often, to death.

Almost anyone could claim to be a doctor in colonial America. For most of the period, no licensing or regulatory boards existed, although some colonies attempted to control the fees which doctors might charge. The vast majority of doctors either taught themselves from whatever medical books were available or served a brief apprenticeship with a practicing physician. Clergymen were often called upon to heal the body as well as the soul, and plantation owners, or their wives, usually "doctored" their slaves using home remedies that were often safer than the doctor's usual bleeding process. Some slaves had more medical knowledge than their owners, and a few received their freedom as a reward. Most whites, however, were afraid to allow slaves to practice medicine on them, lest they accidentally—or purposely—poison them. Surgery was extremely primitive, but no more so than in contemporary Europe. Amputations and other operations were performed without anesthesia—the patient either drinking liquor, taking opium, or literally biting on a bullet. Babies were delivered by midwives, although in 1745 a Dr. John Dupuy of New York (and later other doctors) began to perform this function. Unfortunately, however, the number of women who died in childbirth failed to decrease.

Colonial remedies make strange reading today. For example, "When cold take out the toades, and in an iron mortar pound them very well." Rattlesnake flesh, bear grease, eagles' dung, and all types of herbs and roots were prescribed for various maladies. Apothecaries and doctors blended what would later be called patent medicines. Elixirs and "nostrums" were concocted that claimed to cure everything from asthma to ulcers. Indian remedies such as "Tuscarora rice"—which was claimed to cure tuberculosis—were already popular and were prescribed by the most distinguished colonial physicians (at least up to the middle of the eighteenth century).

This change was caused by the improvement in medical treatment which began at about this time. More Americans went to Europe, particularly the University of Edinburgh, to study medicine. The first American hospital opened in Philadelphia in 1751 and had a mortality rate that was 50 percent lower than that in European hospitals of the period.

During the 1760s the physicians of New York and New Jersey both formed medical societies to examine and license those who wished to practice medicine in their colonies. Dr. John Morgan, an Edinburgh graduate, was the founder and first professor at the medical school—the first in the colonies—opened at the College of Philadelphia in 1765. Two more followed soon after: at King's College in 1768 and at Harvard in 1783. However, as late as the outbreak of the Revolution, only about 5 percent of colonial doctors had an MD degree.

The main advance in American health care came through the gradual acceptance of the practice of inoculation. Cotton Mather had learned from his slave Onesimus that in Africa people were inoculated with smallpox serum; this resulted in a mild form of the disease and immunity from it afterward. Cotton had also read that the same practice was followed in Turkey. In 1721, therefore, when a smallpox epidemic hit New England, Mather convinced Dr. Zabdiel Boylston to inoculate large numbers of Bostonians. Only slightly over 2 percent of those inoculated died, in contrast to a death rate of 15 percent for those who caught the disease naturally.

In spite of these favorable results, Mather was attacked by both physicians and clergymen, and a bomb (which fortunately did not explode) was thrown into his home. Most colonies actually passed laws against inoculation because, as Benjamin Franklin reported, those who were inoculated were not quarantined, so that they spread smallpox among those who were not inoculated. When quarantine did become part of the procedure, and ministers began to agree that disease was not necessarily brought on by the hand of God, inoculation became an accepted practice in the colonies, and smallpox became much less of a killer.

The dental profession did not as yet exist in the colonies. Such work was usually performed by the local barber—or even by the blacksmith. A set of false teeth was difficult to obtain, and a well-fitting set was virtually unknown—as George Washington could testify.

ART

Art in colonial America began, much as science did, as a European phenomenon transported to the New World. However, art was never able to separate itself from its European roots, and as we shall see, the greatest artists of the colonial period felt impelled to return to Europe to fulfill their potential. James T. Adams may have been entirely correct when he entitled his volume on American life between 1690 and 1763 *Provincial Society.*

Painters found few private patrons and no public buildings to decorate in seventeenth-century America. However, some of the wealthier people did want their likenesses preserved for posterity; in the days before photography, this could only be done by a painter. About 400 paintings have survived from seventeenth-century America, but many of them were probably brought from Europe by their owners. Some of the seventeenth-century limners, or portrait painters, were English or Dutch artists who had learned their craft in Europe before coming to the colonies either temporarily or as settlers. Others, such as the sea captain Thomas Smith, were American-born artists who learned to paint by copying prints of European paintings. They often painted standardized male or female bodies in advance and merely added the faces of their clients. When not painting portraits, limners supplemented their income by giving drawing lessons, painting signs for shops and taverns, and even doing ordinary house painting.

By the eighteenth century, however, there was a sufficient number of prosperous colonists who wanted formal portraits of themselves and their families painted in the European manner to support a group of professional artists. These colonists preferred—probably rightfully—even the second-rate European artist (the only type that came to the colonies) to the American-born artist. Early in the eighteenth century, Henrietta Johnston, one of the few woman painters of the period, sailed from England to Charleston. There she enjoyed wide popularity until her death over twenty years later. A Swiss artist, Jeremiah Theüs, succeeded her as the leading artist in Charleston from 1739 to 1774. Charles Bridges, an English painter, made a brief visit to Virginia in 1735 and painted flattering portraits of the daughters of William Byrd and, it is thought, members of other planter families before returning to England. Gustavus Hesselius, a Swedish artist, arrived in Philadelphia in 1711 and, in addition to conventional portraits, painted works based on the Bible and on classical mythology—the first treatments of either of these themes in the English colonies.

The most famous European artist to reach America was John Smibert, an English artist. He arrived in America with Bishop George Berkeley. Smibert's portrait of the bishop and his family soon won him acclaim. Smibert's studio in Boston and his collection of copies of the works of artists such as Raphael, Rubens, Titian, and Poussin soon became a source of inspiration to a new generation of American artists, such as Copley, Peale, and Trumbull.

Even before this time, however, America had produced one outstanding artist, Robert Feke. Feke was born on Long Island in 1705 and was most active between 1740 and 1750. It is not certain whether he had any formal art training, but wealthy Americans in Boston, New York, and Philadelphia were all eager for him to paint their portraits. Dr. Andrew Hamilton of Maryland spoke for most contemporary Americans when in his *Itinerarium,* he described him as "the most extraordinary [artistic] genius I ever knew."

It was the next generation of American artists, however, who were to receive recognition outside the colonies. Their work was influenced by the rococo style of the contemporary English painters Romney, Reynolds, and Gainesborough. The first of these men to win recognition was Benjamin West (1738–1820), a native of

Philadelphia known as the Raphael of America. West settled in England in the 1760s, became president of the Royal Academy, and greatly encouraged the careers of other Americans who came to England. Charles Willson Peale of Maryland (1741-1827), Gilbert Stuart of Newport (1755-1828), and John Trumbull of Connecticut (1756-1843) were all protegés of West. However, all three returned to America and painted the men and events of the Revolutionary and early national periods. Another famous expatriate was John Singleton Copley (1738-1815), who was made a fellow of the Royal Academy in 1766, although he did not leave Boston for England until 1774. Even so devoted a patriot as John Adams had to admit in a letter to Abigail that Copley was "the greatest Master, that ever was in America."

CRAFTS

While colonial painters were deliberately following European conventions, other colonial artisans, most of them unknown, produced works of art in a distinctively American style. Most produced basically utilitarian objects. Those who carved figureheads for ships and weather vanes for homes and barns must have been in demand. The same would be true of the blacksmiths who made the ornamental knockers, andirons, and railings found in and around colonial homes, and of the artisans who carved the likenesses of the deceased, or of fanciful figures, on New England tombstones. Other artists produced silhouettes, which were much prized by those who could not afford oil paintings. Engravers such as William Bartram (the son of the famous botanist) or Henry Pelham (Copley's stepfather) were very popular. Further, Amos Doolittle and Paul Revere won fame for their depictions of the battles of Lexington and Concord and the Boston Massacre, respectively.

Revere came from a long and distinguished line of colonial silversmiths, dating back to Thomas Howard, who began working in Jamestown in 1620. However, to survive, silversmiths needed a sufficient number of customers with taste and the money to satisfy their taste. By the middle of the seventeenth century, such customers could be found in New England, where Robert Sanderson and his partner John Hull won fame in Boston and the surrounding area. They, in turn, trained Jeremiah Dummer and John Coney, who carried on their tradition. Two Huguenot silversmiths, Caesar Ghiselin and John Nys (and later John Richardson), helped make Philadelphia another center of colonial silver making. The third center was New York, where Dutch influence predominated throughout the seventeenth century. Later that style was eclipsed by English patterns, as evidenced in the works of silversmiths such as Myer Myers, the most capable of the New York silversmiths of the eighteenth century.

Most eighteenth-century colonial silverware was based on the English Georgian style but was less ornate. Probably the greatest boon to colonial silversmiths (and to their English counterparts) was the great demand for tea services and numerous other utensils by the ever-increasing middle and upper classes in the cities. By the

FIGURE 22B   (New York Public Library.)

end of the colonial period, New York, Boston, and Philadelphia boasted over 400 silversmiths. In the south, however, the plantation aristocracy continued to give their patronage to English silversmiths.

Furniture making, too, depended on a class of sophisticated and affluent consumers. This group was so small in the colonies during the seventeenth century that those few colonists who were willing and able to purchase fine furniture had to obtain it largely from England. However, by the eighteenth century a sufficiently large group of colonial consumers had developed for furniture making to become a lucrative trade for colonial artisans, particularly in Newport, Boston, Philadelphia, and New York. Colonial furniture makers did not just copy the prevailing eighteenth-century English styles: Queen Anne, Hepplewhite, and Chippendale. They gave their products distinctive and artistic touches which added to their beauty and utility.

235   Colonial Arts and Sciences

Women, too, had the opportunity to express themselves artistically. Woven or patchwork quilts were one of a family's prized possessions. Women often met together for a quilting bee lasting several days, during which they would stitch together quilts of all patterns and colors. Most young girls prided themselves on their samplers. These samplers usually contained the letters of the alphabet; pictures of birds, animals, or flowers; a biblical quotation; and a verse such as

Here you see
What care my Mother
Took of me.*

However, one young lady was honest enough—and bold enough—to complain right on her sampler that she hated every stitch that she put into it.

The arts and sciences of colonial America were based, inevitably, on European concepts and models. American scientists and artists tended to support and expand the theories of Europeans rather than develop original theories and styles. Yet, just as inevitably, the colonial environment and the distance from Europe created certain reorientations and transmutations which ultimately led to distinctive American characteristics: pragmatism and realism in both art and science. Abbé Raynal was woefully inaccurate in his assessment of those Americans who contributed to this transformation.

BIBLIOGRAPHY

BELKNAP, WALDRON P. *American Colonial Painting: Materials for A History.* Cambridge, 1959.
BLACK, MARY, and LIPMAN, JEAN. *American Folk Painting.* New York, 1966.
CASH, P., et al., eds. *Medicine in Colonial Massachusetts, 1620–1820.* Charlottesville, 1981.
CUMMINGS, ABBOTT LOWELL. *The Framed Houses of Massachusetts Bay, 1625–1725.* Cambridge, 1979.
DUFFY, JOHN. *Epidemics in Colonial America.* Baton Rouge, 1953.
HAYWARD, ARTHUR H. *Colonial and Early American Lighting.* New York, 1962.
HINDLE, BROOKE, ed. *Early American Science.* New York, 1976.
KOLLER, JAMES B., ed. *Early American Silver and Its Makers.* New York, 1979.
LOCKWOOD, LUKE V. *Colonial Furniture.* 2 vols. New York, 1921.
MORRISON, HUGH S. *Early American Architecture: From the First Colonial Settlements to the National Period.* New York, 1952.
QUIMBY, IAN M. G., ed. *American Painting to 1776: A Reappraisal.* Charlottesville, 1971.

*From *Child Life in Colonial Days* by Alice Morse Earle. New York: The Macmillan Company, 1899, p. 332.

SHYROCK, RICHARD H. *Medicine and Society in America, 1660–1860.* New York, 1960.

STEARNS, RAYMOND P. *Science in the British Colonies of America.* Urbana, 1970.

WATERMAN, THOMAS T. *The Dwellings of Colonial America.* Chapel Hill, 1950.

WRIGHT, LOUIS B., et al. *The Arts in America: The Colonial Period.* New York, 1966.

23

Everyday Life in Colonial America

The key word in any description of the colonial population is growth. Between 1640 and 1700 the population increased from 26,000 to about 251,000. During the eighteenth century it more than doubled every twenty-five years (at a rate of 2.5 percent a year), reaching about 1 million by 1750 and about 2.5 million at the outbreak of the Revolution. It is estimated that this rate of growth was over twice that of western Europe during the same period. Although immigration played a part in this population growth, the major factor was natural increase. The rate of natural increase for white colonists is placed between 26 and 30 percent a decade, which accounts for most of the 34.5 percent rate of population growth per decade. The higher birth rate in the colonies, coupled with the slightly lower age at marriage of colonial men and women as compared to Europe (see Chapter 18), partially explains the higher rate of colonial population increase.

DEMOGRAPHIC CHARACTERISTICS

A second factor explaining the increase in colonial population was a mortality rate in the colonies of 20 to 25 per 1,000 people; in Europe it averaged about 40 per 1,000. In spite of the high mortality rate for new arrivals in America, and the typically colder winters in the middle and New England colonies, a more ample supply of food and fuel, generally better living conditions, and a more scattered population (which inhibited epidemics) avoided a high death rate from malnutrition and disease—problems that were then still common in Europe. These factors also help explain the significantly lower colonial infant mortality rate and a somewhat lower rate of death in childbirth.

In the southern colonies immigration—in this case the importation of slaves—did have a crucial effect on population growth. About a quarter of a million slaves were imported into the colonies between 1700 and the Revolution (75,000 during the 1760s alone), and probably 90 percent worked in the southern colonies. By the end of the period, blacks made up 40 percent of the population of the five southern colonies, with a high of 70 percent in South Carolina and a low of 15 percent in North Carolina. The southern colonies' share of the total population rose from 42 to 46 percent between 1700 and 1770. An estimated 300,000 to 350,000 white immigrants arrived in the colonies, between 1700 and 1775. Most of them settled in the middle colonies, particularly in Pennsylvania. Thus, this section witnessed the highest rate of population increase during the eighteenth century. The middle colonies' share of the population rose, therefore, from 19 percent in 1700 to 26 percent in 1790.

With two sections increasing their share of the population, New England showed a decline—statistically from 39 to 28 percent—during this seventy-year period. This decline is largely explained by two factors: the relatively small number of immigrants who chose to settle there; and a birth rate of about 40 per 1,000 (considerably lower than that of the other two sections), resulting from the shortage of land and the constriction of other facets of the economy. By 1775, 78.7 percent of English emigrants lived in the thirteen mainland colonies, 17.3 percent lived in the West Indies, and 4 percent lived in Canada. Robert V. Wells states in his study of colonial population, *The Population of the British Colonies in America before 1776,* "It may well be that the confidence inspired by rapidly growing numbers" helped make Americans "willing to risk a physical confrontation with England over economic and constitutional matters."

Two other demographic characteristics of the colonial population are worth noting. First, it was young. After the earliest years of settlement, when primarily adults arrived, between 40 and 50 percent of the colonial population was under the age of sixteen. Also, in the earlier years and in periods of high immigration, men far outnumbered women. However, by 1750 the numbers of white males and females were approximately equal. This was never true of the black population, in which males predominated throughout the colonial period; although in this group, too, the gap continued to narrow.

HOMES AND FURNISHINGS

Numbers tell us very little about a people. We are more interested in how they lived—what their homes were like; what they ate; how they dressed; and what they did for amusement. The first English settlers were unfamiliar with log cabins. Some were forced to live in caves or in mere holes in the ground covered with a sail or any other available material. Others built huts out of boughs and sticks plastered with mud, twigs, and clay. Gradually, however, they began building more permanent homes—the "salt-box" type of house—which was similar to those they had left behind in England. These English-style homes had two rooms on each side of a narrow vestibule. One room was the parlor, the other was the kitchen with a huge fireplace.

The upstairs was divided into two bedrooms. A house of this type might have one central chimney or one outside chimney at each end of the building. Chimneys were first built with timber and daubed with clay, but the danger of fire soon forced the use of stone or brick. Ceilings were low to conserve heat. A sloping roof overhung the first floor. At first most rooms were covered with thatch, but again the danger of fire gradually led to the use of wooden shingles. Doors were often cut horizontally into two parts for better defense in case of attack. Originally windows were covered only by shutters, then with paper soaked in linseed oil, and finally—at least for the well-to-do—with leaded glass. Nails were so costly that in the early years of settlement, colonists burned their old homes down to obtain the nails to be used in their new homes.

Most seventeenth-century houses were built of wood with clapboard siding, but a few, particularly in the southern colonies—where lime was more abundant—were constructed of brick. In either case, interior walls were paneled with wooden boards or plaster and covered with whitewash. At first floors were bare or sanded. These floors were often built in double layers with a filler of sand in between to protect the family from the cold rising from the unheated cellar.

Beginning in the early eighteenth century, the Georgian style of architecture became fashionable in the colonies. Books containing drawings by English architects were used by colonial builders to construct these Georgian homes. The Georgian houses built in the colonies were modified to suit the climate and the materials available there. Georgian homes were larger and more spacious than homes of the previous century. Nomeni Hall, for example, the Carter plantation, was seventy-six feet long, forty-four feet wide, and two stories high. It included a library, a game room, a special dining room for the children, and a thirty-foot ballroom as well as the usual living quarters. As was true of most of the larger plantation homes of the eighteenth century, the kitchen, bakehouse, dairy, and storehouse were in separate buildings as were the laundry, stables, coachhouse, and schoolhouse. The slave quarters were discreetly tucked out of sight.

The exterior of all wooden Georgian homes was painted, and interior walls were covered with fine paneling or wallpaper. Georgian homes typically had a large central hall with two rooms on each side. Georgian staircases were wider and less steep than those in earlier houses, and Georgian windows were larger with clear panes of glass. In addition, Georgian fireplaces were smaller and much more decorative, while doorways in such houses were larger and more ornate than those found in seventeenth-century homes.

Heating the colonial home was a problem. Even the Georgian homes with their two to four chimneys and a fireplace in every room tended to be cold, drafty, and smoky. Later in the colonial period, German immigrants developed an iron stove which vented its smoke through the chimney. Benjamin Franklin improved this stove so that it warmed an entire room without smoking it up. Yet, it should be noted that the Franklin stove rarely warmed a room above 56 degrees in winter.

The colonial fireplace not only provided light and heat, but it also served as a stove. Huge iron or brass pots (some as heavy as forty pounds) and fifteen-gallon copper kettles hung over the fireplace or stood on trivets. Lighting a fire was not easy. Flint and steel were used to ignite the flammable tinder, which was then carefully nurtured into flame. The fire in the fireplace was kept burning night and day. If it accidentally went out, someone would have to go to the nearest neighbor with a pan to bring back some burning coals. This was much easier than starting anew with flint and steel.

Running water was very scarce, and indoor plumbing was virtually unknown in colonial America. Most washing was done in a basin of cool water, and occasionally a person might take a bath in a tub of water heated by hot stones. At first colonial homes were lit by pine knots; these, however, were very smoky and were replaced by tallow candles for most of the colonial period. Candles were placed in candlesticks or candlebeams (chandeliers) hung from the ceiling. Toward the end of the period, the whale-oil lamp or the spermaceti candle, both of which gave much more light, were found in the more affluent homes. The oil was burned in small holders—called Betty or Phoebe lamps—made of pewter or glass.

By modern standards colonial homes were crowded. Three or more children slept in one bedroom—often in one bed. Very young children often slept in cradles or trundle beds in the same room as their parents. Apprentices might sleep in the kitchen on beds which were hooked to the wall and let down at night.

The first settlers were forced to make do with homemade furniture or whatever pieces they brought with them from Europe. The dining-room table was made of planks nailed together, and the family sat on backless benches or stools. Beds were often merely frames which supported a straw mattress. Soon, however, more comfortable furniture was constructed by American artisans or was imported from England. By the middle of the eighteenth century, pieces designed by Hepplewhite, Chippendale, and Sheraton—the leading English furniture makers—were found in the richest homes, and excellent imitations were found in middle-class homes. Storage chests were particularly valued because of the lack of closets in colonial homes.

The story is similar in regard to utensils. Chinaware was rarely found in seventeenth-century homes. Most colonists used pewter utensils; when these wore out, colonists made new ones of wood. In the eighteenth century, however, those who could afford it imported chinaware and glassware from England. However, the colonists were not completely dependent on England for their glassware. You have already read about the Wistar and Stiegel glassworks in America.

Spoons were one of the most important eating utensils, and stews and ragouts were called "spoon meat" because they could be eaten without a fork. Spoons were usually made of pewter, although some frontier families used wooden spoons, and wealthy families attempted to collect silver spoons. Forks were rare in the seventeenth century. John Winthrop had the first fork in the English colonies—a two-tined model then in vogue in Europe. What most colonists could not pick up with a spoon, they picked up with their fingers. This made napkins an essential element in the linen supply of every colonial housewife.

During the seventeenth century, most colonists ate out of wooden trenchers—blocks of wood about four inches deep and a foot square, which were hollowed out to serve as bowls. After dinner the table top was lifted off and washed. Colonial tankards were usually made of pewter, although again, poor families had wooden ones and rich families had silver ones. No matter what they were made of, tankards and other drinking utensils were often passed around from person to person with no concern about germs. Wealthy families also had large silver salt cellars placed in the middle of the table. It was a great honor to sit "above the salt" near the host and hostess rather than "below the salt" with the children and servants.

Food was plentiful in the colonies. Wild turkeys, pigeons, ducks, geese, and many other types of fowl were relatively easy to kill. Deer and other game were plentiful. Preserving the meat was a more difficult problem. Salting was the most popular method, but meat was also smoked and pickled. Fish and shellfish could almost literally be scooped out of rivers, streams, and bays. Corn was the staple cereal. It could be eaten as hominy, pone, succotash, and in myriad other forms. Pumpkins, squashes, turnips, carrots, a wide variety of beans, and sweet potatoes were popular vegetables. (The so-called Irish potato was not then considered to be healthy for man or beast.) Apples, pears, grapes, and many kinds of berries added variety to the colonial menu.

Water was not a popular drink. Beer, ale, wine, brandy, rum, cider, or whiskey—depending on taste and finances—were the most common beverages. Coffee, tea, cocoa, and milk only became popular drinks in the eighteenth century. Sugar was a luxury. Most homes had to be satisfied with sweeteners such as molasses, honey, or maple sugar.

DRESS

As already noted (Chapter 16), in the colonial period dress was closely related to social class. It required considerable wealth to dress in the manner expected of the aristocracy. On formal occasions upper-class men and women wore the finest and brightest silks, satins, velvets, damasks, and laces. The wide skirts and towering hairdos worn by the women made it almost impossible for them to go through a doorway. The men were almost as grand in cocked hats, embroidered coats, ruffled silk shirts, knee britches, silk hose with fancy garters, and pumps with large silver buckles.

Before the end of the seventeenth century, both sexes began wearing elaborate wigs. These wigs were made of human hair, horse hair, goat hair, mohair, or a wide variety of other materials. After wigs went out of style, men began powdering their hair and tying it in a queue in the back. This queue was often wrapped in black cloth because the oil or pomatum men used to hold the powder in their hair often ruined their clothes. Those colonists who wished to keep up with the latest English fashions did so by means of dolls dressed in England with clothes which they could either order from the mother country or attempt to copy at home. Women wore long gloves and masks to protect their complexions from the sun, and both men and women wore muffs to protect their hands.

Of course, the upper classes wore much more practical clothes on ordinary occasions, and the typical farmer or worker was unlikely to have the funds needed to dress himself and his family in expensive clothes. The latter wore garments of wool, leather, and osenbrig, a strong heavy linen. Stockings were made of homespun wool, and shoes of bulky cowhide. On the frontier men wore coonskin caps, deerskin hunting shirts which hung halfway down their thighs, and britches, leggins, and moccasins made of deerskin.

AMUSEMENTS

"All work and no play makes Jack a dull boy" is a saying that can be traced to eighteenth-century Americans. Amusements varied according to social class and location. In rural areas the family had to provide its own entertainment. In the evenings an elder might tell a story, read from the Bible, or lead the family in singing hymns. Attendance at church was as much a social as a religious function. House or barn raisings, plowing bees, sheep shearings, corn huskings, and quilting parties were all occasions for families to come together and socialize.

The social highlight in the countryside was the fair, which was held once or twice a year. The men traded livestock; the women exchanged samples of their food specialties and preserves; and men, women, and children enjoyed games, races, wrestling matches, shooting matches, and other types of athletic contests. Election days, court days, and militia muster days also furnished opportunities for similar activities. All year round, depending on the season, young people and their elders went hunting, fishing, swimming, and skating and played contemporary versions of football, baseball, cricket, and hockey. Small children amused themselves with spinning tops, playing marbles, and engaging in a wide variety of tag games.

In all but the most desolate areas, an inn or tavern was usually within riding distance for the man of the family. There he might play a game of billiards, chess, backgammon, or cards. Or, he might just enjoy his favorite drink, a pipeful of tobacco, and the conversation of his cronies. Taverns were also the usual scenes for the ever-popular cockfights and bear and bull baitings.

The gentry, as far north as New York and Philadelphia, participated in fox hunts, although the pink coats and intricate formalities connected with them later had not yet appeared. However, the most popular equestrian sport for both the gentry and the common people was horse racing. In rural areas these races were informal, but in the towns they were well organized and the scene of heavy betting. Race horses were bred not only by southern planters but also (as noted previously) by the wealthy landowners of Rhode Island.

Dancing was also popular in the colonies. The balls held in the Apollo Room of the Raleigh Tavern in Williamsburgh were justly famous. Most plantation houses included ballrooms where dances were held that often lasted until dawn. The minuet was the fashionable dance, but cotillions and the Virginia reel were probably danced, and enjoyed, even more. Planters may have had dancing masters and trained musicians, but other southerners—including slaves—probably had as much fun dancing to the music of a fiddle, the clapping of hands, and the directions of a caller. Dancing was not confined to the south. By the early eighteenth century, the Quakers allowed dancing schools to open in Philadelphia. Soon after, even New England dropped its ban on "gynecandrical" (or mixed) dancing, which Increase Mather had attacked in "An Arrow against Profane and Promiscuous Dancing" as "scandalous immorality."

Vocal music, particularly the singing of psalms, was popular in colonial America. Even the Puritans, after much debate, allowed women to join in the singing. By the eighteenth century the Bay Psalm Book began to be replaced by newer texts, which also contained musical notes. Also in the eighteenth century, the singing of hymns rather than psalms began to be introduced into church services. This was most characteristic of the Methodist Church, for which Charles Wesley wrote over 6,000 hymns. Just prior to the Revolution, Baptist preachers began to compose new words to popular folk melodies, which developed into the hymns sung at the somewhat later camp meetings and revivals of the early nineteenth century.

As the eighteenth century progressed, a few churches, mainly Anglican, began using organs in their services. However, the finest church music was heard in the churches of the German sects in Pennsylvania—particularly in the Moravian congregations, which had highly trained choirs. They also had organs, and orchestras made up of oboes, flutes, french horns, and trumpets. German settlers remained in touch with the music of their homeland, and Bethlehem, Pennsylvania, became the place to hear the music of Bach, Handel, Hayden, and Mozart.

English and Scotch-Irish settlers on the frontier kept alive the Elizabethan (and even earlier) ballads and Scottish folk songs which they carried with them to America. English songs such as the many versions of *Barbara Allen,* and children's songs such as *Billy Boy, Farmer in the Dell,* and *London Bridge* are still sung today. Contemporary seventeenth- and eighteenth-century songs such as *Rule Britannia* and racy tunes such as *Kiss Me Quick My Mother's Coming* were also popular in the colonies. American composers began writing songs first to commemorate the heroes of the French and Indian War and later (in the 1760s and 1770s) to stir up anti-English feeling. The origin of *Yankee Doodle* is unknown, but the verse "Yankee Doodle came to town riding on a pony" was already popular in 1767. "Father and I went down to camp" probably dates from 1775, when the song virtually became the anthem of the Revolution.

All these songs were played on fiddles, fifes, zithers, dulcimers, and guitars. Many famous Americans played instruments. Franklin played the violin, harp, guitar, and harmonica (not the modern instrument) and composed at least one piece for a string quartet. Washington played the fiddle, and Jefferson and Patrick Henry vied for the title of worst violin player in Virginia. Ladies played the harpsichord and dulcimer, and most towns were plentifully supplied with music masters and music stores. The first chamber music concert was held—surprisingly—in Boston (but by Anglicans) in 1731. In 1762 the St. Cecilia Society was organized in Charleston to support an orchestra. Charleston had earlier been the first American town to have a song recital and to offer performances of light operas such as the *Beggar's Opera* and its many imitators.

At the beginning of the seventeenth century, English citizens of all classes were fond of the drama. However, the hardships of settling a continent, religious opposition (particularly by the Puritans and Quakers), and the lack of urban centers all combined to prevent the growth of theaters in seventeenth-century America.

In the eighteenth century religious opposition to plays continued (though less strenuously), but the other factors were no longer operative—at least along the Atlantic coast. Anthony Aston, an English actor, performed in Charleston and New York in the early years of the century. The honor of having the first theater in the colonies belonged to Williamsburgh, Virginia, which had a playhouse in operation at least by 1718. New York and Charleston were not far behind. The actors in the early theaters were largely local citizens supplemented on occasion by itinerant English actors.

In 1749 the first professional English company arrived in the colonies. It performed plays by Shakespeare, Addison, Congreve, Dryden, Farquar, and other popular English dramatists. This company performed in New York, Annapolis, Williamsburgh, and other towns in Virginia and Maryland, but it was barred from Philadelphia and did not even attempt to enter New England.

A second company headed by Lewis Hallam and his actress wife arrived in Virginia in 1752. They played all the leading cities (the governor of Pennsylvania gave them special permission to perform in Philadelphia) except Boston and Newport. After Hallam's death his widow married David Douglass, who managed the group which became known as the American Company. By the time of the Revolution, Boston was the only important town still refusing to allow the performance of stage plays. Even there plays were occasionally performed under the guise of public readings. Colonial audiences were critical and vociferous, and laws had to be passed in several towns prohibiting the pelting of actors with eggs and other articles of food.

Numerous other amusements were available for those townsfolk who did not enjoy plays. Some were regaled by exhibitions of exotic animals such as lions, tigers, leopards, polar bears, and camels. Others attended shows which featured acrobats, trapeze artists, jugglers, magicians, equestrians, and clowns. Punch and Judy shows were popular, and waxworks exhibiting images of Biblical and historical personalities were well attended. The most spectacular show of the colonial period was the "Microcosm or the World in Miniature," a portable Greek temple in which astronomical phenomena and other exhibits were presented to musical accompaniment.

Finally, numerous holidays broke the monotony of daily life. The anniversary of the discovery of Guy Fawke's plot to blow up the English Parliament was celebrated every November 5 with parades and bonfires. Christmas was celebrated everywhere (except in New England) by church services, and in the south it was marked by the firing of guns. St. Nicholas was known only in New York, and the Christmas tree was completely unknown in the colonies. The first Thanksgiving was celebrated in Plymouth colony in 1621, but later days of thanksgiving were held in various colonies at different times to commemorate happy events or deliverance from evil.

In Massachusetts Commencement Day at Harvard was the occasion for feasting and celebration. In New York City and Albany, slaves were allowed to parade in costume and sing and dance through the streets on Pinkster Day (Pentecost). Slaves in the southern colonies were allowed time off on Shrove Tuesday, Good Friday, Easter, and Christmas. Great events such as the Duke of Cumberland's defeat of the Young Pretender in 1746 or General Wolfe's victories in the French and Indian War were also the cause of parades, bonfires, and general merriment. Also, royal birthdays were dutifully, and joyously, celebrated in all colonies.

In fact, some felt that the colonists were enjoying too many, and too varied, forms of recreation. In 1712 the Boston authorities attempted to persuade the Massachusetts assembly to ban public entertainments lest they corrupt the young. This attempt failed, but sixty-two years later the members of the First Continental Congress felt it necessary to show the seriousness of colonial opposition to English policies by incorporating into their ban on the importation of British goods the additional request that Americans should abstain from "all Horse Racing, and all Kinds of Gaming, Cock Fighting, Exhibitions of Shews, Plays, and other expensive Diversions and Entertainments."

BIBLIOGRAPHY

DULLES, FOSTER R. *America Learns to Play: A History of Popular Recreation.* New York, 1964.

GREENE, EVARTS B., and HARRINGTON, VIRGINIA D. *American Population before the Federal Census of 1790.* New York, 1932.

HUME, IVOR NOËL. *A Guide to the Artifacts of Colonial America.* New York, 1970.

LUCAS, JOHN A., and SMITH, RONALD A. *Saga of American Sport.* Philadelphia, 1978.

RANKIN, HUGH F. *The Theater in Colonial America.* Chapel Hill, 1965.

SUTHERLAND, STELLA H. *Population Distribution in Colonial America.* New York, 1936.

VINOVSKIS, MARIS A. *Studies in American Historical Demography.* New York, 1979.

WARWICK, EDWARD. *Early American Dress: The Colonial and Revolutionary Periods.* New York, 1965.

WELLS, ROBERT V. *The Population of the British Colonies in America before 1776: A Survey of International Census Data.* Princeton, 1975.

24
The Second
Hundred Years' War

Francis Parkman, the classical historian of the struggle between England and France for control of North America, wrote, in *France and England in North America* "The most momentous and far reaching question ever brought to issue on this continent was: Shall France remain here or shall she not?" Actually, this was a rhetorical question. It is rare that one can call a conflict inevitable, but the contest for control of North America is one of the few that falls into this category.

The French and the English fought for control of Acadia (Nova Scotia), Newfoundland, and the adjacent fishing banks since the opening years of the seventeenth century. By the middle of the century, they were fighting for control of the rich fur trade of the area south of the Great Lakes which was dominated by the Iroquois Indians. In 1670 the Hudson's Bay Company was founded, and for almost a century its traders fought bitterly and bloodily with French traders for control of the fur trade in that area. At the beginning of the eighteenth century, English settlers from South Carolina contended with French settlers from Biloxi and Mobile for control of the trade in deerskins and furs with the Indians of the southern frontier. Further, during the entire colonial period, England and France were rivals in the Caribbean.

KING WILLIAM'S WAR

For most of the seventeenth century, the monarchs of both England and France placed domestic and European policies far above colonial considerations, being reluctant to allow the latter to entangle them in war. All was changed, however, when William and Mary ascended the English throne. In 1689, for a wide variety of reasons—dynastic, commercial, and territorial—England joined with Holland, Spain, Austria, Sweden, and a group of German states in the War of the League of Augsburg, or, as it is known in American history, King William's War (1689-1697). This began the conflict that came to be known as the Second Hundred Years' War. (The first Hundred Years' War had been fought between England and France between 1337 and 1453.) Although other objectives were paramount and the major battles of the war were fought in Europe, fighting also took place in America. Under the leadership of the now elderly, but still audacious, Count Frontenac, the French successfully defended Newfoundland against English attacks and occupied most of the trading posts in the Hudson's Bay area. Frontenac also sent raiding parties against the Iroquois Indians in order to win control of the fur trade of upper New York. The destruction of Schenectady in one of these attacks led to the calling of an intercolonial congress by Jacob Leisler (then ruling New York) in May 1690. Representatives of New York, Massachusetts, Connecticut, and Plymouth attended the congress, and Rhode Island, Maryland, and Virginia promised, but did not deliver, support. The congress commissioned Sir William Phips (who, with about 400 Massachusetts troops, had captured Port Royal in Acadia earlier in the war) to attack Canada by sea and agreed that another army would attack by land. Phips's fleet did sail down the St. Lawrence River as far as Quebec, but it failed to capture the town; the overland army disbanded after reaching Lake Champlain. The Iroquois Indians, alarmed by their heavy losses and disgusted at the lack of cooperation among the English colonies, made a separate peace with France. In the West Indies an English fleet captured two French islands, but by the Treaty of Ryswick (which ended the hostilities), it was agreed that all territories acquired in the war should be returned to their original owners.

QUEEN ANNE'S WAR

When King William's War ended, it still had not been decided which nation was to control the Grand Banks or the fur trade—the issues which, to some extent at least, had contributed to its outbreak. Another opportunity to settle these issues soon arose, however, with the eruption of the War of the Spanish Succession, or Queen Anne's War (1702-1713). The war was precipitated by the attempt of Louis XIV to place his grandson on the throne of Spain. England, Holland, and Austria, fearful that a future union between France and Spain would upset the balance of power both in Europe and America, declared war on France and Spain. Once again, the main battles of the war were fought in Europe, but some significant fighting took place in America as well.

France had strengthened its position on the North American continent in the few years between the wars. Forts were built at Detroit, Cahokia (in what is now southern Illinois), Biloxi, and Mobile, which virtually encircled the English settlements. In contrast, the English colonies remained as disunited as ever, and the

English government failed to develop any new procedures to mobilize their personnel and resources for military purposes.

Raids by the French and by the Indians from Acadia against Maine and Massachusetts resulted in a great loss of life. The most severe blow was struck at Deerfield, Massachusetts, where thirty-eight settlers were killed and about one hundred captured. The New Englanders fought back; in 1710 they, in conjunction with an English fleet, captured Port Royal. Hopes arose even of conquering Montreal and Quebec, but the fleet that was sent from England to support the attack was wrecked near the mouth of the St. Lawrence River, and the expedition had to be abandoned. Fighting also took place on the southern frontier during Queen Anne's War. An expedition from South Carolina assaulted St. Augustine but was unable to capture the fort. In return, a fleet of French and Spanish ships attacked Charleston but was driven off. In the West Indies England conquered St. Christophers (St. Kitts) and Nevis. Queen Anne's War had some concrete territorial results in America. The Peace of Utrecht provided that Newfoundland, Acadia, and the Hudson's Bay area be placed under English jurisdiction; and that England be granted the *asiento*, (or right to supply slaves) as well as the right to sell one shipload of goods a year, to the Spanish colonies in America.

For a little more than a quarter of a century, England and France remained at peace. Once again, France utilized the time to strengthen its chain of forts (which now extended all the way to New Orleans) and to build Louisbourg (on Cape Breton Island at the mouth of the St. Lawrence River) to replace Port Royal as a base for French fishermen and privateers. During this period the English colonies did little to strengthen themselves militarily, but the thousands of immigrants who settled there made these colonies a much more formidable opponent than they had been at the beginning of the eighteenth century.

KING GEORGE'S WAR

The period of peace came to an end in 1739 with the outbreak of the so-called War of Jenkins' Ear between England and Spain. Hostilities were precipitated by England's founding of Georgia and the abuse of its trading rights with the Spanish colonies (as exemplified by Captain Jenkins, whose ear was allegedly removed by the Spanish as a punishment for smuggling). The following year events in Europe led France and Prussia to join Spain, and Austria to ally with England. The conflict became known as the War of the Austrian Succession, or—in America—as King George's War (1740-1748).

England once again took the offensive. Admiral Edward Vernon led a successful attack on Porto Bello (Panama), but his attempt to capture Cartegena (Colombia) failed—with a loss of over 2,400 of the 3,000 colonial troops who accompanied him. (In spite of this disaster, Lawrence Washington, George Washington's older half brother, who was one of the few survivors, named his home after the admiral.)

The most glorious English victory—or, really, New English victory—was the capture of the formidable fortress of Louisbourg in 1745. The expedition was suggested by Governor William Shirley of Massachusetts. It was made up of 4,000 New Englanders commanded by William Pepperrell, a Maine merchant, and was financed by a special levy of £50,000 raised by the Massachusetts legislature. It was therefore a terrible shock when, at the Peace of Aix-la-Chapelle, England and France agreed to return all conquests made during the war. Not even generous compensation for the expenses of the expedition and a knighthood for Pepperrell could obscure what to New Englanders seemed to be a callous sacrifice of their interests for questionable benefits in other parts of the world.

THE BACKGROUND OF THE FRENCH AND INDIAN WAR

The arrangements made at Aix-la-Chapelle were more in the nature of a truce than a treaty—particularly as far as North America was concerned. The old rivalries for the fur trade of upper New York and the Great Lakes area continued. The Hudson's Bay Company expanded its activities into what the French considered to be their trading preserves. The boundaries of Nova Scotia were still in dispute, and both England and France claimed St. Lucia and Tobago in the West Indies. However, the most volatile area in the dispute between the two nations was now the Ohio Valley.

In 1748 Conrad Weiser, a veteran Indian trader representing the colony of Pennsylvania, negotiated a treaty with the Miami Indians, who had moved to the Ohio Valley. In it the Indians promised to sell their furs to Pennsylvania traders rather than to the French, as they had done in the past. The Logstown Treaty was a direct challenge to the Canadian economy. In addition, the French realized that English occupation of the Ohio Valley would cut communications between Canada and Louisiana. Therefore, the governor of Canada sent an army of 250 men to the Ohio Valley in 1749 to confirm France's claim to the area and to persuade the Miami Indians to return to their old allegiance. When the Miami Indians refused, a French-led force of Indians drove them, and the English fur traders, out of the valley.

During 1752 and 1753 the French constructed a new series of forts in western Pennsylvania, but England had no intention of surrendering its claim to the Ohio Valley. In 1747 a group of land speculators from England and Virginia organized the Ohio Company, which received a grant from the king of 200,000 acres in the area (with the promise of 300,000 more if enough people settled on their lands). At about the same time, Virginia granted another 500,000 acres to a local venture, the Loyal Land Company. Governor Robert Dinwiddie of Virginia, who was an investor in the Ohio Company, sent George Washington west to warn the French that they were trespassing on English territory. The French politely but firmly denied the English claim, and in the spring of 1754, they built Fort Duquesne at the present site of Pittsburgh. Washington, who was in the vicinity with a body of about 150

Virginia militiamen, attacked a small French force, killing ten soldiers. Both sides then received reinforcements, but Washington's 350 men were no match for 500 French soldiers and 400 Indians, and he was forced to surrender in July 1754. The French and Indian War had begun, although it was two years before it spread to Europe, where England and Prussia fought France, Spain, Austria, and Russia in what is known as the Seven Years' War (1756-1763).

THE FRENCH AND INDIAN WAR

Lawrence H. Gipson, whose studies of this period are considered definitive, called the French and Indian War "The Great War for Empire" because it was fought predominantly for the control of North America and India. Francis Parkman, an earlier historian, had idealized the war as a conflict of civilizations: the Catholic, autocratic French empire against the Protestant, self-governing English empire. Religion played no role in the actual fighting, although the autocratic form of government did give France an advantage in military efficiency, particularly in the first years of the war. In addition, France had a strategically located chain of forts and the support of most Indian tribes, with the exception of the Iroquois. However, the English colonies had a population of 1,200,000, as compared to Canada's (at most) 70,000. In the long run, the superiority of numbers and the increasing effectiveness of the English army and navy proved decisive.

Even before Washington's surrender in 1754, the English government realized that it would have to solve two major problems if it were ever to defeat the French in North America. One of these problems was to retain (or regain) the support of the Iroquois Indians. The Iroquois were complaining that English traders no longer utilized them as middlemen in the fur trade and that English settlers were encroaching on their lands. Nor were they satisfied with the military support they had received in previous wars or the colonies' obvious lack of preparation for the impending conflict.

The second problem was the disunity of the colonies and their reluctance to support military efforts, particularly in the west. In previous wars England had attempted to requisition men and supplies from each colony but had found the system slow, cumbersome, and, in the last analysis, ineffective. As Peter Kalm (a Swedish botanist who visited the colonies in the 1740s) accurately reported in his *Travels into North America:*

> Each English colony . . . may be looked upon . . . as a state by itself. From hence it happens, that in time of war, things go on very slowly and irregularly here: for not only the sense of one province is sometimes directly opposite to that of another; but frequently the views of the governor, and those of the assembly of the same province, are quite different: so that it is easy to see, that, while the people are quarrelling about the best and cheapest manner of carrying on the war, an enemy has it in his power to take one place after another.

To solve these two problems, the Board of Trade convened a colonial conference at Albany in June 1754. The Albany Congress was attended by representatives of Maryland, Pennsylvania, New York, Connecticut, Rhode Island, Massachusetts, and New Hampshire. William Johnson, a fur trader who had married a Mohawk woman and who served as Indian agent for the colony of New York, carried on most of the negotiations with the Iroquois. In an address to the representatives of the Six Nations, he promised them that their grievances "[would] be redressed . . . without any unnecessary delay" if only they would aid the English against the French, "a delusive people, always endeavoring to divide you as much as they can." The Iroquois were also presented with thirty wagons full of trade goods. The Iroquois left the congress without definitely committing themselves to an alliance with the English, but it was felt that their support had been won. This proved to be true only five years later, when the Iroquois decided that the English were going to win the war. Up to that time Iroquois support was intermittent and obtained only at a high cost in money and goods.

To promote colonial unity, Benjamin Franklin and a committee drafted a proposal known as the Albany Plan of Union. The Albany Plan provided for a "grand council" representing all the colonies, to be presided over by a president-general appointed by the king. The council would meet annually to deal with military defense, Indian affairs, and western lands and settlement. Delegates to the council were to be chosen by the colonial assemblies for three-year terms, and colonies would be represented in proportion to their financial contributions to this new colonial government. The president-general was to be vested with a veto power over the decisions of the council. Franklin's plan would have established a form of government in which local affairs would remain under the jurisdiction of each colonial legislature, but problems facing all the colonies would be dealt with by an intercolonial body. However, this attempt to create a federal form of government was unacceptable to both the English government—which feared infringement of its powers—and the colonial assemblies—who felt it deprived them of their authority and might lead to higher taxes and tighter English control over their affairs.

Although the Albany Congress could hardly be called a success, the English government decided to assume the military offensive. General Edward Braddock was ordered to march on Fort Duquesne from his base in Virginia, and expeditions from New York and New England were to attack other French strongholds. Braddock soon realized the futility of the Albany Congress when the legislatures of Virginia, New York, and Pennsylvania refused to vote him the men and supplies he needed. Nor would the Indians join his army when he refused to guarantee that their lands would not be occupied by English settlers. Nevertheless, in June 1755 he set out for Fort Duquesne with an army of 2,500, including about 250 Virginia militiamen under the command of George Washington. Because Fort Duquesne was defended by about only 900 men, including Indian allies, the French decided that their only hope was to ambush Braddock's army. They waited until Braddock's troops were crossing the Monongahela River (about nine miles from the fort) and then attacked. Braddock's army was routed; over 900 men were killed or wounded;

Braddock lost his life; and Washington had two horses shot out from under him but fortunately emerged unscathed. The other English expeditions of 1755 were almost as disastrous. The only exception was the conquest of Acadia, many of whose inhabitants were exiled to Louisiana, where they are still known as Cajuns (Canadians). Nor did the situation improve in the next two years. The able French commander in America, the Marquis de Montcalm, captured Fort Oswego on the southern shore of Lake Ontario and Fort William Henry on Lake George in 1756, and French and Indian raids devastated the New York frontier. In 1758, however, William Pitt assumed the leadership of the English government and gave the war in America top priority. Within the year English troops captured Louisburg and Fort Duquesne (which was renamed Fort Pitt). The Indians then began deserting the French, and in 1759 Fort Niagara, Fort Ticonderoga, and Crown Point all fell to English and colonial troops. In 1760 General James Wolfe laid siege to Quebec. The Marquis de Montcalm, the French commander, was confident that the city was impregnable; however, Wolfe discovered a steep unguarded path above Quebec which led from the St. Lawrence River to the Plains of Abraham. His army of 5,000 climbed to the Plains and then defeated the French army, which came out of its impregnable fortress to meet the British. Both Wolfe and Montcalm died in the ensuing battle. In September 1760 Quebec surrendered to the English. This surrender turned out to be the turning point of the war. Montreal, Detroit, and other western forts fell in 1761. England also conquered Martinique, Guadaloupe, and other French islands in the West Indies. Even the belated entry of Spain into the war in 1762 failed to stem the tide.

By the peace of Paris, signed early in 1763, France ceded Canada and French claims to all lands east of the Mississippi River to England; France also surrendered several West Indian islands to England. Spain ceded Florida to England and, in return, received Louisiana from France. England allowed France to retain two islands in the gulf of the St. Lawrence River, and after prolonged debate as to whether to return Canada or the two valuable sugar islands of Guadaloupe and Martinique to France, finally decided to return the latter.

THE RESULTS OF THE FRENCH
AND INDIAN WAR

The British decision signaled a change in English colonial policy: Previously, colonies had been valued primarily as sources of raw materials; now, with the beginnings of the Industrial Revolution, they were considered more valuable as potential markets for English manufactured goods. This shift of economic emphasis was accompanied by a program of administrative reform designed to reinforce and intensify English military and economic control of its colonies. This policy may be traced back to 1748, when King George's War ended and the Earl of Halifax became president of the Board of Trade. Halifax was determined to reinvigorate the board and to utilize it to assert royal control over all the colonies. The French and Indian War only interrupted this policy; it did not alter it.

However, this intensification of English colonial policy came at a time when the North American colonies had reached a new peak of maturity. As early as 1748 Peter Kalm had noted the ripening of the colonies and wrote in *Travels into North America* that the "English government has therefore sufficient reason to consider the French in North America, as the best means of keeping the colonies in their due submission." Montcalm, too, is supposed to have said just before he died, "England will be the first victim of her colonies."

To Americans the main result of the war was that with Canada and Florida under English control, the mainland colonies (but not the West Indies) were no longer in danger from attack by either France or Spain. The American colonists no longer felt the need for English military protection. This is not to imply that thoughts of independence entered the minds of Americans immediately after 1763. On the contrary, they were at first almost euphoric about sharing the blessings of the glorious British empire and constitution. However, it did mean that if Americans began to feel that England was mistreating them, independence was an option open to them if all means of reconciliation between the colonies and the mother country failed.

The French and Indian War had another result which, like the first, was largely psychological in nature. Never before had the English and the colonists come into such close and protracted contact with each other. Almost immediately a mutual dislike and distrust developed, which was to cloud their relations both during and after the war. The English were furious when colonial assemblies refused to vote much-needed personnel and supplies until the governors gave in to their political demands. Even then the financial aid voted by most colonies was niggardly. Moreover, the colonial troops were so unenthusiastic about the war that General Wolfe described them in a 1758 letter to Lord George Sackville as "in general the dirtiest, most contemptible cowardly dogs that you can conceive." The Americans proved themselves most despicable to the English by carrying on a brisk trade with the enemy all throughout the war.

Conversely, Americans were irked by the arrogance of English naval and military officers, who treated colonial political and military leaders as if they were rustic clowns and who forcibly enlisted Americans in the English army and navy. A basic reason for colonial reluctance to serve under English military leaders was the obvious ignorance of these leaders of the military techniques—such as fighting "Indian style"—necessary to military success in North America. Americans did not appreciate being led into ambushes such as Braddock's in 1755.

Nevertheless, the French and Indian War had more than psychological results. The colonies had matured politically and developed a spirit of self-confidence. By 1750 their control of the "power of the purse" had won them significant victories. However, during the war the necessity of persuading the assemblies to vote the men and supplies so urgently needed by the British government forced many colonial governors to violate their instructions. They allowed the assemblies to appoint public officials, supervise the spending of public funds, and have an important voice in the administration of military affairs.

Two examples of this new spirit could be seen even before the end of the French and Indian War. To prevent smuggling during the war, the British government had utilized writs of assistance. Customs officials were authorized by their commissions to search houses, shops, ships, and warehouses for illegal goods. (A writ of assistance was a court order which authorized sheriffs, constables, and other peace officers to aid customs officials in their search for smuggled goods.) Unlike the procedure with ordinary search warrants, no time limit was placed on writs of assistance, nor was any sworn statement that goods were concealed in such and such a place necessary for issuance of the writs. Several valuable, though illegal, cargoes in the warehouses of Boston merchants were discovered and confiscated. Therefore, when new writs of assistance were issued upon the accession of George III in 1760, a group of Boston merchants challenged their legality. In February 1761 James Otis, an able and eloquent attorney and politician, argued the case before Thomas Hutchinson, chief justice of the Massachusetts Superior Court.

In his arguments Otis expressed political theories which were to be heard again and again between 1763 and 1776. He claimed that writs of assistance led to searches and seizures which were in violation of both the British constitution and natural equity: They were therefore void. Otis lost the battle, the court case, but won the war. Although Hutchinson upheld the legality of writs of assistance, public opinion gradually forced the British authorities to curtail their use.

Another example of this political sophistication occurred in Virginia at about the same time. For years the salaries of Anglican clergymen (among many others) in Virginia were paid in tobacco. In 1758, however, because of a severe drought which increased the price of tobacco to six pence a pound, the House of Burgesses passed the Two Penny Act, making it possible for salaries and debts payable in tobacco to be paid in cash at the rate of two pence a pound of tobacco. This had the effect of cutting the salaries of Anglican ministers by two thirds. They, in turn, complained bitterly to the bishop of London, who persuaded the Privy Council to disallow the Two Penny Act.

In 1759, therefore, the Reverend James Maury brought suit to collect his back salary. Patrick Henry, then a neophyte lawyer, was engaged by the vestry to fight Maury's claim. When the case was finally heard by a jury in 1763, Henry's line of defense was based on John Locke's compact theory of government. According to Maury's own account, Henry declared that as long as the king provided for the welfare of his subjects, he was entitled to their obedience; but when he disallowed a law that was obviously in the public interest (the Two Penny Act), he "degenerated into a tyrant and forfeits all rights to his subjects' obedience." Whether because of Henry's argument or because of colonial resentment toward royal disallowance, the jury—although it found in favor of Maury—voted him only one penny in damages.

The French and Indian War also encouraged the economic development of the colonies. For the duration of the conflict, the laws against colonial manufacturing were not enforced. With the English army in great need of supplies, it would have been ridiculous not to have taken advantage of the rich manufacturing resources of the colonies. By the end of the war, America had more forges and furnaces than England, and the quality of the iron and steel produced in the colonies compared favorably with the English products. The colonial shipbuilding industry also boomed. During the war years American fishermen took control of the invaluable Grand Banks away from their English competitors. American fur traders also continued their profitable activities throughout the war. American farmers, too, thrived because of the demand for their wheat, corn, beef, pork, cattle, horses, tobacco, rice, and indigo from friends and foes alike. In essence, the French and Indian War had shown the colonists how boundless American prosperity might be if unhampered by English mercantile restrictions.

However, the colonies were not left alone. Quite the contrary, at the conclusion of the war, English merchants, manufacturers, fur traders, and land speculators were all insistent that their government guarantee that English, not American, business interests reap the lion's share of the profits that were now available in North America.

BIBLIOGRAPHY

DOWNEY, FAIRFAX. *Louisbourg: Key to a Continent.* Englewood Cliffs, N.J., 1965.

FREGAULT, GUY. *Canada: The War of Conquest,* Margeret Cameron, trans. New York, 1969.

JACOBS, WILBUR R. *Diplomacy and Indian Gifts: Anglo-French Rivalry Along the Ohio and Northwest Frontiers, 1748–1763.* Stanford, Cal., 1950.

LEACH, DOUGLAS E. *The Northern Colonial Frontier, 1607–1763.* New York, 1966.

McDERMOTT, JOHN F. *The French in the Mississippi Valley.* Urbana, 1965.

NEWBOLD, ROBERT C. *The Albany Congress and Plan of Union.* New York, 1955.

PECKHAM, HOWARD H. *The Colonial Wars, 1689–1762.* Chicago, 1964.

WOODS, PATRICIA DILLON. *French-Indian Relations on the Southern Frontier, 1699–1762.* Ann Arbor, 1980.

25
The Road
to Revolution

In 1818, in a letter to Hezekiah Niles, John Adams gave as his considered opinion that "the radical change in the principles, opinions, sentiments, and affections of the people was the real American Revolution." And Adams made it clear that this revolution had taken place before, and was a prerequisite to, approval of the Declaration of Independence. Modern historians of the Revolution, particularly Bernard Bailyn, have emphasized this point by indicating that it was not the specific legislation passed by Parliament which precipitated the Revolution but rather the belief by the American people that these laws were part of a conspiracy to strip them of their basic political rights.

THE ANGLICAN BISHOP
CONTROVERSY

One of the best examples of how sensitive Americans were to what they perceived as threats to their liberties was the controversy over the appointment of an Anglican archbishop for the colonies. For years the Society for the Propagation of the Gospel in Foreign Parts, with the support of a few aggressive Anglican clergymen in America, had pressed for such an appointment. In the 1760s the bishop of London actively supported them, fearing that otherwise the Church of England would be unable to compete with the numerous dissenting churches which were flourishing in the colonies. While the modern reader would view the appointment of an archbishop as a strictly religious matter, to colonial Americans, including Anglicans (who wanted to retain lay control of their churches), it was considered an essentially political issue. Americans agreed with the warning of the Reverend Jonathan Mayhew* that the appointment of an Anglican bishop would result in the "enslaving both bodies and souls of men."

The controversy became even more heated when Parliament passed the Stamp Act and other revenue measures affecting the colonies. Americans feared that Parliament would levy an additional tax to support the Anglican bishop. The fact that the same groups—royal officials and Anglican clergymen—who supported Parliament's revenue measures also advocated sending a bishop to America intertwined the two issues in the public mind. Congregational and Presbyterian ministers utilized their pulpits to make sure that their congregants understood the dangers which faced them if an Anglican bishop arrived in America. At no time during the 1760s or 1770s did the English government ever officially recommend such an appointment. Yet, the debate raged unabated. After 1776 Patriots and Loyalists alike agreed with John Adams, who, in a letter written to Jedediah Morse in 1815 credited the controversy with causing Americans to think seriously about "the constitutional authority of Parliament over the colonies."

THE PROCLAMATION OF 1763

Various other—more substantive—issues clouded the relations between England and its North American colonies after the French and Indian War. The first source of friction was the issuance of the Proclamation of 1763. Seven years earlier, by the Treaty of Easton, the colony of Pennsylvania had promised not to allow settlement on Indian lands west of the Appalachian Mountains. The English government supported this treaty in order to detach the Indians from their alliance with the French. However, in spite of this agreement, settlers were trespassing on Indian lands and unscrupulous fur traders were cheating the Indians out of their furs. Likewise, Sir Jeffrey Amherst, the commander-in-chief of the British troops in America, further irritated the Indians by building forts in their territory and refusing to give them the gifts which they had formerly received from the French.

Most importantly, the Indians had no intention of allowing their fate to be determined by treaties signed in Europe or to accept a European way of life. In the early 1760s a Delaware Indian named Neolin led a crusade for a return to the earlier Indian way of life and the abandonment of European values, tools, and rum. The combined defense of their lands and their way of life was undertaken by Pontiac, a chief of the Ottawa Indians, in May 1763. In alliance with numerous other northern tribes, Pontiac destroyed most of the English western outposts but was unable to capture Detroit, Niagara, or Pittsburgh. Pontiac's Conspiracy, as this bloody Indian war was called, continued for over two years until dissension among the Indians forced Pontiac to make peace.

*In *A Discourse Concerning Unlimited Submission and Non-Resistance to the Higher Powers.* (1750)

Pontiac's Conspiracy precipitated the issuance of the Proclamation of 1763. Its purpose was to prevent the Indians from being exploited by white settlers or unscrupulous fur traders. Temporarily, at least, settlement west of the Appalachian Mountains was to be barred, the fur trade was to be strictly regulated, and future land purchases were only to be made with the approval of royal—not colonial— officials. Its primary purpose was to bring peace to the frontier, but the Board of Trade also hoped that by restricting Americans to the coastal area, the mother country would be better able to control them.

While not welcome, the Proclamation of 1763 was not, at first, a major cause of difficulty between the colonists and the mother country. It was only in the 1770s, when after much debate in government circles, it became clear that the line of settlement (although modified slightly) was to be virtually permanent and that the English were to be favored in any future land grants, that colonial resentment over the proclamation reached its height. Potential settlers (of whom there were many), land speculators, and fur traders felt that Americans were being cheated out of the opportunity of enjoying—or exploiting—the western lands which they had helped to conquer.

THE SUGAR ACT

Peace with the Indians was concluded by 1766, but the British government decided that it was necessary to maintain an army of 10,000 men to defend the frontier. It also decided, in the light of a national debt that had grown from £75,000,000 to about £140,000,000 during the war and a heavy tax rate which most English citizens found burdensome, that the American colonists must bear at least part of the £300,000 annual cost of this army. The colonists disagreed sharply with both aspects of this decision. No British army had been stationed in America while France had been a threat. Why should it be needed now? In addition, Americans now asked why they should pay for an army they neither wanted nor needed. They were confident that they could easily handle the Indians themselves. Hadn't they done so ever since the colonies were settled?

George Grenville, a Whig who became George III's chief minister in 1763, decided that a reasonable tax on sugar imported from the non-English West Indies would supply about £45,000 toward the support of the British army in America as well as improve the economic position of the English West Indies. The Sugar Act was passed by Parliament in 1763 with the purpose of "defraying the expenses of defending . . . the said colonies and plantations; . . . and more effectively preventing the clandestine conveyance of goods to and from the said colonies and plantations." The act actually lowered the duty on molasses from six pence to three pence, but other provisions made it clear that the collection of this duty, unlike the earlier one, was going to be strictly enforced. Customs collectors were ordered to take up residence in America (in the past they had often remained in England and sent a deputy instead); additional naval ships were sent to patrol the American coast; and the powers of the admiralty courts were strengthened.

The passage of the Sugar Act dismayed the people of the northern colonies—particularly the merchants. They were already suffering from a postwar depression caused by the termination of military subsidies and contracts and the loss of profits from privateering and illegal trade. Northern merchants predicted that the Sugar Act would destroy the rum distilling, fishing, and lumber industries, cut off their best supply of hard money, and thus lessen the importation of goods from Great-Britain.

The colonists protested against the Sugar Act on constitutional as well as economic grounds. The most vociferous of these protests came from the Boston town meeting in which Samuel Adams asked:

> If taxes are laid upon us in any shape without our having a legal Representation where they are laid, are we not reduced from the character of free Subjects to the miserable State of tributary Slaves?

This reference to the threat of slavery was to become a frequent, and sincere, refrain in the years to come.

James Otis expressed similar sentiments and the New York assembly claimed that it was its right to be exempted from all Parliamentary taxes. Other colonies were more tentative in their protests against the Sugar Act; most of the language of the act (with the exception of the clause which earmarked the revenue for the army) was similar to that of earlier Parliamentary acts regulating trade, to which no objection had been voiced. Also, colonial protests were soon transferred to a new and much more ominous act of Parliament: the Stamp Act.

THE STAMP ACT

Stamp duties had been known in England since 1694; they raised substantial sums of money at a very low cost to the government. In 1764 Grenville announced that stamp duties were also to be collected in America unless the colonists would suggest some alternative method of raising revenue in America. When no such suggestions were forthcoming, Parliament passed the Stamp Act in March 1765, to go into effect the following November. The Stamp Act required that stamps be attached to all types of legal documents, business papers, licenses, pamphlets, newspapers, almanacs, printed sermons, playing cards, and dice. Stamps were to be paid for in hard money, and violators were to be tried in admiralty courts, where no jury trials were granted. The £60,000 which it was hoped the act would raise was to be allocated to the support of the British army in America.

The passage of the Stamp Act was a grave error on the part of the English government. Never before had Parliament attempted to tax the colonies directly.

This function had always been reserved to the colonists' own assemblies. In addition, the stamp duties hit colonial opinion leaders—merchants, lawyers, printers, ministers, and tavern keepers—the hardest. The delay between the passage of the Stamp Act and the time it was to go into effect gave them ample opportunity to mobilize opposition to it.

This opposition took place on several levels simultaneously. The "low road" was taken by the Sons of Liberty—groups of farmers, small shopkeepers, artisans, seamen, unskilled workers, and apprentices. Once these groups were referred to as the rabble or the mob. Now they were organized and led by merchants, planters, and lawyers and were acclaimed for using force—or the threat of force—to compel the stamp masters, all Americans, to resign their commissions and thus nullify the act. In Boston they ruined the homes of Andrew Oliver, the stamp master, and Thomas Hutchinson, the lieutenant governor. Stamp masters in other towns experienced similar difficulties. By November 1765 no stamp master remained at his post.

Opposition to the Stamp Act was also based on constitutional principles. One of the most influential discussions of the issues was contained in a pamphlet *Considerations on the Propriety of Imposing Taxes in the British Colonies* written by Daniel Dulany of Maryland. Dulany first attempted to demolish the English doctrine of virtual representation. According to this doctrine, a member of Parliament represented the economic interests of the entire empire and not just a geographical district. Thus, Parliament had the right to tax the colonies even though they had no direct representation in that body. English proponents of the doctrine insisted that the colonies were in the same position as the people of English cities such as Manchester, who elected no representatives to Parliament but, being virtually represented, were completely under its jurisdiction.

Dulany, however, contended that colonial interests were so distinct from English interests that no English person was capable of representing American interests in Parliament. Only the presence of American representatives (which he did not advocate) could legitimize certain types of Parliamentary taxation of the colonies. Dulany (unfortunately, as it turned out) made a distinction between two types of taxes: internal and external. He explained that Parliament had the right to levy external taxes—import and export duties—on goods entering or leaving the colonies, which were intended more to regulate trade than to raise a revenue. However, he believed that "a right to impose an internal tax [such as the stamp duties] on the colonies without their consent *for the single purpose of revenue* is denied." In Dulany's opinion such a tax could only be levied by the colonial legislatures, and not by Parliament.

Dulany's distinction between internal and external taxes was not universally accepted in America. Patrick Henry in the Virginia House of Burgesses introduced a set of resolutions which, in effect, completedly denied Parliament's right to tax the colonies. One of his resolutions found in the *Journals of the House of Burgesses of Virginia* stated that

> The General Assembly of this Colony have the only and sole exclusive right and power to levy taxes and impositions upon the inhabitants of this colony. . . .

and another warned that

> The inhabitants of this colony are not bound to yield obedience to any law or ordinance whatever, designed to impose any taxation whatsoever upon them other than the laws or ordinances of the General Assembly aforesaid.

Neither of these resolutions was passed by the House of Burgesses, but they were circulated among the colonies; and when—upon the request of the Massachusetts General Assembly—the Stamp Act Congress met at New York City in October 1765, it agreed with Patrick Henry. In the Declaration of Rights and Grievances drafted by John Dickinson of Pennsylvania, the members of the Stamp Act Congress declared their "Allegiance to the Crown of Great Britain" and "all due Subordination to that August Body the Parliament of Great Britain" but still protested that "no Taxes ever have been, or can be Constitutionally imposed on them but by their respective Legislatures." However, the main significance of the Congress was that American opposition to the Stamp Act was so intense that nine colonies were willing to brave the wrath of the English government by meeting together to protest it.

The colonists did not rely only on mob violence or constitutional theory to combat the Stamp Act. Colonial merchants agreed to limit their imports from England. City women organized themselves as Daughters of Liberty, made clothing and other articles for their families, and punished merchants who failed to cooperate with the boycott. In a relatively short period this boycott was felt by English merchants and manufacturers who, in turn, put heavy pressure on Parliament to repeal the Stamp Act. Grenville had been dismissed as chief minister in July 1765 for reasons entirely unconnected with the Stamp Act. He was replaced by a ministry headed by the Marquis of Rockingham, the leader of another Whig faction. Rockingham persuaded Parliament to repeal the Stamp Act and to reduce the duty on molasses to one penny a gallon.

William Pitt's speech in Parliament in January, 1766 urging repeal of the Stamp Act offers a lucid presentation of the English supporters of the colonial point of view. Pitt described the doctrine of virtual representation in Parliament for America as "the most contemptible idea that ever entered into the head of a man." He also accepted the distinction between external and internal taxes and claimed that for Americans to yield to arbitrary taxation would be "to submit to be slaves." Yet, Pitt still claimed that Parliament could "bind their [American] *trade,* confine their *manufactures,* and exercise every *power* whatsoever, except that of taking their money out of their pockets without their consent." Other English politicians were even less willing to abandon completely Parliament's right to tax the colonies. Therefore, at the same time that Parliament repealed the Stamp Act, it passed the

Declaratory Act. This act affirmed Parliament's power to "bind the colonies and people of America . . . in all cases whatsoever."

Americans initially ignored the potential threat of the Declaratory Act and celebrated the repeal of the Stamp Act. However, the passage of the Quartering Act by Parliament in 1765 stirred up new controversy. This act required that colonies find quarters for British soldiers stationed in America in inns or barns (but not in private homes) if regular barracks were not available. Colonists were also to supply these soldiers with bedding, cooking utensils, condiments, and liquor. This was standard procedure in England. However, the assembly of New York, which was the headquarters of the army, considered the Quartering Act another attempt at Parliamentary taxation and, at first, completely refused to comply. In the debates on the question, it was repeatedly asked why an army that was supposed to protect the colonies from Indian attack should be stationed along the Atlantic coast. To these Americans it seemed that the army had been assigned a completely new and different duty—to destroy American liberties. The New York assembly grudgingly yielded only after it had been suspended by the English government. Nevertheless, neither New York nor any other colony ever fully met the requirements laid down by the Quartering Act.

THE TOWNSHEND ACTS

A change in the leadership of the English government helped create additional tension between the mother country and its North American colonies. In August 1766 domestic economic problems forced Rockingham to resign. A new Whig ministry headed by William Pitt (now Lord Chatham) and the duke of Grafton came into power. With Pitt now in the House of Lords and unwell in mind and body, Charles Townshend, the Chancellor of the Exchequer, soon became the dominant member of the ministry. Opposition to further domestic taxation led Townshend once again to attempt to raise a revenue from the colonies.

Townshend thought that he would take advantage of the distinction (made by Dulany and accepted publicly before a Parliamentary committee by Benjamin Franklin) between internal and external taxes by levying customs duties—external taxes—on lead, paints, paper, glass, silk, and tea imported from England into the colonies. The £40,000 expected to be raised by the Townshend Acts would be used to support the English troops in America and, in addition, to pay the costs of colonial administration in America. At the same session of Parliament, the customs service was tightened up still further.

Most Americans had never accepted the distinction between internal and external taxation. The Stamp Act Congress had made it clear that it objected to any tax that raised a revenue in the colonies. Only taxes for the regulation of trade were acceptable. These views were repeated in *Letters From a Farmer in Pennsylvania* written by John Dickinson. He, too, warned that acceptance of Parliamentary taxation would make Americans "as abject slaves as France and Poland can shew in wooden shoes, and with uncombed hair . . . ."

Similar views were expressed by Samuel Adams, who wrote the Circular Letter of February 11, 1768, sent by the Massachusetts legislature to all the other colonies. Adams stressed the point that if governors and judges no longer depended on the colonial assemblies for their salaries, Americans would lose their freedom. This, together with the reform of the customs service, could only result—for the first time in colonial history (with the possible exception of the short-lived Dominion of New England)—in effective enforcement of the Navigation Acts.

At first the English government gave every indication of enforcing the Townshend Acts. Lord Hillsborough, who held the newly created post of secretary of state for the colonies (another sign of the government's intention to strengthen its control over the colonies) ordered the Massachusetts legislature to rescind the Circular Letter. When the legislature refused, Hillsborough ordered the governor to dissolve the legislature and had several regiments of troops transferred to Boston. However, once again nonimportation of English goods proved effective, thanks to the support of the Daughters of Liberty. Accounts from virtually all colonies testify to the zeal with which American women boycotted British goods—particularly tea. Therefore, by the end of 1769 (Townshend had died two years earlier) the ministry, again in deference to English merchants and manufacturers rather than to American constitutional theory, repealed all the Townshend duties except the tax on tea. The latter was retained as Lord North told Parliament on March 5, 1770 "as a mark of the Supremacy of Parliament, and an efficient declaration of their right to govern the Colonies."

Ironically, the Townshend Acts were repealed on the same day as the famous Boston Massacre. As might be expected, bad feelings and incidents of petty violence had taken place between the people of Boston and the British soldiers who had been transferred there. This situation was aggravated by the fact that off-duty soldiers competed with Bostonians for odd jobs around the docks. On March 5, 1770, a mob began to harass the sentry at the customs house. Captain Thomas Preston gathered some soldiers and came to the sentry's aid. However, the mob was not cowed and continued to buffet the soldiers with missiles. Suddenly, someone (almost certainly not Captain Preston) yelled "Fire" and the soldiers shot at the mob. Crispus Attucks, a black seaman who may have been the first to strike a soldier, and four others were killed. Only the withdrawal of the British troops from Boston proper (to which they did not return until 1774) prevented a major riot.*

Samuel Adams and his few followers, who sincerely hoped for a separation between the colonies and the mother country, never allowed the Boston Massacre to be forgotten. However, most Americans rejoiced over the repeal of the Town-

---

*At the later jury trial (at which the soldiers were defended by none other than John Adams), Captain Preston was completely exonerated, and only two of the soldiers involved were found guilty—and then merely of manslaughter.

shend Acts, and for almost four years their satisfaction seemed justified. The committees of correspondence organized by Samuel Adams to publicize any British injustices perpetrated in the colonies had nothing very serious about which to write. The most sensational event of the period was the capture and burning of the English revenue ship the *Gaspee* when it went aground near Providence, Rhode Island, in 1772. Although the English government established a commission, no one was ever punished for the affair.

THE TEA ACT AND ITS REPERCUSSIONS

The period of calm came to a sudden end in 1773 when Parliament passed the Tea Act. Since 1770 the ministry had been headed by the Tory, Lord North, who was George III's personal nominee for the position. North had attempted to pursue a conciliatory policy toward the colonies. He had no intention of sabotaging this policy when he tried to solve the financial difficulties of the British East India Company by allowing it to export tea to the colonies without paying the usual customs duties and middlemen's fees. This made it possible for the company's tea to be sold in America more cheaply than the Dutch tea commonly smuggled into the colonies—even after the colonists paid the three pence a pound tea tax which survived the repeal of the Townshend Acts.

Lord North expected Americans to appreciate this bargain, but he was completely mistaken. The Tea Act united economic interest and constitutional principle. Merchants with large supplies of tea on hand faced ruin from what they viewed as monopolistic competition. In addition, paying the tea tax would legitimize Parliament's claim that it had the right to tax the colonies. Once again the Sons of Liberty saw themselves facing imminent slavery. The Daughters of Liberty began serving their families "liberty tea" made from dried raspberry or currant leaves.

When the ships bearing the East India Company's tea arrived in most American towns, they were either forced to return to England, or their tea was stored without being sold. In Boston, however, Lieutenant Governor Hutchinson was determined that the tea be unloaded and sold. Samuel Adams and his followers were just as determined not to allow the tea to be marketed. When Hutchinson refused to yield, the Bostonians decided to take drastic action. On the night of December 16, 1773, a group of about sixty men gathered at Fulton's carpenter shop, where Mrs. Fulton and her sister helped disguise them as Mohawk Indians. The "Indians" then boarded the three tea ships and dumped more than £10,000 worth of tea into Boston harbor before returning to the Fulton's to wash away the telltale signs of their escapade. (Sarah Fulton was henceforth known as the mother of the Boston Tea Party.) Many people were aware of the decision not to allow the tea to be landed, and—with no troops in town—the "party" was well attended. Hundreds of men and women stood on Griffin's Wharf enjoying the proceedings.

English reaction was immediate and violent. Lord North at first planned to prosecute only those directly involved, but when he found this to be impossible, he decided to punish the city of Boston and the colony of Massachusetts. In spite of the warnings of Pitt and Edmund Burke, who (rightly) feared that Lord North's tactics would only unite all the other colonies behind Massachusetts, an overwhelming majority in both houses of Parliament supported a series of laws known collectively as the Coercive, or Intolerable, Acts.

In March 1774 Parliament passed the Boston Port Bill, which closed the port of Boston to all trade except for food and fuel until compensation was paid to the East India Company. The Port Bill was followed by the Administration of Justice Act, which provided that officials who suppressed riots could be tried in England if they did not expect a fair trial in the colonies. To Americans this seemed to be a device to ensure that such persons would go unpunished. A third act—the Massachusetts Government Act—amended the charter of Massachusetts. It took the power of selecting the council away from the legislature and gave it to the governor. The governor was also given the power to appoint and remove judges, sheriffs, and other law enforcement officials and to limit town meetings to one a year. Massachusetts received a new governor: General Thomas Gage, the commander-in-chief of the British forces in America. The last of the Intolerable Acts—a revised Quartering Act—ordered local authorities to provide quarters for British troops at the scene of any disturbance and not at a more distant location, as before.

In June 1774 Parliament passed the Quebec Act, which—though not part of the Intolerable Acts—was just as bitterly resented by the colonists. The Quebec Act extended the boundaries of the province of Quebec southward to the Ohio River and westward to the Mississippi. The area could be ruled by a governor and council appointed by the king—with no representative assembly. Catholics were to enjoy full religious rights, and French civil law was to be in effect. The Quebec Act did much to ensure the loyalty of French Canadians to the British during the Revolution; but to the English colonists, the Quebec Act seemed to be part of a malicious plot to prevent them from settling their western lands, settling the lands instead with Catholics who would support British despotism.

THE FIRST CONTINENTAL CONGRESS
AND THE OUTBREAK OF VIOLENCE

As Pitt and Burke had foreseen, the Intolerable (and Quebec) Acts rallied the other colonies to support the people of Massachusetts. Foodstuffs from as far away as South Carolina were hurriedly transported to Boston. A meeting of all the colonies was called to discuss ways and means of reversing the punitive policy of the British government. The majority of the delegates to the Continental Congress (where every colony but Georgia was represented) believed that Parliament was guilty of exceeding its authority over the colonies. Even those few delegates, such as Joseph Galloway of Pennsylvania, who accepted the British view in theory, realized that formal steps should be taken to transform the empire from a unitary into a federal empire.

Therefore, Galloway proposed that the congress petition the British authorities to create an American legislature. This would be elected by the colonial assemblies but presided over by a president-general (who would possess a veto power) appointed by the king. All measures which affected all the American colonies would have to be approved by this American legislature as well as by Parliament. Local affairs would remain under the jurisdiction of the colonial assemblies. Galloway's Plan of Union, which attempted to set up the machinery to make the British empire a federal empire in fact as well as in (American) theory, was debated at the Continental Congress, never again considered, and finally deferred by a vote of six colonies to five.

In fact, relations with Great Britain had deteriorated to the point where the majority of the delegates were no longer willing to accept the high degree of Parliamentary control over the colonies that Galloway's plan would have permitted. Nor did they have any confidence that Parliament would agree to share its authority with any colonial legislature. Therefore, the members gave their approval to a set of more radical principles: the Suffolk Resolves—passed by an extralegal body in the county which included Boston. By approving these resolves, Congress gave its support to the formation of the Continental Association, which would enforce nonimportation, nonexportation, and nonconsumption of English goods. Congress also agreed to the formation of a force of minutemen to protect colonial rights by military means if necessary. Yet, although in a Declaration of Rights adopted October 14, 1774 the members of the Continental Congress violently attacked Parliament's attempts to tax them and the Intolerable Acts as being violations of "the immutable laws of nature, the principles of the English constitution, and the several [colonial] charters or compacts," they still recognized Parliament's right to regulate "our external commerce."

Lord North, however, fortified by an increased Parliamentary majority and the king's advice to him on September 11, 1774 that "the colonies must either submit or triumph," was determined to take a hard line. The appeals of Burke and Pitt for reconciliation lest, as Pitt expressed it, "the kingdom be undone" were again ignored. New Englanders were forbidden to fish off the Grand Banks or to trade with any foreign nation (later other colonies were included in this ban). Reinforcements were sent to the British army in America. The best offer North would make to the colonies was that if they would voluntarily contribute a sum satisfactory to the English government toward the cost of their administration and defense, Parliament would not exercise its own taxing power over them. This token gesture of conciliation only confirmed colonial fears that Parliament was determined to procure a revenue from them in one way or another.

There followed shortly the order to send troops to Lexington and Concord to destroy the military stores being collected there by the colonials. Paul Revere and William Dawes soon spread the word, and a handful of minutemen met the British at Lexington on the morning of April 19, 1775. Shots rang out, the minutemen withdrew, and the British moved on to Concord where another skirmish took place. Casualties in these battles were light. However, by the time the British troops were able to return to Boston, over 70 of their men were killed and over 170 wounded by the embattled American farmers who fired at them all along the route. Nor did the Americans hesitate to continue the fight. In May colonial troops captured Fort Ticonderoga in upstate New York and seized much-needed artillery. In June the Americans occupied Breed's Hill, which overlooked Boston. When 2,500 British troops attempted to capture the hill, they were twice beaten back. Only when the Americans ran short of ammunition did they make an orderly retreat to Bunker Hill (for which the battle was named) and then to Cambridge. British casualties were over 1,000; American casualties less than 400. Although the hill was taken, Americans were greatly encouraged by the Battle of Bunker Hill because it indicated that they were able to hold their own against British troops.

THE SECOND CONTINENTAL
CONGRESS AND INDEPENDENCE

It was, therefore, a far different climate in which the members gathered for the Second Continental Congress in May 1775. This time all thirteen colonies were represented, but feelings were still decidedly mixed. Congress voted to organize and raise funds for a Continental army with George Washington at its head. Yet, even the *Declaration of Causes of Taking-up Arms,* which the Second Continental Congress approved on July 6, 1775, though announcing the intention of Americans "to dye Freemen rather than live Slaves," denied any "ambitious designs of separating from Great Britain." At the same time Congress sent the so-called Olive Branch Petition to the king in which it begged him to effect "a happy and permanent reconciliation" so that Americans might once more be "the most dutiful subjects, and the most affectionate colonists."

By now the members of the Continental Congress had reached the point where they denied Parliament any authority whatsoever over the colonies. They considered their only political link with Great Britain to be the person of the king. Even those—and they were still few—who hoped for independence from Great Britain, realized that Americans were not yet ready to accept any attacks on the authority or the good will of the monarch. However, King George, not only ignored the Olive Branch Petition but proclaimed that the colonies were in a state of rebellion and dispatched additional troops to America.

Many thoughts—some confused and some contradictory—must have been going through the minds of Americans at this time. Thomas Paine, a young Englishman who had only been in the colonies two years, published in January 1776 a pamphlet called *Common Sense,* which coalesced all these ideas, added a few new ones, and arrived at the conclusion that American independence was necessary and attainable.

Paine was the first to place the blame for the colony's plight squarely upon the king. He denounced King George as "the hardened, sullen-tempered Pharoah of England" who was inciting Parliament to deprive Americans of their rights. Paine went on to condemn the British constitution and the institution of monarchy as "fit only for the dark and slavish times" in which they originated. Paine painted an inspiring portrait of a free, independent, and prosperous American republic uncontaminated by the vice and corruption, and secure from the conflicts, of the Old World. He pointed out how ridiculous it was for a huge continent peopled by a young, rapidly growing population to remain under the domination of a tiny, jaded island.

Common Sense made a tremendous impression on the colonials. They (and some English Whigs) were by now convinced that a conspiracy existed to reduce both Americans and the English to slavery. This belief was shared by people as different as Samuel Adams and John Dickinson. As Bailyn pointed out, this conspiracy theory was not developed in America but was an integral part of English political thought of the first half of the eighteenth century. When in power, English politicians believed that their opponents were constantly conspiring to overthrow them. However, more importantly, politicians in the opposition (which included the more radical Old Whigs and to a lesser extent the extreme Tories) believed that wicked and desperate ministers were plotting to subvert the balance between King, Lords, and Commons—in other words, the constitutional compromises which had developed out of the seventeenth-century revolutions. The Old Whigs pointed—correctly—to the bribery and "influence" of the House of Commons indulged in so successfully by Sir Robert Walpole, the first prime minister (1721-1742), and his successors. They believed that unless checked, these ministers would ultimately destroy English liberties.

This essentially seventeenth-century political philosophy was even more accepted in America than it was in the mother country. The basic reason for this cultural lag was the feeling, common to most Americans, that they had never been accorded the full rights and protections won in the Glorious Revolution by their fellow subjects in England. Allusions to the loss of liberty by the people of other nations may also be found in colonial writings all through the eighteenth century. It is therefore not surprising that when the English government began to reinforce its control over the colonies, its actions were interpreted by Americans as a deliberate plot by the ministry to enslave them—leaving independence their only viable alternative.

English actions, as well as Paine's writing, impelled Americans to declare their independence. At the end of 1775, news arrived that the king had proclaimed America to be in a state of rebellion. This was followed by the Prohibitory Act, which placed an embargo on American trade and ordered the capture of all American ships found on the high seas. Lord Dunmore, the governor of Virginia, seemed to be inciting racial violence when he offered freedom to slaves whose masters were in revolt against Great Britain. Lastly came word that the British government intended to use German mercenaries to subdue the colonies. These threats so frightened and angered the members of the Continental Congress that they ordered all American ports to be opened to foreign trade. And on June 7, 1776, Richard Henry Lee, on instructions from the Virginia Assembly, presented three resolutions to the Continental Congress:

FIGURE 25A   (Library of Congress.)

That these United Colonies are, and of right ought to be, free and independent states.

That it is expedient forthwith to take the most effectual measures for forming foreign alliances.

That a plan of confederation be prepared and transmitted to the respective colonies for their consideration and approbation.*

During the debates on these resolutions, no member of the congress openly opposed them. However, some members (such as John Dickinson, who still hoped for reconciliation) urged further delay until the colonies had formed a confederation and won the support of foreign nations. Proponents of the resolutions argued that the colonies were already de facto independent and that a confederation and foreign aid could only be expected after independence was declared. After much debate the Congress decided that a committee made up of Robert Livingston (New York), Roger Sherman (Connecticut), Benjamin Franklin, and John Adams, chaired by Thomas Jefferson, should compose a document explaining why the colonies were justified in declaring their independence.

When composing the Declaration of Independence, Jefferson largely followed Locke's compact theory that governments were formed by the "consent of the governed" to protect the people's "unalienable rights" of "Life, Liberty and the pursuit of Happiness." Therefore, when the king (the authority of Parliament is no-

*Journals of the Continental Congress V, 425.

where recognized in the Declaration) degenerated into a tyrant who ignored or violated these rights, the people were forced to exercise their "right of revolution." In
order to prove that this right of revolution was not being resorted to prematurely,
Jefferson went on to list thirty-nine examples of the king's despotism. The declaration then included Lee's independence resolution and concluded with the delegates' promise to support it with their "Lives . . . Fortunes and . . . sacred Honor."

When the declaration was presented to the Continental Congress on July 2,
1776, the delegates of all the colonies except New York (who abstained because of
lack of instructions) first voted to approve independence and then, two days later,
approved an edited version of the declaration itself. The colonies were now independent. It remained to be seen if they could maintain their independence against
the assault of the greatest military power of the period.

BIBLIOGRAPHY

BAILYN, BERNARD. *The Ideological Origins of the American Revolution.* Cam-
    bridge, 1967.
BECKER, ROBERT A. *Revolution, Reform, and the Politics of American Tax-
    ation, 1763–1783.* Baton Rouge, 1980.
BRIDENBAUGH, CARL. *Mitre and Scepter: Transatlantic Faiths, Ideas, Person-
    alities, and Politics, 1689–1775.* New York, 1962.
JENSEN, MERRILL. *The Founding of a Nation: A History of the American Revo-
    lution, 1763–1776.* New York, 1968.
KERBER, LINDA K. *Women of the Republic: Intellect and Ideology in Revo-
    lutionary America.* Chapel Hill, 1980.
LABAREE, BENJAMIN W. *The Boston Tea Party.* New York, 1964.
MAIER, PAULINE. *From Resistance to Revolution: Colonial Radicals and the
    Development of American Opposition to Britain, 1765–1776.* New York,
    1972.
MORGAN, EDMUND S., and MORGAN, HELEN M. *The Stamp Act Crisis: Pro-
    logue to Revolution.* Chapel Hill, 1953.
NASH, GARY B. *The Urban Crucible: Social Change, Political Consciousness, and
    the Origins of the American Revolution.* Cambridge, 1979.
NORTON, MARY BETH. *Liberty's Daughters: The Revolutionary Experience of
    American Women, 1750–1800.* Boston, 1980.
PECKHAM, HOWARD H. *Pontiac and the Indian Uprising.* Princeton, 1947.
SHAW, PETER. *American Patriots and the Rituals of Revolution.* Cambridge,
    1981.
SOSIN, JACK M. *Whitehall and the Wilderness: The Middle West in British Colo-
    nial Policy, 1760–1775.* Lincoln, 1961.
WHITE, MORTON. *The Philosophy of the American Revolution.* New York, 1981.
ZOBEL, HILLER B. *The Boston Massacre.* New York, 1970.

26
The Revolutionary
War

In December, 1776, Washington wrote to his brother Augustine:

> You can form no idea of the perplexity of my situation. No man, I believe,
> ever had a greater choice of difficulties, and less means to extricate himself
> from them. However, under a full persuasion of the justice of our cause, I can-
> not entertain an Idea, that it will finally sink, tho' it may remain for some
> time under a cloud . . .

From these few words one can appreciate the blend of realism and optimism
which made George Washington the ideal person to lead the divided and militarily
ill-prepared American people to ultimate victory in the Revolutionary War.

MILITARY ADVANTAGES
AND DISADVANTAGES

Very few people, inside or outside of America, could have expected that the thirteen
colonies would have any realistic chance of winning their independence. In the
Seven Years' War (French and Indian), England had proven itself the mightiest
military power in Europe. Its army was well trained and well equipped, its navy
controlled the seas, and its financial system was well able to assume the burden of a
war. In addition, England expected aid from the Loyalists and the Indians. The
United States, on the other hand, had an army and navy in name only and faced
financial chaos.

However, England's advantages were more apparent than real. At the start of the Revolution, its regular army numbered only about 15,000 and depended heavily on German mercenaries. These mercenaries often decided, after seeing the prosperity of their fellow countrymen in America, to desert rather than face possible death in a quarrel that did not concern them. The English navy had also deteriorated seriously since 1763. Ships were not properly maintained, and political interference had ruined the morale of officers and men alike.

The Loyalists were eager to fight for their mother country, but English army officers looked down on them. At first Loyalists were ignored or utilized only as spies or guides. Later, however, about 50,000 of them were allowed to join the English army, while others formed special fighting units of their own. Loyalist efforts were often coordinated with Indian attacks on the frontier—particularly in New York, Pennsylvania, and what later became Tennessee. However, neither the Iroquois of the north nor the Cherokees of the south were properly utilized by the English, and they did not play as effective a role in the contest as their numbers and experience warranted.

America's size, distance from England, and—paradoxically—its disunity were to lead (with the aid of its allies) to ultimate victory. Time and time again English strategists failed to take America's size and lack of roads into consideration when planning their campaigns. England had great difficulty in supplying its army in America at a distance of 3,000 miles. During the French and Indian War, much of the English army's supplies were obtained from the colonies rather than from the mother country. Obviously, this was much more difficult—if not impossible—during the Revolutionary War. Further, in many ways American disunity, although certainly inimical to military effectiveness, made it impossible for the English to win the war. For example, when the English army captured New York and Philadelphia, New England and the southern states fought on undeterred. Likewise, when the southern states were overrun by the English, the other sections of the country were able to carry on the war just as before. The United States could only be conquered if and when England occupied all sections simultaneously—a feat which was beyond its strength.

England failed to take into consideration that men who used guns regularly could, in a relatively short period of time, be turned into an effective army. It is estimated that as many as 400,000 Americans fought in the Revolutionary War at one time or another either in the state militias or in the Continental army. Black Americans also fought in the Revolutionary War. They distinguished themselves at Lexington, Concord, and Bunker Hill. However, when the Continental army was formed, blacks were barred from enlisting lest armed blacks encourage slave revolts. Two factors soon brought about a reversal of this policy. One factor was the action of Lord Dunmore, the governor of Virginia, who promised freedom to any slave who would join his army. Other English commanders later repeated this offer, and thousands of slaves did flee to the English armies during the course of the war. The other, and even more important, factor was the shortage of troops, which plagued the Continental army throughout the war. To fill their quotas of men, all states accepted black recruits—both slave and free. By 1783 about 10,000 black men had fought on the American side in the Revolutionary War.

American women played an important part in the war éffort—both directly and indirectly. Deborah Sampson Gannett enlisted in the Continental army as a man, served on active duty for over a year, and was wounded twice. Only a bout of fever led to the discovery that she was a woman and ultimately to an honorable discharge and a pension of eight dollars a month. Margaret Corbin and Molly Hays (better known as Molly Pitcher for providing water to the troops at the battle of Monmouth) also participated in battles and won pensions for their heroism. Other women served as couriers, often under very difficult conditions. Also, some served the army as part-time spies, scouts, and nurses.

A number of women performed less glamorous—but equally valuable—services. Catherine Greene, the wife of General Greene, allowed their home to be used as a hospital for men inoculated with smallpox and shared her husband's sufferings at Valley Forge. Esther Reed and (after Reed's premature death at age thirty-four) Sarah Franklin Bache headed Philadelphia's campaign to raise funds for much-needed clothing and supplies for the Continental army. Women's organizations in other colonies followed Philadelphia's example. Women's groups also spearheaded

FIGURE 26A (New York Public Library.)

the fight against inflation and profiteering. Abigail Adams wrote her husband about a female riot in which a group of women seized a load of coffee from an avaricious merchant. In other incidents merchants were similarly punished for overcharging for sugar and tea. Finally. women played a crucial role in the war by running farms and businesses, often quite successfully, while their husbands and fathers were serving in the armed forces.

The Americans developed an "instant navy" by adding a few guns to the many merchant ships that were available. As early as March 1776, a small fleet of eight American ships captured valuable cannon and ammunition from as far away as New Providence Island in the Bahamas. The most famous naval exploits of the war were performed by John Paul Jones. The defeat of the *Serapis* by Jones's ship the *Bonhomme Richard* is well known. Even more important was his victory over numerous English merchant ships in their home waters. Before the war was over, over 2,000 English ships were captured by the Continental navy and American privateers.

England greatly underestimated France's desire and capacity for revenge, which stemmed from the latter's defeat in the Seven Years' War; it also miscalculated the emnity against England which had developed in numerous European nations because of the wars fought since 1689. The help in money and naval support which the United States was to receive—particularly from France, Spain, and Holland—proved crucial to the outcome of the war. Finally, due credit must be given to George Washington, whose character and example—even more than his military skills—were major factors in winning American independence. Washington did not win many battles, but he saw to it that an American army always remained in the field, thus making ultimate English victory impossible.

THE CAMPAIGNS OF 1776–1777

The military history of the American Revolution may be dealt with relatively briefly. In March 1776 the English army—now commanded by General William Howe—evacuated Boston, leaving the New England states in safety (except for sporadic raids) for the remainder of the war. Earlier, American troops under the command of Generals Richard Montgomery and Benedict Arnold had made a gallant but unsuccessful effort to conquer Canada. Although Montgomery captured Montreal, weather, smallpox, and the English army saved Quebec. No other military operations were undertaken against Canada, although members of the Continental Congress continued to hope that Canada would voluntarily join the United States.

In June 1776 an English army failed to take Charleston, but by the end of the year, New York City and most of New Jersey were under English control. During the fighting in this area, it seemed that the Revolution was fated to come to a speedy and unsuccessful close. Howe's troops decisively defeated Washington's smaller and poorly trained army but twice allowed it to escape what seemed to be certain capture. Only Washington's victories over small detachments of English troops at Trenton and Princeton preserved some vestiges of American morale.

The English strategy for the year 1777 was to cut New England off from the rest of the United States by sending an army of 7,000 under General John Burgoyne down from Canada. He was to be joined by an army from New York City (which was to march up the Hudson River) and another force (which was to be sent from Philadelphia by General Howe). However, Howe did not capture Philadelphia—his main objective—until September, and Burgoyne received no reinforcements either from him or from General Henry Clinton in New York. New Englanders, however, recognized the threat to their safety, and in October 1777 Burgoyne found himself surrounded near Saratoga, New York, by an American army of 17,000 men under the command of General Horatio Gates. After vainly attempting to break through the American lines, Burgoyne surrendered his entire army.

Burgoyne's surrender has rightly been termed the turning point of the war—not that it was such an overwhelming military victory—but it did convince France that the United States would ultimately win the war. The French government, therefore, signed two treaties with the United States: one recognizing it as a soverign nation; and the other pledging to support it militarily if war should break out (as it soon did) between England and France. In 1779 Spain joined the war as an ally of France, though not of the United States. Later Russia, Sweden, Denmark, and Holland formed the League of Armed Neutrality to protect their ships against seizure by the English navy. Foreign financial support was as important (if not more important) in helping the United States win the war. By 1780 the paper money issued by the Continental Congress had become almost worthless, and only the infusion of French and Dutch gold made it possible to continue financing the war effort.

THE CAMPAIGNS OF 1778-1781

In spite of the American victory at Saratoga, Washington and the remnants of his army spent the winter of 1777-1778 under almost unbearable conditions, while Howe and his men rested in warmth and comfort in Philadelphia. However, the time at Valley Forge had been put to good use. Baron von Steuben, who was actually only a captain in the Prussian army, performed the invaluable task of drilling Washington's men, turning them into trained soldiers. In 1778 the arrival of a French fleet forced General Clinton (who had replaced Howe) to evacuate Philadelphia and return to New York.

However, the most important fighting of 1778 took place in the west. With the encouragement of the English and the Loyalists, Indians had been successfully attacking settlements all along the frontier. Governor Patrick Henry of Virginia sent George Rogers Clark and a band of less than 200 men west to intimidate the Indians. This he did successfully by capturing English posts at Kaskasia, Cahokia, and

Vincennes in present-day Illinois and Indiana. The conquest of these forts and the capture of the English commander in the area, Colonel Henry Hamilton, discouraged the Indians from further raids. In addition, Clark's victories gave the United States support for its claim (at the peace conference following the war) to the land west of the Appalachian Mountains.

For the remainder of the conflict, most of the action took place in the southern states. An English army occupied Georgia in 1779, and in May 1780 captured Charleston along with 5,000 men and 300 cannon. Later that same year the defeat of General Gates's army at Camden, South Carolina, exposed North Carolina and Virginia to English conquest. Fortunately, an English force of 1,100 was badly defeated at King's Mountain in northern South Carolina, and General Charles Cornwallis, the English commander, delayed his advance. However, soon after, General Daniel Morgan defeated the English at Cowpens, North Carolina, and Cornwallis went in pursuit of him. At this juncture General Nathanael Greene assumed command of the American troops in the south. Although defeated by Cornwallis at Guilford Court House, Greene, with the help of a contingent of troops under the command of the Marquis de Lafayette, proved more than a match for Cornwallis.

When Cornwallis led his army to the Yorktown peninsula in expectation of its being transported to New York by an English fleet, Washington saw the opportunity he had long awaited. He requested that the Comte de Grasse, the commander of the French fleet in the West Indies, blockade Chesapeake Bay. In the meantime he ordered Lafayette to cut off Cornwallis's lines of retreat to the Carolinas while the main American army was being transported to Virginia. When de Grasse defeated an English fleet at the mouth of the Chesapeake Bay, Cornwallis found his army of 7,000 surrounded by 8,800 American and 7,000 French troops—with no hope of evacuation by sea. Cornwallis had little choice: After holding out for three weeks, he surrendered on October 17, 1781.

PEACE NEGOTIATIONS

Lord North is supposed to have exclaimed, "Oh, God! It is all over."—and he was absolutely correct. Although peace negotiations dragged on for over a year, no further important battles took place in North America. Upon North's resignation in March 1782, first the Marquis of Rockingham and then, when he died, the Earl of Shelburne, assumed the reins of government. Despite the king's protests, they were determined to end the war. However, they both hoped that the United States would accept some form of homerule within the British empire. (Such an offer had been made by Lord North in 1778, but the Continental Congress rejected it when the Franco-American alliance was signed.) This illusion was quickly shattered by the American peace commissioners Benjamin Franklin, John Jay, John Adams, and Henry Laurens.

The peace negotiations were further complicated by the fact that the Franco-American treaty provided that neither party would negotiate or make peace without the consent of the other. The Americans were aware, however, that France and (particularly) Spain were eager to limit the extent and power of the new nation. They therefore negotiated a treaty with England and then presented it to France as a virtual *fait accompli*. The final treaty recognized America's claim to the lands west of the Appalachian Mountains and made the Mississippi River the western border of the United States. The southern boundary of the United States was set at the thirty-first parallel, the northern border of Florida (which was returned to Spain). Americans were allowed to fish off the Grand Banks and to land on Newfoundland to dry their catch. The English government promised to evacuate its forts in the northwest. In return, the United States agreed to facilitate the payment of the prewar debts owed by Americans to English merchants and to compensate Loyalists for their property losses. The greatest disappointment in the treaty for the United States was that American merchants were no longer accorded the special privileges of trading with the West Indies that they had enjoyed as English subjects. Palatable or not, France had little choice except to agree to the treaty and the Peace of Paris was ratified by all combatants in 1783.

DOMESTIC EFFECTS
OF THE REVOLUTION

Cornwallis's army had surrendered to the tune of a then popular song, "The World Turned Upside Down." However, the American Revolution was not followed by the social and economic upheavals such as those resulting from the later French and Russian revolutions. Nevertheless, important changes did take place in the new nation. The Revolution had also been a civil war. A quarter of the population had been willing to endanger their lives and property by remaining loyal to England. Geographic factors played an important role in this decision. In the south Virginia and Maryland were strongly Whig; Georgia and South Carolina, strongly Tory; and North Carolina, mixed. In the north New England was predominantly Whig (although even here 1,100 Tories left with Howe when he evacuated Boston); while the middle colonies, particularly New York, were mixed. Former officeholders, royal officials, and Anglicans (outside of Virginia) remained loyal to England to a much higher degree than members of other groups. Debtors were almost always strong Patriots as were most small farmers, city workers, and shopkeepers. Otherwise, it is very difficult to generalize. Large landowners, rich merchants, lawyers, and doctors were found on both sides. Most ethnic groups were split, with the exception of the Highland Scots, who remained consistently loyal to England.

During the war many Loyalists fought for the preservation of the empire; some fled to English-occupied territory, and many merely retired to the country and attempted to keep as low a profile as possible. The new states passed laws confiscating Loyalist property and the Loyalists themselves were subject to sporadic persecution. After the war about 80,000 to 100,000 Loyalists left the United States. Most went to Canada, although some settled in England or in the West Indies.

Gradually, state laws against them were rescinded or relaxed, and many Loyalists were able to return to their homes and once again become active and respected members of their communities. No better example may be given than Edward Shippen, who, although he was the father-in-law of the notorious Benedict Arnold, became chief justice of the Pennsylvania supreme court.

In spite of the return of so many Tories, the popularization, or radicalization, of American politics which had taken place during the 1760s and 1770s could not be undone. During that period politicians who openly showed their fear and dislike of the "mob" lost their seats in the colonial assemblies (and later became Loyalists). Those who replaced them—for example, Patrick Henry, Richard Henry Lee, and Thomas Jefferson in Virginia—although still of the gentry class, sympathized with ordinary citizens and realized the necessity of winning their support in the struggle against the English government. Thus, the common folk had a greater opportunity to participate in, and make their views known to, the extralegal assemblies which were organized in all colonies during 1774-1775.

This struggle for democracy has given rise to the concept of a double revolution—one meant to win independence from England and the other to democratize American politics and society. The latter goal was attained, to some extent, in all the states. Suffrage requirements were lowered: Ownership of personal as well as landed property entitled a man to vote in some states, and two states allowed all taxpayers to vote. Also, although much of the land of the confiscated Loyalist estates was acquired by speculators, some was granted to formerly landless Americans, who thus became eligible to vote. However, officeholding tended to remain in the hands of the aristocracy. Nevertheless, the number of farmers elected to state legislatures more than doubled, and fewer merchants and lawyers were elected to legislatures than in the pre-Revolutionary period.

After the Revolution all the southern states passed laws officially separating church and state. The highpoint of the disestablishment movement was Jefferson's Statute of Religious Liberty, which went into effect in Virginia in 1786. This statute declared

> ... that no man shall be compelled to frequent or support any religious worship, place or ministry whatsoever, nor shall be enforced, restrained, molested, or burthened in his body or goods, nor shall otherwise suffer on account of his religious opinions or belief; but that all men shall be free to profess, and by argument to maintain, their opinion in matters of religion, and that the same shall in no wise diminish, enlarge or affect their civil capacities.

The middle states (except for four counties of New York) never had established churches. However, the New England states, with the exception of Rhode Island (which never had an established church), refused to sever their official ties with the Congregational Church. Yet, even in these states non-Congregationalists were no longer forced to contribute to the support of the established church.

The Revolution also led to independence for American religious denominations. Obviously, Anglicans could no longer remain part of the Church of England. Therefore, in 1784 Samuel Seabury was ordained as the bishop of the Protestant Episcopal Church in the United States. In the same decade American Methodists organized the Methodist Episcopal Church under the leadership of Francis Asbury and Thomas Coke; and Father John Carroll of Maryland became the head of the Catholic Church in the United States. Later the Presbyterians, the Baptists, and the Dutch Reformed Church also organized separate American churches.

Another step toward democracy was taken through a series of laws which finally abolished the already declining practices of primogeniture and entail. Entail limited the inheritance of an estate to a specific individual or class of individuals (such as sons or the eldest son) in order to keep it intact within a family. Entail was abolished shortly after 1783. Primogeniture, which had required that all property—both real and personal—be bequeathed to the eldest son, was banned by the end of the eighteenth century, although some states still gave the eldest son a double share of the estate. Both of these practices were abolished partly because they savored too much of the aristocratic English tradition and partly because the ready availability of land in America made such practices unnecessary.

All during the 1760s and 1770s, Americans had accused England of attempting to make them slaves. This accusation inevitably led to the questioning of the morality of African slavery. As early as 1764 James Otis had written in *The Rights of the British Colonies Asserted and Proved,* "The Colonists are by the law of nature free born as indeed all men are, white or black." In 1775 Benjamin Franklin and Dr. Benjamin Rush founded an antislavery organization, and Thomas Paine attacked slavery in *Common Sense.* During the Revolutionary War slaves in Massachusetts and New Hampshire petitioned for their freedom, claiming that they deserved their liberty for the same reasons that other Americans were fighting for their independence.

Thus, the morality of slavery was brought into serious question. As might be expected, this questioning led to more concrete action in the north than in the south. In 1780 Pennsylvania, which had a long history of Mennonite and Quaker opposition to slavery, passed a law which provided for the gradual abolition of slavery. In 1783, in the Quock Walker case, the Massachusetts supreme court interpreted the clause in the state constitution that "all men are born free and equal" to mean that slavery was illegal in Massachusetts. The other New England states also abolished slavery during the 1780s. The middle states followed their example, although New York did not formally outlaw slavery until 1799.

Slavery did not remain unchallenged in the southern states either. In the early 1780s Virginia passed several laws to encourage the manumission of slaves. Although these statutes were later repealed, about 10 percent of the slaves in Virginia and Maryland were free by 1800. Virginia, and all the other southern states except South Carolina and Georgia, also attempted to curtail the slave trade by placing heavy duties on slaves imported into their states.

In contrast to black Americans, women, who had also contributed significantly to the war effort—both on the home front and on the battlefield—failed to benefit from the Revolution. Abigail Adams had requested in a letter of March 31, 1776, that her husband John "remember the Ladies" when creating a new government. He, however, retorted two weeks later, "We know better than to repeal our masculine systems." All the leaders of the Revolution, except Thomas Paine, and certainly most women, agreed with Mercy Otis Warren, (the author of a three-volume history of the American Revolution) who wrote a friend in 1791 that "the subordination of women was necessary and natural."* The law codes which were drafted in the newly independent states tended to grant married women and widows fewer legal rights—such as signing contracts and retaining control of their doweries—than they had during the colonial period. At a time when more men than ever were becoming eligible to vote, no state, except New Jersey, which allowed it from 1790 to 1807, allowed any woman to vote.

The American Revolution was only a beginning in the transformation of American social life. John Adams was right in 1776 when he claimed that members of the Continental Congress were in favor of modifying rather than destroying existing political institutions.

BIBLIOGRAPHY

ALDEN, JOHN R. *A History of the American Revolution.* New York, 1969.

BROWN, WALLACE. *The Good Americans: The Loyalists in the American Revolution.* New York, 1969.

FERGUSON, E. JAMES. *The Power of the Purse: A History of American Public Finance, 1776–1790.* Chapel Hill, 1961.

FOWLER, WILLIAM M. *Rebels Under Sail: The American Navy during the Revolution.* New York, 1976.

GRAYMONT, BARBARA. *The Iroquois in the American Revolution.* Syracuse, 1972.

MACKESY, PIERS. *The War for America, 1775–1783.* Cambridge, 1964.

MAIN, JACKSON TURNER. *The Sovereign States, 1775–1783.* New York, 1973.

MORRIS, RICHARD B. *The Peacemakers: The Great Powers and American Independence.* New York, 1965.

QUARLES, BENJAMIN. *The Negro in the American Revolution.* Chapel Hill, 1961.

ROYSTER, CHARLES. *A Revolutionary People at War: The Continental Army and American Character, 1775–1783.* Chapel Hill, 1979.

SHY, JOHN. *A People Numerous and Armed: Reflections on the Military Struggle for American Independence.* London, England, 1976.

SMITH, PAUL H. *Loyalists and Redcoats: A Study in British Revolutionary Politics.* Chapel Hill, 1964.

STINCHECOMBE, WILLIAM C. *The American Revolution and the French Alliance.* Syracuse, 1969.

VAN ALSTYNE, RICHARD W. *Empire and Independence: The International History of the American Revolution.* New York, 1965.

*However, Mrs. Warren believed that this subordination was not natural but necessitated by the difference in education received by men and women.

27

Governments for a New Nation

In 1775 General John Sullivan of New Hampshire recommended giving the people a full voice in their own government. A year later a conservative Virginian, Carter Braxton, replied that such a plan would only lead to anarchy and recommended an aristocratic form of government. Those responsible for the development of constitutions, both state and national, during the Revolutionary period were faced with these two alternatives. As so often happens in such cases—they compromised.

STATE CONSTITUTION MAKING

After 1776 the new states (with the exception of Connecticut and Rhode Island, who were satisfied with modifying their old colonial charters) were faced with the necessity of drawing up constitutions which expressed their political beliefs and goals. The state constitutions framed during this period were both a reflection of, and a reaction to, the experiences of Americans under English rule.

One example of this was the American demand for a written constitution embodied in a single document. England itself did not have such a document and was loath to grant one to any of its colonies. In deciding how a state constitution was to be drafted and approved, Americans institutionalized the Lockean phrase "by the consent of the governed" through the invention of the constitutional convention. By electing a group of delegates with the sole duty of drafting a constitution, the people showed that sovereignty belonged to them. Once a constitution was drafted, it had to be approved by the qualified voters of the state. In the 1770s few states went through the complete procedure of calling constitutional conventions and then presenting the constitutions they drafted for a popular vote. Some states called a constitutional convention but omitted popular ratification. In other states the state legislature drafted the constitution but it was submitted to the voters for ratification. Only Massachusetts in 1780 went through the complete process. Nevertheless, the tradition was established and gradually became an integral part of American political procedure.

The eleven state constitutions drafted during this period shared several characteristics. All established governments with three branches: executive, legislative, and judicial. The executive branch, however, was stripped of virtually all its powers. The Pennsylvania constitution omitted the office of governor entirely and placed the executive power in a council of twelve elected by the people. In the other states the office of governor was retained, but terms were limited to one year; governors had no veto power at all; and in most states governors could no longer call or adjourn sessions of the legislature, grant pardons, or make any appointments without the consent of the legislature. The reason for these drastic changes is obvious: The royal governors, with—in theory at least—almost unlimited powers, had been considered the archenemies of the rights of the people.

Second, the new state constitutions (Pennsylvania and Georgia were temporary exceptions) followed English and colonial precedents and provided for bicameral legislatures. The members of the lower house were always elected by the people, generally for only a one-year term. The members of the upper house, usually called a senate, were also elected by the people, but for a longer term than assembly members. Generally, the seats in these legislatures were redistributed so that the western areas were accorded more equitable representation than they had enjoyed during the colonial period. These legislatures now controlled most of the powers formerly held by the royal governor, and in most states one, or both, houses of the legislature elected the new governor. In the majority of the states, the legislature also appointed the members of the judiciary.

Lastly, state constitutions contained a bill of rights. Included among these rights were freedom of speech, press, and assembly; freedom of religion; the right to bear arms; speedy trial by jury; and immunity from excessive bail, cruel and unusual punishment, general search warrants, and ex post facto laws. Most of these rights were borrowed from English documents such as the Magna Carta, Petition of Right, and Bill of Rights. The main criterion for their selection, however, was the popular feeling that these particular rights had either been ignored or violated by the English or colonial governments.

THE ARTICLES OF CONFEDERATION

While all these changes were taking place on the state level, the delegates at the Continental Congress were attempting to agree on some sort of central government, which was necessary if only to prosecute the war and deal with foreign governments. As early as July 1776, John Dickinson chaired a committee which prepared a report outlining a plan for a central government. However, it was not until November 1777 that Congress approved a much modified version, which came to be known as the Articles of Confederation. The Articles of Confederation can be assessed properly only if one recalls that its authors were reacting to alleged Parliamentary tyranny and thus believed that the less government, the better. The governing body under the Articles of Confederation was the Congress, a unicameral legislature elected annually, in which each state had two to seven delegates but—regardless of wealth or population—only one vote. Congress was given sole authority to declare war and conduct foreign relations. It also had the power to supervise Indian affairs, coin money (although each state also retained this power), regulate weights and measures, and establish post offices. Routine matters were decided by a majority vote. For crucial matters the votes of nine states were required, and the Articles themselves could only be amended by a unanimous vote. Congress was deliberately not granted the power to tax or the power to regulate commerce; these had been the major bones of contention between the colonies and the English government. It could merely request funds from the states. More often than not, these requests were ignored.

No executive or judicial departments were provided for by the Articles of Confederation. It did, however, create the Committee of the States—made up of one member of each state delegation—to function when Congress was not in session. This committee was headed by a president who could serve for only one year out of every three. Other committees (some antedating the Articles of Confederation) such as the Marine (or Naval) Committee, the Treasury (or Finance) Committee, and the Foreign Affairs Committee (usually headed by a superintendent or secretary) also gradually began to assume executive functions. Officially, however, they were only authorized to act under instructions from Congress, which greatly reduced their efficiency.

WESTERN LAND LAWS

Even this frame of government, which merely created a loose confederation of thirteen independent states, required more than three years to be approved by the states. One of the main objections to the Articles of Confederation was that it failed to provide for the cession of the western lands of those seven states whose charters granted them lands extending west of the Appalachian Mountains. The six states which had fixed boundaries feared that they would eventually be overwhelmed by their potentially gigantic neighbors. They believed that these lands had been won from England by all the states and that they should be the common property of the United States. With Virginia setting the example, the seven states surrendered their rights to their western lands, and in 1781 Maryland became the thirteenth state to approve the Articles of Confederation.

Once the western lands were turned over to the central government, Congress had to decide how this huge area was to be settled and governed. In 1784 Thomas Jefferson drew up a plan for the Northwest Territory which divided it into ten districts and allowed the settlers of each district self-government from the start. It also granted them the right to form themselves into a territory with a voting representative in Congress when their population reached 20,000, and it ensured that they would be admitted as a state as soon as the population reached the level of the smallest existing state. Jefferson suggested that slavery be forbidden in the Northwest Territory, but Congress refused to accept this aspect of his plan or to stipulate exactly how many districts were to be formed. Even though his plan was accepted in principle, the Ordinance of 1784 never went into effect, partly because not all the land had been ceded to the central government and partly because of eastern opposition to the creation of so many new states.

In 1785 Congress passed a land ordinance which divided the Northwest Territory into seven ranges—each six miles wide. These ranges were divided into six-mile-square townships, which were further subdivided into thirty-six sections of 640 acres each. Four sections in each township were to be retained by the central government, and the income from a fifth section was to be used to support public education. Land sales were to begin in the easternmost range and then to proceed west in an orderly manner. No one was to be allowed to buy less than one section (640 acres), and the minimum price for the land was set at a dollar an acre. Congress hoped that the sale of these lands would provide a revenue to support the central government, but potential settlers were unwilling—or unable—to pay $640. Therefore, they merely squatted on the western lands.

Land speculators were interested in purchasing these western lands, but they knew that they could only attract settlers if a system of government was put into operation in the Northwest Territory. In 1787, therefore, to encourage the sale of land and also to maintain its own authority over the west, Congress passed the Northwest Ordinance. This ordinance authorized the creation of three to five states, but instead of allowing the settlers to govern themselves, Congress appointed a governor, a secretary, and three judges to rule them. When a district's population reached 5,000 adult males, it became a territory; adult males who owned fifty acres or more were eligible to elect members to a legislature and to send one nonvoting delegate to Congress. When the population of a territory reached 60,000, it was authorized to draft a constitution and apply for admission as a state. Although the Ordinance of 1787 offered somewhat less self-government to the settlers than the Ordinance of 1784, it forbade slavery in the Northwest Territory, and guaranteed the settlers religious freedom and other civil rights.

The Congressional land laws of 1784–1787 laid down two basic principles which guided American western policy for over a century. Most importantly, they announced that the United States would treat the settlers of its western lands as first-class American citizens who, when they were numerous enough, would be entitled to form states and enjoy the same rights and privileges as the residents of the thirteen original states. Americans came to take this privilege for granted, forgetting that it was completely contrary to eighteenth-century European, including English, precedents.

The second principle formulated by these land ordinances was that settlement of the west should be undertaken in an orderly manner, much as had been practiced in New England. Settlers could not, as they had in the southern states, purchase irregular plots of land, selecting only the most fertile soil. Instead, they had to buy solid blocks of already-surveyed land, taking the bad with the good. In spite of opposition from many settlers, this method of disposing of western lands was essentially incorporated into all subsequent land laws.

The land ordinances passed by Congress only began to solve the nation's numerous western problems. The Iroquois Indians had lost most of their military power when they supported (by and large) the English during the Revolutionary War. However, in spite of the provisions of the Treaty of Paris, England retained control of its forts in the Northwest Territory, and with its support the western tribes were strong enough to resist attempts at American settlement of the area, except in southern Ohio and Indiana. At no time during the Confederation period was the United States strong enough to remedy this situation.

In the southwest conditions were no more satisfactory. Under the leadership of Alexander McGillivray—a half-Indian, half-Scottish chief of the Creeks—the Creeks, Cherokees, Choctaws, and Chickasaws fought all attempts at white settlement in Tennessee and western Georgia. These Indians were supported by Spain, whose control of New Orleans was a grave threat to the already-existing American settlements in Kentucky and Tennessee. Lacking adequate roads, farmers of these two areas could transport their corn and wheat to market only by floating them on flatboats down the Mississippi River and then transshipping them at New Orleans to ocean-going vessels which carried them to ports along the Atlantic coast.

In 1784, in order to gain control of the Yazoo strip—a large territory between Georgia and West Florida which was claimed by both Spain and the United States— Spain closed the Mississippi River to American shipping. No settlement of the boundary dispute could be reached, but Don Diego de Gardoqui, the Spanish envoy, did offer special trading privileges to the United States if it agreed to prevent its citizens from navigating the Mississippi River for twenty-five years. When John Jay, the American negotiator, presented this proposed accord to the Congress of the Confederation in 1786, all seven northern states, hopeful of commercial profits, voted to approve it. Five southern states voted to disapprove, and Delaware abstained. Since the Articles of Confederation required a vote of nine states to approve a treaty, the so-called Jay-Gardoqui Treaty never went into effect. Nevertheless, the very fact that the United States was too weak to protect American shipping on the Mississippi River and that a majority of the states were willing to sacrifice the vital interests of the settlers of Kentucky and Tennessee, made these frontier settlers think about either independence or an alliance with Spain.

ECONOMIC PROBLEMS

The new nation also faced a wide variety of economic problems. By 1784 the United States was suffering from a serious depression. Commercial ties between England and the United States were not broken as easily as political ties. Americans were used to buying English goods, which usually were a better buy than those of France or other would-be European competitors. English merchants saw to it that this advantage was retained by cutting prices and extending generous credit to their American customers. The virtual dumping of English goods on the American market effectively undermined the growth of American industry and forestalled European competition. On the other hand, in spite of American pleas (which were seconded by Pitt the Younger and other English statesmen), the United States was not allowed to retain the same trading privileges with England and its colonies that it had enjoyed as part of the British empire. This meant that heavy import duties severely damaged the lucrative trade between New England and the middle states with the English West Indies. The withdrawal of bounties almost ruined the naval supply industry of North Carolina and the rice and indigo industries of South Carolina and Georgia. Enforcement of the Navigation Acts hurt New England's fisheries and shipyards. Also, the loss of slaves during the war led to a serious decline in the tobacco production of Virginia and Maryland.

Most Americans were hard hit by this economic crisis and responded with complaints and riots. The states reacted to these protests in varying ways. Many issued paper money—much of which rapidly declined in value. They also issued "stay" laws, which prevented creditors from collecting their debts. A moratorium on the collection of taxes was also put into effect in many states. By 1786, however, economic conditions were already improving. The United States began to develop profitable trade relations with France, Holland, Sweden, and China, and agriculture was rapidly recovering.

Still, the outbreak of the most serious protest—Shays' Rebellion, in August 1786—obscured these facts. Massachusetts had not passed any "stay" laws or delayed the collection of taxes. On the contrary, the farmers of western Massachusetts were infuriated by the fact that their taxes had increased and were payable in hard money only. When their protests were ignored, these farmers, under the leadership of Daniel Shays—a former captain in the Continental army—seized control of the county courts and prevented them from foreclosing on their farms for nonpayment of taxes or other debts. When they also threatened the arsenal at Springfield, the government of Massachusetts appealed for help to the Congress of the Confederation. Congress, however, had no army or possibility of raising one. Finally, by the end of February 1787, the Massachusetts militia was able to put down the rebellion without outside assistance.

THE CONSTITUTIONAL CONVENTION

Shays' Rebellion frightened many Americans. As Washington wrote to General Henry Knox of Massachusetts on December 26, 1786, "Who besides a Tory could have foreseen or a Briton predicted" such an outbreak? Those Americans known as nationalists because they argued the necessity for a strong central government almost welcomed Shays' Rebellion: It appeared to prove their contention. Nationalists had varied, and often interwoven, motives for desiring a strong central government. Those who owned land or wanted to settle in the west felt that only a strong national government could defeat the Indians and make western expansion possible. Those who owned the approximately $28 million worth (at face value) of government securities believed that only a strong national government could ever pay its debts. Manufacturers, merchants, and urban artisans realized that only a central government with the power to regulate commerce could protect them against foreign competition and win them better trading rights from England and other European nations. Other Americans claimed that only a strong central government could prevent the United States from degenerating into anarchic and bellicose groups of states arguing over boundaries, tariffs, and the value of their paper money.

Even many of those who did not join the nationalistic camp agreed that the Articles of Confederation should be strengthened by giving Congress the power to tax and regulate commerce. As early as 1781, and several times thereafter, Congress recommended that it be empowered to levy a 5 percent import tax, but it could never secure the approval of every state. This continued the situation in which each state was free to levy whatever import duties it wished and created dissension between those states which had good ports and those which did not. A similar controversy between Virginia and Maryland over the navigation of the Potomac River led to a conference, first at Alexandria, Virginia, and then at Mount Vernon (Washington's home) in 1785. Realizing that other states shared an interest in commercial affairs, Virginia invited all of them to a convention at Annapolis, Maryland, in 1786. Representatives of only five states attended this convention, but they agreed that conditions in the United States were so perilous that a convention of all the states should meet in Philadelphia the following year "to render the constitution of the Federal Government adequate to the exigencies of the Union."* Congress gave its approval to this project in February 1787, and in the following May the meeting that came to be known as the Constitutional Convention was called to order.

Fifty-five delegates from twelve states (Rhode Island refused to attend) attended the Constitutional Convention. Stalwarts such as John Adams and Thomas Jefferson were absent because they were representing the United States in Europe; and Samuel Adams, Patrick Henry, and Richard Henry Lee declined to attend because they opposed the attempt to create a powerful central government. Nevertheless, the delegates were a distinguished group of men who had served in their state governments and/or the national congress. The youngest of these delegates, Jonathan Dayton of New Jersey, was twenty-six; the oldest, Benjamin Franklin, eighty-one; and the average age was forty-two. The delegates chose George Washington to preside over the convention and decided that their debates should be kept secret. All present agreed that the central government needed strengthening, and very early in the meeting they concluded that this could be done only by drafting an entirely new constitution.

*From *Proceedings of the Annapolis Convention,* September 14, 1786.

Therefore, on May 29 Edmund Randolph introduced the Virginia, or "Large State," Plan, which had been largely developed by James Madison. The Virginia Plan provided for a bicameral legislature: The number of representatives in the lower house would be based either on "quotas of contribution, or [on] the number of free inhabitants." The lower house would elect the members of the upper house from among those nominated by their state legislatures. Both houses of the legislature would select the president and the judges who would staff a system of federal courts. The Virginia Plan gave Congress the power to veto state laws and to employ troops to force the states to obey federal laws. Under this plan each individual member of Congress would have one vote. This meant that the large and/or wealthy states would dominate the federal government.

For this reason William Paterson introduced the New Jersey, or "Small State," Plan. Superficially, the New Jersey Plan seemed only to be a revision of the Articles of Confederation. Under this plan a unicameral legislature was retained, with each state having one vote. However, this legislature was to be empowered to levy taxes and regulate interstate and foreign commerce. A plural executive, elected by Congress, would enforce the laws and appoint federal officials, including the members of a single federal court. Significantly, the New Jersey Plan also provided for the coercion of a state that violated a federal law or treaty.

Alexander Hamilton proposed a plan which would have created an omnipotent federal government with powers far beyond those envisioned in either the New Jersey or Virginia plans. This plan was far too extreme for the delegates who, by a vote of seven states to three (the New Hampshire delegates had not yet arrived at the convention), agreed to favor the Virginia Plan over the New Jersey Plan. Nevertheless, it was obvious to all that numerous modifications would have to be made in the plan if it were to be approved by the entire convention.

The first, and most important, of these modifications was the Great Compromise suggested by Roger Sherman of Connecticut. This compromise provided for a bicameral Congress with representation in the lower house based on population. However, each state would have the same number of representatives in the upper house. An accompanying compromise between the northern and southern states stipulated that a state's population for both representation and taxation would be defined as all whites plus three-fifths of its slaves. (The south had originally wanted all their slaves counted for purposes of representation but none for purposes of taxation.) Another compromise between north and south prevented the federal government from using its power to regulate commerce to prohibit the importation of slaves into the United States before 1808.

The new Congress was given all the powers exercised by the Congress of the Confederation, with the addition of the crucial powers to levy taxes and regulate commerce. However, to satisfy the south, Congress was forever prohibited from levying an export tax. This removed the fear of the southern states that such a tax would increase the price of the tobacco and other crops which they exported to Europe. In addition, the federal government now had the sole authority to coin money and to negotiate treaties with foreign nations. The new federal government also incorporated a system of courts, headed by a supreme court, to adjudicate cases arising from the Constitution, treaties, and federal laws and to settle controversies between states or the citizens of different states.

Article VI of the Constitution stated that the

> . . . Constitution, and the Laws of the United States, shall be the supreme Law of the Land; and the Judges in every state shall be bound thereby, any Thing in the Constitution or Laws of any State to the Contrary notwithstanding.

With these words the delegates at the Constitutional Convention abolished the loose alliance of states which had been in existence under the Articles of Confederation. No longer was it necessary to give the federal government the power to coerce states or veto their laws as suggested in the Virginia and New Jersey plans. Article VI accomplished the purpose without outraging state sensibilities.

One of the most difficult problems facing the Constitutional Convention was in deciding how the president should be selected. If Congress or the state legislatures chose the president, it would seriously undermine the latter's authority. Election by the people was considered too democratic. Therefore, the delegates designed the electoral college system, which is still in use today. The Constitution made the president commander-in-chief of the armed forces; gave the president the power, with the consent of the Senate, to make treaties and to appoint ambassadors, judges, and other public officials; and authorized the chief executive to veto acts of Congress. In spite of the fact that this veto could be overridden by a two-thirds vote of both houses of Congress, the president was a much more powerful executive than most contemporary state governors. Perhaps the expectation that Washington would be the nation's first chief executive made the delegates to the convention more generous than they might otherwise have been.

The authors of the Constitution envisioned the House of Representatives as the protector of the rights of the people. Its members would be popularly elected every two years and would have the sole power to initiate money bills. In addition, the Constitution guaranteed every state a republican form of government and outlawed titles of nobility; bills of attainder (legislative acts which deprive a person of property and civil rights because of a sentence of death); ex post facto laws (laws that would apply to actions committed before the laws were passed); religious tests for officeholding; and the suspension of the writ of habeas corpus, except when the public safety was endangered.

The drafters of the Constitution ignored European political theory, which insisted that sovereignty was unitary and indivisible. Instead, strongly influenced by the way in which the British empire worked in practice, they created a form of government in which sovereignty was shared by the state and federal governments. Both levels of government were, within their spheres of authority, to operate directly upon the individual citizen. The federal government had only the powers granted to it either explicitly or by implication through the "necessary and proper clause" which concludes Article I, Section 8, of the Constitution—all other powers were reserved to the states

THE RATIFICATION STRUGGLE

Once the wording of the Constitution was polished, largely by Gouverneur Morris, a member of the Pennsylvania delegation, the document was signed by thirty-nine of the forty-two delegates then present. Knowing that unanimous approval of the states was impossible and that the state legislatures were unlikely to transfer so many of their powers to a federal government, the Constitution provided that it would go into effect when ratified by special conventions in any nine states. After some debate—particularly over the fact that the vote of only nine states would change the nation's form of government—the Congress of the Confederation voted to approve the ratification procedure outlined in the Constitution.

In 1887 in a letter to the Committee in charge of the celebration of the Centennial Anniversary of the American Constitution, William Gladstone, the British Prime Minister, was to write:

> I have always regarded that Constitution as the most remarkable work known to me in modern times to have been produced by the human intellect, at a single stroke (so to speak), in its application to political affairs.

However, a century earlier large numbers of Americans known as Antifederalists had many doubts about and objections to the document produced at Philadelphia. It has often been claimed that the Federalists had a monopoly of the talented and wealthy Americans of the period. Yet, Madison himself had to admit ruefully that there were many individuals of wealth and ability among the Antifederalists.

Basically, the Antifederalists contended that the United States covered too large an area for its freedom to be safe under a federal form of government. They feared that the federal government would ultimately run roughshod over the rights of the states and of individuals. The omission in the Constitution of a bill of rights was cited as clear proof of the latter contention. Patrick Henry warned that the powers of the president were so extensive that the executive might turn into a king. Governor Clinton of New York argued that the American economy was beginning to make significant improvements under the Articles of Confederation—improvements which might be endangered by a change in the government. Other Antifederalists charged that the Constitution did not properly observe the doctrine of separation of powers; deplored the six-year term of senators; and expressed fear of the potential power of the federal court system.

Although the Federalists, as the Nationalists now called themselves, were outnumbered, they were far better organized and were far more active than their opponents. In most states, particularly in the smaller ones, the Federalists easily won control of the ratifying conventions. Delaware, New Jersey, and Georgia approved the Constitution unanimously. In Pennsylvania the vote was 46 to 23 in favor; and in Connecticut, 128 to 40. In Massachusetts the struggle was much more difficult, but after John Hancock and Samuel Adams were won over, the convention approved the Constitution by a vote of 187 to 168. When Maryland (63 to 11), South Carolina (149 to 73), and New Hampshire (57 to 47 after initially disapproving the Constitution) ratified the Constitution, it had won approval by the necessary nine states.

However, it was obvious to both Federalists and Antifederalists that the new government could not go into operation unless and until both Virginia and New York joined the fold. In June 1788 Virginia approved the Constitution by a vote of 89 to 79 after the Federalists promised that a bill of rights would be added. In New York the opposition was worn down by Virginia's ratification, the arguments in *The Federalist* (written by James Madison, Alexander Hamilton, and John Jay), and the practical argument that New York would be economically isolated unless it joined the Union. Even then the New York convention only approved the Constitution by a vote of 30 to 27.

North Carolina at first rejected the Constitution but later approved it by a vote of 195 to 77. In May 1790 Rhode Island reluctantly approved the Constitution by a vote of 34 to 32, after first rejecting it in a popular referendum (the only one held in any state) by a vote of 2,708 to 237. If other states had held referendums, authorities agree that these popular votes would also have been negative.

Some historians have viewed the adoption of the Constitution as a reaction to the democratic tendencies of the American Revolution. However, closer scrutiny of the evidence disproves this contention. Followers of Daniel Shays welcomed the Constitution, while local elites who controlled county or town elections opposed it. If those who drew up the Constitution were conservative, it was only in the sense that they looked toward the structure of the British empire as they believed it to have been—or believed that it *should* have been—before the Revolution. Yet, a decisive change had taken place: the acceptance of the theory that sovereignty rested with the people. This was as revolutionary a doctrine—and in practice much more crucial—than the declaration in 1776 that "all men are created equal." When the drafters of the Constitution chose the words "We the People of the United States" to introduce the Constitution, they opened up new vistas and new possibilities of political liberty for all mankind. As George Washington wrote in a letter to the Congress of the Confederation (September 17, 1787) recommending the Constitution:

> Individuals entering into society, must give up a share of liberty to preserve the rest. . . . It is at all times difficult to draw with precision the line between those rights which must be surrendered, and those which may be reserved . . .
> In all our deliberations on this subject we kept steadily in our view, that which appears to us the greatest interest of every true American, the consolidation of our Union, in which is involved our prosperity, felicity, safety, perhaps our national existence.*

*From Max Farrand (ed.), *The Records of the Federal Convention of 1787*, Vol. II, 666–67. By permission of Yale University Press.

BIBLIOGRAPHY

ADAMS, WILLI PAUL. *The First American Constitutions: Republican Ideology and the Making of the State Constitutions in the Revolutionary Era.* Chapel Hill, 1980.

DOUGLASS, ELISHA P. *Rebels and Democrats: The Struggle for Equal Political Rights and Majority Rule during the American Revolution.* Chapel Hill, 1955.

EIDELBERG, PAUL. *The Philosophy of the American Constitution.* New York, 1968.

HOFFMAN, RONALD, and ALBERT, PETER J. (eds.). *The Sovereign States in an Age of Uncertainty.* Charlottesville, Va.: University of Virginia Press, 1982.

JAMESON, J. FRANKLIN. *The American Revolution Considered as a Social Movement.* Princeton, 1926.

JENSEN, MERRILL. *The New Nation: A History of the United States During the Confederation, 1781–1789.* New York, 1950.

MAIN, JACKSON TURNER. *Political Parties Before the Constitution.* Chapel Hill, 1973.

McDONALD, FORREST. *E Pluribus Unum: The Forming of the American Republic, 1776–1790.* Boston, 1965.

MacLEOD, DUNCAN J. *Slavery, Race and the American Revolution.* Cambridge, 1974.

RACKOVE, JACK N. *The Beginning of National Politics: An Interpretive History of the Continental Congress.* New York, 1979.

ROSSITER, CLINTON. *The Grand Convention.* New York, 1966.

RUTLAND, ROBERT A. *The Ordeal of the Constitution: The Antifederalists and the Ratification Struggle of 1787–1788.* Norman, Okla., 1966.

SZATMARY, DAVID. *Shays' Rebellion: The Making of An Agrarian Insurrection.* Amherst, 1980.

WOOD, GORDON S. *The Creation of the American Republic 1776–1789.* Chapel Hill, 1969.

Index

Williams, Roger, 74, 75, 77, 200
Winslow, Edward, 219
Winthrop, John, 71–73, 75, 77, 155, 168, 186, 220, 240
Winthrop, John, Jr., 159, 228
Winthrop, John, IV, 228
Wise, John, 198
Wistar, Caspar, 160
Wistar, Richard, 160
Witchcraft, 196–98
Witherspoon, John, 219
Wolfe, James, 252, 253
Women:
    in arts and crafts, 160, 232, 235
    education of, 207, 211
    Indian, 17–18, 21
    legal status, 188–89, 280
    pioneer, 131
    in Portuguese empire, 37
    in Revolutionary War, 273–74, 279–80
    roles of, 187–88

    voting rights, 107
    writers, 221–22
Wood, Peter H., 85
Wood, William, 219
Woolen Act, 128, 154, 158
Woolman, John, 122, 222
Workers, 160–62
Writing, 13

Y

Yale College, 214, 216
Yamasee Indians, 85
Yazoo strip, 285

Z

Zenger, John Peter, 224–25
Zinzendorf, Nicholaus Ludwig von, 199